EDEXCEL
A LEVEL
HISTORY

*Active*Book included

Paper 3:
Lancastrians, Yorkists and Henry VII, 1399–1509

Dr Helen Carrel
Series editor: Rosemary Rees

ALWAYS LEARNING

PEARSON

Published by Pearson Education Limited, 80 Strand, London, WC2R 0RL

www.pearsonschoolsandfecolleges.co.uk

Copies of official specifications for all Edexcel qualifications may be found on the website:
www.edexcel.com

Text © Pearson Education Limited 2016

Designed by Elizabeth Arnoux for Pearson

Typeset and illustrated by Phoenix Photosetting, Chatham, Kent

Produced by Out of House Publishing

Original illustrations © Pearson Education Limited 2016

Cover design by Malena Wilson-Max for Pearson

Cover illustration © Mary Evans Picture Library/Interfoto/Friedrich

The rights of Helen Carrel to be identified as author of this work have been asserted by her in
accordance with the Copyright, Designs and Patents Act 1988.

First published 2016

21

10 9 8

British Library Cataloguing in Publication Data
A catalogue record for this book is available from the British Library

ISBN 978 1 447 985396

Printed in the UK by Ashford Colour Press Ltd

Websites

Pearson Education Limited is not responsible for the content of any external internet sites. It is essential
for tutors to preview each website before using it in class so as to ensure that the URL is still accurate,
relevant and appropriate. We suggest that tutors bookmark useful websites and consider enabling
students to access them through the school/college intranet.

A note from the publisher

In order to ensure that this resource offers high-quality support for the associated Pearson
qualification, it has been through a review process by the awarding body. This process confirms
that this resource fully covers the teaching and learning content of the specification or part of
a specification at which it is aimed. It also confirms that it demonstrates an appropriate balance
between the development of subject skills, knowledge and understanding, in addition to preparation
for assessment.

Endorsement does not cover any guidance on assessment activities or processes (e.g. practice
questions or advice on how to answer assessment questions) included in the resource nor does it
prescribe any particular approach to the teaching or delivery of a related course.

While the publishers have made every attempt to ensure that advice on the qualification and its
assessment is accurate, the official specification and associated assessment guidance materials are
the only authoritative source of information and should always be referred to for definitive guidance.

Pearson examiners have not contributed to any sections in this resource relevant to examination
papers for which they have responsibility.

Examiners will not use endorsed resources as a source of material for any assessment set by Pearson.

Endorsement of a resource does not mean that the resource is required to achieve this Pearson
qualification, nor does it mean that it is the only suitable material available to support the qualification,
and any resource lists produced by the awarding body shall include this and other appropriate
resources.

Contents

How to use this book

STRUCTURE

This book covers Paper 3, Option 30: Lancastrians, Yorkists and Henry VII, 1399–1509 of the Edexcel A Level qualification.

You will also need to study a Paper 1 and a Paper 2 option and produce coursework in order to complete your qualification. All Paper 1/2 options are covered by other textbooks in this series.

EXAM SUPPORT

The examined assessment for Paper 3 requires you to answer questions from three sections. Throughout this book there are exam-style questions in all three section styles for you to practise your examination skills.

Section A contains a compulsory question that will assess your source analysis and evaluation skills.

A Level Exam-Style Question Section A

Study Source 5 before you answer this question.

Assess the value of the source for revealing the character of Richard II and the reasons for his deposition in 1399.

Explain your answer, using the source, the information given about its origin and your own knowledge about the historical context. (20 marks)

Tip

Ensure you consider not only the significance of the lords appellant, but also factors such as Richard's use of a private bodyguard of men from Cheshire.

Section B contains a choice of essay questions that will look at your understanding of the studied period in depth.

A Level Exam-Style Question Section B

How significant was the challenge posed by John Oldcastle's rebellion in 1414 to the government of Henry VI? (20 marks)

Tip

Ensure that you consider the threat posed by Oldcastle's rebellion in the context of Henry V's imminent departure to France.

Section C will again give you a choice of essay questions but these will assess your understanding of the period in breadth.

A Level Exam-Style Question Section C

How far do you agree that, throughout the period 1399–1509, maintenance was the key problem facing late medieval English kings? (20 marks)

Tip

Make sure you consider key changes in how maintenance was controlled by the crown during this period, as well as other problems late medieval kings faced, such as popular rebellion or threats from foreign powers.

The Preparing for your exams sections at the end this book contains sample answers of different standards, with comments on how they could be improved.

FEATURES

Extend your knowledge

These features contain additional information that will help you gain a deeper understanding to the topic. This could be a short biography of an important person, extra background information about an event, an alternative interpretation, or even a research idea that you could follow up. Information in these boxes is not essential to your exam success, but still provides insights of value.

EXTEND YOUR KNOWLEDGE

Archaeological evidence for the death of Richard III
In 2013, a venture by the Richard III Society, the University of Leicester and Leicester City Council resulted in a major dig in Leicester to find a Franciscan Priory called Greyfriars, where historical records indicated that Richard III had been buried after the Battle of Bosworth. The remains of Richard III were discovered. The skeleton showed severe injuries, particularly to the skull, but Jo Appleby from the University of Leicester has argued that only minor facial disfigurement was caused as Henry Tudor wished Richard to be identified to prevent any later claims that he had survived the battle.

It is clear from the bones that some of the injuries occurred when Richard was not wearing armour. It is likely that Richard was killed, then stripped of his armour and that some damage was then inflicted on the corpse post-mortem. This suggests that Richard's enemies engaged in some form of humiliation of the corpse.

Knowledge check activities

These activities are designed to check that you have understood the material that you have just studied. They might also ask you questions about the sources and extracts in the section to check that you have studied and analysed them thoroughly.

ACTIVITY
KNOWLEDGE CHECK

Henry VII's financial policies and his security on the throne

1 Consider the statement: 'Henry VII's financial policies undermined rather than strengthened his security'. Write a one-minute speech either agreeing or disagreeing with the statement, giving evidence to support your views. Then listen to a speech giving the alternative viewpoint from another member of your class and take notes.

2 Draw up a table comparing the significance of the Yorkshire rebellion of 1489 and the Cornish rebellion of 1497. Remember to focus on the importance of the events, rather than just describing everything that happened. Once you have completed this, write a paragraph explaining which event was more significant in your view and why.

Summary activities

At the end of each chapter, you will find summary activities. These are tasks designed to help you think about the key topic you have just studied as a whole. They may involve selecting and organising key information or analysing how things changed over time. You might want to keep your answers to these questions safe – they are handy for revision.

ACTIVITY
SUMMARY

The influence of key personalities on the politics of 1449-60

1 Draw and complete a table charting the key achievements and failures of Henry VI, Margaret of Anjou, the duke of Suffolk, the duke of Somerset, the duke of York and the earl of Warwick. How reliable is the available source material when assessing their characters?

2 On a piece of A3 paper, create a timeline that covers the key battles of the period 1449-61, including details of why each battle was significant (especially which key figures were killed/taken prisoner/escaped). Draw a red rose by battles that were victories for the Lancastrians and a white rose by battles that were a victory for the Yorkists.

Thinking Historically activities

These activities are found throughout the book, and are designed to develop your understanding of history, especially around the key concepts of evidence, interpretations, causation and change. Each activity is designed to challenge a conceptual barrier that might be holding you back. This is linked to a map of conceptual barriers developed by experts. You can look up the map and find out which barrier each activity challenges by downloading the progression map from this website: www.pearsonschools.co.uk/historyprogressionsapproach.

progression map reference

 THINKING HISTORICALLY Cause and consequence (6c)

Connections

Work in groups or individually and answer the following:

1 Read Source 1 (page 114). How are Aristotle's beliefs about women exercising power and influence in government similar to criticisms of Queen Margaret in the 15th century?

2 Look at Source 2 (page 114).
   a Why is the artist depicting a woman beating her husband? Is he criticising the woman in this image?
   b How is this image similar to the views expressed by those criticising Margaret of Anjou?

3 Read Source 3. What long-standing ideas about women (for example from classical authors like Aristotle) was Waurin influenced by when writing this account of the queen's behaviour?

4 Why it is important for historians to see these links across time and be able to explain how causal factors can influence situations much later in time?

Getting the most from your online ActiveBook

This book comes with three years' access to ActiveBook* – an online, digital version of your textbook. Follow the instructions printed on the inside front cover to start using your ActiveBook.

Your ActiveBook is the perfect way to personalise your learning as you progress through your A Level History course. You can:

• access your content online, anytime, anywhere
• use the inbuilt highlighting and annotation tools to personalise the content and make it really relevant to you.

Highlight tool – use this to pick out key terms or topics so you are ready and prepared for revision.

Annotations tool – use this to add your own notes, for example links to your wider reading, such as websites or other files. Or, make a note to remind yourself about work that you need to do.

*For new purchases only. If the access code has already been revealed, it may no longer be valid. If you have bought this textbook secondhand, the code may already have been used by the first owner of the book.

Introduction
A Level History

WHY HISTORY MATTERS

History is about people and people are complex, fascinating, frustrating and a whole lot of other things besides. This is why history is probably the most comprehensive and certainly one of the most intriguing subjects there is. History can also be inspiring and alarming, heartening and disturbing, a story of progress and civilisation and of catastrophe and inhumanity.

History's importance goes beyond the subject's intrinsic interest and appeal. Our beliefs and actions, our cultures, institutions and ways of living, our languages and means of making sense of ourselves are all shaped by the past. If we want to fully understand ourselves now, and to understand our possible futures, we have no alternative but to think about history.

History is a discipline as well as a subject matter. Making sense of the past develops qualities of mind that are valuable to anyone who wants to seek the truth and think clearly and intelligently about the most interesting and challenging intellectual problem of all: other people. Learning history is learning a powerful way of knowing.

WHAT IS HISTORY?

History is a way of constructing knowledge about the world through research, interpretation, argument and debate.

Building historical knowledge involves identifying the traces of the past that exist in the present – in people's memories, in old documents, photographs and other remains, and in objects and artefacts ranging from bullets and lipsticks, to field systems and cities. Historians interrogate these traces and *ask questions* that transform traces into *sources of evidence* for knowledge claims about the past.

Historians aim to understand what happened in the past by *explaining why* things happened as they did. Explaining why involves trying to understand past people and their beliefs, intentions and actions. It also involves explaining the causes and evaluating the effects of large-scale changes in the past and exploring relationships between what people aimed to do, the contexts that shaped what was possible and the outcomes and consequences of actions.

Historians also aim to *understand change* in the past. People, states of affairs, ideas, movements and civilisations come into being in time, grow, develop, and ultimately decline and disappear. Historians aim to identify and compare change and continuity in the past, to measure the rate at which things change and to identify the types of change that take place. Change can be slow or sudden. It can also be understood as progressive or regressive – leading to the improvement or worsening of a situation or state of affairs. How things change and whether changes are changes for the better are two key issues that historians frequently debate.

Figure 1 Fragment of a black granite statue possibly portraying the Roman politician Mark Antony.

Debate is the essence of history. Historians write arguments to support their knowledge claims and historians argue with each other to test and evaluate interpretations of the past. Historical knowledge itself changes and develops. On the one hand, new sources of knowledge and new methods of research cause *historical interpretations* to change. On the other hand, the questions that historians ask change with time and new questions produce new answers. Although the past is dead and gone, the interpretation of the past has a past, present and future.

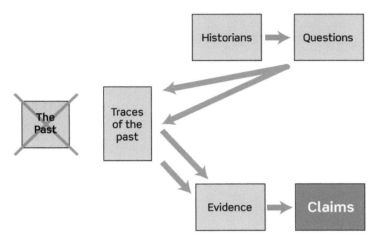

Figure 2 Constructing knowledge about the past.

THE CHALLENGES OF LEARNING HISTORY

Like all other Advanced Level subjects, A Level history is difficult – that is why it is called 'advanced'. Your Advanced Level studies will build on knowledge and understanding of history that you developed at GCSE and at Key Stage 3 – ideas like 'historical sources', 'historical evidence' and 'cause', for example. You will need to do a lot of reading and writing to progress in history. Most importantly, you will need to do a lot of thinking, and thinking about your thinking. This book aims to support you in developing both your knowledge and your understanding.

History is challenging in many ways. On the one hand, it is challenging to build up the range and depth of knowledge that you need to understand the past at an advanced level. Learning

about the past involves mastering new and unfamiliar concepts arising from the past itself (such as the Inquisition, Laudianism, *Volksgemeinschaft*) and building up levels of knowledge that are both detailed and well organised. This book covers the key content of the topics that you are studying for your examination and provides a number of features to help you build and organise what you know – for example, diagrams, timelines and definitions of key terms. You will need to help yourself too, of course, adding to your knowledge through further reading, building on the foundations provided by this book.

Another challenge is to develop understandings of the discipline of history. You will have to learn to think historically about evidence, cause, change and interpretations and also to write historically, in a way that develops clear and supported argument.

Historians think with evidence in ways that differ from how we often think in everyday life. In history, as Figure 2 shows, we cannot go and 'see for ourselves' because the past no longer exists. Neither can we normally rely on 'credible witnesses' to tell us 'the truth' about 'what happened'. People in the past did not write down 'the truth' for our benefit. They often had clear agendas when creating the traces that remain and, as often as not, did not themselves know 'the truth' about complex historical events.

A root of the word 'history' is the Latin word *historia*, one of whose meanings is 'enquiry' or 'finding out'. Learning history means learning to ask questions and interrogate traces, and then to reason about what the new knowledge you have gained means. This book draws on historical scholarship for its narrative and contents. It also draws on research on the nature of historical thinking and on the challenges that learning history can present for students. Throughout the book you will find 'Thinking Historically' activities designed to support the development of your thinking.

You will also find – as you would expect given the nature of history – that the book is full of questions. This book aims to help you build your understandings of the content, contexts and concepts that you will need to advance both your historical knowledge and your historical understanding, and to lay strong foundations for the future development of both.

Dr Arthur Chapman
Institute of Education
University College London

QUOTES ABOUT HISTORY

'Historians are dangerous people. They are capable of upsetting everything. They must be directed.'
Nikita Khrushchev

'To be ignorant of what occurred before you were born is to remain forever a child. For what is the worth of human life, unless it is woven into the life of our ancestors by the records of history.'
Marcus Tullius Cicero

Lancastrians, Yorkists and Henry VII, 1399–1509

In 2012, archaeologists from the University of Leicester excavated a car park and discovered a male skeleton showing ten injuries, demonstrating that he had died as a result of being stabbed in the face and the side of the head. There was also evidence of injuries apparently designed to humiliate the victim, including a pelvic wound which was likely to have been caused by a weapon thrust upwards through the buttock, although it was undoubtedly the head wounds which proved fatal. The corpse was then thrown into a hastily dug grave below a church, probably with the hands still bound. Once the corpse had been removed, the bones were DNA tested and the body was proved to be that of Richard III, perhaps England's most controversial medieval king.

This archaeological find caused a media frenzy that indicated the ongoing public's fascination with 15th-century English history. At the heart of this period was the 'Wars of the Roses', a name given to a civil war that took place from 1450 to 1485 between two rival families claiming the throne – the Yorkists and the Lancastrians. It was this war that ended with Richard's brutal death on the battlefield and the rise of the Tudor dynasty to the throne. The period involves political intrigue, noble rivalries, child killing, battles, murder, accusations of witchcraft and one of the great royal romances of history – the marriage of Edward IV to Elizabeth Woodville. It is not difficult to understand why this period continues to grip the 21st-century imagination and has been the subject of numerous television documentaries and books. Dramatists and novelists have found the topic appealing, most famously William Shakespeare, who wrote eight plays on the subject. Some of England's most famous historical characters date from the 15th century. Henry V was the famous war hero of the Battle of Agincourt in 1415, when English archers defeated the French with spectacular success. His son, Henry VI, was noted for his periods of insanity, as England fell into the grip of civil war while different noble factions sought to control the throne. Edward IV, the first Yorkist king, was noted for his womanising and, aside from his controversial marriage to a relatively poor widow, allegedly seduced merchants' wives in London to obtain cash for his military campaigns. None of these colourful individuals compare to the two kings who ended the Wars of the Roses, however: Richard III and Henry VII. Richard III has long been suspected of ordering the killing of his two nephews, the 'Princes in the Tower', who were aged ten and twelve at the time of their mysterious disappearance. The evidence against him, however, is inconclusive and the fate of the two boys has remained a hotly contested mystery, with the Richard III Society being formed in the 1920s to try to clear his name. Meanwhile, Henry VII (Richard's successor) has been credited by some as being the first 'modern' ruler, using tighter financial controls and much higher

1399 – Richard II deposed by his cousin, who becomes King Henry IV

1420 – Treaty of Troyes, making English kings heirs to the French throne

1444 – Treaty of Tours signed, reducing English claims in France

1461 – Henry VI deposed; Edward of York seizes throne and becomes Edward IV

1470 – Edward IV removed from throne; Henry VI reinstated

1475 – Edward IV invades France but instead of fighting signs Treaty of Picquigny

1485 – Battle of Bosworth. Richard III killed. Henry Tudor crowned King Henry VII

1509 – Henry VII dies and his son becomes King Henry VIII

1399
1420
1444
1461
1470
1475
1485
1509

1377

1377 – Edward III dies; his grandson, Richard II, becomes king

1413

1413 – Henry IV dies; his son, Henry V, becomes king

1422

1422 – Henry V dies. His son, Henry VI, becomes king of England and France

1450

1450 – Jack Cade's rebellion

1464

1464 – Edward IV secretly marries Elizabeth Woodville, thus angering the French king and the earl of Warwick

1471

1471 – Henry VI removed from the throne; Edward IV becomes king again

1483

1483 – 9 April: Edward IV dies

Summer: Edward IV's sons ('The Princes in the Tower') disappear in mysterious circumstances

26 June: Richard III proclaims himself king

1499

1499 – Henry VII's son, Prince Arthur, marries the Spanish princess, Katherine of Aragon

levels of spy surveillance to control his nobility. While such claims may well be exaggerated, there can be little doubt that the Tudor dynasty which Henry VII brought to the throne has remained a potent image of government stability after civil war.

Figure 1 *The Plucking of the Red and White Roses* by Henry Arthur Payne, painted in 1910. This artwork was created as part of the decoration of the East Corridor in the Houses of Parliament in Westminster. It depicts a (probably fictional) scene in London, where Richard Plantagenet (the duke of York) chooses a white rose (to become the symbol of the Yorkists) while his enemy, the duke of Somerset, chooses a red rose, which becomes the badge of the Lancastrians. Their various supporters then pick sides by plucking either a red or a white rose. The events as shown here are unlikely ever to have occurred, but were popularised by a scene in Shakespeare's play *Henry VI: Part I*, Act II, scene iv. The fact that this scene was chosen to decorate the modern-day parliament indicates the ongoing political significance of the Wars of the Roses, as well as the romanticised legends that have developed around the period.

3.1 Changing relationships between crown and the nobility: 'over-mighty subjects'

KEY QUESTIONS

- Were major landholders more important as props to the crown or as potential rivals?
- How significant was retaining to political stability?
- How well did the crown cope with the challenges of local disorder?

INTRODUCTION

The 15th-century political system was one that focused on 'personal kingship', a phrase coined by modern scholars to reflect the fact that much of the late medieval political system was based on the individual role of the monarch and his relationships with leading noblemen within the kingdom. In the political and religious ideology of the time, the king was born to the role through hereditary right and the coronation ceremony emphasised that he was chosen by God for the role. To disobey the king, therefore, was not only a crime in legal terms, but also a sin. This ideal view, however, had been put to the test on several occasions in the past, but never more so than in late medieval England. In this period, two factors particularly undermined the authority of the crown. The first was that in 1399, the throne had been seized by force by Henry Bolingbroke (later King Henry IV), demonstrating very publicly that an unpopular king (Richard II) could be deposed by a powerful noble, undermining the principle that the position of the king, as God's anointed, was inviolable. The second was that by the 1450s it became increasingly clear that Bolingbroke's grandson, Henry VI, was mentally incapable of decision making, throwing the entire system of personal kingship into chaos. The civil war that followed, usually described as the Wars of the Roses, provides historians with both a fascinating and illuminating insight into power relations between the monarchy and leading noblemen, highlighting the conflicting loyalties at play in late medieval England. The result of this conflict was exceptionally historically significant, not least as it ended with the Tudor dynasty ascending the throne.

WERE MAJOR LANDHOLDERS MORE IMPORTANT AS PROPS TO THE CROWN OR AS POTENTIAL RIVALS?

According to Sir John Fortesque, a leading 15th-century judge, it was the duty of an English medieval king 'to maintain the peace both outward and inward'; in other words, it was his role to ensure the kingdom was free from *outward* threats, such as foreign invasion, but also *inward* dangers,

---

1399 – Richard II deposed by Henry Bolingbroke, who is crowned Henry IV, the first Lancastrian king

1415 – Conspiracy against Henry V, called the 'Southampton Plot', is crushed by the king

1422 – August: Henry V dies unexpectedly and the English throne is inherited by his baby son, Henry VI

1395	1400	1405	1410	1415	1420	1425	1430	1435	1440

1413 – Henry IV dies and the throne is inherited by his son, Henry V

1420 – May: Henry V negotiates the Treaty of Troyes, an agreement with the French which is highly advantageous to the English. This treaty makes Henry heir to the French throne.

2 June: Henry V marries Catherine of Valois, daughter of the French king, as part of the agreement at Troyes

such as rebellion or offences against law and order. As a medieval monarch had no police force or large standing army to enforce his will, he instead needed to demonstrate his authority by two key methods:

- Firstly, he needed to show military ability, by personally leading successful armies either against rebels within England or against foreign forces. It is no coincidence that the monarchs of the late Middle Ages who were perceived as 'good kings' were those who won famous victories in battle, such as Edward III at Crecy in 1346 and Henry V at Agincourt in 1415.

- Secondly, he needed to assert his position as a judge, both in the sense that he was the head of the legal system, hence crimes were offences against the *king's* law and disturbances disrupted the *king's* peace. This was crucial in terms of settling quarrels between leading noblemen, who were often jockeying for land, wealth or position.

Both of these roles were neatly summarised in the images on the 'Great Seal' used by monarchs to authorise important legal documents, which contained images both of the king as a warrior, riding into battle on horseback, and as a judge, seated upon a throne holding the **orb** and **sceptre** as symbols of his legal and spiritual authority.

KEY TERMS

Orb
A globe made from precious metal and topped with a cross. It is held by a monarch on ceremonial occasions and represents sovereignty and justice.

Sceptre
A rod or staff, again made from precious metal, that is held by a monarch as part of their royal regalia.

SOURCE 1

This is the Great Seal of Henry V. Similar images can be found on other monarchs' seals from the late medieval period. The Great Seal showed the two idealised images of a king: as a judge (similar to contemporary images of Christ sitting in judgement, emphasising that this was a God-given role); and as a warrior, defending his realm.

1444 – The duke of Suffolk negotiates the Treaty of Tours, a controversial truce with France

1453 – 17 July: English defeated at the Battle of Castillon and lose all territory in France except Calais. Duke of Somerset arrested.
August: Henry VI suffers total mental collapse
13 October: Henry VI and Margaret of Anjou have a son, Prince Edward

1470 – Readeption of Henry VI

1471 – Edward IV restored to throne

1485 – Richard III defeated by Henry Tudor at Battle of Bosworth. Tudor declared Henry VII.

| 1445 | 1450 | 1455 | 1460 | 1465 | 1470 | 1475 | 1480 | 1485 | 1490 |

1450 – May: The duke of Suffolk is murdered
June to July: Jack Cade's rebellion

1455 – May: First Battle of St Albans fought between York and Somerset supporters. York victorious, but cannot translate success into lasting political gains.

1461 – 29 March: Decisive York victory at the Battle of Towton. Edward of York proclaimed King Edward IV.

1483 – Edward IV dies and his sons disappear. His brother, Richard of Gloucester, becomes Richard III.

Nobleman

Names in this period can sometimes be confusing because, firstly, sons often had the same names as their fathers and, secondly, noblemen were often referred to not by their surname, but by the place mentioned in their title. Therefore, Richard Neville, earl of Warwick, might be referred to as 'Neville' or as 'Warwick' yet it does mean the same person. Understanding this point will help you considerably with your reading and also make it easier to use book indexes on the topic. If searching for a particular noble, remember to search under both the surname and the place name of their title to ensure you find all the references.

Magnate

A senior noble, such as a duke or earl, who would usually hold extensive landed estates and have direct access to the king.

Lord

When used with a capital 'L', this is a title for someone's name, such as Lord Scales. When used without a capital, however, 'lord' describes someone of senior rank, who provides patronage and assistance to those of a lower rank. Contemporaries, therefore, might refer to someone of a senior rank who provided them with protection or assistance as 'my lord' or 'my good lord'.

The personality of the king was very important in the late medieval period. Indeed, the reign of Henry VI was to prove how inadequate the 15th-century political system was in coping with an inactive monarch. Nonetheless, it was clear that it was essential for a monarch to delegate authority and duties to others, particularly noblemen, in order for the realm to function properly. As major landowners, **noblemen** (also known as **magnates**) had a key role in terms of communication; they were expected to keep the king informed about the situation in the region under their influence and to inform and carry out the king's wishes. Importantly, too, noblemen were required to raise troops from their tenants when the king required it and it was the changing relationship between **lords** and their followers that have often been held responsible for the disorder and bloody reputation of 15th-century England.

Lands and offices of the state

Although the personality of the king and relationships with leading nobles were at the heart of the medieval political system, there were also established bureaucratic systems and official government roles. There were a number of key government departments:

- The Exchequer dealt with matters of royal finance and was headed by a treasurer. The Exchequer was primarily involved in the collection of revenues, notably from taxes.

- The Chancery was the legal section of medieval government and clerks in the Chancery wrote up important legal documents, such as royal charters. This section held the Great Seal, which was required to authenticate these documents. The head of the Chancery was the chancellor and for most of the medieval period this role was held by a bishop, reflecting the important role that the Church had in government.

- The Office of the Privy Seal developed in the early 14th century and reflected the growing bureaucratisation of the Chancery, as this department now held the Great Seal almost permanently. Therefore, the king needed a seal for his own use to authenticate key documents he sent out while moving around the country. The key official was the Keeper of the Privy Seal and throughout the late medieval period this role was held by a senior clergyman, usually a canon, dean or bishop. Although the Office was based in London, the Keeper usually travelled with the king and was one of his key advisers.

- The King's Chamber was originally a reference to the king's private rooms, and this reflected the very personal nature of medieval kingship. It was also effectively a government department, however, and was headed by a chamberlain who often had very considerable control over who could see the king and how royal finances were spent. The exact role of the Chamber and chamberlain varied somewhat between reigns, depending on the preferences of the monarch in question.

While these departments dealt with bureaucratic matters, for decisions of national importance, such as foreign diplomacy and defence, it was expected that the king would take advice from a group of councillors, mainly drawn from the nobility. Councils met to discuss government policy, as well as to administer justice, take measures to maintain order within the realm, to assist the smooth-running of trade, and to issue warrants, letters and proclamations to advertise and explain their decisions to the wider population. The term 'council' in the period was used rather flexibly, but there seems to have been two key forms:

- The Great Council could be made up of any of the lords who served in parliament and who were available at the time to give the king advice. Potentially, therefore, it was a large body, often upwards of 125 men. It was in fact the institution from which parliament had developed in the 13th century, but it continued to be used throughout the late medieval period. The advantage of the Great Council over parliament was that it could be called at shorter notice and with less formality, making it a speedier way of dealing with problems or emergencies. This informality, however, meant that the record keeping was much less complete and so the sources for council meetings are very patchy, making it difficult for historians to understand fully the workings of this important body. Nonetheless, it appears that the king usually also had a greater influence over the individuals who could be called to these meetings, whereas when parliament was called it was entirely a matter of lordly status. The Great Council was usually called to discuss important matters of state, such as war or key government policy decisions.

- The Continual Council was a much smaller group of the king's closest advisers. It dealt with much of the everyday governance of the realm. In 1377, when Richard II came to the throne, the Council seems to have become more formalised and a fixed post of the Clerk of the Council was established to record its decisions. During the same reign, a system of salaries for the councillors was set up which suggests they were official appointments. This change was probably the result of the fact that Richard was a child at the time of his accession to the throne, and so previously less-formal arrangements needed to be consolidated during the king's minority. It was usual in the late 14th century for the key members to be the three major officers of state – the chancellor, the treasurer and the keeper of the Privy Seal.

Key officers of state were appointed by the king and served as members of his household, often travelling with him as he moved around the country, although they would also have held their own landed estates. Many of these roles had a financial responsibility, notably the chancellor and treasurer, but other posts were predominantly responsible for matters of security: the Constable of the Tower of London, for example, was a post usually held by a leading lord and involved ensuring the safety of this important royal palace and treasure-house. The Captain of Calais, meanwhile, managed the substantial English army based in this city, which was a significant military role (see also page 130). Importantly, all these roles gave the holder both various forms of additional income and also access to the king, whom they were expected to advise about important matters of state, such as whether to go to war and key laws to pass.

The importance of the king taking good advice was widely recognised by contemporaries, and considered crucial that monarchs did not listen to a narrow set of views. It was also likely to be unpopular if a king was seen to favour the advice of lesser nobles over the guidance of the great magnate, something demonstrated most clearly in 1406 when parliament criticised Henry IV for this; they pressured him into removing the knights and esquires from the council and instead relying more strongly on great landowners. In part, this reflected innate late medieval class consciousness, but there were also important practical reasons for a monarch to take soundings from leading nobles; they were, after all, the major landowners and had control and often considerable local loyalty in the areas where their estates were based. Highly successful and well-established monarchs, such as Edward III, could often seek the advice of lesser men without criticism, but this was much less likely in the case of a monarch such as Henry IV, who was a fairly recent usurper.

The advice leading nobles gave, however, was not above criticism and it was considered particularly dangerous if a small clique was dominating a weak king. This was one of the major criticisms made against Henry VI, who was widely regarded as too dominated by the dukes of Somerset and Suffolk in the 1440s. It must also be remembered, however, that owing to the fact that it could be considered treason to criticise the king personally, it was usual for negative comments about government to instead focus on the monarch's 'evil councillors', who made much less controversial scapegoats for blame. This type of political rhetoric must be borne in mind when analysing primary sources offering political commentary from the period.

The king communicated his will to the regions formally via royal proclamations, which were sent out to different parts of the country by messengers and which were legally binding. Laws were enforced locally by not only nobles, but also lesser landowners, a social class called the **gentry**. The latter group often acted as law-enforcement officers in the role of **sheriffs** or **Justices of the Peace**. Additionally, the king could call parliament at any time and summonses were sent around the country to call members of parliament to attend. Parliament was divided into the Lords (a group which consisted of both the lords spiritual, who were bishops in the Roman Catholic Church, and lords temporal, who were noblemen) and the 'Commons' (who were lower-ranking property owners, a mixture of wealthy merchants, lawyers and members of the gentry). Parliament was involved in advising the king and in passing laws. Crucially, it was also essential if the king wished to raise money via taxation, as it was an established principle that taxes could not be charged without the consent of both the Lords and the Commons. It was only acceptable for the king to ask for taxation to assist with defence, and members of parliament also became hotly critical of the monarch if they felt the money was in fact being used for other purposes.

KEY TERMS

Gentry
A social class of more minor landowners than the nobility, but this group would not have participated in any form of agricultural labour. They included professionals, such as lawyers.

Sheriff
The leading law-enforcement officer in a region.

Justice of the Peace (JP)
An official who presides over and judges legal cases heard at a local level.

Church patronage

When studying late medieval society and politics, it is important to give due consideration to the role of the Church, an institution that had enormous influence, not only in terms of religion, but also in terms of the control of land and political influence. The Church as an institution was staffed by two groups: the regular clergy were monks, nuns or friars (sometimes simply known as 'the religious') who took lifelong vows of chastity, poverty and obedience and who lived as members of **religious orders**; while the secular clergy were priests and deacons who lived in parishes or in cathedral chapters, mixing with the wider population more freely. As an institution, the Church owned a large amount of land, much of which was controlled by monastic houses, and the clergy claimed tax exemptions on their income, a point that caused considerable friction between the crown and the Church throughout the Middle Ages. The Church also ran its own law courts and both the secular and regular clergy had a significant legal privilege called the 'benefit of the clergy', which was the right to request trial in a church rather than a secular court. This 'benefit' was subjected to considerable abuse, as church courts could not impose the death penalty, and so it was much in demand for those who wished to avoid the extreme penalty of the law.

KEY TERM

Religious order
In the Catholic context, this is an organisation of monks, nuns and friars who take vows of poverty, chastity and obedience to a superior within the Church and who live in communities together as religious brothers or sisters.

Relations with the papacy

In this period, prior to the Reformation, all churches in England were Roman Catholic and, in theory at least, the Catholic clergy's first allegiance was not to the king but to the pope in Rome, a figure who not only had spiritual authority over matters of church doctrine, but who could also exercise considerable political influence by granting or withholding his religious approval to or from a particular king. The benefits of papal approval were evident, for example, in 1485, when Henry Tudor claimed the throne and was assisted by a legal document from Pope Clement VII which publicly stated that, in the eyes of the Church, Tudor was the rightful king of England. The pope was also important as his permission was required if a king or noble wished to marry within the **prohibited degrees of consanguity**. This meant marrying a blood relation, such as a cousin, which strictly speaking was

forbidden by **canon law**. As medieval royalty and the nobility often arranged marriages among the same small social class, however, it was sometimes difficult to avoid marrying blood relations and so **papal dispensations** were necessary to ensure these important political matches were completely legal. Again, Henry VII provides an example of this, as he wished to marry Elizabeth of York for political reasons, but they were both great-great-grandchildren of John of Gaunt, the 14th-century duke of Lancaster. Fortunately, Pope Clement VII was helpful in this matter and the wedding took place in 1486.

SOURCE
2
Image from a legal manuscript showing the 'Tree of Consanguinity'. This was a fairly standard type of diagram which showed the prohibited degrees of consanguinity (blood relationship), which would prevent a marriage without permission from the pope. After 1215, the Church forbade marriages between a range of blood relations, including second cousins.

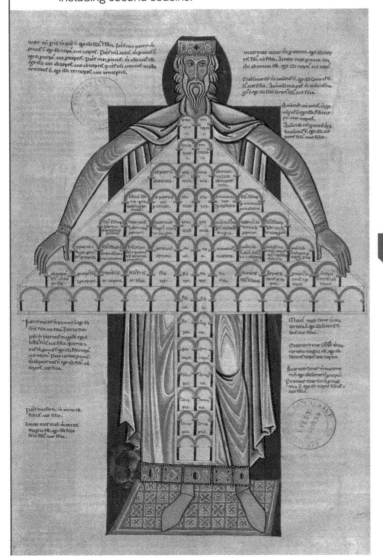

KEY TERMS

Prohibited degrees of consanguity
'Consanguity' means 'a blood relationship'. According to Church law, it was forbidden to marry relations and legal treatises set out in great detail exactly which relationships were forbidden.

Canon law
Ecclesiastical law, in the medieval context, that was laid down by the pope and the Roman Catholic Church.

Papal dispensation
A legal document issued by the pope that gives an exemption from a particular aspect of canon law.

In the 12th and 13th centuries, a key area of tension between the papacy and the English monarchy had been who should choose which men had key clerical appointments, with famous clashes on the matter during the reign of King Henry II (r. 1154–89) and King John (r. 1199–1216), the latter refusing to accept the preferred papal candidate for Archbishop of Canterbury, a dispute which resulted in the king being **excommunicated** and the entire country being placed under **interdict** from 1209 to 1213. By the later Middle Ages, however, a certain level of informal compromise had been reached (see Extract 1), especially in relation to the important matter of the appointment of bishops. Officially, when a bishop died, a group of clergymen called the '**cathedral chapter**' held an election to find a suitable candidate, and once this was done the

KEY TERMS

Excommunicate
In the medieval context, to exclude someone from participation in the sacraments of the Roman Catholic Church. By committing certain serious sins, such as murder, an individual can effectively excommunicate themselves from the Church and cannot afterwards receive the Eucharist, for example, until attending confession and being absolved. More relevant in the medieval political context, however, are official proclamations of excommunication made by the pope or other senior churchmen, when an individual was publicly excommunicated from the Church and not permitted to receive the sacraments until they had repented and this had been accepted by the pope or other senior members of the clergy.

Interdict
In the Catholic Church, this is a type of ecclesiastical punishment which excludes a certain individual or group from particular rites of the Church. In the reign of King John, therefore, when England was placed under interdict, no one was allowed to receive certain sacraments.

Cathedral chapter
A group of clergy who staffed a cathedral and met together to take key decisions about their church and the surrounding diocese.

candidate was subject to the approval of the king, his ecclesiastical superior (an archbishop in the case of a bishop, or the pope in the case of an archbishop) and the man himself. While in theory the king was only supposed to object to the chapter's choice on grounds of real significance, in reality, during the 15th century, kings usually imposed their choice of candidate upon the Church, for reasons of political expediency. While the majority of the clergy were of importance only within their local communities, the loyalty of bishops was especially important to kings as they could take a significant role in politics. They had an automatic seat in the Lords in parliament, and were often involved in government offices, most notably as the chancellor, who ran the legal section of government administration.

EXTRACT

From J.A.F. Thomson, *The Transformation of Medieval England, 1370–1529* (2014). Here, the historian discusses the potential for disputes between the papacy and the English monarchy in relation to clerical appointments and jurisdictions.

Many of these disputed matters were not formally resolved [by the late 15th century], but in practice one can see that a working system developed, as pope and king alike recognized the desirability of a measure of compromise. Agreement was tacit rather than explicit and there were still intermittent crises, but these should not obscure the fact that on many practical matters there was often substantial co-operation. The Pope might theoretically claim supremacy over all Christians, but could still appreciate that little was to be gained by alienating the secular ruler, while a king could realise that with papal goodwill he could enhance his authority over an important section of his subjects.

Church careers and political advancement

Given their potential usefulness in terms of political advancement, high-ranking church positions were often sought after for those seeking a public career. Some members of the gentry found them particularly useful; the most famous example of this was William Wykeham, a man whose only claim to gentility was being the grandson of a Hampshire knight, who, through a judicious mixture of royal and church patronage, became Bishop of Winchester and chancellor of England. Similarly, John Morton, another man of gentry origins, advanced his career through the Church by becoming a canon lawyer and then moving into royal service. After the Tudor victory at Bosworth, he was made chancellor by Henry VII and the following year, at the king's instigation, the pope allowed him to be made Archbishop of Canterbury. Both examples indicate that a role in the Church was a very useful way to begin a political career, but to move to the great offices of state, royal approval was the crucial factor. It should not be assumed, however, that all churchmen were ambitious former members of the gentry; indeed, leading noble and royal families also put their sons into the Church, especially younger sons who were not needed to continue the family line. Examples of **cardinals** with royal blood were Henry Beaufort, an illegitimate grandson of Edward III, and Thomas Bourchier, a legitimate great-grandson.

'Over-mighty subjects' and 'under-mighty monarchs': noblemen as necessary props to the crown but also potential rivals

Throughout the 15th century, a recurring political theme was that noblemen acted both as a key prop to the power of the crown, but also as potential rivals to the king. These were the '**over-mighty subjects**' described by Sir John Fortescue in the 15th century, who could easily come to have undue influence over a weak or '**under-mighty monarch**', or even go so far as to challenge the king's claim to the throne.

KEY TERMS

Over-mighty subject
First used in the 15th century by the lawyer Sir John Fortescue and has been adopted by modern historians. It refers to a noble who became too powerful and influential with the king, and was therefore able to steer his patronage and matters of national policy to a very great extent, in a manner which ultimately was likely to cause conflict among the nobility in general.

Under-mighty monarch
Again, a phrase coined in the 15th century and now used widely by modern scholars. It refers to a weak monarch who was unable to overrule leading nobles when necessary and who was too easily influenced by individual subjects when taking key decisions.

This situation was made all the more fraught by events in 1399, which were to undermine future kings' claims to the throne for three generations. King Richard II had come to the throne at the age of ten in 1377. Despite showing early promise as a monarch, the final two years of his reign were marked by a growing rift between the crown and many influential members of the nobility, a time traditionally described as a period of **tyranny** in English history. One of the most disgruntled figures of the later period of Richard's reign was the king's cousin, Henry Bolingbroke, who had been exiled and lost his inheritance. In 1399, while Richard was fighting rebels in Ireland, Henry returned from exile in France and seized the throne, taking Richard prisoner when he returned to defend his crown. The **usurper** was crowned King Henry IV in October 1399 and Richard died while held prisoner in Pontefract Castle in February 1400, probably having been murdered. The Lancastrian dynasty of kings had begun.

KEY TERMS

Tyranny
Cruel or oppressive rule, often where an individual leader takes arbitrary decisions and reprisals against those whom they dislike, outside the normal rule of law.

Usurper
Someone who seizes the throne by force.

A key problem was now faced by Henry IV and his successors. The first was that Henry had seized the throne by force and upset the legitimate line of succession. Even if Richard had voluntarily **abdicated**, as the Lancastrians (no doubt falsely) claimed, the fact that Henry Bolingbroke took the throne by force made something of a mockery of the **hereditary claim** to the throne, particularly as there were alternative claimants. It is unsurprising, therefore, that Henry IV faced a number of rebellions, the most serious of which occurred in 1403 and involved the united forces of a leading Welsh rebel, Owain Glyndwr, and Henry Percy, the earl of Northumberland (also known as 'Henry Hotspur'). This uprising, however, was defeated by the king at the Battle of Shrewsbury in the same year; Hotspur was killed in the fighting and his lands were forfeited to the crown.

KEY TERMS

Abdicate
To resign as a monarch.

Hereditary claim
A claim (in this case to the throne, but it could also be to money, land or titles) that is inherited from one's family.

Crushing conspiracy by force: examples for the reigns of Henry V and Henry VII

While historians have on occasion exaggerated the level of violence in this period, there can be no doubt that the use of force was a very important aspect of control during the 15th century. As the example of Richard II's usurpation proved, even a king with a strong legitimate claim to the throne via hereditary right could be deposed if he lost popularity and if there was a powerful nobleman willing to challenge his authority with an army. Unsurprisingly, therefore, violent uprisings occurred against every monarch in this period and were often led by members of the nobility. In order to keep his throne, therefore, a king was obliged on occasion to use force against rebellious subjects and two kings who did this to particularly good effect were Henry V and Henry VII. These instances, therefore, provide a useful insight into the workings of violent power in the 15th-century political system.

The Southampton Plot: conspiracy against Henry V in 1415

Despite his problems, King Henry IV was successful in leaving a relatively secure throne to his eldest son, who became Henry V when his father died following a prolonged period of ill-health in 1413. Henry V is undoubtedly the quintessential 'good king' of popular folklore, a reputation owed largely to his outstanding military victories in France during the **Hundred Years War**. The first two years of his reign, however, showed resurgence in anti-Lancastrian sentiment, which culminated in 1415 with the '**Southampton Plot**' that aimed to kill Henry V and replace him on the throne with Edmund Mortimer, the earl of March. The leaders of the revolt were Richard of Conisburgh, third earl of Cambridge; Henry Scrope, third Baron Scrope of Masham; and Sir Thomas Grey.

These insurgents sought to involve various groups within the kingdom who were dissatisfied with Lancastrian rule, including Scottish and Welsh rebels, the earl of Northumberland and his men, and a group of religious dissidents called **Lollards**. It is also possible that there was French encouragement of the rebellion, as Henry V was at the time planning an invasion of France and so they may have hoped internal strife would distract him from this military endeavour. The leaders of the rebellion do not seem to have informed their proposed candidate for kingship, the earl of March, of their aims until fairly late on in proceedings and he proved an unsatisfactory conspirator, ultimately betraying the plot to Henry V. The leaders were arrested and imprisoned in Southampton Castle, where they confessed and were swiftly tried and executed as traitors to the crown. Their heads were displayed publicly as a warning to others and this quick and ruthless treatment of the plotters effectively helped to deter any further rebellions during his reign. Henry was not only authoritarian, however; he also showed wisdom in offering a pardon to the earl of March, who probably had known of the plot for some time before he betrayed it to the king. This act of mercy ensured March's absolute loyalty to Henry for the rest of his reign. By the late summer of 1415, the king felt sufficiently secure to continue his planned invasion of France, where he won a surprise and highly celebrated victory at the famous Battle of Agincourt, a display of military skill that considerably enhanced his popularity and authority back in England.

Crushing of conspiracy by Henry VII: the execution of Warwick in 1499

Henry VII was the first Tudor monarch. His rise to power had been bloody; in exile from England for most of his life, he had invaded from Brittany in the summer of 1485 and fought King Richard III for the throne at the Battle of Bosworth.

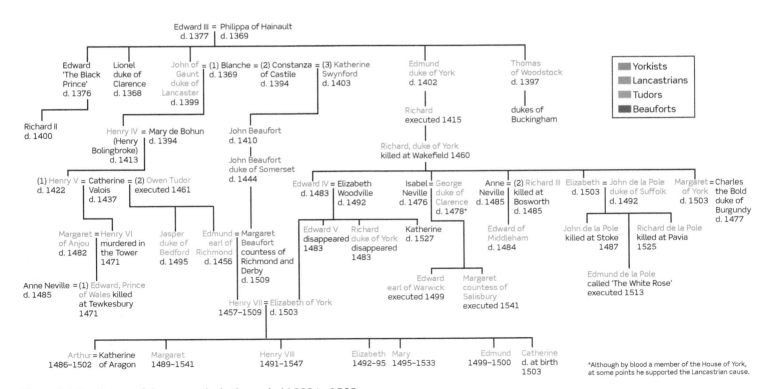

Figure 1.1 Family tree of the monarchy in the period 1399 to 1509.

Richard III was killed, his body stripped and mutilated, and Henry was declared king by his exultant troops. Despite this military victory, however, the legitimacy of his claim to the throne was undoubtedly shaky; his mother, Lady Margaret Beaufort was a descendent of John of Gaunt, duke of Lancaster and brother to Edward III, but from a relationship Gaunt had with his long-standing mistress, Katherine Swynford. While Gaunt had later married Swynford and his heirs were legitimised, there can be little doubt the situation was far from ideal for a potential claimant to the throne. In addition, rumours abounded that Henry's father, Edmund Tudor was also illegitimate and, scandalously, actually the blood-uncle of his wife and Henry's mother, Margaret. If true, these rumours would have made Henry's parents' marriage illegal and forbidden in the eyes of the Catholic Church.

Given these extensive problems with his claim to the throne, it was obvious that alternative candidates to the throne would emerge once Tudor claimed it in 1485. The most dangerous of these in terms of a legitimate claim was the 14-year-old Edward, earl of Warwick, the son of George, duke of Clarence. To prevent problems from this quarter, Henry had the boy imprisoned in the Tower of London, where he lived in reasonable comfort although he was deprived of his freedom. During 1485–86, there were some small rebellions, but the first major threat to Henry came in the form of the 1486 Simnel Conspiracy.

Lambert Simnel was the ten-year-old son of an organ maker, who was encouraged by an Oxford priest called Richard Symonds to pretend that he was Edward, earl of Warwick. In fact, as mentioned above, the real earl was imprisoned in the Tower but, because he had not been seen, rumours began to circulate that he had either escaped or been murdered. Symonds chose to manipulate these rumours by arguing that Simnel was the rightful heir to the throne. Yorkist sympathisers, embittered by their defeat at Bosworth, backed the plan, which gained particular support in Ireland, which was inclined to be more sympathetic to the Yorkist cause for these reasons:

- The earl of Warwick was the grandson of Richard, duke of York, who had been popular in Ireland since his lieutenancy in 1447.

- Irish leaders, including Walter Fitzsimmons, Archbishop of Dublin, and the earl of Kildare, wished to cause difficulties for the new king, because Henry VII would not confirm their positions as he was uncertain of their loyalty.

- Irish leaders were keen to gain greater powers to govern Ireland with less interference from the English crown.

- Some supporters may have wished to gain land through the rebellion.

Additionally, Richard III's sister, Margaret, dowager duchess of Burgundy, offered her support to the rebellion to get revenge against Henry for the Battle of Bosworth. She sent an army of 2,000 men and, in response, the Irish crowned Simnel king in a ceremony in Dublin in 1487.

When Henry learned of the rebellion, he acted swiftly, arresting any key figure with Yorkist connections, regardless of their involvement in this particular uprising, including Elizabeth Woodville and her son, the marquis of Dorset. He also publicly displayed the real earl of Warwick to scotch rumours about his escape and, when the army supporting Simnel landed in Lancashire in June 1487, the king met them at the Battle of Stoke. King Henry VII won decisively and a number of Yorkist leaders were killed, while the young Lambert Simnel was pardoned and given a job working in the palace kitchens. The scale of the rebellion highlighted, however, the fragility of the Tudor claim on the crown and indicated early unease within the reign of Henry VII.

Henry VII's relationship with the nobility continued to be a fraught one and, in the 1490s, a fresh threat to the king came in the form of another pretender, called Perkin Warbeck, who claimed to be Richard of Shrewsbury (also known as Richard, duke of York), the younger of the two 'princes in the Tower' who disappeared in 1483 and are thought to have died. Warbeck again gained support from pro-Yorkist factions, including significant support from the French king and Margaret of Burgundy. James IV of Scotland, too, saw the potential of Warbeck to make trouble for Henry VII and so went as far as to arrange for the pretender to marry Lady Catherine Gordon, a cousin of the Scottish king, in order to strengthen his position. During the 1490s, Warbeck attempted to invade England three times, but ultimately he was a troublesome failure for all concerned. In 1497, he managed to raise a rebel army of a few thousand and besiege the city of Exeter, but this ended in failure and in August he gave himself up and was mercifully treated by Henry VII, who allowed him to live under house arrest within the English court with his Scottish wife. In 1498, however, Warbeck attempted to escape to cause further uprisings and this time he was caught and imprisoned in the Tower.

TIMELINE: REBELLION AGAINST HENRY VII

1485
Tudor victory at the Battle of Bosworth

Henry VII imprisons Edward, earl of Warwick in the Tower of London

1487
Pretender Lambert Simnel crowned king by the Irish in Dublin. Henry arrests all those in England with Yorkist connections and displays real earl of Warwick publicly

June: Army supporting Simnel lands in Lancashire

Henry VII defeats Simnel's troops at the Battle of Stoke

1491
December: Perkin Warbeck arrives in Cork, Ireland, and is persuaded by Yorkists there to impersonate the younger son of Edward IV, Richard of Shrewsbury

1492
March: King of France promotes Perkin Warbeck as the rightful King of England

November: England and France make peace terms, so the French stop backing Warbeck

Warbeck supported by the dowager duchess of Burgundy who confirms that he is her long-lost nephew

1493
Some English nobles begin plotting with Warbeck

Henry VII cuts off trade with Burgundy

Early 1495
Robert Clifford betrays those involved in the Warbeck Plot to Henry VII. Various English nobles arrested and tried.

July: Warbeck makes an unsuccessful invasion attempt on England. He then sails to Ireland.

November: Warbeck welcomed in Scotland by James IV of Scots

1496
January: King James IV arranges Warbeck's marriage to Katherine Gordon, a distant royal relation by marriage

Warbeck and James plan joint invasion of England

September: Warbeck and James invade England, but Warbeck quickly withdraws. Henry VII plans counter-invasion of Scotland.

1497
May: Cornish Rebellion against Henry VII. Insurgents call on Warbeck to lead them.

June: Henry defeats rebels at Blackheath

17 September: Warbeck and rebels besiege city of Exeter, but flee as the royal army approaches

October: Warbeck captured and confesses

1498
9 June: Warbeck escapes, but is later recaptured

18 June: Warbeck condemned to life imprisonment in shackles in the Tower of London

1499
Summer: During his imprisonment, Warbeck meets a fellow inmate, the earl of Warwick. The two men plot together.

August: Plot betrayed to Henry VII

23 November: Warbeck hanged at the Tyburn in London

28 November: Edward, earl of Warwick, executed for treason at Tower Hill

While in captivity, Warbeck met a fellow prisoner, Edward, earl of Warwick. The exact nature of the two men's discussions is unknown, but in 1499 they were tried for plotting to escape from the Tower together and in November both men were executed, Warbeck being hanged as a commoner while Edward retained the noble privilege of being beheaded on Tower Hill. The evidence against Edward, earl of Warwick remains unclear and it may well have been a charge that was politically motivated to ensure that he could not be used as a further focus of rebellion against the Tudor regime. The fact that such a course of action was deemed necessary indicates that Henry VII was still fearful for his position and keen to remove all possible rivals to the throne.

ACTIVITY
KNOWLEDGE CHECK

The necessary qualities of a late medieval king

1 Draw a mind map of the key qualities of a successful medieval king.

2 Add examples to the mind map of when a king displayed this quality. For example, in 1415 at Agincourt, Henry V displayed his ability as a successful military commander.

3 Make notes on how Henry V responded to the Southampton Plot and Henry VII to the rebellions of Lambert Simnel and Perkin Warbeck. In different colours, highlight examples of when the king showed mercy, and when he used force. Write a paragraph analysing the advantages and disadvantages of using each method.

HOW SIGNIFICANT WAS RETAINING TO POLITICAL STABILITY?

Control of land was crucial to political power in the late Middle Ages and to understand this it is necessary to understand the **feudal system** and how it was disintegrating in this period. Classic English feudalism, which was an important form of political and social control prior to the 14th century, involved the following:

- A lord, who was a noble, or sometimes a leading member of the regular clergy, who held a substantial amount of land.

- A vassal, the person who was granted possession of part of that land by the lord.

- A fief, the land granted to the vassal.

Feudal relationships had obligations on both sides. A lord was expected to provide his vassals not only with the use of the fief, but also with protection from attacks by interlopers and a certain level of legal protection if the vassal got into trouble with the law. It was a matter of honour that the lord would provide these services, with considerable emphasis on the principles of 'good lordship' in contemporary writing. In return, a vassal was required to take an **oath of fealty** (loyalty) to the lord in a special ceremony. This oath meant that the vassal could not take up arms against his lord and was required to come to his aid to fight if the lord called upon him to do so (the vassal was the lord's **retainer**). Increasingly, vassals might have a range of other obligations including, but not limited to, attending the lord's local court or acting as an adviser. Importantly, the traditional feudal relationship was hereditary, with families of vassals having a long-term commitment to their lord.

KEY TERMS

Feudal system
A name given by modern historians to the social relationships between individuals of unequal social rank in early and high medieval society, which involved the granting of the use of land (called a fief) and an oath of loyalty to a lord.

Oath of fealty
A vow of loyalty taken by someone of lower social status, who promised to support and serve someone of higher social status. This was sometimes also described as 'doing homage'.

Retainer
A member of the gentry who was loyal to his lord, often over the monarch. Retainers would wear the colours of their lord.

Livery, maintenance and bastard feudalism

During the 14th and 15th centuries, the feudal system was gradually disintegrating. This change has been described by influential historians such as Charles Plummer and K.B. McFarlane as 'bastard feudalism', although McFarlane disagreed with the view that the shift in medieval social relationships was essentially a negative development, as the wording of this term might suggest. The traditional feudal system was proving problematic because, firstly, as estates were divided through inheritance and marriage, lords did not always have enough property to provide numerous vassals with land, and, secondly, feudal holdings descended through the vassal's family line, which gave the lord no control over the type of vassal he had to serve him. Therefore, lords in the late medieval period increasingly moved away from a system of vassalage with *land* at its core, to a system where lords increasingly made annual *cash* payments in return for military and non-military services instead. In this system, men who served the lord were individually known as retainers, and as a group they were called his retinue or **affinity**. To distinguish his followers, a lord often gave each of them a distinctive badge or item of clothing, called a livery, which was designed to advertise their link to a particular lord and in this way to advertise the lord's power. Unlike traditional feudalism, this was not a hereditary system, with a focus instead on a personal relationship between a man and his lord and, sometimes, a written contract, called an indenture, replaced the oath of fealty ceremony. Instead, these indentures usually bound a man and lord together in a relationship of mutual dependence and loyalty for the lifetime of the parties concerned only, rather than being a hereditary bond passed down the generations.

KEY TERM

Affinity
An alternative term for 'retinue', this word is often preferred by more recent historians, partly as there is a suggestion in the current scholarship that formalised, paid contracts of indenture were less widely used than previously believed. Instead, some scholars now argue that the bond between lord and follower was often more informal in nature and depended upon local social and political networks.

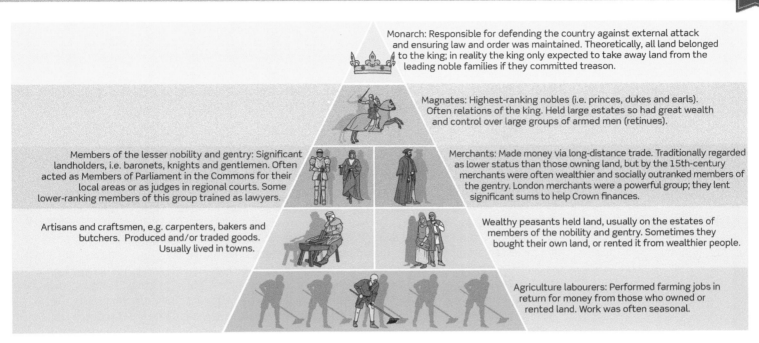

Monarch: Responsible for defending the country against external attack and ensuring law and order was maintained. Theoretically, all land belonged to the king; in reality the king only expected to take away land from the leading noble families if they committed treason.

Magnates: Highest-ranking nobles (i.e. princes, dukes and earls). Often relations of the king. Held large estates so had great wealth and control over large groups of armed men (retinues).

Members of the lesser nobility and gentry: Significant landholders, i.e. baronets, knights and gentlemen. Often acted as Members of Parliament in the Commons for their local areas or as judges in regional courts. Some lower-ranking members of this group trained as lawyers.

Merchants: Made money via long-distance trade. Traditionally regarded as lower status than those owning land, but by the 15th-century merchants were often wealthier and socially outranked members of the gentry. London merchants were a powerful group; they lent significant sums to help Crown finances.

Artisans and craftsmen, e.g. carpenters, bakers and butchers. Produced and/or traded goods. Usually lived in towns.

Wealthy peasants held land, usually on the estates of members of the nobility and gentry. Sometimes they bought their own land, or rented it from wealthier people.

Agriculture labourers: Performed farming jobs in return for money from those who owned or rented land. Work was often seasonal.

Figure 1.2 The social structure and landholding relationships in late medieval England.

SOURCE 3

This is the Dunstable Swan Jewel, currently housed at the British Museum in London. It is a very expensive, high-class version of a livery badge, designed to show allegiance to the House of Lancaster, and specifically to Henry IV's son, the Prince of Wales, in the early 15th century. It is made of white enamel fused over gold, and is the only surviving example of such a costly livery badge, although documentary records show that other similar items existed in wealthy noble families. Supporters of lower social rank and servants would have had livery badges with similar symbols, but made from cheaper materials which are less likely to have been preserved.

Maintenance
This was the system of a lord developing retinues or affinities based upon his personal relationship with them, and often cash payments, rather than a hereditary feudal tie based on land. Formal contracts, called indentures, sometimes formalised this arrangement, which was usually for the lifetime of the two parties involved.

The new system, usually described as a system of **maintenance** by historians, clearly had considerable advantages for the lord: it was, for example, easier to stop paying a disobedient retainer than to confiscate a troublesome vassal's land. More importantly, it gave the lord and retainer considerably more control over whom they chose to bind themselves to, although in the continually shifting loyalties of the Wars of the Roses it is likely that many came to regret their choices. Nonetheless, the flexibility of the arrangements should not be exaggerated, as men in a retinue had to have someone to act as their protector, something contemporaries referred to as being a man's 'good lord'. Therefore, if the lord died, members of the retinue were liable to look to his heir or replacement for their next leader.

The traditional view of the Wars of the Roses has been that this new, more fluid system of social relationships was a key factor in causing civil unrest, as it reflected a more widespread destabilisation of society. Certainly, the loyalty of large retinues to individual noblemen could be a factor in making them 'over-mighty', as in effect they could be used as private armies. Two factors, however, need to be kept in mind when evaluating this view. Firstly, retinues were needed if lords were to provide the necessary number of armed men for the king's wars. Clearly, this was a more important factor in the later medieval period because of the large amount of fighting in France during the Hundred Years War. Secondly, contemporaries regarded it as essential that great nobles had large followings; a magnate, for example, would be expected to have a large number of servants who resided in his household, as well as a retinue of men bound to him via indentures. There did seem to be contemporary criticism, however, when lords failed to control these retinues, or extended them unduly with groups of men paid a fee and given a livery, but who actually had fairly little connection with the lord and who were therefore difficult for him to control. This last group, often referred to as 'liverymen' in the primary sources, were viewed with suspicion and there were complaints that they caused disturbances to the peace, could be used by the nobleman to intimidate rivals or even the king, and were not necessarily loyal in their service, as some took fees from more than one lord.

Statutes against retaining in 1468 and 1504

There has been considerable debate among historians about the extent to which this shift towards cash relationships has been responsible for a breakdown in law and order in the late medieval period, but certainly contemporaries were concerned regarding the development of private retinues. This was evidenced by parliamentary legislation of the period, which sought to distinguish between necessary retainers and the more widespread granting of liveries to a larger and less controlled group. Parliament legislated on this point on a number of occasions during the 14th century, with three such Acts being passed in the 1390s, which presumably reflects contemporary concern regarding the growing instability of Richard II and therefore potential lawlessness within the realm. The fact that such legislation had to be frequently repeated in the 15th century argues for its ineffectiveness and certainly it must have been difficult to enforce for both practical reasons and as the wording of much of the legislation was complex and vague.

One of the more famous pieces of legislation to control retinues was passed in 1468 by Edward IV. This outlawed the practice of retaining except for legal advisers, domestic servants, estate officials and, rather vaguely, those in 'lawful service'. Unsurprisingly, the reference to 'lawful service' proved a major loophole and the practice of maintenance among the great lords continued unabated. This was partially, no doubt, because, while kings might criticise the lawlessness of some retinues, they remained aware that in reality they were essential for the medieval political and military system to function. Retinues were usually the basis of national armies sent to fight in France, as occurred in 1475 and 1492.

Importantly, too, the liverymen of nobles who were loyal to the king could prove highly beneficial to a monarch in helping to put down uprisings, as Henry VII discovered in 1487 during a rebellion which attempted to make a ten-year-old boy called Lambert Simnel king. The conspirators (falsely) claimed Simnel was Edward IV's nephew and the rightful heir to the throne. As events like the Simnel Conspiracy highlighted, therefore, retinues had both the potential to make and break a monarch's power. Hence, a late medieval king had a tricky balancing act to achieve: on one hand, he needed to maintain sufficient popularity among nobles so that he could be sure of the support of the majority in times of difficulty; on the other hand, he needed to assert his authority sufficiently to ensure that he was not challenged by them for the throne, or that they did not use their wealth and power to create disorder in the kingdom. One king who formulated a novel method for resolving this problem was Henry VII, who in the parliament of 1504 passed a statute that lords had to receive written permission in the form of a licence from the king to retain men and to provide a list of retainers for his approval. Those who disobeyed this law were liable to be fined, and certainly enormous sums were levied on those who retained men illegally. Nonetheless, for loyal associates of Henry VII, such as his councillor Sir Thomas Lovell, it remained possible to develop extensive affinities.

ACTIVITY
KNOWLEDGE CHECK

Retaining in the late medieval period

1 Draw a flow diagram to show how the medieval feudal system worked.

2 Re-read the section called 'Livery, maintenance and bastard feudalism' and write one-sentence definitions of the words in bold, in your own words.

3 Make two lists, one on advantages of the system of retaining and maintenance, and one on the disadvantages. Then write a paragraph, explaining your view on this statement: 'For medieval society as a whole, the benefits of the late medieval practice of retaining outweighed the costs.' You could also debate this statement with a partner or as a class.

HOW WELL DID THE CROWN COPE WITH THE CHALLENGES OF LOCAL DISORDER?

The Neville–Percy dispute in the North

The most infamous example of feuding was found in the North of England, between the Nevilles and the Percies, two leading noble families who had substantial territorial claims in Yorkshire, the Lake District and other northern counties. Both families had grown to prominence in the late 14th century. In 1377, Henry 'Hotspur' Percy was made the earl of Northumberland. The Nevilles, meanwhile, gained power and prestige via their involvement in wars against the Scots and by the 15th century were headed by Richard Neville, earl of Salisbury. The proximity of the two families' estates made it almost inevitable that they would be rivals in matters of land and prestige. In 1403, however, the Percies faced a serious setback when Hotspur lived up to his name and led a rebellion against King Henry IV, thus dying a traitor and ensuring that his estates were forfeit to the crown (see page 16). In the short term, this was a disaster for the family. Nonetheless, between 1416 and 1440, Hotspur's grandson, also called Henry Percy, managed by patient negotiation to recover most, although not all, of the lost estates. By the mid-15th century, the Percies were once again serious rivals to the Nevilles in the North.

By contrast, the fortunes of the Neville family had been largely successful during the first half of the 15th century. The head of the family, Richard Neville, earl of Salisbury, was by the 1440s a member of the king's council and an important adviser to the king. His son, also called Richard Neville and later known as 'the kingmaker', made a highly advantageous marriage to the wealthy heiress Anne Beauchamp. In 1449, and aged only 21, the younger Richard inherited the title of earl of Warwick via marriage, along with vast estates, especially in the Midlands. This growing ascendancy of the Nevilles increased Percy resentment and set the stage for more serious conflict, but it was, in fact, the younger sons of both families who were to take the leading role in the major conflicts of the 1450s. On the Percy side, the key protagonists in the quarrel were the earl of Northumberland's sons, Thomas, who became Lord Egremont in 1449, Ralph and Richard, while on the Neville side were the earl of Salisbury's sons, Thomas and John.

Planned assassination at the wedding of Thomas Neville to Maud Stanhope

The main trigger of the violent conflicts of 1453 and 1454 was the marriage of Thomas Neville to Maud Stanhope. Maud was the niece and co-heiress of Lord Cromwell, who had been rewarded with substantial estates for his service to Henry VI, including the two former Percy manors of Wressle in Yorkshire and Burwell in Lincolnshire. At the time of the engagement, Northumberland was engaged in legal proceedings to take this land back from Cromwell and so the news that they would now be inherited via marriage by a member of the Neville family was infuriating for the Percies.

In June and July 1453, Egremont and John Neville were actively hostile to one another and there were outbreaks of violence between the rival retinues, which led to Henry VI repeatedly summoning them to appear before him to explain their actions. Henry VI was so weak and ineffective in this period, however, that the men disregarded these royal commands with impunity. During the summer of 1453, it became increasingly obvious that the crown was not in control of the situation, and this was confirmed in August by Henry VI's complete mental collapse. In this fraught situation, the controversial Neville-Stanhope marriage took place, and it was on 24 August 1453, as the Nevilles were returning from the wedding party, that a large force led by Egremont and Richard Percy ambushed them and attempted to assassinate Salisbury and a number of other members of his family, including the newly-weds. It is unclear if the earl of Northumberland knew of, and had approved, this plot of his sons. It is certain, however, that the retinues involved on both sides must have been substantial, as 710 Percy retainers were named in subsequent legal proceedings. No doubt owing to the skill and size of their own affinity, the Nevilles were able to escape this attack. Despite attempts at legal redress, violence on both sides continued into the autumn and winter.

This assassination attempt not only illustrates the extent to which law and order had broken down during Henry VI's reign, but also demonstrates how local rivalries and national politics were interlinked. Henry VI's mental breakdown in August 1453 caused a political crisis in terms of who should now govern in his stead during the period of his illness. The obvious candidate was the king's closest adult male relation, Richard, duke of York, who was keen to act as Defender and Protector of the Realm. The Nevilles supported his claim. York, however, was not a popular man and Henry VI's queen, Margaret of Anjou, was particularly anxious that he should not be given control, as she feared he would try to oust her baby son from his position as heir to the throne. Margaret worked with the duke of Somerset to exclude York and they were supported in this endeavour by the Percies, who appear to have been motivated largely by the Nevilles' support for York. As part of their plotting, the Percies convinced the young Henry Holand, duke of Exeter to support their cause, on the grounds that Holand was also in a land dispute with Lord Cromwell.

During early 1454, tensions on both a local and national level ran high. In January, the leading noble opponents arrived in London for parliament armed, as a significant and threatening show of strength. The parliament was tense and focused on who should rule during the king's illness. On 27 March, the decision was taken to make the duke of York Protector of the Realm, placing the Nevilles, as his supporters, in a very strong position. This was cemented almost immediately when York appointed a Neville – Richard, earl of Salisbury – as chancellor. Unsurprisingly, the Percies reacted with anger to the news. By

May, Lord Egremont, the duke of Exeter and other rebels were attempting to gain support in Yorkshire, Lancashire and Cheshire for an armed rebellion against the new Protectorate. On 19 May, York himself arrived with strong military support, including the backing of Lord Cromwell. The rebel leaders were forced to flee, but it proved difficult to implement legal redress against the insurgents' supporters as local law officers could find themselves at risk when trying to make arrests in the Percy strongholds of the North. Nonetheless, by July, York had managed to capture Exeter and imprison him in Pontefract Castle. There was a recurrence of Neville–Percy violence in the autumn of 1454, in the environs of Stamford Bridge, but there is considerable scholarly debate concerning the exact date or location of this outbreak.

SOURCE 4

Image of Richard, duke of York (1411–60) in a painted glass window from St Lawrence's church in Ludlow, Shropshire.

During the winter of 1454–55, the political tide began to turn against York and this was speeded up by Henry VI's recovery from his illness in 1454. King Henry, always easily influenced, was quickly persuaded to release a number of those made prisoners during York's Protectorate, including the duke of Exeter and the duke of Somerset. Partly as a reaction to this, York began to plot to regain his influence over Henry VI and he successfully took up arms against him in May 1455 at the First Battle of St Albans. During this battle, the head of the Percy family, the earl of Northumberland was killed, while Egremont was captured and imprisoned. Exeter, who had not fought, was later seized by York again. The duke of York's victory was, however, once again short lived; Yorkshire remained a hotbed of lawlessness, Egremont escaped from prison by 1456 and Exeter was apparently released. Nonetheless, the Percies and Exeter remained too weak to renew hostilities and had considerably less motivation to rebel as York's power and influence decreased from 1456 onwards.

On 25 March 1458, both sides took part in a highly theatrical and public ceremony of reconciliation in London, known as 'Loveday', at the request of Henry VI, which was designed to end the enmity caused by the First Battle of St Albans. Each faction had to pay substantial damages to those they had offended and the erstwhile enemies, Margaret and York, and the earl of Salisbury with the new earl of Somerset, walked hand-in-hand to a service at St Paul's Cathedral. This demonstration of goodwill and peace, however, was to prove short lived, and by the following year the Wars of the Roses had begun again in earnest.

Local disorder in the reign of Henry VI: the Bonville–Courtenay dispute in the South West, 1451–61

Although the disputes in the North were the most infamous of the period, clashes between rival families also occurred elsewhere in the country, which again influenced and were influenced by the fraught political situation surrounding Henry VI's weak grip on power. In the South West, there were clashes between the Courtenay family (the earls of Devon, who were traditionally dominant in the area) and the Bonvilles, a family who were lords of Harington and whose wealth and prominence grew during the 15th century. Although the earls of Devon were undoubtedly very wealthy compared to the majority of the population, they were by the 1430s among the poorest families of their rank. When the young Thomas Courtenay, thirteenth earl of Devon, came of age he was fully aware of the threat to his position as pre-eminent local nobleman from William, Lord Harington, who by now owned one of the most valuable estates in the South West. In 1437, therefore, when the king appointed Bonville as Royal Steward in Cornwall for life, it was seen by Courtenay as a serious threat to his regional authority. This triggered a campaign of violence by the retinue of the earl of Devon against that of Lord Harington and his affinity.

During the late 1430s and early 1440s, Bonville had increasing influence at court and at this time supported the duke of Suffolk and Queen Margaret in national politics. In 1449, this alliance succeeded in gaining for Bonville his elevation to the peerage, when he became Baron Bonville of Chewton. This was another blow to the cause of Thomas Courtenay. In response, the earl of Devon allied with the rival faction, led by the duke of York. The summer of 1451 saw battle between the two local rivals, with the earl of Devon placing Taunton Castle, the Bonville stronghold, under siege, a situation which was only stopped by the personal intervention of the duke of York who clearly felt the situation was getting out of hand.

During 1452–55, Bonville exercised considerable dominance in the West Country and he clearly had the full support of King Henry VI, who personally stayed at Bonville's home during the summer of 1452. During this period, Bonville not only was confirmed as Steward of Cornwall, but also appointed constable of Exeter Castle, a post traditionally within the influence of the earls of Devon. As the duke of York and his supporters gained ascendancy in their bid to influence the king, it is evident that Bonville shifted his support towards the Yorkists and away from the queen's party. This change in loyalties was cemented in around 1455, by the marriage of Bonville's grandson to Katherine, daughter of Richard Neville, earl of Salisbury, who was allied with the Yorkist cause in this period. This advantageous match was no doubt another cause of Thomas Courtenay's growing hostility towards the Bonvilles. On 23 October 1455, the earl of Devon's son and other members of the Courtenay affinity attacked and murdered one of Bonville's senior councillors, Nicholas Radford. This marked the beginning of a very violent period in the history of the South West, which continued into 1456.

In 1458, the thirteenth earl of Devon died and the new earl, another Thomas Courtenay, was Radford's murderer, so not a conciliatory figure. Worryingly for Bonville, Courtenay quickly found favour with the queen, a situation which pushed Bonville further into the rival camp of the duke of York. In 1460, both William Bonville's son and grandson fought alongside York at the Battle of Wakefield and all three were killed. In February 1461, the Yorkists, now led by Edward, the new duke of York, fought against the queen's Lancastrian forces at the Second Battle of St Albans. Bonville himself was too old to fight, but he was made responsible for ensuring that King Henry VI, at this time a captive of the Yorkist faction, was kept securely guarded. Unfortunately for Bonville, the Yorkists were defeated; their leader, the new duke of York, was forced to flee for his life and the king was freed by the Lancastrians. At the instigation of Queen Margaret and the earl of Devon, Bonville was subjected to a mock trial after the battle and was subsequently executed.

A Level Exam-Style Question Section C

'The key factor in upholding the king's authority in the years 1399–1509 was his relationship with the nobility.'

How far do you agree with this statement? (20 marks)

Tip

Make sure that you consider not only the king's relationship with leading nobles, but also factors such as the role of the gentry, especially in parliament, and the importance of foreign policy.

A Level Exam-Style Question Section C

How far do you agree that, throughout the period 1399–1509, maintenance was the key problem facing late medieval English kings? (20 marks)

Tip

Make sure you consider key changes in how maintenance was controlled by the crown during this period, as well as other problems late medieval kings faced, such as popular rebellion or threats from foreign powers.

Being a member of the gentry during the Wars of the Roses: the experience of the Paston family

While the great noble disputes of the 15th century were undoubtedly of great national importance, the experience of a less exalted family, the Pastons, has been one that has excited the imagination and added personal colour to the study of the Wars of the Roses for generations. The Pastons were an upwardly mobile gentry family based in Norfolk and are of considerable significance to modern historians as almost their entire collection of letters survives. In a period when letter-writing was obviously the mainstay of communication between family members at any distance, this has provided scholars not only with unparalleled evidence for the interplay of local and national politics of the period, but also a unique insight into the interpersonal relations of a lively 15th-century family.

During the 14th and 15th centuries, the Pastons rose from peasant to gentry status. In 1440, John Paston I was a lawyer who made a highly advantageous marriage to Margaret Mauteby. Through his marriage, John became a confidante and legal adviser to a wealthy local Norfolk knight, Sir John Fastolf, the real-life persona of the character 'Falstaff' in Shakespeare's plays. When Fastolf died in 1459, John Paston claimed to be the main beneficiary thanks to a nuncupative will (that is, a will that was delivered orally and written down later). Unsurprisingly, this was widely contested by the other executors and resulted in legal wrangling with Fastolf's two other heirs, Thomas Howes and Sir William Yelverton. As the national political situation became more fraught in the early 1460s, when Edward IV usurped the throne, the dispute concerning Fastolf's will descended into violence. This is often seen as a classic example of local quarrels getting out of control during the political turmoil of the Wars of the Roses.

Tension concerning the disputed inheritance was made more significant as two noble families, the Mowbrays (earls of Norfolk) and the de la Poles (earls of Suffolk), had strong territorial interests in the estates claimed by the Pastons and both seem to have used the crown's weakness and the political upheavals of the period as an opportunity to further their own claims at the expense of their less-powerful neighbours. In 1461, for example, the duke of Norfolk seized Caister Castle for a period, while in 1465 the duke of Suffolk laid claim to two disputed Norfolk manors of Hellesdon and Drayton and had his men attack and rob the properties, causing very considerable damage (see Source 5). During the legal disputes regarding the Fastolf inheritance, John Paston ended up in Fleet Prison in London on two occasions in 1464–65.

SOURCE

5 Margaret Paston to her husband, John, writing in 1461 shortly after she visited Hellesdon manor to inspect the damage following the attack on it by the affinity of the duke of Suffolk. From N. Davies (ed.), *The Paston Letters* (1983).

I was at Hellesdon upon Thursday last past and saw the place there, and in good faith there will no creature think how foul and horribly it is arrayed but if they saw it. There cometh much people daily to wonder thereupon, both of Norwich and of other places, and they speak shamefully thereof... Ye have the more good will of the people that it is so foul done.

Although John Paston I had allied primarily to the Yorkist cause during the Wars of the Roses, this does not seem to have prevented Edward IV's brother-in-law, Anthony Woodville, Lord Scales, from claiming Paston's property in the king's name in January 1466. This could be taken as supporting evidence for the widespread contemporary view that the family of Queen Elizabeth Woodville were grasping and sought to use their connections with the king for their own benefit. However, it should also be noted that the Pastons were an extremely ambitious and quarrelsome family, who were rarely blameless in the disputes with which they became embroiled. Certainly, the strain of the Fastolf dispute on John Paston I was considerable, and may well have contributed to his early death in May 1466. At this time, the matter was still unresolved and his two sons, both also called John, therefore inherited a complex legal dispute, which focused upon the manors of Caister Castle (in Norfolk) and Cotton and Caldecott Hall (in Suffolk).

EXTEND YOUR KNOWLEDGE

The problems of the evidence from the Paston letters

There is a traditional scholarly view of the later Middle Ages as an intrinsically violent and anarchic age. According to this interpretation, the 15th century was a period of political and social decline, and was a highly violent period. The classic work of this kind was *The Waning of the Middle Ages* by Johann Huizinga, which focused on the history of France and the Netherlands, but a similar theme was noticeable in the historiography of England, with the late medieval period being regarded very much as the 'poor relation' of the Tudor age, which was seen to represent a return of order and stability. To a large extent, the works of Shakespeare were responsible for the widespread nature of this view, as the playwright produced history plays for Tudor monarchs and so the scripts unsurprisingly seek to emphasise the problems that faced England during the Wars of the Roses, in order to highlight the comparative strength of his patron's dynasty.

More recently, scholars have again turned their attention to the question of the level of violence during the Wars of the Roses and how much the conflicts impacted upon everyday life for those living in England. Professor Michael Hicks, for example, has argued that 'the Wars of the Roses were superimposed upon a peaceful realm' arguing that, in general, battles caused relatively little impact on the surrounding areas except for during the years 1461–70. Key sources for this debate have been three collections of gentry letters from the period, those by the Paston, Stonor and Plumpton families. Certainly, the Pastons were heavily interested in, and influenced by, the dramatic events of the civil war, particularly through their claim to the Fastolf inheritance. In the words of Professor Christine Carpenter, however, these missives are 'the most lurid and the most atypical' and so have 'reinforced existing beliefs about the barbarity of the period'. Much less dramatic are the letters of the other two families, who were less involved, suggesting that the Pastons were unusually preoccupied with national affairs. When considering this correspondence as a source, therefore, it is important to give due consideration to the typicality of the events described.

John II, the eldest son, had become associated with the Yorkist cause from 1461, when he joined the **king's household**. Although not an immediate success, by the mid-1460s he seems to have become well connected, even taking part in a jousting tournament with the king and Lord Scales in 1467. It was no doubt in part owing to these connections that shortly following his father's death he received confirmation of his ownership of Caister Castle, despite Lord Scales' early attempts to seize Paston property in that year. Problems concerning the inheritance, however, continued when in October 1468 Fastolf's other trustees, Yelverton and Howes, sold their rights to the inheritance to the more formidable duke of Norfolk. As the national political situation again deteriorated in 1469, with rebellion in the North and Clarence and Warwick conspiring against Edward IV, Norfolk took advantage of the crisis to further his own interests. He besieged Caister for five weeks, eventually forcing the defenders led by John Paston III (the younger brother) to surrender.

SOURCE

From a letter to John Paston II from his mother, Margaret Paston, dated 14 September 1469. Here, Margaret describes how the Pastons and their supporters were besieged by the duke of Norfolk and his retinue at Caister Castle, when the duke sought to claim the property. She is also clearly dissatisfied with her eldest son's behaviour in relation to the threat. Daubeney and Berney, mentioned in the letter, are two supporters of the Pastons. From N. Davies (ed.), *The Paston Letters* (1983).

I greet you well, letting you know that your brother and his fellowship stand in great jeopardy at Caister, and lack food; and Daubeney and Berney be dead, and divers other greatly hurt, and they fail gunpowder and arrows, and the lace sore broken with guns of the other party, so that, unless they have rapid help, they are likely to lose both their lives and the place, to the greatest rebuke to you that ever came to any gentleman, for every man in this country marvels greatly that you suffer them to be so long in so great jeopardy without help or other remedy.

... Therefore, as you will have my blessing, I charge you and require you that you see your brother be helped in haste... Do your best now, and let me send you no more messengers for these matters, but send me by the bearer of [this letter] more certain comfort than you have done by all the others that I have sent before.

God keep you. Written the Tuesday next before Holy Cross Day [14 September], in haste.

By your mother.

SOURCE

7 On 15 September 1469 (the next day), John Paston II replied in this way to his mother. From N. Davies (ed.), *The Paston Letters* (1983).

Mother, on Saturday last week, Daubeney and Berney were alive and merry, and I suppose there came no man out of the place to you since that time who could have informed you of their deaths. And in relation to the fierceness of the duke or of his people,... I think it was concluded that truce and abstinence of war should be had before he departed, which shall endure until Monday next coming [18 September]. And by that time I think that truce shall be taken till that day a week afterwards, by which time I hope of a good decision.

But, mother, I feel by your writing that you deem in me that I should not do my best unless you wrote to me some bad tidings; and, mother, if I had need to be hurried with a letter in this [time of] need I would be too slow a fellow. But, mother, I ensure you that I have heard ten times worse tidings since the siege began than any letter you wrote to me, and sometimes I have heard very good tidings too... But whether I had good tidings or ill, I take God as my witness that I have done my best as I would do for any similar case, and I shall do until there be an end of it... I never knew a matter in my life that I could have been so troubled and sorry for. With God's grace, it shall be remedied well enough, for by my oath I had sooner lose the manor of Caister than the poorest man's life therein. Therefore I beseech you to send me word what money and men you think that I am likely to get in that area, for the hasty gaining of money and men shall be to the getting and rescuing of it [Caister Castle], and the saving of most men's lives, if matters go that way ...

John Paston, Knight.

KEY TERM

Readeption
In this context, it means regaining the throne after losing it, as Henry VI did in 1470.

A Level Exam-Style Question Section C

How far do you agree that the Wars of the Roses were little more than the violent escalation of private feuds? (20 marks)

Tip

Make sure that, in addition to discussing the feuds outlined here (such as the Neville–Percy dispute), you also discuss when nobles disagreed over areas of national policy, such as the war with France.

In terms of local and national politics, 1470 was a complex year. At this time, John II managed to reach an accommodation with his opponents via legal compromise on the ownership of various manors, but the duke of Norfolk continued to occupy Caister Castle regardless. By this stage John II had developed some associations with the earl of Oxford, who was an influential Lancastrian, and so the family altered their allegiance away from the Yorkists. By this means, the Pastons succeeded in having Norfolk removed from Caister briefly, but their change in loyalty quickly proved to be an ill-judged step, as Henry VI's **readeption** was short lived. Soon both the Paston brothers found themselves fighting on the losing side at the 1471 Battle of Barnet and shortly afterwards Norfolk felt confident enough to once again reoccupy Caister. Fortunately for the Pastons, they were not considered important enough figures to be a target of much recrimination from Edward IV and both were pardoned after the battle, with John II spending considerable time serving the king in Calais between 1473 and 1477. When the duke of Norfolk died in January 1476, the Pastons were finally able to gain both practical and legal possession of Caister. John II was not, unfortunately, able to enjoy his victory for long, as in 1479 he died of plague caught during a stay in London, and he was succeeded as head of the family by his younger brother.

ACTIVITY
KNOWLEDGE CHECK

Understanding the experience of the Pastons

1 Write short descriptions of the characters of the following members of the Paston family, including evidence to support your opinions: John Paston I (the father); John Paston II (the eldest son); John Paston III (the younger son).

2 For each character you have described, explain how their lives were influenced by the weakness of Henry VI and the key events of the Wars of the Roses.

The readeption of Henry VI in 1470 and the return of Edward IV in 1471

One of the periods of greatest instability during this time was 1470–71, when Richard Neville, sixteenth earl of Warwick was at the forefront of English politics. This period is seen as a classic example of an 'over-mighty subject' seeking to dominate the king and is crucial to understanding how Warwick came to be known from the 16th century as 'the kingmaker'. As discussed earlier, Neville was an exceptionally wealthy magnate and accordingly had access to a very large private retinue. This support was all the more dangerous as many members of the affinity had a long-standing loyalty to his family and a strong sense of identity fostered in part by the ongoing hostility with the rival Percy retinue. In 1460, Warwick had used his power and influence to back Richard, duke of York's claim to be heir to the throne, but the Yorkists had faced a temporary setback when Richard was killed at the Battle of Wakefield in December 1460. Quickly, however, York's son and heir, Edward of March, proved himself to be an able military tactician and with Warwick's vital assistance in March 1461 the Yorkists won a resounding victory over the Lancastrian forces at the Battle of Towton. Edward was crowned king while Henry VI, the queen and their young son Prince Edward were forced to flee to Scotland.

SOURCE

8 A description of Henry VI, written by John Blacman, precentor (a type of chaplain) at Eton College, one of Henry VI's foundations. Blacman knew Henry VI personally, acting as his personal priest and witnessing Henry VI's actions as he set up Eton College. This source was originally written as a Latin essay called 'Compilation of the meekness and good life of Henry VI'. It was certainly written after Henry VI's death, and probably Blacman was writing in around 1483. Blacman viewed Henry as a truly spiritual man and this piece of writing was designed to further a campaign to have Henry VI canonised as a saint in the Roman Catholic Church, a campaign which continued into the early 16th century, but which was ended by the Reformation. From M.R. James (ed. and trans.), *Henry the Sixth* (1919).

It is written that we are to praise no man before his death, but that in the end shall be the exposing of his works... I have therefore thought fit to treat of some matters to the praise of God and of the serene prince King Henry VI now deceased... He was a simple man, without any crook of craft or untruth, as is plain to all. With none did he deal craftily, nor even would say an untrue word to any...

This king Henry was chaste and pure from the beginning of his days... He was wont utterly to avoid the unguarded sight of naked persons,... Therefore this prince made a covenant with his eyes that they should never look unchastely upon any woman. Hence it happened once, that at Christmas time a certain great lord brought before him a dance or show of young ladies with bared bosoms who were to dance in that guise before the king, perhaps to prove him, or to entice his youthful mind. But the king... very angrily averted his eyes, turned his back upon them, and went out to his chamber, saying: 'Fie, fie, for shame, forsooth ye be to blame.'

Against the pest of avarice with which so many are infected and diseased, even princes of the earth, this king Henry of whom we speak was most wary and alert... Never did he oppress his subjects with unreasonable exactions as do other rulers and princes, but behaving himself among them like a kind father, relieved them from his own [money]... rather than that they should pine in poverty, trodden down by his harshness.

... The same prince when in the end he lost both the realms, England and France, which he had ruled before, along with all his wealth and goods, endured it with no broken spirit but with a calm mind, making light of all temporal things, if he might but gain Christ and things eternal... He also customarily wore a long gown with a rolled hood like a townsman, and a full coat reaching below his knees, with shoes, boots and foot-gear wholly black, rejecting expressly all curious fashion of clothing... to confirm his notable devotion to God, many who yet survive and were once of his household say that he was wont almost at every moment to raise his eyes heavenward like a denizen of heaven or one rapt, being for the time not conscious of himself or of those about him, as if he were a man in a trance or on the verge of heaven...

In the first decade of his reign, Edward IV had to grapple with the tricky problem of patronage. As the new king was reluctant to alienate too many Lancastrian supporters, he confiscated only relatively modest amounts of land from former enemies and so some of his followers were disappointed with their rewards. This resentment was increased as the earl of Warwick was one of the few to be lavishly rewarded for his assistance to the Yorkist cause. Edward and Warwick, however, became increasingly alienated during the 1460s. A key cause of this was disagreement over the king's highly unsuitable, and secret, marriage to Elizabeth Woodville in May 1464. The new queen was English, from the gentry class, a widow with two sons, and her whole family had been Lancastrian supporters until her union with Edward. It ended any prospect of Edward marrying a French princess for diplomatic reasons, a match which Warwick had worked hard to promote. The clandestine marriage infuriated the French king, and made Warwick feel humiliated and betrayed. Additionally, Queen Elizabeth's very large family quickly became noted for greed and a very significant proportion of royal patronage flowed in the direction of her father and siblings.

Another figure to resent Edward and his wife was the king's brother, George, duke of Clarence. In fact, Clarence had been a major beneficiary of the new Yorkist regime, but he bitterly resented the growing influence of the Woodvilles and also generosity shown towards the third and youngest brother, Richard, duke of Gloucester. Disillusioned with Edward, therefore, Clarence began to seek support from Warwick and the two men arranged that Clarence should marry Warwick's eldest daughter Isabel. Edward, however, refused to allow the match, exercising the king's right to withhold permission for marriages involving the higher nobility. Furious, Clarence and Warwick began to conspire together and in 1469 Warwick encouraged two popular rebellions against Edward in the North of England. These revolts were led by two rebels calling themselves 'Robin of Redesdale' and 'Robin of Holderness', pseudonyms used to mask their real identity. Warwick intended these uprisings to distract King Edward's attention while Clarence sailed to Calais to marry Isabel Neville and also to plan how to seize the throne from his brother.

Clarence and Warwick returned to England with troops in July 1469 and intercepted the earl of Pembroke, one of Edward's principal supporters, defeating him at the Battle of Edgecote, after which Pembroke was captured and executed. On hearing the news, the rest of Edward's troops deserted and Edward himself was forced to flee, but he was quickly taken prisoner by Warwick. Warwick now attempted to rule England himself, in Edward's name, while the king was in captivity. Unsurprisingly, such an eccentric measure failed miserably, indicating that Warwick had overestimated magnate support for his cause. In the face of a Lancastrian uprising in the North West and unco-operative nobility, Warwick was forced to release Edward IV from custody. Although the king was not in a strong enough position to punish Warwick immediately, enmity between the two men was inevitable. Once peace was restored, Warwick therefore began plotting again, in March 1470 secretly encouraging a rebellion by Sir Robert Welles in Lincolnshire against Edward. This resulted in the Battle of Losecoat Field, where they were soundly beaten by the king and his troops. This year saw a number of private quarrels also being settled by violence, with some escalating into pitched battle, as occurred in 1470 at the Battle of Nibley Green, where the Berkeleys and the Talbots fought concerning a disputed inheritance.

THINKING HISTORICALLY   Change (7a)

Convergence and divergence

Local unrest, 1399–1509				
1403-16	**1415**	**1453**	**1461**	**1469**
Percies lose power in North, while Nevilles gain authority.	Southampton Plot.	August, planned assassination of Nevilles following Neville-Stanhope marriage.	Duke of Norfolk seized Caister Castle, which was claimed by the Pastons.	Popular rebellions in the North led by 'Robin of Redesdale' and 'Robin of Holderness'.

National political change, 1399–1509				
1403	**1413**	**1453**	**1461**	**1469**
Henry IV wins the Battle of Shrewsbury.	Henry IV dies and is succeeded by his son, Henry V, who begins to prepare for war with France.	September 1453 to December 1454, Henry VI's first mental collapse.	Henry VI deposed and Edward IV becomes king.	Clarence and Warwick invade England from Calais and defeat Edward's troops at the Battle of Edgecote.

1 Draw a timeline across the middle of a landscape piece of A3 paper. Cut out ten small rectangular cards and write the above changes on them. Then place them on the timeline with the local unrest above the line and national political change below. Make sure there is a lot of space between the changes and the line.

2 Draw a line and write a link between each change within each strand, so that you have five links that join up changes in the local unrest part of the timeline and five that join the national political change. You will then have two strands of change: local and national policy.

3 Now make as many links as possible across the timeline between local unrest and national political change. Think about how they are affected by one another and think about how things can link across long periods of time.

You should end up with something like this:

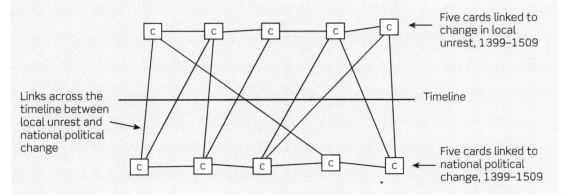

Answer the following:

4 How far do different strands of history interact with one another? Illustrate your answer with two well-explained examples.

5 At what point do the two strands of development converge (i.e. when do the changes have the biggest impact on one another)?

6 How useful are the strands in understanding the instability of royal power in the Wars of the Roses?

Encouraged by the level of turmoil within England, Warwick and Clarence fled to France in the hope of enlisting support from Louis XI. The French king, surprisingly, managed to persuade Clarence, Warwick and their erstwhile bitter enemy Margaret of Anjou to form an alliance in order to restore Henry VI to the throne. This agreement was confirmed by the **betrothal** of Margaret's son, Prince Edward, to Warwick's youngest daughter, Anne Neville, a marriage which took place in December 1470. Louis' aim was to break the English alliance with Charles, duke of Burgundy, which had been strengthened in 1468 when Edward IV had married his sister, Margaret, to Charles.

Warwick returned to England in September 1470, and Edward IV was forced to flee to Burgundy, along with a number of his leading supporters. The Lancastrian king was released from prison by Warwick, as agreed with Margaret of Anjou, and there followed Henry VI's readeption to the throne. England now supported France in the quarrel between Louis XI and Charles the Bold of Burgundy. This high-handed decision on the part of Warwick and Margaret enraged parliament, who had not been consulted about this major change in foreign policy, which was liable to have a significant, negative impact on English trade. Burgundy, meanwhile, was now prepared to help fund Edward's plans to retake the English throne.

In March 1471, Edward returned from Burgundy, where he was reconciled with his brother, the duke of Clarence, who had become disillusioned with Warwick because he would not support his candidature for the throne. The reunited York brothers met Warwick's forces in April 1471 at the Battle of Barnet, where Warwick was killed, and this was followed shortly afterwards by another Yorkist victory at Tewkesbury where a number of leading Lancastrians were killed, the most significant of whom was Margaret of Anjou's son, Prince Edward. The young prince's death effectively put an end to Lancastrian hopes and was a decisive factor in bringing stability to Edward IV's reign post-1471. Shortly afterwards, Henry VI himself died in captivity, probably murdered on Edward's orders. The only leading Lancastrian supporters to escape were Henry VI's half-brother, Jasper Tudor, and his nephew, Henry Tudor, earl of Richmond. These two fled to France where, for the time being at least, they were to remain a negligible force.

KEY TERM

Betrothal
An agreement and promise to marry someone – like an engagement.

Causes of the readeption of Henry VI in 1470 and restoration of Edward IV in 1471

1 Create two lists:

   a) Reasons for Warwick to support Edward IV, and

   b) reasons for Warwick to rebel against Edward IV.

2 Draw a flowchart or timeline, detailing key events between 1469 and 1471. (There will be multiple events in each year.)

3 Highlight the two key events you think are most significant in causing Edward IV's downfall in 1470 and write a paragraph justifying your choices.

4 Working with a partner, decide which were the most significant reasons for Edward IV's ability to return to the throne in 1471. Write them down, with an explanation of their importance.

5 What had happened between 1469 and 1471 that would make Edward IV more secure in his second reign than in his first? Make a list of factors.

Increased control of the localities in the 1470s

The experience of the Pastons in the 1470s (see page 26) is indicative of the increased political stability of the nation experienced during the second reign of Edward IV, which was in large part due to the deaths of leading Lancastrians, and especially Henry VI's son and heir, Prince Edward, in 1471. This removed the possibility of a continuing Lancastrian dynasty and the Yorkists' position was also strengthened by the death of Henry VI in May of that year, which removed the alternative candidate for the throne with the strongest dynastic claim. This, combined with King Edward's greater experience and the absence of Warwick's over-mighty influence, made for an easier decade in terms of national politics, which had a calming influence on the heated local politics of regions such as Norfolk.

During his second reign, Edward was acutely aware of the need to bring the localities under greater royal control. He had begun this process in the 1460s, but returned to this task in 1471 with new vigour, which was no doubt a result of his recent experience of rebellion and betrayal. His key development was regional councils, which were held in addition to the 'great' and 'continual' councils which were a mainstay of 15th-century politics. The most significant was the Council of the North, which was based first in Sheriff Hutton and later in the city of York. This was established in part to co-ordinate protection for the area from the very real threat of Scottish raids or actual invasion across the border. In addition, the northern counties were noted in this period for their lawlessness, not least as the area was particularly affected by a long-standing feud between two important noble families in the area, the Nevilles and the Percies (see page 23 for full details of

this conflict). The area was also deemed too far from London to be effectively controlled from the capital. The northern council had very similar powers to the king's council, and was designed to provide effective and speedy justice in the area. King Edward IV made his youngest brother, Richard of Gloucester, the most powerful figure in the Council of the North and Gloucester was a highly respected figure in the region because of this. To assist Richard and ensure he was seen as an authority figure in the North, in 1472 Gloucester married Anne Neville, the dead earl of Warwick's daughter and widow of the Lancastrian Prince of Wales. The elevation of his younger brother was both a reward for Richard's loyalty, but also ensured that this troubled area was brought under direct Yorkist supervision, ensuring most of the earl of Warwick's former vast estates in the North would be held by someone the king could trust. The marriage to Anne Neville was also a means of ensuring that former members of Warwick's retinue were more likely to be loyal to the Yorkist regime.

SOURCE

Ranulf Higden, a monk in 14th-century Chester, wrote a history of the world entitled *Polychronicon* or 'Universal Chronicle'. In this work, he described the differences between the North and South of England in this way:

All the language of the men of Northumberland, and especially of Yorkshire, soundeth so that the men of the South country may scarcely understand the language of them, which thing may be caused by the proximity of their language to that spoken by barbarians, and also by the great distance of the kings of England from [the North], since those kings mostly frequent the South, and only enter the North when accompanied by a large number of their retainers. There is also another cause, which is that the South is more abundant in fertility than the North, has more people, and more convenient harbours.

EXTRACT

2

Professor Carpenter is an academic historian based at the University of Cambridge and here she is discussing Richard of Gloucester's marriage to Anne Neville and his role in the North of England.

This was the start of the rise to northern 'super-power' of Richard of Gloucester. Partly his elevation was a reward for his loyalty between 1469 and 1471 but it was also a solution to the northern problem that had proved all but insoluble in the 1460s. The north was always a difficult area to rule. It was unstable and there was the constant need to defend the border against the Scots; it was the only part of England which could be described as a militarised region. It needed constant attention, but kings could rarely spend much time there. It therefore required a royal deputy, but he had to have territorial power or he would be ineffectual. That normally meant a Neville or a Percy, with the result that the great military offices along the border were too often turned into pawns in local politics. The best solution was always to use a northern noble who was closely attached to the king and would be acting as much in the king's name as in his own. Gloucester, once he had the Neville lands in the north, was the perfect candidate.

Similarly in Wales, King Edward needed to ensure strong, loyal local leadership, as this was an area prone to rebellion and was a Lancastrian stronghold. This region included the **Principality** of Wales as well as the **marcher lordships**, which were counties on the modern Anglo-Welsh border. In theory at least, Wales owed allegiance to the English monarch and since 1301 it had become customary for the region to be governed by the king's eldest son, who assumed the title of the Prince of Wales, although in reality if the prince was a child the area was governed by leading noblemen in his entourage. Edward IV therefore made his infant son and heir, also called Edward, the Prince of Wales and earl of Chester in June 1471 and a loyal Yorkist council, including a strong Woodville influence, was created for the young prince to rule in his name while he was still a child. The influence of other, arguably more unstable figures in Wales, such as the earl of Pembroke and the duke of Buckingham, was decreased as they were gradually excluded from power in the area.

ACTIVITY
KNOWLEDGE CHECK

Edward IV and regional control

Read Extract 2 and answer these questions:

1 According to Carpenter, what were the two reasons for Richard of Gloucester's marriage to Anne Neville?

2 What were the key reasons for Edward IV setting up regional councils in the following areas?

   a) The North.

   b) Wales.

Conclusion

The traditional idea expressed in the **historiography** of 'over-mighty subjects' being responsible, through their greed and selfishness, for the Wars of the Roses is an appealing one. More recently, historians such as John Watts and Christine Carpenter have made important revisions to this view, arguing that leading 15th-century nobles were less to blame and that the late medieval political system simply could not function with an 'under-mighty' monarch for an extended period of time, as was proved during the reign of Henry VI. Certainly the long-term mental instability and inherent ineffectiveness of Henry VI presented the political community with a unique problem. Indeed, given how spectacularly the king failed militarily and in terms of general governance, it is unsurprising that nobles began to vie with one another for power, particularly given the lingering memory of the fact that Henry's grandfather, as first Lancastrian monarch, was himself a usurper. This inherent lack of leadership was certainly largely responsible for the level of noble and gentry feuding that certain areas, such as Northumberland, the South West and Norfolk, suffered. More surprising, perhaps, is the fact that Edward IV lost the throne in 1470 to such an obviously disastrous king as Henry VI. That such an idea could even be contemplated indicates the power and determination of the earl of Warwick in particular, as well as the extraordinary propensity towards betrayal displayed by George, duke of Clarence. The fact that such a situation was short lived was predictable, however, and Edward IV's second reign was made considerably more secure by the death of the Lancastrian heir at the Battle of Tewkesbury and of Warwick himself at the Battle of Barnet, both in 1471. As a response to his experience of rebellion, Edward appears to have been determined to expand his control of the outer-lying regions of the realm via the Councils of the North and of Wales and here he had a certain level of success, as indicated by the fact that in 1483 he died a natural, if somewhat unexpected, death.

KEY TERMS

Principality (or princedom)
An area ruled over by a prince, even if most of his wealth/estates are based outside the principality. The Principality of Wales included Angelsey, Caernarfon, Merioneth, Cardigan and Carmarthen.

Marcher lordship
A Marcher lord was a noble appointed to govern estates in the area on the English–Welsh border (called the Marches), which was a region that saw considerable conflict in the Middle Ages. A marcher lordship was the region he governed. These lordships each had a slightly different system of government from England and from each other and, as a group, the Marcher lords were powerful and periodically problematic during the Wars of the Roses especially.

Historiography
In this context, the term refers to the body of historical research and debate on a particular topic.

THINKING HISTORICALLY Cause and consequence (7c)

The value of historical explanations

Historical explanations derive from the historian who is investigating the past. Differences in explanations are usually about what the historians think is significant. Historians bring their own attitudes and perspectives to historical questions and see history in the light of these. It is therefore perfectly acceptable to have very different explanations of the same historical phenomenon. The way we judge historical accounts is by looking at how well argued they are and how well evidence has been deployed to support the argument.

Approach A	Approach B	Approach C
Civil war is caused by a weak, unpopular monarch, who fails to lead effectively. A system dependent on monarchy is only as good as the individual in charge.	Civil war is caused by the greed and selfishness of rival members of the nobility. These figures take advantage of a monarch's weakness for their own ends.	Civil war is caused by military failure abroad, which not only creates a sense of national humiliation but also usually has followed a period of high taxation.

Work in groups of between three and five. (You will need an even number of groups in the class.)

In your groups, devise a brief explanation of the Wars of the Roses, of between 200 and 300 words, that matches one of the approaches above. Present your explanation to another group who will decide on two things:

1 Which of the approaches is each explanation trying to demonstrate?

2 Considering the structure and the quality of the argument and use of evidence, which is the best of the three explanations?

3 If you choose a 'best' explanation, should you discount the other two? Explain your answer.

ACTIVITY SUMMARY

National and regional conflict in the 15th century

1 For the reigns of Henry VI and Edward IV, make notes under these headings:

   a) Leading nobles and their influence during the reign.

   b) Key successes/strengths.

   c) Key weaknesses/failures.

   d) Key events in local disputes involving the Nevilles and Percies, Bonvilles and Courteneys, or Pastons.

2 Which was the most significant rebellion: the Southampton Plot in 1415, that of Lambert Simnel in 1486 or Perkin Warbeck in the 1490s? Write a paragraph explaining your answer.

3 Which 15th-century dispute has the greatest national political significance: the Neville–Percy feud in the North, the Bonville–Courtenay quarrel in the South West or the problems faced by the Pastons in East Anglia? Write a paragraph explaining the reasons for your answer. Remember to evaluate the seriousness of the dispute, not simply describe what happened in each case.

WIDER READING

Allmand, C.T. *Henry V*, Yale University Press (1997)

Bremner, I. 'The reign of Richard II, 1377 to 1399', BBC History website (2011). Available online at www.bbc.co.uk/history/british/middle_ages/richardii_reign_01.shtml#twelve

Carpenter, C. *The Wars of the Roses: Politics and the Constitution in England, c.1437–1509*, Cambridge Medieval Textbooks (1997)

Grant, A. *Henry VII*, Routledge (1985)

Griffiths, R.A. 'Local rivalries and national politics: the Percies, the Nevilles and the Duke of Exeter, 1452–1455', *Speculum* 43 (1968). Online access available at www.jstor.org, for which your school will need a password.

Horrox, R. 'Kingship and Queenship' in Marks, R. and Williamson, P. (ed.) *Gothic: Art for England*, Victoria and Albert Museum (2003)

Ibeji, M. 'Paston Family Letters' (2011). Available at www.bbc.co.uk/history/british/middle_ages/pastonletters_01.shtml

Mortimer, I. *The Fears of Henry IV: The Life of England's Self-Made King*, Vintage (2008)

Pollard, A. 'Percies, Nevilles and the Wars of the Roses', *History Today* 43:9 (1993). Available online at www.historytoday.com for subscribers.

Ross, C. *Edward IV*, Yale University Press (1997)

Watts, J. *Henry VI and the Politics of Kingship*, Cambridge University Press (1999)

Wolffe, B. *Henry VI*, Yale University Press (2001)

3.2 Changes in the sinews of power

KEY QUESTIONS

- How significant was royal income for the successful expression of political power in late medieval England?
- Did parliament act as a prop or a curb to royal power?
- Was war or diplomacy of the greatest benefit to the English crown in the period 1399–1509?

INTRODUCTION

A mainstay of medieval moralising art and literature was the concept of the 'Wheel of Fortune'. This image depicted the idea that one day things could be going very well for an individual, they would be at the top of the wheel, being successful and admired, but very quickly Fortune might spin the wheel, ensuring that they sank back down the social and political ranks. Given the chequered royal history of the 15th century, it is no surprise that this image was popular at the time, with Source 1 showing an example from a manuscript originally intended for King Henry VI, although, poignantly, he was deposed in 1461 before the book could be presented to him. Owing to the fickleness of political circumstances, monarchs were understandably keen to make their position as secure as possible. Brute force was an important factor in establishing a reign, and it could play a role in consolidating power, but alone it was not enough. Three other interlocking areas were very important for 15th-century monarchs: their wealth; the support of parliament; and successful foreign policy.

HOW SIGNIFICANT WAS ROYAL INCOME FOR THE SUCCESSFUL EXPRESSION OF POLITICAL POWER IN LATE MEDIEVAL ENGLAND?

Royal finance was one of the key challenges for monarchs in the period 1399–1509. The crown had a number of sources of income, including land, taxation, customs, feudal dues, pensions, fines and loans. It required a wide network of officials and administrators to ensure that this money was paid in a timely fashion. This was important for maintaining royal authority, as the king then used this money for a range of purposes which were central to providing effective government and thereby ensuring that his own position was secure. The key government areas of expenditure can be divided into normal costs and exceptional outlay and are listed on page 38.

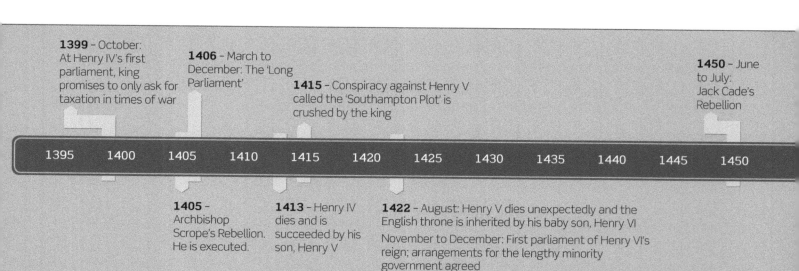

1399 – October: At Henry IV's first parliament, king promises to only ask for taxation in times of war

1406 – March to December: The 'Long Parliament'

1415 – Conspiracy against Henry V called the 'Southampton Plot' is crushed by the king

1450 – June to July: Jack Cade's Rebellion

1395   1400   1405   1410   1415   1420   1425   1430   1435   1440   1445   1450

1405 – Archbishop Scrope's Rebellion. He is executed.

1413 – Henry IV dies and is succeeded by his son, Henry V

1422 – August: Henry V dies unexpectedly and the English throne is inherited by his baby son, Henry VI

November to December: First parliament of Henry VI's reign; arrangements for the lengthy minority government agreed

SOURCE 1

A miniature from John Lydgate's *Troy Book and Siege of Thebes* showing the 'Wheel of Fortune'. It was created c1457–60 as a gift from Sir William Herbert to Henry VI. By 1461, however, Herbert had changed his allegiance to the Yorkists and Henry VI was deposed, so the manuscript passed into the collection of the Percy family, as William Herbert's daughter married Henry Percy, the fourth earl of Northumberland.

1453 – July: Battle of Castillon. English lose Hundred Years War.

13 October: Henry VI and Margaret of Anjou have a son, Prince Edward

1475 – Edward IV gains annual income from France as a result of the Treaty of Picquigny

1499 – Marriage between Prince Arthur and Katherine of Aragon

1502 – Prince Arthur dies

| 1455 | 1460 | 1465 | 1470 | 1475 | 1480 | 1485 | 1490 | 1495 | 1500 | 1505 | 1510 |

1461 – Spring: Henry VI deposed and Edward IV crowned king

1485 – August: Battle of Bosworth. Richard III killed and Henry Tudor becomes King Henry VII.

1504 – Parliament rejects Henry VII's request for some traditional feudal fees

1509 – April: Henry VII dies

Routine expenditure

- Maintenance of the king, his family and the royal household, the latter being a large organisation including retainers, servants and advisers. While some of this expenditure on lavish clothes and food may seem extravagant, it is important to remember that contemporaries expected kings to live in a very opulent style and this was regarded as crucial to maintaining their authority at home and respect for the English crown abroad. Therefore, in 1450, one of the criticisms made by angry subjects during **Cade's Rebellion** was that the king was so in debt he could not pay for food and drink for his household.

- Regular defence costs, including protection of the Scottish and Welsh borders, and security in overseas areas which the English claimed, such as Ireland and sections of France, most notably Calais.

- Administration, including costs of employing staff in key government departments like the Exchequer and Chamber, funds for calling parliament, running law courts, etc.

KEY TERM

Cade's Rebellion
A large, popular uprising in the summer of 1450 led by a man calling himself Jack Cade, although he also used other aliases. The rebels focused particularly on London and published a list of grievances against the government. These particularly concerned the poor management of war with France, high levels of royal debt, and the fact that the king was manipulated and poorly advised by self-interested nobles. For more information, see Chapter 5, page 119.

Exceptional expenditure

- Finance for key ceremonial costs, including coronations, royal baptisms, weddings, etc.

- Exceptional defence costs, which might include money for an invasion or to repel attacks on English territories in France, especially during the Hundred Years War. This was to become a major outlay, especially during the reign of Henry VI, which contributed very substantially to the problems of the reign.

Income

During the period 1399–1509, there was a decline in the traditional incomes enjoyed by the king, mostly because of a fall in tax revenue from the wool trade. Under the Lancastrian kings, this became a serious problem because of very high defence costs: Henry IV had difficulties with rebellions in Wales and Scotland, while his son Henry V waged an expensive war in France. Although Henry V was very militarily successful, the costs of acquiring and maintaining his conquests overseas were huge and by the end of the reign parliament expressed unease about the state of the royal finances; indeed, Henry V was to die heavily in debt, and after he died in 1422 his jewellery and ships had to be sold to pay back money to creditors of the crown. The most catastrophic reign in terms of finance, however, was that of Henry VI, owing to the king's personal ineptitude and the costly

and unsuccessful war with France. According to historian Charles Ross, by 1433, the accumulated debts of Henry V and Henry VI meant that the crown was in debt to the tune of £225,000 and by 1450, when the English suffered some of their heaviest defeats in the Hundred Years War, this figure had risen to £372,000. To put this in perspective, Christine Carpenter has argued that in the 1430s the entire cost of regular defence to the crown was c£25,000 each year.

Unsurprisingly, Henry's financial crisis provoked strong public criticism, most forcefully from Cade's rebels in 1450, who succinctly pointed out that 'he owes more than ever any King of England ought'. Consequently, regaining financial solvency was a priority for his successor, Edward IV. During his first reign (1461–70), Edward took a range of measures to increase the efficiency of crown lands and to improve relations with key creditors, such as London merchants, who were more prepared to lend money at reasonable rates to Edward than they had been to the weak Henry VI. Edward also engaged in a range of unpopular measures for raising money, such as forced loans and gifts, particularly to pay for a proposed invasion of France during his second reign in 1474. These methods were of very dubious legality and caused considerable criticism from contemporaries. The king's gamble, however, paid off in financial terms at least, as he invaded France and then, instead of fighting, used his troops as a key diplomatic weapon in obliging the French king to sign the 1475 Treaty of Picquigny, which gave Edward an annual pension from France of £10,000 per annum. This, combined with improved royal revenues from customs and land, meant that by 1483 Edward died solvent. The next king's reign was too short, from 1483 to 1485, to have significant financial impact, but after this Henry VII was to substantially build upon Yorkist financial stability to ensure the crown was wealthy and secure. By 1509, Alexander Grant has estimated that Henry had increased annual royal income by 40 percent from its rate under Edward IV. To secure a better understanding of royal financial management, however, and how it impacted upon the king's authority, it is necessary to consider each form of income in turn.

Land

Patronage was a crucial demonstration of royal power in the late medieval period and the granting of land was an especially delicate matter. In theory, all land belonged to the king and he could grant it to whomever he wished. These individuals in return were expected to be loyal to him; this was the basis of the feudal system established after 1066. In reality, however, it was considered extremely important that a certain level of stability was maintained within the kingdom and kings were obliged to recognise the hereditary claims of noble families. Indeed, failure to do so could be catastrophic, as was the case in 1399 when Richard II disinherited Henry Bolingbroke, duke of Lancaster, and in response Henry overthrew the king. Consequently, kings did not always have substantial amounts of land to hand out to those they wished to reward or promote and this was one of the key attractions for the nobility of the Hundred Years War with France; the periods when England was victorious, most notably under Henry V, meant that new conquests provided the king with French land to distribute to his followers. When new territory overseas was not available, however, kings needed to provide their leading subjects with land in England.

One method of a monarch gaining land was forfeiture. When an individual lord was found guilty of treason, he was not only liable to be executed, but also to give up his lands to the crown. These lands could provide the crown with a significant increase in wealth, or could be given to other, hopefully more worthy, recipients. Edward IV's brothers, for example, profited substantially from the death of the earl of Warwick in 1471, while Richard, duke of Gloucester also made substantial gains when his brother, George, duke of Clarence was found guilty of treason in 1478. In the most extreme circumstances, Acts of Attainder were passed against those who committed treason, which meant that the land was lost to that family permanently, unless the Act was repealed. Obviously, this was potentially a very powerful method of control available to monarchs, as land gave nobles and their heirs status and power, so losing their estates permanently was a considerable threat. Henry VII showed himself to be very aware of the power and value of Acts of Attainder: when he became king, after his troops killed Richard III at the Battle of Bosworth in 1485, he was careful to date his reign in official records to the day before the battle had taken place. This meant that those who had supported Richard could be classed as traitors and potentially have their lands seized by the crown. Nonetheless, attainting enemies was not always a wise course of action during the complex politics of late medieval England, as it meant that the disinherited heirs had little to lose and much to gain from further rebellion. Often, therefore, the guilty individual's heirs could eventually regain their lands, by a subsequent show of loyalty and payments to the crown, as Henry Hotspur's grandson did between 1416 and 1440.

Given the fraught political situation of the Wars of the Roses, the crown periodically gained considerable estates owing to forfeiture after important battles, when leading nobles or gentry were either killed or found guilty of treason for fighting on the losing side. These windfalls, however, were normally used to reward the king's supporters and so these lands often did not financially benefit the crown in the long term. When forfeited land was not available, kings had the difficult task of rewarding their followers from relatively limited resources. One option was to grant away crown lands, properties also described as **royal demesne**. This was property held by the monarch directly, rather than having another lord. As part of the king's income came from crown lands, selling or granting away such property was a topic of considerable political tension, particularly under Henry VI, who was widely regarded as so mentally unstable that he was not able to make reasoned decisions and so was vulnerable to exploitation by greedy opportunists.

KEY TERM

Royal demesne
Also sometimes referred to as 'ancient demense' or 'domain'. All land that had belonged to the crown since 1086, when the Domesday Book recorded landholdings for the first Norman king, William I ('William the Conqueror'). Tenants who lived on this land could claim special legal privileges, but also had the disadvantage of being obliged to pay a higher tax rate.

To what extent was the Duchy of Lancaster an advantage for Henry IV?

Until 1399, crown lands did not make a substantial contribution to national finances and were instead primarily used to support members of the extended royal family. The usurpation of Henry Bolingbroke, however, changed this, as when he came to the throne he retained the very substantial lands he had held as the duke of Lancaster. The Duchy estate was so valuable it required its own administrative council, which was staffed by its own chancellor, chamberlain, two chief stewards, a receiver general, an attorney general, two auditors and a clerk of the council. Henry IV appears to have been keen to make a clear division between his position as king and his private position as duke of Lancaster, and a **charter** from 1399 states that the Duchy would continue to be treated in exactly the same way as if he had never become king. This indicates Henry's insecurity on the throne following his usurpation, as presumably such a measure was designed to ensure that should he lose the throne, his descendants would retain their Lancastrian inheritance. This charter had an important legal impact; indeed, from as early as 1405 royal judges were making a division between crown possessions and the lands which Henry IV held privately.

KEY TERM

Charter
A legal document from a monarch or government that grants specified legal privileges or rights to a body such as a town, university, company or, in this case, landed estate.

While such legal niceties were important, they did not alter the political ramifications of the king's ownership of such substantial private property. The Duchy of Lancaster was, in theory at least, a great benefit for the king, as it gave him a substantial source of private income, as well as retinues on whose loyalty he could rely. Given parliament's propensity for criticising the expenditure of Richard II, it is understandable that Henry IV sought to increase his own popularity by telling parliament that, owing to his extensive private properties, he would be able to finance his own requirements and would only seek money from taxation in times of war. This statement may well have been one Henry was later to regret, as from then on parliament was very keen to emphasise that now the king should 'live of his own'. The exact meaning of this phrase has been debated by historians, with the traditional view being that it meant the king should meet various costs from his own lands rather than asking for money from taxes. J.A.F. Thomson, however, has argued that contemporaries did agree that the king needed money from customs and taxes, but were simply critical of a practice called 'purveyance', where the king could seize his subjects' goods for his own use. While this may well have been the case, there can be little doubt that the personal wealth of the Lancastrian kings, as well as the rather weak political position of Henry IV as a usurper, did mean parliament was less likely to be forthcoming with taxation for his use. Indeed, they frequently met the monarch's later requests for financial support with the argument that the king should farm his own land to greater profit and live from this income. This was difficult for Henry to do as, from 1347 onwards, the period saw repeated outbreaks of the **Black Death**, which led to major shortages in agricultural workers. This meant that experienced labourers were hard to find and, despite legislation seeking to limit wages to pre-Black Death levels, in practice agricultural workers were often able to demand higher wages. Consequently, most landlords experienced a reduction in income in this period.

EXTRACT

From J.A.F. Thomson, *The Transformation of Medieval England, 1370–1529* (2014). Thomson analyses the various sources of medieval royal revenue.

The greater part of the king's resource in the later Middle Ages came from... various taxes and quasi-taxes, such as forced loans and benevolences. There was one further substantial source of royal revenue, the estates which the Crown owned and exploited directly. Traditionally, it has been thought that the demands which were sometimes made in the later Middle Ages that the king should 'live of his own' implied that the yield from these lands should normally suffice for his needs and that he should not demand more from his subjects, but recent work has made it almost certain that contemporaries did not take so limited a view of the King's 'own'. What was particularly attacked was the practice of purveyance for the royal household, whereby the king might arbitrarily take his subjects' goods for his own use.

According to research undertaken by Helen Castor, under Henry IV the average annual income of the Duchy for the king was £11,000. In the first instance, this was used to support the king and members of the royal family. The fact that Henry IV's younger sons did not have children meant that this family was smaller and so there was now surplus property. Some of this land was used as a form of patronage to provide income for favoured members of the royal household, but the remainder increasingly came to be used to contribute to government finances, even though the two were kept legally and administratively separate. On average, therefore, the Duchy contributed £1,120 per annum to government finances.

Henry V confirmed his father's charter that the Duchy should be regarded as the personal property of him as duke of Lancaster, rather than a crown estate, but made various practical changes which made the Duchy much more closely linked to royal finances. In particular, he placed the Duchy's private administrative council under the close supervision of crown officials and sought to increase further the profitability of the farming of the estate. In this, he was successful and average annual revenue from the Duchy increased under Henry V to £13,000. He also ensured that a higher proportion of the money, on average £4,400 each year, supported government finances.

Henry VI's reign has less complete surviving records of the Duchy finances, so exact statistics are difficult to obtain. Nonetheless, it is clear that this period saw a significant reduction in the annual government income from the Duchy. In a public statement to parliament in 1433, for example, the treasurer highlighted that the lands provided an annual income of only £4,953 to the crown and that of this £2,544 was consumed in costs of the estate, leaving only £2,409 as profit. In part, this was because the Duchy revenues suffered from the lack of the strong personal leadership of the king throughout the reign, firstly because of Henry VI's minority and later because of his mental instability. This meant that there was little close supervision of Duchy finances, so the land was utilised less productively and some money was lost through corruption. Other factors, however, also contributed to the situation. Most significant was the marriage agreement between Henry V and Catherine of Valois, which had been a key part of the Treaty of Troyes. In 1420, it had been agreed that Catherine would receive an annual income of 20,000 crowns as part of the marriage settlement and, from 1422 onwards, it was arranged that this would partly be funded by the Duchy lands, a situation which continued until her death in 1437. Later, substantial revenues from Duchy lands were diverted to fund Henry's pet projects – his educational foundations of Eton College and King's College, Cambridge. This combination of circumstances contributed to the financial difficulties of Henry VI's reign, which were substantially worsened by the growing monetary demands of the Hundred Years War.

A similar pattern has been noted by Helen Castor in the three kings' relationship with the Duchy affinities. In ideological terms, private ownership of the Duchy of Lancaster created a problem for Henry IV, which was significant in the context of the political instability of the period: the king was the head of the judicial system and was supposed to arbitrate in cases of disputes between leading nobles over land or tenants. Obviously, however, it was very difficult for a monarch to seem objective in such matters if he himself had a vested interest in particular areas of the country, as he was also that region's 'special good lord'. Henry IV, with the understandable uneasiness of a recent usurper, sought to maintain the very personal loyalty of his Lancastrian retinues who had proved so important to claiming the throne in 1399. Henry V was more confident in his position as king, and so ensured he not only maintained the loyalty of his father's retinue, but also widened his scope for patronage by including new men into his service as part of the Duchy affinity. This allowed him to broaden his influence and gain new loyal followers who did not distinguish his role as duke from that of king.

Unfortunately, much of this good work came undone during the reign of Henry VI. During the royal power vacuum created by the king's personal inadequacies, regional lords were required to not only manage their own lands and retinues, but also to enforce royal authority in the area. Clearly, such an arrangement was untenable in the long term, as it essentially required nobles accustomed to functioning in the essentially competitive world of 15th-century territorial politics to self-regulate and to seek the common good, not their own personal advancement. In addition, Henry VI was clearly not the man to manage effectively a large affinity. Consequently, areas where Duchy lands were substantial often saw conflict. In East Anglia, for example, where Duchy estates were significant but where the king's trusted confidante the duke of

Suffolk also held authority, law and order broke down in the 1440s when the duke of Norfolk sought to challenge Suffolk's power in the region. In essence, the territorial conflicts which were an established part of late medieval land-holding society required an active king to adjudicate and manage rivals, and under Henry VI such a moderating and disciplining influence did not exist.

EXTRACT

2 Historian Helen Castor analyses the key problems of Henry VI's reign, particularly in relation to the Duchy of Lancaster.

The problem of the public and private aspects of the king's authority reasserted itself strongly during the crises of Henry VI's reign, since the two elements could only be combined into a workable unity through the active participation of the king. Because of the almost complete passivity of Henry VI, the polity had to find ways of directing itself, and the public authority of the crown was therefore managed by a succession of private interests. This situation produced a redoubling of the original problem. Whereas previously it had been the king who had to maintain his public authority while simultaneously controlling his private resources, now private individuals were attempting to embody the authority of the crown in order to carry out the same task in place of a king who was failing to assert his own will. The tensions produced by this hybrid authority, formed from a compound of public and private, royal and non-royal interests, played an important role in the disorder which developed during the late 1440s and 1450s, in regions where the king was a substantial landowner.

What happened to income from Duchy lands after the fall of the House of Lancaster?

In 1461, when Henry VI was overthrown and Edward IV seized the throne, the new king claimed that, although the Duchy of Lancaster was to be held separately from other royal possessions, nonetheless it was forfeit to the crown and was to be held by the kings of England from then on. Edward also took a range of measures to alter the management of royal estates, designed to improve the efficiency of their administration and size of returns. While the financial situation was improved from Henry VI's reign, nonetheless Charles Ross has estimated that the income from all crown lands, including but not limited to the Duchy, was no more than £10,000 per annum in the late 1470s and early 1480s. To some extent, this was less important after 1475, as at this time Edward negotiated a new treaty with the French which provided him with a substantial annual pension. Nonetheless, it is notable that Henry VII's drive for increased financial efficiency was much more effective, as discussed below.

ACTIVITY
KNOWLEDGE CHECK

Henry IV, his successors and the Duchy of Lancaster
1 What were the advantages and disadvantages of the Duchy of Lancaster becoming united with crown lands in 1399? Overall, do you think it was more a benefit or a problem for Henry IV, V and VI?
2 Do you think that Henry IV was wise to promise parliament he would 'live of his own'? What do you think motivated him to make this promise?
3 Read Extracts 1 and 2. Summarise the views of each historian in no more than two sentences.
4 What were the key changes implemented by Edward IV and Henry VII to the management of crown lands?

Patronage and resumption

'Resumption' was the term used by contemporaries to describe an Act of parliament which removed land from a lord and took it back into crown ownership. Reasons varied, but Acts of Resumption were passed by parliament at various points in the late 14th and 15th centuries in order to regain lands that had been **alienated** by the king, perhaps unwisely. In 1404, for example, parliament petitioned Henry IV to resume all crown lands granted away by the monarch since 1367, although the king, no doubt realising how unpopular such a measure could make him among those losing land, showed very little enthusiasm for such a measure.

KEY TERM

Alienated
Granted to another individual and thus lost as a source of royal income.

The monarch who had the least concerns regarding giving away land was Henry V as, thanks to significant military victories in the Hundred Years War, he had the luxury of newly conquered lands in France to reward his nobles with. As the English began to suffer defeats against France under the rule of Henry VI, pressure on royal estates grew. This problem was made worse by Henry VI's weak mental state, which made him an easy target for noblemen seeking to gain favours, and the king gave away substantial amounts of land. During the early 1450s, therefore, parliament sought to curb this problematic generosity through **Acts of Resumption.** This was a significant curtailment of the king's power and, according to J.A.F. Thomson, was a key turning point in crown finance, as neither Yorkists nor Tudors endangered their power with such high levels of generosity. Indeed, when Edward IV ascended the throne in 1461, he passed an Act of Resumption which gained him many of the land grants made by Henry VI. This made a substantial difference to the crown's wealth, and Edward added to it further with his own personal wealth as duke of York, which included the Duchy of York and the Earldom of March. Indeed, according to Charles Ross, a conservative estimate of the increase in income to the crown from these new lands would be £30,000, which was more than the total royal revenues raised in the last years of Henry VI's reign.

KEY TERM

Act of Resumption
A piece of parliamentary legislation that recalled grants of land made by the king into crown ownership.

Henry VII also began his reign with an Act of Resumption, although this was less wide-ranging than Edward IV's, which reflected the fact that the Yorkist kings had not been as profligate with grants of land as Henry VI. He did, however, gain the substantial estates of the defeated Richard III, as well as several estates forfeited by Yorkist supporters. Characteristically, Henry was to make the greatest financial gains from crown lands of all the kings of the period 1399 to 1509. Compared to the maximum of £10,000 per annum raised by Edward IV,

Henry achieved a yearly revenue of £42,000 from these properties by the early 16th century. This was in part due to the fact that Henry had a very small royal family to support, in contrast to Edward IV, who was extremely generous not only to his two brothers, but also to his wife's very large family. Henry, however, did not have the same number of relations and was not so generous. His wife, for example, was given land worth only about two-thirds of that which Edward IV had given his queen, Elizabeth Woodville. Similarly, Henry kept the revenues from his younger son's land himself in contrast to royal practice prior to 1485 and also reabsorbed Arthur's revenues after he died. Regime change, then, made a very important contribution to the growth of royal income under the Tudors. Indeed, Alexander Grant has estimated that Henry VII's total income was probably over £100,000 annually, whereas the next most financially successful king, Edward IV, raised between £60,000 and £65,000. Henry's motivations were undoubtedly political; he was strongly aware that he had gained and continued to maintain power largely because he ended civil war and the problems caused by 'over-mighty subjects'. It was extremely important to royal policy, therefore, that as far as possible the king remained financially solvent and so was not beholden financially or politically to his leading nobles.

Custom duties

Although in terms of status and control of the nobles, land was arguably the most crucial aspect of a king's income, in purely financial terms the most lucrative source of money was from custom duties. These were fees levied on imported or exported goods and it was a long-standing **royal prerogative** that the king gained income from these charges.

> **KEY TERM**
>
> **Royal prerogative**
> The formal rights and powers of the crown.

Custom charges on wool remained the most lucrative from 1399 to 1509 and were charged in two ways. Firstly, an 'ancient custom' of 6s 8d was charged on each sack of wool and, from 1353 onwards, a 'subsidy' was added, which was a changing amount set by parliament and charged on wool imports. The wool subsidy was the single largest payment to the royal coffers in the 14th and 15th centuries and by the 1360s it became accepted that the monarchy would receive this money as a matter of course. This reflected a shift in the late 14th and 15th centuries towards making custom duties a source of regular income for the crown, rather than an exceptional boon granted by parliament in times of emergency.

The crown in the 15th century faced the serious problem of a reduction in income from wool. The period saw raw wool exports fall from c21,000 sacks in 1390 to c8,500 sacks in 1510. This was partly a result of a major trade recession c1440 to 1480, which was a major trade recession. The government also lost income as, increasingly, wool centres in England were not exporting the raw product to the continent but instead were manufacturing woollen cloth, an industry which was less heavily taxed. Henry IV and Henry V both had difficulty balancing royal revenue with expenditure, with Henry V leaving the crown in debt when he died in 1422. During Henry VI's minority, the king's finances had become so unsound that the treasurer, Lord Cromwell, declared the true state of the royal finances to parliament in the hope of obtaining more sympathy – and revenue – from them. Covering the years 1429–32, this statement showed that outgoings included around £25,000 on regular defence (including protecting the Scottish and Welsh borders, and securing the traditionally English-held strongholds in Calais), over £23,000 on administration and more than £14,000 on his household. This high level of outgoings meant that the crown revenues were running an annual deficit of nearly £16,000.

The problem was worsened by an increase in piracy in the Channel as England suffered defeats in the Hundred Years War during the 1440s and 1450s, which meant considerable disruption to trade and the collection of customs. The decline in royal income from wool during the 15th century, especially in the period 1430–53 when costs of foreign war were very high was, according to Christine Carpenter, the basis of the considerable financial problems of Henry VI's reign. Indeed, the fact that the total annual revenue of the crown fell from £90,000 in the reign of Henry IV to less than £24,000 in the late 1450s indicates the level of financial crisis faced by Henry VI's government, which was greatly exacerbated by the loss of France and associated trade, as well as the king's ill-advised alienation of crown lands. This made Henry very dependent on loans from leading subjects, notably Cardinal Henry Beaufort and Richard, duke of York, which largely remained unpaid and added to the sense that 'over-mighty subjects' could seek to control the king.

Edward IV inherited this problem and in the 1460s the royal annual income from customs did not increase. During Edward's second reign, however, there were two key changes. Firstly, up to 1471, parliament retained some control over the money obtained via the wool subsidy, as it could vary the amount levied on each sack of wool depending on the defensive needs of the realm. After this year, however, the subsidy became a fixed amount, thus reducing Edward IV's dependence on parliament. According to J.A.F. Thomson, the move towards greater acceptance and standardisation of custom duties was a response to a growing acknowledgement among the political community that it was not feasible for the monarch to finance government policies through his own personal wealth and funds alone. This may also reflect a tacit acknowledgement that allowing leading members of the nobility to effectively bankroll the government was unwise, as had been proved particularly in the reign of Henry VI. This is not to say that individuals engaged in trade did not sometimes seek to avoid such charges illegally, or that they did not object at times to the amounts levied, but broadly speaking there was, firstly, an acceptance of the monarch's right to place charges on trade and, secondly, it was considerably less likely to spark widespread rebellion in the way that other, direct forms of taxation sometimes could. The 1381 Peasants' Revolt which was partly an uprising against the new poll tax collection is the obvious case in point. In the 1470s, Edward's government successfully negotiated a number of commercial treaties with neighbouring countries, and via diplomacy improved relations with a number of England's continental neighbours, most notably France. This meant that trade improved again and so there was some increase in royal revenue from customs.

Obviously, one method of raising money that was always likely to be uncontroversial as far as the indigenous population was concerned was to tax foreigners more heavily than native inhabitants. From 1303 onwards, something called a 'new' or 'petty' custom was charged to foreign merchants, whether they lived abroad or were resident in England. Originally, this fee was an additional 50 percent on top of the ancient custom payable on wool, wax and leather, but from 1347 this was extended to include imported cloth. All other wares were charged at 3d in the pound. In addition to these fees, all foreign merchants except those belonging to the **Hanseatic League** were obliged to pay 'poundage', which was a duty paid on all **non-staple goods** that were imported or exported via English ports.

Wine was an important import in the 14th and 15th centuries. In this period, it was unsafe to drink water and only the destitute did so. Therefore, various forms of alcohol were consumed as the fermenting process ensured that the liquid was safe to drink. The most common beverages were ale or beer, but by the 15th century wine was widely drunk by higher social orders. Indeed, the trade was one reason why England's holdings in France were so economically significant and why defeats in the Hundred Years War during the 1450s were politically damaging to Henry VI, who was responsible for losing important wine-producing regions including Gascony.

ACTIVITY
KNOWLEDGE CHECK

Royal revenue from land and customs and its impact on royal power

Using an A3 sheet of paper, construct a graph. (Sometimes this type of diagram is described as a 'living graph.') On the horizontal axis, label the dates from 1399 to 1509, in divisions of approximately five years. Label the vertical axis 'Royal income and power' and number it 1–10. Then complete the following tasks:

a) In one colour, draw a line to represent royal income from customs (especially the wool custom). The number one represents low income and the number ten represents high levels of income.

b) In a different colour, draw a line to represent royal income from land. In particular, mark key changes in royal land ownership, such as Acts of Resumption at the start of Edward IV and Henry VII's reigns. Label these key changes with a brief note, explaining what happened at this point.

c) In another colour, draw a line representing royal power and authority, assuming one is very little authority and ten is a high level of authority.

d) Add a key.

e) Write a paragraph explaining the impact of finance from land and customs upon royal authority in the period 1399–1509. Explain carefully which kings were particularly successful/unsuccessful in managing finance and how this impacted upon their reigns.

KEY TERMS

Hanseatic League
Also referred to as the German Hanse or Hansa. This was a group of cities and countries along the coast of Northern Europe that dominated the Baltic trade. They had a mutual agreement regarding trade and defence. Merchants from member states had special legal and diplomatic privileges as they travelled along trading routes, and the League had its own legal system and form of military protection.

Non-staple goods
In the medieval context, the term 'staple' refers to the system of taxation and custom collection. Therefore, 'staple goods' were those subject to various custom duties, including the ancient custom and the new, or petty, custom. The term 'non-staple goods' refers to those wares that were not liable for these traditional charges, but which could be subject to other forms of taxation, such as poundage.

Feudal rights

The term 'feudalism' is how modern historians refer to a system of landholding used from the Norman Conquest in 1066 to the 13th century. In essence, all land belonged to the king, who then divided it out among his tenants-in-chief (usually the greater nobles), who in turn divided their estates among their tenants, this process continuing down the social ladder. The tenant at the bottom of the hierarchy did agricultural work on the land directly, while any lords who came between this lowly tenant and the king were described as mesne lords and were of increasingly high standing. Each tenant held the property 'in service' to their mesne lord (and, ultimately, the king), which meant they had responsibilities to him in return for being able to live on the land. Acts of 'service' varied depending upon an individual's status and the size of property held. At the lower end, tenants were

KEY TERMS

KEY TERMS

Serf
A person legally bound to a particular lord who owned the land on which he or she lived.

Array
In a military context, this means the arrangement and organisation of troops. In the reign of Edward I (r. 1272–1307), the practice of the king issuing 'commissions of array' began, which gave regional lords the authority to raise an army in the name of the king during times of national emergency.

Muster
Similar in meaning to 'array', a muster in a military context means a gathering together of troops for service.

Mercenary
A professional soldier who will fight for any cause in return for payment.

classified as 'unfree' **serfs** who had to perform agricultural labour on the lord's personal lands. By the mid- to late 14th century, however, this type of tenure was greatly in decline and most land was held by free tenants, who could be responsible for one or more of the following forms of duty to his lord:

- **Personal service**: this could include serving one's lord with his wine at dinner or holding his banner in battle.

- **Payment of rent**: under the traditional feudal system, this usually had been paid in kind, often in the form of military service or in farm produce. From c1300, however, rent was usually paid in cash.

- **Military service**: under the feudal system, each tenant-in-chief was obliged to provide one or more knights or other military personnel to serve the king or mesne lord as required. From the early 14th century onwards, this method declined. It was replaced by a system where lords were authorised by the king to raise forces in the name of the crown and then contracts, often called 'indentures' or 'commissions' of **array** or **muster**, were sent out, giving the details of how many soldiers each lord needed to provide. These troops were usually found from within the lord's affinity, although sometimes **mercenaries** would be employed, especially for battles overseas. To a large extent, this change was caused by the greater manpower resources required to support English kings as they fought the Hundred Years War (1337–1453). This conflict needed more fighting men who were required to spend longer periods abroad, and the older system of raising an army was not adequate to meet these new demands. In addition, it reflected a more general shift towards cash payment for retainers, rather than hereditary feudal ties based on land between lords and their followers (see Chapter 1, page 20). Contemporary moralists were often critical of this new, cash-focused and non-hereditary system, regarding it as a key cause of the changing loyalties and disorder associated with the Wars of the Roses. There was probably some truth in this, and certainly during the civil war it was often very difficult for soldiers and retainers to know where their loyalties should lie. Nonetheless, the key factor was probably not a lack of hereditary ties between lord and man, but instead simply the fact that cash payment for military service allowed lords to keep larger affinities, which was dangerous as they effectively could be used as private armies and allowed leading nobles to become 'over-mighty subjects' too easily. The problem of unrest and a decline in royal control was also increased as the war with France meant a large proportion of the population had direct fighting experience, which made them more dangerous in times of popular rebellion. This was particularly evident, for example, in 1450 during Cade's Rebellion, when the insurgents were joined by angry and humiliated soldiers returning to England from defeat in France.

EXTEND YOUR KNOWLEDGE

The status of serfs
Serfs could not move away from the land they were assigned and had to perform labour services (usually in the form of agricultural work) not only on the land on which they lived, but also on property that provided food for the lord directly. Serfs also had to have permission from the lord to marry or to educate their children. Unlike classical slaves, however, the body of a serf could not be bought or sold; they were instead tied to the property on which they lived.

The decline of serfdom was speeded up considerably by the 1348–49 outbreak of the Black Death, which killed so many that traditional ties to lords and the land were often broken. Increasingly, serfdom became heavily resented and to refer to someone as a 'serf' became an insult.

One source of royal income came from the king's traditional feudal rights over his tenants living on crown lands. For example, like other feudal lords, the king gained a fee when his tenant's eldest daughter got married. In addition, as monarch, the king had greater feudal rights than any other lord over his tenants, such as the 'right to the wardship of idiots', which meant that the king took the profits of all lands held by those suffering from a permanent mental disability, less the tenant's living costs. Monarchs could also request feudal aids for the knighting of the king's eldest son and the marriage of the king's eldest daughter, with the consent of parliament. Henry VII was famously ruthless in extracting the financial benefits of this tradition when, in 1504, he proposed to parliament that he should be granted customary feudal fees on the occasion of the marriage of his daughter, Princess Margaret, and the knighting of his eldest son, Prince Arthur. Not entirely surprisingly, parliament opposed this suggestion, as Arthur had been knighted five years earlier and was already dead, and Margaret had been married in the previous year. S.B. Chrimes has suggested that this was motivated less by a desire for this particular fee than a general attempt by the king to investigate how far-reaching in practical terms his prerogative rights were. Nonetheless, this case has done little to alleviate the widespread view that he was a particularly avaricious king.

While all kings took advantage of these aspects of the royal prerogative, they were less significant than custom duties or various forms of direct taxation; in 1433, for example, a year for which there are unusually good financial records, revenue from feudal dues was just over seven percent of total royal income. Nonetheless, there was periodic concern to ensure that the king received all the money he was owed from this source. Henry VI's minority government launched various investigations to ensure the correct payment of feudal dues, the most comprehensive being in 1427, although Ralph Griffiths has argued that overall the minority council were careless with this source of royal income and manipulated it to support factionalism rather than strengthening the crown. The management of royal income improved under Edward IV, thanks to the introduction of more efficient management systems administered through the Chamber rather than the Exchequer (see page 46), methods which were then improved on further by Henry VII.

Profits of justice

A key element of the king's role was the maintenance of law and order within the realm. It was also obviously crucial that this system of law enforcement was efficient enough to ensure that payments owing to the crown were made. By 1399, a complex system of courts and royal administration had developed to organise this. The central courts were based at Westminster and included the court of the Exchequer, which heard cases relating to the crown's revenue. Its judges were the barons of the Exchequer, who by the late Middle Ages were professional lawyers. Clearly, for the king to maintain a healthy income, it was necessary that those who broke the law in relation to payments to the crown were pursued through legal channels and therefore the court of the Exchequer was important to ensure royal financial solvency.

Other courts were important not only in terms of law enforcement, but also as a source of royal income. While the popular image of the criminal justice system in medieval England remains one of torture, mutilation and the death penalty, in reality many people who were found guilty of offences were simply punished by a fine and, when the conviction took place in the royal courts, this money accordingly went to the king's coffers.

In 1874, the historian J.R. Green made the highly influential argument that Edward IV and Henry VII created a 'new monarchy', in other words, that these two kings substantially altered the role of a king and how the politics and the finances of the realm were managed. In Edward's case, this focused mainly on his use of new forms of loans and taxation (discussed in Chapter 6). Most subsequent scholarship, however, focused on changes made by Henry VII, with Alexander Grant in particular arguing the first Tudor reign saw the birth of a more 'modern'

form of government, particularly in terms of his management of finances. These bonds were payments to the crown by members of the nobility in return for either privileges or as fines which were imposed upon those whose loyalty to the king was questionable, or who were liable to quarrel violently with another noble family. The payment of bonds was not new, but Henry increased their use considerably and during his reign more than half the peerage was obliged to pay money to the crown as security for their good behaviour, with some nobles being forced to agree to more than one bond. These payments were not always called in, but the nobles in question lived under continual threat of being forced to sacrifice huge amounts of money if they offended the king in any way. In addition, a noble could be made to pay an annual sum in lieu of the whole amount, which provided a considerable addition to the royal finances as well as very effectively ensuring loyalty to the king. These demands were of dubious legality, as they effectively allowed punishment of potential offences rather than actual ones. Predictably, therefore, such measures were unpopular and, although Henry VII remained in power until his natural death in 1509, it is notable that one of his key architects of this policy, Edmund Dudley, was swiftly tried and killed for his involvement in this unpopular policy just a few days after the king died.

Taxation

The form of royal income that had the greatest impact on a monarch's expression of political power in late medieval England was direct taxation. This was undoubtedly the most controversial method of a king raising money. According to custom, such taxation had to be agreed by parliament and was usually to meet the costs of defending the realm, a reason which included war overseas, most frequently in France (see page 46).

In response to a request for money from the monarch, it was most usual for parliament to grant 'the tenths and fifteenths', a phrase that originally had referred to taxation on movable goods. This form of taxation could only be levied if both houses of parliament had agreed to it. In theory, those living in the countryside paid the crown a fifteenth of the value of their movable goods, while those living in towns and cities, or who lived on royal demesne land, paid the higher rate of one-tenth of the value of their possessions. In 1334, however, royal officials assessed counties or towns rather than individuals; from this point onwards the phrase referred to this fixed sum, which continued to be charged to each community. There were a number of problems with this system, which weakened its usefulness to the monarchy:

- The system of charging a county or town with a fixed levy made the system inflexible. In particular, there had been a severe drop in population in this time, owing to frequent outbreaks of the Black Death from 1347 onwards. Therefore, there were fewer people to pay the taxes, which made the burden on individuals much heavier. Some communities, in desperation, petitioned the crown asking for relief, with periodic success, but it is often difficult for historians to distinguish genuine pleas from those seeking to avoid paying taxes that they could actually afford.

- It is highly likely that tax evasion occurred, but it is difficult to discern this as obviously it was not recorded in the official documentation. Parliament frequently complained, however, that the expected sums were not in fact received by the Crown.

- In general, a prominent local man was put in charge of collecting taxes in the area and, in theory at least, was liable to make up the difference to the crown if he did not collect enough, although this penalty was not always incurred in practice. This gap between the anticipated income and reality could mean that the king was unable to raise enough money to support his policies, especially in relation to war, which could be highly problematic in military and political terms and could weaken his reputation for authority both at home and abroad.

A key difficulty faced by monarchs during the Hundred Years War (1337–1453) was that the costs of the conflict were usually high, the main exception being a period of truce in the 1360s. Kings such as Henry V, who were militarily highly successful, had relatively little difficulty in obtaining the necessary grants of taxation from a grateful parliament, whereas there was liable to be far more criticism when the English were suffering defeats. The parliament of November 1450, for example, held after the English loss of Normandy, was highly critical of Henry VI's government and especially Edmund Beaufort, duke of Somerset, who was the military leader in France. When the war was going badly, particularly in the mid-15th century, taxes were more resented and therefore harder to collect. This lack of funds then obviously hindered the war effort, making this a downwards spiral. This situation was particularly evident with the attempts to collect the tenth and fifteenth granted by parliament in 1449. Although parliament had taken the precaution of changing payment thresholds to make the tax less harsh upon the poor, royal officials still experienced huge difficulty in collecting the money owed and by 1453 it is estimated that only around three-quarters of the total had reached the crown.

Given the problems associated with the tenth and fifteenth taxation, and its failure to provide adequate income for sustained war overseas, it is unsurprising that the period saw some experimentation with different forms of taxation. This was evident in the reign of Henry VI. In 1428, for example, a tax was imposed upon parishes and in 1431 a tax on land. The fact that neither of these measures was renewed suggests they did not prove particularly successful. The reign also saw an attempt to introduce income tax in 1435, described as a 'subsidy'. Such measures reflected the growing cost of maintaining English control in France. Income tax was also used by Edward IV in 1472–73 to raise money for a planned invasion of France. Contemporaries tended to look unfavourably on this form of taxation, however, and this suspicion seems to have influenced the collection of Edward's 1472–73 levy, which only gathered half of the anticipated amount of £60,000. Edward needed this money for his invasion of France in 1474–75 (see page 58), but after 1475 Edward IV, Richard III and Henry VII all benefited considerably from the need to spend less on war. Gaining consent for taxation from parliament was therefore less of a political issue in the later stages of the period.

(see page 58)

EXTEND YOUR KNOWLEDGE

Why was changing the tax system so difficult in the later Middle Ages?

For all the faults of the system of tenths and fifteenths, there were two key problems with changing the system. Firstly, the 1381 Peasants' Revolt had been sparked by England's first use of the poll tax. The violence of this rebellion against the ruling elite (especially leading tax collectors) remained infamous throughout the 15th century and was very much in the memory of those making political decisions. Class division was increased by Cade's Rebellion in 1450, a major popular rising against perceived oppression of the lower orders by the ruling elite. Secondly, medieval society was essentially conservative and did not easily welcome innovation; it was therefore considerably politically easier to get a tax accepted if it was traditional, than if it was perceived as novel and, therefore, possibly illegal.

The role of the Exchequer and the Chamber

The medieval Exchequer was the bureaucratic institution that dealt with matters of royal finance. Its primary functions were to receive, store and pay out money on behalf of the crown, and to audit the royal accounts. The Chief Officer of the Exchequer was the treasurer and subordinate to him was the Chancellor of the Exchequer. Until the 14th century, officials in the Exchequer were usually members of the clergy, but this tradition decreased in the late Middle Ages. Local officers (usually sheriffs) were in charge of collecting taxation and other forms of revenue from the localities. They brought the money gathered to the Lower Exchequer, where an official called the Chamberlain of the Exchequer presided. In return, the sheriffs received a piece of marked wood, called a 'tally', which acted as a receipt for the amount they had paid. Tallies were then taken to the Upper Exchequer, where they were checked by the clerks to ensure the correct amount of money had been handed in by each locality. These returns were recorded in medieval manuscripts called the pipe rolls. (See Sources 2 and 3.) The bureaucratic hierarchy was complex and focused on preventing fraud. This meant that, while it usually functioned in an honest fashion, it was slow to process and audit money. Consequently, Edward IV developed an alternative financial department, under the management of the Chamber.

'The King's Chamber' was originally a phrase that referred to the king's private apartments, where he slept, washed and dressed. Because of the nature of personal kingship, however, this private area could also be a place where the king met with his closest advisers and made political decisions. Consequently, the member of staff in charge of this area – the chamberlain – was a highly influential figure, as he largely controlled access to the king. As a government department, the Chamber's importance increased from the beginning of the 14th century, particularly under Edward II, when it gained its own income and permanent staff. The Chamber also had a financial role. Traditionally, while the Exchequer organised and audited royal income, the Chamber arranged the spending of this money, as directed by the king, although increasingly this division broke down in the 15th century.

SOURCE 2

A section of a medieval pipe roll. This was a medieval manuscript used by the Exchequer to record the receipt of money collected from each region.

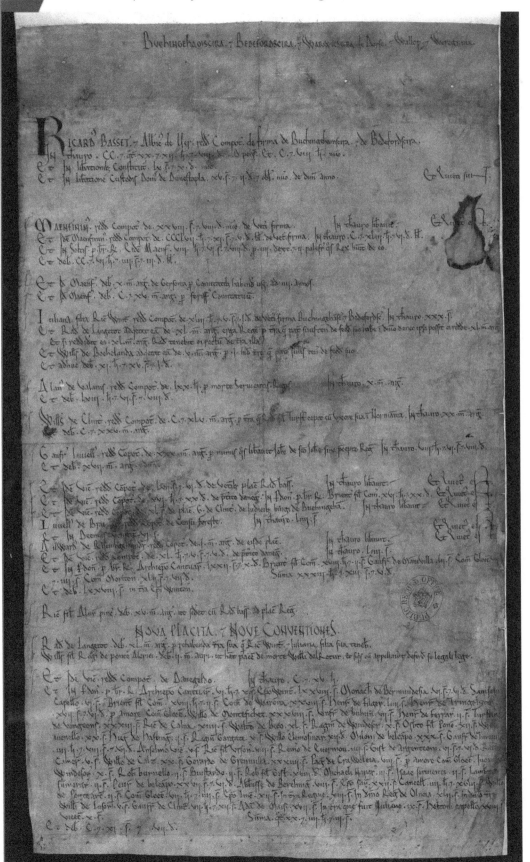

It is difficult to generalise about the precise activities of the Chamber, as each monarch used it in a slightly different way. Nonetheless, it is clear that Edward IV made a key alteration in the roles of the Exchequer and Chamber, making the latter the leading financial department. He particularly favoured it as a speedy method of circumventing the slower bureaucracy of the Exchequer officials, increasingly using it to control royal income and expenditure. The increased flexibility provided by this system enhanced Edward's financial position, allowing him to restore the crown finances during his second reign from the precarious state they were left in by Henry VI. This meant that the monarchy was solvent by the 1480s, despite Edward's reputation for personal extravagance. In the upheaval of the Tudor takeover in 1485, Exchequer officials reinstated the old system, but once Henry VII became established he returned to the use of Chamber finance, and the greater control this gave the king over royal revenues was influential in helping him to increase crown income and gain a strong reputation as an intelligent financial operator.

SOURCE

3

This image represents the 15th-century Exchequer of Ireland, which was modelled on the English Exchequer. The word 'exchequer' originates from the chequered cloth on the table. Each square represented a value – pounds, shillings, pence and other amounts. The people around the table were financial officials writing out accounts, and the staff of the treasurer and the sheriffs, who were heatedly discussing the audit.

Taxation, the Exchequer and the Chamber

1 In no more than 20 words (writing in full sentences), explain the relationship between taxation, parliament, the king and defence.

2 Draw a flowchart explaining the development of the roles of the Exchequer and the Chamber in the period 1399–1509.

DID PARLIAMENT ACT AS A PROP OR A CURB TO ROYAL POWER?

Parliamentary representation and local relations with the crown

Since 1265, the English parliament had been made up of representatives from both towns and the countryside (sometimes referred to as the 'shires'). These representatives could be summoned by the king whenever he chose and the composition of parliament was as shown in Figure 2.1.

The Lords consisted of two groups

1) Lay noblemen with a hereditary right to a seat in parliament because of their landholdings and family background.

2) Bishops, who had an automatic right to a seat as representatives of the Church. Members of the Upper House were summoned personally to parliament by writ from the monarch.

The Commons consisted of two groups

1) Town representatives (usually merchants and lawyers).

2) 'Knights of the shire' – gentry representatives of the countryside. All members of parliament in the Commons were chosen by the wealthier male members of their local communities.

Figure 2.1 The composition of parliament.

Representatives to the Commons were chosen by a small electorate, composed entirely of adult males who owned fairly substantial property in the county. In 1376, the Commons had for the first time chosen a leader from among themselves, to speak to the king and Upper House on their behalf, and from then on this role became traditional and formalised as the 'Speaker of the Commons'. During the reign of Richard II and under the Lancastrian kings, parliament's role developed substantially and it is notable that, while the language used by the Commons towards the king was usually deferential, in reality there were often significant challenges from the Lower House to the monarch's autonomy. Throughout the late medieval period, parliament had two primary roles: to assent to the king's requests for taxation and as a legislative body, each of which are discussed in turn here.

Parliament and legislation

In terms of law making, parliament had a more innovative role than it did in terms of taxation. Instead of simply agreeing to what the king had already decided, the Commons were expected both to listen to the king's ideas about legislation and also to put forward their own suggestions about which laws should be passed. As part of this, they were expected to inform the king via petitions of particular problems currently being experienced by people in different regions of the kingdom. Parliamentary petitions took two forms:

- A personal petition was a formal request from an individual, family, group or area for assistance from the crown to remedy a particular problem. For example, a town might request parliamentary permission to take measures to combat vagrancy or illegal trading in the area. These petitions can be particularly illuminating evidence in relation to areas that were experiencing a breakdown in law and order.

- A Commons petition was a formal request from the Lower House to the crown to deal with a particular problem affecting the kingdom as a whole, or a region within the kingdom. This type of petitioning began in the early 14th century and by the end of the century had become firmly established.

Petitions were important as the king's response to these documents became law, thus giving the Commons a significant role in shaping the legislative process. It should be noted, however, that the king had the right to refuse to grant what was requested, a response which was fairly commonplace. He could also organise for his own bills to be presented, thus allowing the crown to steer the law-making process as well.

Parliament and taxation

From the 13th century onwards, the crown's traditional sources of revenue were gradually reduced and there were fairly frequent financial demands on the country's income because of war. At the same time, it became an established custom that parliament had to agree to taxes being collected and, from the 1260s onwards, this included the consent of both the lords and the Commons. This increased the importance of the Lower House substantially and, from 1325 onwards, no parliament met without both Chambers being summoned. It was conventional that taxes were only levied by parliament in the case of urgent necessity for **the common good** and usually defence of the realm was cited as the reason why money was required. The level of control the Commons had over taxation was limited, however, as they did not have the right to refuse the crown money if the king demonstrated genuine need, particularly in relation to defence. Nonetheless, they could use the request as an opportunity to negotiate regarding the amount of taxation granted and also to voice concern regarding the management of the kingdom.

KEY TERM

The common good
This phrase is used frequently in late medieval political literature to indicate that something or someone is acting in the public interest.

TIMELINE: KEY DEVELOPMENTS IN THE ROLE OF PARLIAMENT

1376
Commons choose Speaker to represent their views to the king and the Lords

1386
'Wonderful Parliament' of Richard II, when parliament threatens the king with deposition if he does not attend and had the chancellor forcibly removed

1399
Richard II deposed and his cousin, Bolingbroke, becomes Henry IV

1404–6
Parliament demands appointment of special 'treasurers for war', who are to oversee the receipt of taxation and ensure it is not used instead by the royal household

1406
'Long Parliament' meets at Westminster on 1 March 1406 and sits until 22 December. The king's illness means that this parliament is instrumental in transferring many of the king's powers to his son, Prince Henry. 31 articles are drawn up to control the king's financial expenditure.

1413
Henry IV dies and is succeeded by his son, Henry V

1415
In gratitude for the king's victory at Agincourt, parliament grants Henry V tonnage and poundage for life and makes other tax grants

1422
August: Henry V dies and is succeeded by Henry VI, who is nine months old

November to December: During the first parliament of Henry VI's reign, arrangements for the lengthy minority government are drawn up

1454
March: Parliament declares Richard, duke of York 'Defender and Protector of the Realm' for the first time

1455
February: Henry VI recovers his health and the First Protectorate of Richard, duke of York, ends

November: Following Yorkist victory at the First Battle of St Albans, the Second Protectorate of Richard, duke of York, begins

1456
February: York's Second Protectorate ends

1461
Henry VI deposed by the new Edward IV

1470
Readeption of Henry VI

1471
April: Edward IV regains throne and his second reign begins

1475
Treaty of Picquigny between England and France. This provides Edward IV with an annual pension, thus substantially reducing his dependence on parliament for finance.

1478
George, duke of Clarence, brother to Edward IV, is tried in parliament for treason and found guilty

1483
Edward IV dies. Edward V disappears, assumed dead. Richard III takes the throne.

1485
Battle of Bosworth. Henry VII takes the throne

1504
Parliament rejects Henry VII's claim for financial support relating to the knighting of Prince Arthur and the marriage of Princess Margaret, and reduces the amount he seeks in taxation. This is the last parliament of the reign.

1509
Henry VII dies

This most dramatically occurred during the 1376 'Wonderful Parliament' of Richard II, when the chancellor, Michael de la Pole, was forcibly removed from office, but other governments were criticised by parliament. In 1450, for example, charges were brought against William de la Pole, duke of Suffolk, who was the English military commander in France at the time of the loss of Normandy. In their complaints, parliament included almost all of its typical criticisms of unpopular government ministers, including corruption, financial mismanagement, military incompetence, oppression, misuse of taxes and poor appointments. Statements of grievance against ministers were perhaps particularly inclined to be so comprehensive because it was considered important that the king himself was not criticised. Indeed, the monarch himself was rarely personally attacked, as this would amount to treason, and so instead objections tended to focus on '**evil councillors**' around the monarch, who were blamed for misleading him. This political rhetoric can make it initially difficult when reading the primary sources to discern the difference between cases where particular officials, such as the chancellor, were particularly disliked and when they were instead being scapegoated to save royal embarrassment in the case of an unpopular monarch.

KEY TERM

Evil councillor
A phrase used in late medieval political literature to refer to an adviser to the king who was deemed either by the public or by parliament to be incompetent or malicious.

It is evident that the Commons, in particular, valued the opportunity offered by parliament to discuss key concerns affecting the realm, as evidenced by the frequent petitions that it should become customary for the king to summon parliament at least annually. In reality, however, as historian J.S. Roskell has pointed out, the frequency of meetings of parliament was primarily dictated by the king's financial needs. For Henry IV, royal financial needs were a very pressing problem and he had a rather

EXTRACT 3

From S.J. Payling, 'Middle Ages: Parliament and Politics Before 1509', *The History of Parliament: British Political, Social and Local History* (2014). Here, the historian Payling discusses the power and limitations of the late medieval parliament.

By the end of the medieval period, Parliament was, in both structure and function, the same assembly that opposed the Stuarts in the seventeenth century. It bargained with the Crown over taxation and formulated local grievances in such a way as to invite legislative remedy, and, on occasion, most notably in 1376, it opposed the royal will. Yet this is not to say that Parliament had yet achieved, or even sought, an independent part in the polity. The power of the Lords resided not in their place in Parliament, but in the landed wealth of the great nobility. For the Commons, a favourable answer to their petitions remained a matter of royal grace, yet they were under an obligation to grant taxation as necessity demanded (a necessity largely interpreted by the Crown); and their right of assent to new law was a theoretical rather than a practical restraint on the King's freedom of legislative action. Indeed, Parliament amplified rather than curtailed royal power, at least when that power was exercised competently. Not only were the Crown's financial resources expanded by the system of parliamentary taxation, so too was its legislative force.

fraught relationship with parliament. Henry IV was hindered by the stigma of having forcibly overthrown the last king, Richard II, as well as suffering due to ill-health, both factors reducing his support in the country. Although he asked for considerably less money in taxation from parliament than his son, he was subject to significantly more criticism. This was most notable in the 'Long Parliament' of 1406, which lasted 23 weeks in total and ended with very bitter exchanges between the king and Commons regarding taxation (see page 50).

EXTRACT 4

From J.S. Roskell, 'The Place of Parliament in the King's Government', in J.S. Roskell, L. Clark and C. Rawcliffe (eds), *The History of Parliament: the House of Commons, 1386–1421*, (1993). Here, Roskell evaluates the relationship between the monarch and parliament in the 15th century.

The basic function of Parliament remained, as before, to serve the King and kingdom, but the former took priority, the interests of the kingdom being, of course, subsumed among his personal concerns. If, as occasionally happened, Parliament made pretence to be an organ of control, this was, as a general rule, only when the royal authority was being weakly or uncertainly exercised (largely because of the monarch's own incapacity or youthfulness)...

With King and subjects, government and governed, locked in an embrace of mutual dependence, information had constantly to be exchanged and, as regards both internal and external matters, views expressed. Parliament always provided a sounding-board whether relations between King and people were serene or strained, although in the latter case meetings were especially necessary. If unpopular domestic policies excited suspicion or led to division, or if the King's management of foreign affairs met with disapproval in certain quarters, Parliament was the place where differences would most likely be resolved. And if, at a more humdrum level, serious complaints were made about the royal administration either central or local, Parliaments offered an ideal opportunity for their ventilation, with common petitions, for which the Commons were to become chiefly responsible, able to secure legislative remedies for specific grievances, provided the Lords assented and the King withheld his veto.

ACTIVITY
KNOWLEDGE CHECK

Comparing interpretations of the role of parliament
Read Extracts 3 and 4 and answer these questions.

1 What is Payling's view of the role of parliament in this period? Does he regard it as a prop or a curb to royal power? Explain your answer.

2 In two sentences, summarise Roskell's view of the role of parliament in relation to the crown. Focus on whether he regards medieval parliament as a prop or a curb to royal power.

3 Compare Extracts 3 and 4.

   a) How do Payling and Roskell differ in their interpretation of whether parliament assisted or hindered the crown during the later Middle Ages?

   b) What evidence do they give to support their opinions?

   c) Which interpretation do you find most convincing and why?

Use both the extracts and your own knowledge to support your answers.

The parliament of 1406

Henry IV's relationship with parliament has been the subject of particular scholarly interest. The traditional view among historians has been that he had a very fraught relationship with the Commons, largely owing to his position as a usurper and the fact he was unable to make good his promise 'to live of his own' and so had to ask parliament for taxation on a number of occasions. There is certainly some evidence to support this. According to one **chronicle**, Henry IV was sent a letter by Philip Repyndon, the Bishop of Lincoln, unfavourably comparing the enthusiasm that had greeted Henry as he took the throne in 1400 with the growing unease regarding the king's financial management by 1401: 'joy has turned to bitterness, while evils multiply themselves everywhere, and hope of relief fades from the grieving hearts of men'.

KEY TERM

Chronicle
Chronicles were usually written by monks, although they could also be authored by lay people. They provide a history of a country, area or institution (like a monastery) year by year and generally include a mixture of information about national and local politics, the economy, social conditions, the weather and gossip.

Background causes of friction between the Commons and Henry IV

A key reason for the king's early financial distress was the fact that the French king refused to recognise Henry IV as the rightful monarch of England, causing a crisis in Anglo-French relations. This was unsurprising as Richard II's widow was a French princess, but it led to various serious problems that were long-term causes of the tensions that arose in the 'Long Parliament' of 1406:

- Piracy in the Channel caused problems for trade. From 1402, the situation deteriorated as the French and Scottish formed an alliance against the English, increasing hostilities at sea. England was penalised for its involvement in piracy by the Hanseatic League, who placed considerable restrictions on English merchants doing business in the Baltic.

- In 1404, there were two French naval attacks on the south coast of England, which increased criticism of the king. The need for repairs also reduced the taxes these areas could pay.

- The French began to use the domestic upheaval in England as an opportunity to threaten English territorial holdings in France, most notably Calais, Aquitaine (where Richard II had been very popular, having grown up in Bordeaux) and Gascony. The defence of Aquitaine alone is estimated to have cost the English government the substantial sum of £1,300 per annum between 1400 and 1403.

- As a result of the costs of war, in October 1404 parliament granted substantial taxation to the king, including two collections of the tenths and fifteenths as well as a new form of tax on land. This was the most tax granted at any time in Henry IV's reign and it was granted by the Commons on condition that two named 'treasurers of wars' received the money and accounted for it to the next parliament.

Problems facing Henry IV in 1405

The year 1405 was a critical one for Henry IV, who faced two serious threats. First, a number of leading nobles, including the earl of Northumberland, Earl Marshal Thomas Mowbray and Lord Bardolf, openly rebelled against Lancastrian rule in late May and June. Particularly concerning was the involvement in the revolt of Archbishop Richard Scrope of York. Although Scrope's motivations for rebellion are somewhat unclear, it is evident that he was heavily critical of the government's financial management, preaching publicly in York Minster against taxation. Archbishop Scrope and Thomas Mowbray raised an army of several thousand men, but disbanded this force when they were met by the earl of Westmorland, who promised them that their grievances would be heard. In reality, however, the king was furious with Scrope and he was tried, found guilty and beheaded on the same day, 8 June, just outside the city of York.

EXTEND YOUR KNOWLEDGE

The political and religious impact of the execution of Archbishop Richard Scrope of York
Although not unprecedented, the execution of an archbishop was extremely unusual and controversial, as clergymen were not usually subject to the death sentence. It was probably partly Scrope's popularity and partly resentment against the Lancastrian regime in Yorkshire that gave rise to a belief after the archbishop's death that miracles were being worked at his tomb because he was a holy martyr, rumours which caused considerable embarrassment to the king and his advisers.

The government was obliged to ban people from bringing gifts to his tomb, and to cover the grave with stones and logs to prevent public access. While Scrope was never officially recognised as a saint by the Roman Catholic Church, he was popularly known as 'Saint Richard Scrope' in the north of England. The fact that Henry IV fell ill so soon after Scrope's death was frequently cited by contemporary moralists as evidence of divine disapproval of the king's decision to kill the archbishop.

The strain of dealing with this insurrection seems to have taken its toll on Henry IV's health, and he became incapacitated for a week immediately after Archbishop Scrope's execution. He apparently recovered, however, and by mid-August was heading to Wales to subdue the second key threat to him in 1405 – a rebellion there led by Owain Glyndwr. It was being supported by the French king, who had sent 2,500 troops to assist the rebels. Henry was unable to eradicate the Welsh and French threat and this provided an uneasy backdrop to the parliament of 1406, which was summoned to deal yet again with the king's strained financial situation in March of that year.

What happened during the 'Long Parliament' of 1406?

The 1406 parliament was called 'long' because it first met at Westminster on 1 March 1406 and sat until 22 December, with a three-week Easter break in April and a break from mid-June to mid-October for the harvest. The deliberations were so prolonged firstly because there seems to have been considerable heated debate regarding taxation and, secondly, because Henry's health suddenly deteriorated rapidly, making him incapacitated for significant periods of time. There is debate in the historiography regarding whether or not this parliament was particularly hostile to the king, but there does seem to be evidence to suggest that Henry made some attempts to **pack** parliament and ensure Lancastrian supporters were chosen as representatives of the shires in the Commons. Certainly the Speaker of the Commons, Sir John Tiptoft, was a long-standing Lancastrian supporter who had served Henry prior to his seizure of the crown and it is evident that he used this role in part to curb some criticism of Henry IV's regime.

KEY TERM

Pack

The practice of trying to ensure a certain faction's supporters are in the majority in the Commons in parliament. Monarchs, in particular, sometimes manipulated those who were chosen as parliamentary representatives of the shires to ensure an outcome favourable to them in key decisions.

The exact nature of Henry IV's illness remains unknown, but it is clear that the illness was extremely debilitating, preventing the king from attending parliament or indeed ruling effectively at times. In 1406, arrangements were made for the succession to the throne by the monarch's son, Henry, Prince of Wales, indicating that there was an expectation in this year that the king would die.

When news of the king's illness reached parliament, the meeting was initially postponed in the hope that the king would recover but, by 22 May, Henry IV himself recognised that he was not able to govern alone and so asked parliament to appoint a council to assist him. Accordingly, 17 councillors were chosen, but there were considerable concerns about the ability of both the king and this group of advisers to manage government finances. The debate was very heated and it was only in mid-November that an agreement was reached. The key aspects of this settlement were as follows:

- A new, smaller council was set up to govern in the king's name, which was headed by Henry, Prince of Wales and included the three key officers of state, who were the chancellor, treasurer and Keeper of the Privy Seal. In addition, Archbishop Arundel, the bishops of Winchester and London, Edward, duke of York and John Beaufort, earl of Somerset were to be members.

- A document containing 31 articles was drawn up, detailing rules for controlling the crown's financial expenditure.

What was the significance of the 1406 parliament?

The new council seems to have been much more successful at managing finances and mainly used the Exchequer to ensure that taxes were spent on defence rather than the costs of the royal household. Additionally, they took measures to reduce the cost of the royal household and, as a result, were able to obtain a grant of taxation from parliament the following year with ease. There were also a number of achievements in foreign policy that, in turn, reduced pressure on finances: notably the capture by the English in 1406 of Prince James, heir to the Scottish throne, which gave the government a very valuable bargaining chip when dealing with Scotland. Another of England's enemies, the duke of Orléans, was murdered in November 1407, which helped to trigger civil war

in France and thus reduced pressure on the English holdings of Gascony and Calais.

In terms of domestic politics, the most significant result of the 1406 parliament was the tension it caused between Henry IV and his eldest son and heir, Henry, Prince of Wales. The prince had a strong following in Wales, where he had spent much of his time once his father came to the throne, fighting against Glyndwr's rebels. His retinue included the earls of Arundel and Warwick as well as members of the Beaufort family, a powerful group who had previously been allied to the king himself. Henry IV was disillusioned by the fact that these men increasingly supported the prince, who they saw as the monarch of the future. He also resented the fact that the prince was taking such a prominent role in running the country, while his own health severely limited his practical involvement in government. Throughout his illness, the king's most loyal supporter was Archbishop Arundel, who had supported Henry IV both as a friend and a political adviser since the usurpation and continued to do so throughout his reign.

ACTIVITY
KNOWLEDGE CHECK

The relationship between Henry IV, his son and the nobility

1 List those who, after 1406, were increasingly supporting Prince Henry, rather than his father. In each case, briefly explain why they were more loyal to the Prince of Wales than to the king.

2 a) Make a bullet-point list of the factors which made the 1406 parliament significant to the political stability of the Lancastrian dynasty. Place the most significant factor (in your opinion) at the top, and the least significant factor at the bottom.

b) Write a paragraph explaining why you have put the factors in this order.

Henry V's relationship with parliament

In general, Henry V had a considerably less tense relationship with parliament than his father had. This is evidenced by the fact that parliament met frequently to discuss finance for the Hundred Years War, assembling twice in the years 1414, 1416 and 1421, for example. Nonetheless, the meetings were often brief, lasting between three and four weeks. Henry certainly showed some tact in handling parliament early in his reign. It is notable, for example, that in 1413, the first parliament of the reign, the Commons had made complaints regarding the maintenance of law and order and the king responded in the parliament of the following year by taking various strong measures against lawlessness. In addition, in 1414, clearly under royal instruction, Bishop Henry Beaufort gave the opening sermon and in this speech emphasised the need for restoring justice both at sea and on land, but reassuring parliament that the king would make no request for a tenth and fifteenth in the hope that they would help him financially on future occasions.

Nonetheless, it is clear that the key reason for Henry's largely easier relationship with parliament was his popularity, mainly created by his military victories in France. After hearing the news of English victory at Agincourt in 1415, London went wild with enthusiasm for the monarch and magnificent processions were organised for his homecoming. Joining in the spirit of the occasion, the opening sermon of the March 1416 parliament praised Henry's victory and granted him tonnage and poundage for life. It is notable, however, that the king did not immediately use this as an opportunity to press a tenth and fifteenth taxation to consolidate his victories, probably a wise decision given that the taxes granted by the previous parliament were still being collected. Consequently, he was in a much stronger position to ask for a larger grant when parliament met again in October.

Despite Henry's judicious dealings with parliament, it is evident that by the end of the reign, costs of war with France were taking a heavy toll, as shown by the high levels of royal debt in the early 1420s. In addition, the king was frequently abroad and his lengthy absences caused some public concern. He did not, for example, personally attend any parliament in the years 1417 to 1420, although three took place. In May 1421, there was clearly considerable unease about how Henry's conquest of France the previous year should be financed and it is notable that there is some suggestion in the records that Henry may have requested a tenth and fifteenth which was either declined or deferred to the following parliament. The extent to which Henry V would have been able to maintain his own French victories had he lived longer is a point of considerable historical speculation, but it is clear that when he died in 1422 and his baby son became Henry VI, the 'golden years' of an entirely amicable relationship between a popular king and his parliament were already on the wane.

Comparing Henry VI and Edward IV's relationships with parliament

Given the unstable character of Henry VI, it is difficult to ascertain how much of relations between the crown and parliament were of the king's own making, and the extent to which government policy was shaped by others. This problem is exacerbated by the tradition of criticising 'evil councillors' rather than the king himself. Nonetheless, it is clear that Henry VI's relationship with parliament was a fraught one. From 1422 until his deposition in 1461, 22 parliaments were held in Henry's name, and one was held in November 1470 during the readeption. The parliaments of the 1440s and early 1450s focused mainly on the key issues of defence, especially in relation to France, associated questioning and criticism of the king's advisers and on the parlous state of the royal finances. In the instance of the trial of Henry's favourite, Suffolk, in 1450 for example, it is evident that parliament was not acting in accordance with the king's wishes, although given the level of rebellion in the country at this time, it could be argued that such measures were necessary to maintain some semblance of royal control. It is clear that at times parliament did undermine the king's authority – most notably the so-called 'Parliament of Devils', which occurred in November 1459 and was packed with Lancastrian supporters with the clear purpose of attainting the duke of York and his supporters, especially the earl of Salisbury, the earl of Warwick and York's eldest son Edward of March (later Edward IV). All these Yorkist leaders fled the country, but the bitterness with which they were treated, including the confiscation of their lands and attainders passed against them, effectively gave these men very clear motivations for further rebellion. This led to the Yorkists invading England and defeating Lancastrian troops at the Battle of Northampton in July 1460. Although this was not a decisive win, by the following year the Yorkists had defeated Henry VI and Edward IV took the throne.

Edward IV appeared to have a considerably more harmonious relationship with parliament than his predecessor. To a large extent, this was owing to the fact that he was less dependent upon taxation for defence and, consequently, during his 23 years in power parliament was called only six times, although these sessions were often lengthy. In addition, Edward went to some trouble to pack the Commons for meetings that were likely to be controversial, by pressurising local electorates to return preferred royal candidates or even tampering with the **electoral returns**. The clearest example of this type of manipulation was found in 1478, when Edward wanted a compliant parliament to ensure that his brother, the duke of Clarence, was convicted of high treason. On this occasion, according to Charles Ross, of the 27 shires represented in parliament, 23 were represented on this occasion by at least one member of staff from the royal household. Such interference in local electoral choices occurred periodically but not frequently during the period 1399–1509, and was surprisingly uncontroversial, perhaps reflecting the fact that contemporaries did regard parliament very much as a servant of the king's will.

Like other kings, Edward used parliament primarily as a forum to increase his income. This was most controversial in the parliaments of the 1460s and early 1470s, when he was raising funds for a planned invasion of France. Many contemporaries had understandable doubts about this policy, given the recent military history of the Hundred Years War. It is no coincidence, therefore, that Edward was granted a tenth and fifteenth in the parliament of 1468, and in 1469 rebels against the king voiced criticism of this heavy taxation. Once returned to power in 1471, Edward faced considerable difficulties in gaining the requisite money from parliament to pursue his military policy against the French and a parliament which sat through the period 1472–75 granted him four tenths and fifteenths, but clearly with reluctance, insisting that the money could only be handed over when definite plans for the French invasion were made. This invasion, though disappointing from a military perspective, had a lucrative outcome for Edward and his French pension made him largely independent from parliament for financial support until his death in 1483.

Edward IV did undoubtedly acquire a reputation for greed during his lifetime. It was perhaps partly to distance himself from this image, as well as to strengthen his claim to power, that Richard III chose not to request taxation in the only parliament of his reign, held in 1484. Given the brevity of his time as king, however, it is very difficult to reach any informed assessment about what his relationship with parliament was like.

A Level Exam-Style Question Section C

'The key factor in limiting royal power in the years 1399–1509 was the king's relationship with parliament.'

How far do you agree with this statement? (20 marks)

Tip

When answering this question, ensure that you consider evidence from the full range of dates mentioned and focus on themes of change and continuity in your writing.

WAS WAR OR DIPLOMACY OF THE GREATEST BENEFIT TO THE ENGLISH CROWN IN THE PERIOD 1399–1509?

Foreign war, if one can forgive the wordplay, was something of a double-edged sword for late medieval monarchs. On one hand, it was seen as the king's sovereign duty to protect his realm from outside threats and it is notable that the country was particularly prone to rebellion or hostile parliaments when there was a threat of invasion, especially from France, Wales or Scotland. For example, Richard II faced the Peasants' Revolt in 1381 after a number of serious French raids on the south coast, while Henry IV faced the Archbishop Scrope's rebellion in the same year as a revolt in Wales from Owain Glyndwr. Kings, once they were of age, were expected to act as military leaders and fight personally in battles. Doing so proved their skills as a warrior and commander, as demanded by medieval concepts of honour, and also provided the opportunity for their men to conquer foreign territory, which was an important source of income for many nobles in this period.

On the other hand, foreign war was a costly and uncertain business; just as victories enhanced a monarch's reputation, defeats, especially if they were seen to be the result of poor leadership or dishonourable conduct, could seriously damage a king's status. In addition, war had to be funded through taxation and parliament had to agree to these grants. As the Commons often used requests for taxation as an opportunity to raise grievances concerning the government of the realm, gaining money in this way could be problematic, especially for a monarch in a weak political position.

Henry V, Henry VI and the Hundred Years War

In terms of foreign war, Henry V was the most successful monarch, conquering large amounts of land in France and massively increasing his popularity with the nobles, who often benefited substantially from these victories. The Treaty of Troyes, which was signed in 1420 and made Henry V heir to the French throne, was the high point of the Hundred Years War for England and was the culmination of a series of important military victories, the most spectacular being those at Harfleur and Agincourt in 1415 and Rouen (the capital of Normandy) in 1419 (see also Chapter 4). Arguably, however, Henry V secured his excellent reputation as the quintessential 'good king' by dying in 1422, shortly after he signed this triumphant treaty. It is very unlikely that the English could have maintained control of these vast areas of land indefinitely. Henry V, therefore, bequeathed to his baby son the glorious title of 'King of England and France', but there can be little doubt that this was a poisoned chalice. Problems in France were to overshadow Henry VI's reign and the need for continuing requests to parliament for taxation to further the war effort made his regime very vulnerable to criticism (see also pages 118–20).

KEY TERM

Armagnacs
One of the rival factions in a civil war in France which ran between 1407 and 1435. The conflict was between two rival dynasties seeking to take the French throne, the Armagnacs (who supported the House of Orléans) and the Burgundians (who supported the dukes of Burgundy).

During Henry VI's minority, the king's uncle, John, duke of Bedford, had the difficult role of trying to maintain the English conquests in France and enforcing the terms of the treaty. This was particularly tricky as, while the treaty had been widely accepted in the north of France, it was bitterly resented in much of the south, where the **Armagnacs** supported the claim of the French Dauphin, Charles, to the French throne. Initially, however, Bedford was successful in 1424, convincingly defeating the dauphin's French–Scottish army at the Battle of Verneuil. Nevertheless, the military situation rapidly changed as the English turned their attention towards Orléans in the late 1420s. This change in fortunes is often attributed to the role not of a seasoned military leader, but instead to an uneducated peasant girl – the famous Joan of Arc.

Joan of Arc was a teenage peasant girl from the village of Domremy, which lay in lands claimed by the duke of Burgundy but which had always remained loyal to the claim of the French Dauphin, Charles. She claimed to hear the voices of God and the saints telling her it was her mission to save France and, during 1429, she led Charles' forces successfully against the English, winning a number of important victories for the French that led to the dauphin being crowned King Charles VII of France in July 1429, while Joan looked on.

Although Joan of Arc's role in the Hundred Years War was brief (she was only active between 1429 and 1431), the fact that she was successful in ensuring the dauphin was crowned was highly significant: by 1435, Philip, duke of Burgundy, abandoned his allegiance to the English and instead declared his loyalty to Charles, which meant that the English had little hope of making the Treaty of Troyes a workable reality.

This was to become a long-standing problem for Henry VI, as his very public failure to live up to the memory of his father was one factor in undermining him. Given his young age in the 1420s and 1430s however, it was his advisers rather than the king personally who were held responsible. It is also unlikely that in the long term this would have been so problematic had Henry VI shown himself as competent in other areas of government, such as managing finance or the nobility, but given his uniform weakness it became another area for criticism as he grew to adulthood.

In practical terms, the English government came to realise that a new treaty with France was required. This was agreed at Tours in 1444 (see page 113). Negotiated primarily by Edmund Beaufort, duke of Somerset and William de la Pole, duke of Suffolk, this agreement attempted to secure more lasting peace by arranging a marriage in 1445 between Henry VI of England and the French princess, Margaret of Anjou. Problematically, however, the treaty surrendered the hard-won region of Maine to France, a clause which was so controversial that it initially had to be kept secret because of fear of public outcry in England. When news of this arrangement emerged in 1447, it created considerable public hostility towards Henry VI and his French wife Margaret, as well as to his key advisers in this matter, Somerset and Suffolk.

The significance of English losses in France in the Hundred Years War

The truce was not to last. In 1449, an English force attacked Fougères in Brittany, looting the town. The reasons for this attack are unclear, and it was an extremely unwise move. Charles VII declared that he therefore was no longer bound by the terms of the Tours truce. Charles had effectively reorganised his army and the French fought very successfully against the English, defeating them in Normandy and Gascony by 1450. Despite the valiant efforts of one English commander, John Talbot, who managed to regain Bordeaux, these victories proved a death knell for English interests in France. The final blow came on 17 July 1453, when Talbot's army was routed at the Battle of Castillon. Quickly, all of the English territories in France fell, except Calais.

The defeats of the early 1450s can be regarded as a disaster for England, as well as a personal catastrophe for King Henry VI. In 1450, the king was dealing with not only news of the loss of Normandy and Gascony, but also a widespread peasant rebellion in the south of England led by a figure called 'Jack Cade'. While the rebels had a range of grievances, the poor handling of the war and level of royal debt was high on their priority list and their ranks were swollen by soldiers recently returned from France, who were very disillusioned by their military defeats there.

The decline in royal authority had also contributed to a major breakdown in law and order in the north of England owing to an ongoing feud between the Nevilles and the Percies. The final blow to Henry, however, came on learning the news of the English defeat at Castillon, which seemed to trigger a complete mental and physical collapse in the English king. It is unclear exactly what illness Henry was suffering from, though some scholars now argue that it was a form of catatonic schizophrenia. Contemporary accounts, however, make it clear he fell into a complete stupor for 17 months and was apparently incapable of speaking, reasoning or understanding what was said to him. The political ramifications of this were great, as it was unclear when (or if) the king would recover or who should rule the country in the meantime. Henry had no children, although his wife was pregnant and gave birth to a prince, Edward, during the period of the king's illness. Henry, however, did not recognise or respond to his child when the baby was brought to him (see Source 4).

SOURCE

 4

Letter from John Stodeley, dated 19 January 1454; the intended recipient is unknown. Here, Stodeley gives an account of the political situation at this time. In the letter, he begins by describing how Henry VI did not seem aware of the birth of his own son, owing to his mental collapse in this period, and then discusses the 1453–54 parliament. It would have been traditional for the king to give a blessing to his son at this first meeting, thus recognising that the baby was his own son. From J. Gairdner (ed.), *The Paston Letters*, Vol. II (1904).

As touching tidings, let it please you to know that at the Prince's [i.e. the baby, Prince Edward] coming to Windsor, the Duke of Buckingham took him in his arms and presented him to the king in a goodly manner, beseeching the king to bless him and the king gave no manner of answer. Nevertheless, the Duke waited still with the Prince by the king, and when he could get no manner of answer, the Queen came in, and took the Prince in her arms and presented him in the same way as the Duke had done, desiring that he should bless it [i.e. the baby], but all their labour was in vain, for they departed from there without any answer or glance saving only that once he looked on the Prince and cast down his eyes again, without any more.

Item, the Cardinal [i.e. John Kempe, Chancellor of England and Archbishop of Canterbury] has charged and commanded all his servants to be ready with bow and arrows, sword and buckler, crossbows, and all other raiment of war, such as they can take action with to await upon the safeguarding of his person...

Item, the Queen has made a bill of five articles desiring those articles to be granted; the first is that she desires to have the whole rule of this land; the second is that she may appoint the chancellor, the treasurer, the privy seal and all other officers of this land, with sheriffs and all other officers that the king should appoint; the third is that she may give all the bishoprics of this land and all other benefices belonging to the king's gift; the fourth is that she may have sufficient livelihood assigned to her for the king and the prince and herself. But as for the fifth article, I cannot yet find out what it is.

Item, the Duke of York will be in London next Friday exactly, at night, as his own men tell for certain, and he will come with his household men, of decent appearance and able men. And the Earl of March [i.e. Edward, Earl of March, Richard of York's son and the future King Edward IV] comes with him, but he will have another fellowship of good men that shall be at London before him...

During the king's period of incapacity, great tensions arose between the duke of Somerset and the duke of York, both of whom wished to control government. During the autumn of 1453, both Somerset and the queen endeavoured to exclude York from power. In early 1454, Margaret of Anjou apparently made a bid to gain the right to rule as regent in the king's name (see Source 4). The idea of Margaret ruling, however, was very unpopular: she was noted for her divisive tendencies and her French origins were distrusted, particularly given recent events in the Hundred Years War. Perhaps more importantly, there was widespread suspicion of a female ruling, something which was unprecedented within English politics, although in France the example of Blanche of Castille provided Margaret with a possible role model. It was perhaps concern about the queen's possible move, as well as the death of the chancellor, John Kemp, Archbishop of Canterbury, in March that made parliament more favourable towards the case of the duke of York. On 27 March, York was to become the 'Defender and Protector of the Realm' during the period of the king's illness.

A Level Exam-Style Question Section C

To what extent was involvement in foreign war the factor most likely to bring change to a monarch's financial position in the period 1399–1509?
(20 marks)

Tip

Ensure that you consider not only foreign war in terms of taxation, but also factors such as its impact on trade. Also consider the role of other factors, such as the monarch's relationship with parliament and the profitable farming of crown lands. The focus of Section C questions is on change, but questions may be more or less implicit.

SOURCE

5

Description of King Henry VI's recovery from illness in a letter from Edmund Clere to John Paston I, dated 9 January 1455. Edmund Clere was a neighbour of the Pastons. Please note that the reference to 'my Lord Prince' in the text refers to Prince Edward, who had been born during the time of the king's illness. Cited in the *Edinburgh Magazine*, 1787.

Blessed be God, the king is well amended, and has been since Christmas Day; on Saint John's Day [27 December] commanded his almoner to ride to Canterbury with his offering, and commanded the secretary to offer at Saint Edward [the Confessor's tomb in Westminster Abbey]. And on the Monday afternoon, the Queen came to him and brought my Lord Prince with her. And then he asked what the Prince's name was, and the Queen told him Edward; and then he held up his hands and thanked God therof. And he said he never knew him till that time, nor had an idea of what was said to him, nor where he had been while he had been sick until now. And he asked who [the Prince's] godfathers were, and the Queen told him.

And she told him that the Cardinal [John Kemp, Archbishop of Canterbury] was dead, and he said he did not know this until now; and he said that one of the wisest lords in this land was dead.

And my Lord of Winchester and my Lord of Saint John were with him on the morrow... and he spoke to them as well as he ever did; and when they came out they wept for joy.

And he says he is in charity with all the world, and so he wishes that all the lords were. And now he says matins [prayers] of Our Lady and evensong, and hears Mass devoutly.

ACTIVITY
KNOWLEDGE CHECK

The illness and recovery of Henry VI, 1453–54

1 What were the key political problems facing Henry VI during the 1450s?

2 In your view, would the birth of Prince Edward in October 1453 strengthen or weaken the king's position? Give reasons for your answer.

3 Read the first paragraph of Source 4. Why do you think the duke of Buckingham and the queen were so anxious to get a response from Henry VI?

4 Read Source 5.

   a) What impression is given of Henry VI's attitude towards the Church and religion in this source?

   b) What does the source tell you about Henry's understanding during the time of his illness?

Foreign diplomacy and the Treaty of Picquigny, 1475

The memories of spectacular victories in France during the reigns of Edward III and Henry V were an important aspect of the English political psyche in the 15th century. It is therefore unsurprising that a monarch such as Edward IV might attempt to regain some of this military glory as a method both of protecting his realm, gaining personal glory and, of course, the political security which came with it. The outcome of Edward's invasion of France in 1474 was therefore surprising and for many contemporaries, dishonourable for the king.

Edward began to plan to invade France in 1468, obtaining taxation for this cause from parliament, but the projected attack did not go ahead, causing considerable resentment about the waste of money that probably helped Warwick and Clarence gain support for their rebellion in some quarters during 1469. During the 1470s, however, Edward IV resumed his preparations for a large-scale invasion of France. By 1474, he had secured an alliance with Burgundy against France and he was granted a special tax of one-tenth of all income from land by the parliament of November 1472, which was to pay for 13,000 archers for the campaign. In addition, the king tried various other, less conventional, methods of acquiring money to support the planned war, which were largely responsible for his subsequent reputation as an avaricious monarch who took money unfairly from his subjects. In particular, Edward began to raise money through **benevolences**. Edward went to considerable trouble to acquire these gifts, personally touring his kingdom and requesting money from his wealthier subjects – requests that were extremely hard to refuse. Indeed, the king was so pressing that rumours circulated about the rather dubious tactics he was prepared to use to gain the cash he wanted.

KEY TERM

Benevolence
A benevolence was a 'gift' of money from a subject or group of subjects to the king.

According to some sources, for example, wealthy London merchants were particularly generous because their wives persuaded them to be – female support having been obtained by Edward granting them sexual favours! Whether this particular tale is true or not, it is indicative both of Edward's much-noted personal charm and lustfulness, which appears to have crossed class barriers, and also his willingness to use that charm to manipulate money from his subjects.

After lengthy preparations, Edward finally crossed to Calais on 4 July 1475 with a substantial army. The planned military campaign did not, however, go ahead. This was partly because Edward's ally, Duke Charles of Burgundy, proved unsupportive, but also because the very able diplomat and politician, King Louis XI of France, effectively managed to buy off the English invaders. Louis and Edward met on a bridge over the Somme at Picquigny and signed a treaty there. The key terms of this treaty were:

- a seven-year truce between the two countries

- the marriage of the Dauphin Charles (Louis XI's eldest son and heir to the French throne) to Edward's eldest daughter, Elizabeth

- France to pay the English £15,000 immediately and then £10,000 annually in the form of a pension.

The consequences of the treaty at home in England were fairly predictable: Edward and his army were heavily criticised for what was seen as a dishonourable settlement and many were very angry that their taxes and benevolences (which, needless to say, were not returned) had been wasted. Indeed, such was the unpopularity of the benevolences that the first Commons petition of Richard III's first (and only) parliament requested that they never be levied again, a promise which the new king made, but was later, in effect, to renege on. Nonetheless, the French settlement of 1475 was extremely advantageous for Edward, as the pension allowed him to manage without further appeals to parliament for taxation to meet his costs until 1482, when war with Scotland required an army to be raised. In this way, he neatly circumvented the need to give parliament a licence to 'advise' or critique his rule, and gave himself considerable financial certainty that helped him to secure his hold on the throne more firmly.

SOURCE

6 From 'The Great Chronicle of London'. Although the authorship of this chronicle is not certain, it was definitely written by someone involved in the civic government of London during the late 15th century. The author may well be Robert Fabyan, a wealthy London draper (cloth merchant) who served as a London alderman in this period. He was a prominent figure in civic government, but is best remembered for his chronicles, which cover both matters directly concerning London and national affairs.

The king intending his royal voyage into France, considering that late days he had charged as in the xiith year of his reign, his subjects with notable sums of money used a policy to fore days, by none of his noble progenitors put in use. For after he had known the good minds of his lords and nobles of his land he called before him the mayor, and showed to him his royal purpose with sundry other circumstances, and finally demanded of him what he would of his free will depart with him toward his said voyage. The which granted unto him with a glad pretence £30. The which grant his grace well and thankfully accepted, and after the mayor's good will thus to him known, his grace sent for the aldermen one by one, so that some granted £20 and twenty mark and some £10. And when he had thus dealt with the aldermen, he then sent for the head commoners, of the which for the more party he had granted the wages of half a soldier for a year, whereof the charge was £4 11s 3d. And that done he rode into Essex, Suffolk and Norfolk and other countries of this land and entreated the people so favourably that he had more money by those means than he should have had by two fifteenths. It was reported that as he passed by a town in Suffolk and called before him among other a rich widow and asked her what her good will should be toward his great charge, and she liberally had granted to him £10, he thanked her and after took her to him and kissed her, the which kiss she accepted so kindly, that for that great bounty and kind deed, he should have £20 for his £10. And thus by his own labour and other solicitors that he assigned in his stead [such] as the Bishop of Ely [then] Dr. Morton and others he gathered notably sums of money with the which all provision was made in all goodly haste for the said voyage.

THINKING HISTORICALLY Cause and consequence (7a&b)

Questions and answers

Questions that historians ask vary depending on what they think is important. It is the questions that interest us that define the history that is written. These questions change with time and place. Different historians will also come up with different answers to the same questions, depending on their perspectives and methods of interpretation, as well as the evidence they use.

Below are three historians who had different areas of interest.

G.L. Harris	Anne Curry	J.R. Green
Died in 2014 aged 89. He was a scholar with a particular interest in parliamentary, financial and administrative history.	An active historian, presently working at the University of Southampton. She has a particular interest in military history, leading projects on the Medieval Soldier and Agincourt.	19th-century historian. He was interested in the liberties of ordinary people and how these could be undermined by the individual power of monarchs.

These are some key events in late medieval England:

The 'Long Parliament'	The loss of England's French territories	Changes in the use of the Chamber and Exchequer
The Battle of Agincourt	Extension of the vote for those who owned property worth over 40 shillings	The Treaty of Picquigny

Work in groups of between three and six to answer these questions:

1 Which of these events would have been of most interest to each historian? Explain your answer.

2 Each take the role of one historian and devise a question that would interest them about each of the events.

3 Discuss each event in turn. Present the questions that have been devised for each historian and offer some ideas about how they would have answered them.

4 For each event, decide as a group which question is the most interesting and worthwhile of the three.

Answer the following questions in pairs:

5 Identify the different ways that each historian would approach writing an account of the Wars of the Roses.

6 In what ways would Green and Curry differ in their explanations of the significance of the Hundred Years War? What would be the focus of their arguments?

Answer the following questions individually:

7 All three historians may produce very different accounts and explanations of the same piece of history. Of the three historians, whose account would you prefer to read first? Explain your answer.

8 Do the differences in these accounts mean that one is more valid than the others?

9 Explain why different historical explanations are written by different historians.

10 Explain why different explanations of the same event can be equally valid.

The Spanish Marriage, 1499

Although most histories of England's late medieval foreign policy tend to focus on relations with France, another important factor in international diplomacy in this period was relations with Spain. This was particularly true in the late 15th century, when Spain was ruled by King Ferdinand II of Aragon and his wife and second cousin, Queen Isabella I of Castile – a couple often referred to jointly as 'the Catholic monarchs', a title granted to them by Pope Alexander VI in 1494 in recognition of their defence of the Catholic faith. Their five children made politically significant foreign marriages and, as part of these diplomatic endeavours, the youngest daughter, Katherine of Aragon, was married to Henry VII's eldest son, Prince Arthur, in 1499.

Prince Arthur was not in fact the first choice of the Catholic monarchs, who would have preferred a French alliance for their eldest daughter – which, for diplomatic reasons, would have precluded an English match for their youngest. The French king rejected the Spanish overtures, however, and in 1487 ambassadors from Spain arrived in England to negotiate the match. Henry VII was extremely keen to form the alliance; the security of the Tudor dynasty was still very uncertain, as Henry's claim was tenuous and was, in practice if not in theory, mainly based on his victory at the bloody Battle of Bosworth in 1485. Therefore, a marriage between his eldest son and a Spanish princess would be highly advantageous, gaining the Tudors the prospect of military support from abroad, as well as strengthening the family's royal status immeasurably. Perhaps realising the English king's keenness for the match, the Spanish negotiated firmly during 1488 on the financial basis of the match, wishing to provide Katherine with a smaller financial outlay than the English hoped for. Ultimately, however, the two countries' mutual enmity towards France ensured that the agreement went ahead, with the usual proviso that the children should wait until both came of age before being married. In 1489, a treaty was drawn up creating a political alliance between Spain and England, as well as a number of trading agreements.

In fact, the planned marriage almost never took place owing to disagreements that occurred in the 1490s surrounding the rebellion against Henry VII, led by the pretender to the throne, Perkin Warbeck. Warbeck managed to gain considerable international support for his cause, particularly in areas that were hostile to England such as Scotland, Ireland, France and Austria. Shaken by this, Henry initially accused Ferdinand and Isabella of supporting Warbeck, but they quickly took action to reassure him and a **proxy marriage** took place between Arthur and Katherine in May 1499. Katherine herself journeyed to England in 1501, when her groom was 14 and she was 17. She came with an entourage of 60 people, including her **duenna**, Doña Elvira, bishops and chaplains, ladies-in-waiting, cooks, a butler, her fool and her pages. Henry and Arthur travelled to meet Katherine, joining her at Farnborough, Hampshire, on 4 November. When the Spanish ambassador rather coyly insisted on observing the Spanish practice of keeping the bride away from her groom prior to the marriage, Henry allegedly insisted on seeing her even if she were in bed before introducing his son to her. After this rather abrupt meeting, she then travelled to London, where she was met with customary pageants and the marriage was solemnised at St Paul's Cathedral.

What were the political consequences of the Spanish marriage?

As the incident of Katherine and Arthur's first meeting suggested, there were tensions between the English and Spanish entourages regarding sexual etiquette, perceptions of female modesty and the consummation of the marriage. The Spanish ambassador to England, Doctor De Puebla, argued that the marriage should not be consummated immediately, requesting that Katherine remain in London while Arthur resumed his duties of Prince of Wales at Ludlow. This may have been a deliberate ploy by the Spanish to keep the marriage unconsummated for as long as possible, as only once sex had taken place was a marriage binding in the eyes of the Catholic Church. This request may well have reflected Spain's continuing unease about the Tudor regime. Henry VII, however, was strongly in favour of consummation, presumably to ensure, firstly, that the marriage was made valid and, secondly, in the hope of gaining a grandson to inherit the throne and thereby to support his dynastic claims to the throne. He therefore sent the young couple to Wales in December 1501. Their marriage proved very brief, however; on 2 April 1502, Arthur died.

Given that the marriage had taken so long to arrange and was politically and economically significant, it was highly problematic when it was cut short due to Arthur's untimely death. Both the Catholic monarchs and Henry VII were keen to ensure the alliance between England and Spain continued and therefore it was quickly suggested that Katherine should marry Arthur's younger brother, Henry. Unfortunately, the Church did not allow marriage between a former brother and sister-in-law. Therefore, the couple needed special permission from the pope to marry (called a papal dispensation), which arrived in 1504. The wedding was delayed, however, because of the death of Katherine's mother, Isabella, in November. This created a change in the international political scene, as the heir to Castile was Katherine's eldest sister, Juana, who was married to Archduke Philip, the ruler of the Low Countries. Isabella, however, had tried to disinherit Juana and had instead named her husband, Ferdinand, as governor of Castile in her will. Henry VII decided to attempt to keep his options open in relation to which side England should support and so sent money to help Philip's claim, and put the marriage negotiations on hold, but he did not publicly put an end to his alliance with Ferdinand.

KEY TERMS

Proxy marriage
The practice, not uncommon among royal families in the Middle Ages when important diplomatic marriages were at stake, of conducting a marriage ceremony when either the bride or groom was not there. Usually, this was because the two people lived in different countries and for diplomatic reasons the ceremony needed to go ahead quickly. Therefore, a 'proxy' (that is, someone else) would stand in for either the bride or groom and take the vows on their behalf.

Duenna
An older woman employed by an aristocratic family to act as a chaperone to young women and girls within the household. The role was specifically aimed at ensuring female modesty and that (in the case of unmarried women) chastity was observed. A duenna in the royal household was a figure of importance and the individual herself would have been of noble birth and of impeccable reputation.

The death of Philip in 1506 meant that Ferdinand's claim became much stronger, but Henry VII decided to consider marrying his son to another European leader, rather than committing to the Spanish alliance. To justify this, he highlighted the fact that Ferdinand had not paid the second instalment of Katherine's dowry and, again, financial wrangling between the two countries was bitter. The death of Henry VII in April 1509, however, changed the situation once again and his son, the new King Henry VIII, took a different direction in foreign policy. Finally, on 11 June 1509, Katherine of Aragon married Henry VIII and became Queen of England.

ACTIVITY
KNOWLEDGE CHECK

Foreign diplomacy, the Treaty of Picquigny and the significance of the Spanish marriage for the Tudor regime

1 Write a definition of a 'benevolence' and explain why these payments were unpopular.

2 Write a paragraph answering the question: 'Did the Treaty of Picquigny support or reduce the personal authority of Edward IV?'

3 Make notes under these headings:

a) Reasons why Henry VII wished to promote the match.

b) Reasons why the Spanish royal family were uncertain about the marriage.

c) Advantages of the marriage settlements for the English government.

d) Problem of Perkin Warbeck.

e) Political consequences of the marriage.

A Level Exam-Style Question Section C

'The period 1399–1509 provides clear evidence that foreign diplomacy usually had more successful outcomes than foreign war in providing England with political stability.'

To what extent do you agree with this statement? (20 marks)

Tip

Remember that you gain marks in this type of essay for the careful organisation of your ideas on paper, so take care to ensure you have clear sections on both diplomacy and foreign war, rather than continually switching between the two topics.

Conclusion

The period 1399–1509 marked a surprising level of continuity in the core structure of political power and royal finance, with the role of parliament in granting taxation in particular being firmly established by the beginning of the 15th century. Indeed, the fact that institutions of government such as parliament, the Chancery and the Exchequer continued to function so effectively during a period of civil war and dynastic upheaval is itself a testament to how well established they were in this period, and how ingrained their importance was in the bureaucratic and political culture of the time. The relationship between parliament and individual monarchs varied, and was based primarily on three interlocking factors – their personal reputation, their foreign policy and their level of financial solvency. Kings who were perceived as having the ability to defend and, in some cases, to further England's territorial ambitions were popular and more rarely forced to argue with parliament regarding funding. Less successful or less powerful monarchs were much more likely to have their reign criticised by parliament, or to struggle to raise taxes.

ACTIVITY
SUMMARY

The relationship between finance, parliament and royal power

1 Draw a mind map of the different forms of income available to monarchs reigning in the later Middle Ages. Colour-code or group these sources of financial support into the following categories:

a) Sources of income that were uncontroversial.

b) Sources of income that might lead to criticism of a monarch or his advisers.

c) Sources of income that were highly controversial.

2 Create a graph showing how the power of parliament changed between 1399 and 1509. Label and explain the key events on your graph.

3 In note form, summarise the key features of the relationship between the king and parliament during these reigns:

a) Henry IV.

b) Henry V.

c) Henry VI.

d) Edward IV.

e) Henry VII.

4 Write a paragraph discussing the significance of the Treaty of Picquigny and a paragraph discussing the significance of the Spanish marriage. In your view, which event had a more positive impact on the following:

a) The reputation of the English monarchy at home.

b) The reputation of the English monarchy abroad.

WIDER READING

Allmand, C.T. 'Henry V (1386–1422)', *Oxford Dictionary of National Biography*, Oxford University Press (2004). Online edn, Sept 2010, www.oxforddnb.com/view/article/12952

Bellamy, J.G. *Criminal Law and Society in Late Medieval and Tudor England*, Palgrave Macmillan (1984)

Brown, A.L. and Summerson, H. 'Henry IV (1367–1413)', *Oxford Dictionary of National Biography*, Oxford University Press (2004). Online edn, Sept 2010, www.oxforddnb.com/view/article/12951

Castor, H. *The King, the Crown, and the Duchy of Lancaster: Public Authority and Private Power, 1399–1461*, Oxford University Press (2000)

Lander, J.R. *The Wars of the Roses*, The History Press (2007)

Payling, S.J. 'Middle Ages: Parliament and politics before 1509'. Available online at www.historyofparliamentonline.org/periods/medieval

Ross, C. *Edward IV*, Yale University Press (1997)

Thomson, J.A.F. *The Transformation of Medieval England 1370–1529*, Routledge (2014)

3.3

The crises of 1399–1405

KEY QUESTIONS

- To what extent was Richard II responsible for the crisis of 1399?
- How significant was Bolingbroke's usurpation of the throne in relation to the problems of his early reign?
- To what extent was the Lancastrian monarchy secure by 1405?

INTRODUCTION

The psychology of Richard II (r. 1377–99) is an intriguing topic. Both medieval commentators and modern historians have discussed all aspects of his personality, evaluating not only his political abilities, but also speculating upon his mental stability and sexuality. It is certainly clear that he was a king who was easily able to alienate those around him. Nonetheless, he is both a fascinating and important figure, not only because of his own eccentricities, but also because his reign tested the stability of the medieval political system and its concept of loyalty to a monarch to its limits. This chapter examines the extraordinary circumstances of Richard's rise to the throne as a 'child-king' and the dramatic methods by which he lost not only the kingdom to his cousin, Henry Bolingbroke, who was to become the first Lancastrian king, but also his life. Bolingbroke's usurpation of the throne created a dangerous precedent for medieval kings, introducing the idea that an unpopular monarch could be put aside in favour of a more-able candidate, even if this person had a weaker hereditary claim to power. This change in attitude towards kings and the nature of their power was a key factor in the early instability of Henry IV's reign, but also had longer-term consequences, being a latent cause of much of the Wars of the Roses that broke out later in the century.

TO WHAT EXTENT WAS RICHARD II RESPONSIBLE FOR THE CRISIS OF 1399?

The reasons for Bolingbroke's seizure of the throne from Richard II

The long-term causes of the 1399 crisis

Richard was the son of two great medieval 'celebrities'. His mother, Joan of Kent, was a famous beauty of the day, being known to contemporaries as 'the Virgin of Kent', probably a sarcastic reference to her three marriages and chequered romantic history. His father, Edward of Woodstock, often known as

1377 – Edward III dies and his ten-year-old grandson becomes King Richard II

1382 – Richard II marries Anne of Bohemia

1385 – July: The king leads his first military campaign to Scotland, leading to a quarrel with John of Gaunt

1388 – The 'Merciless Parliament' tries de la Pole and de Vere along with other royal favourites for treason, despite the king's opposition to this

1375	1380	1385	1390

1381 – Peasants' Revolt

1383 – William de la Pole appointed chancellor by Richard II

1386 – October: 'Wonderful Parliament' impeaches de la Pole

1389 – John of Gaunt returns to England

'The Black Prince', was the eldest son of Edward III and a highly successful warrior. In 1376, however, disaster struck the royal family. The Black Prince died, apparently of dysentery, and was followed to the grave in 1377 by his elderly father. In July 1377, therefore, the ten-year-old Richard was crowned king at Westminster Abbey and the next day the Bishop of Rochester, Thomas Brinton, preached a sermon to a noble congregation, emphasising the importance of showing loyalty to their child-king. The anxiety of the political community concerning the dangers of a boy on the throne was evident.

Given the king's youth, it was clear that much of the actual governing of the kingdom would have to be done by others, initially at least, and this inevitably caused tensions among the leading nobles, who had few precedents to guide them in this situation. Key figures were the king's uncles, John of Gaunt and Thomas of Woodstock, as well as a number of knights in the royal household. Control over decisions made in the young king's name was a matter of considerable concern, as is evidenced from the parliamentary records of the period. This matter was especially sensitive given that taxation in the early years of Richard II's reign was unusually high in order to finance military campaigns in France and Scotland, but it was obvious that these endeavours were going badly. Indeed, the period of 1377–81 saw a number of French raids on the south coast of England, increasing public hostility towards the king's councillors.

In 1381, these tensions overflowed into one of the most famous and dramatic protests of English history, the so-called 'Peasants' Revolt'. Violent attacks were made on both local and national leaders, and especially those, like John of Gaunt, who were blamed for the imposition of an unpopular new form of taxation called the **poll tax**, as well as England's lack of success in the war with France. The rebellion began in Essex and spread rapidly to other areas of the country, with protestors converging on London and demanding to speak directly to the king himself, claiming that he was being deceived in his advice by 'evil councillors'. The 14-year-old Richard acquitted himself in front of the thousands of insurgents with a surprising level of confidence, assuring them that he heard their complaints and that he would grant charters of freedom and pardon for their revolt, thereby persuading them to disperse. His generosity was not to last, however; within a fortnight, Richard had witnessed the executions of a number of rebels and had formally revoked his pardons, presumably on the recommendation of his councillors.

The events of 1381 were not only the result of public hostility towards the poll tax, but also a symptom of the growing class tension that had developed in England since the first outbreak of the Black Death in 1347. This disease, now identified as strains of bubonic and pneumonic plague, is estimated to have killed 30–45 percent of the population in its first outbreak, with further episodes occurring periodically throughout the century. Although the psychological trauma caused by this disease was no doubt devastating, peasant survivors often found their living conditions considerably improved as a result. There followed an agricultural labour shortage, allowing workers to demand higher wages and use this greater wealth to finance increased leisure time, as well as better food, clothes and other consumables. This new-found social mobility was fiercely resisted by the gentry and nobility; indeed, in 1350, the Statute of Labourers was passed by parliament, which legally required wages to be limited to pre-Black Death levels, and greatly restricted worker mobility and the amount of time off that agricultural labourers could have. This law, regularly repeated by parliament

KEY TERM

Poll tax
A tax where each liable adult is charged the same amount regardless of wealth.

1397 – Earls of Gloucester, Warwick and Arundel arrested for treason. Gloucester dies at Calais; Warwick imprisoned; Arundel executed.

1399 – May: Richard II leaves England to lead military expedition to Ireland
June to July: Henry Bolingbroke invades England
13 October: Henry IV's coronation

1395 — 1400 — 1405 — 1410

1396 – Richard II betrothed to Isabella of France, seven-year-old daughter of the French king. Twenty-eight-year truce agreed with France in the Hundred Years War.

1398 – Mowbray and Bolingbroke both exiled

1400 – February: Richard II dies, possibly murdered
September: Owain Glyndwr leads Welsh rebellion

1405 – Archbishop Scrope's rebellion

1403 – Henry ('Hotspur') Percy's rebellion. Rebels defeated and Hotspur killed at Shrewsbury.

for the subsequent two centuries, was bitterly resented by workers and was a key underlying cause of their hostility towards the ruling classes and Richard II's so-called 'evil councillors'.

The revolt of 1381 was deeply frightening for the political leaders of the day, and may well have contributed to Richard's increasingly hysterical emphasis on absolute obedience as his reign progressed. The rebellion marked, however, a coming of age for the young king, as he had publicly shown his courage and ability to deal with a hostile crowd in front of his knights and nobles, many of whom were criticised for their own cowardice during the rebellion. This move towards adulthood was also marked by Richard's marriage in January 1382 to Anne of Bohemia (1366–94), the sister of Wenceslas IV, the **Holy Roman Emperor**-elect and king of Bohemia. The match was arranged by leading members of the English government, including Michael de la Pole and Simon Burley, presumably in the hope of gaining the Empire's support against the French in the Hundred Years War. Certainly, Wenceslas drove a hard bargain for his sister's hand, providing her with no dowry, as was traditional, and obliging Richard to commit to a loan of 80,000 florins (around £12,000, an enormous sum at the time). While the marriage appears to have been happy and committed, from a political perspective it was a failure for England, with the public being sharply critical of the high cost of the marriage terms as well as Richard's extreme generosity towards Anne's Bohemian relations and servants. In addition, the hope of a military alliance between the Empire and the English against the French failed to materialise.

Richard's failings as an adult monarch

Over-generosity to those whom he personally favoured was to be a defining feature of Richard's reign, and a key cause of his fall from power. As he emerged from his **minority**, Richard promoted a number of his favourites to important positions. In itself, this was not inherently a problem; all medieval kings were expected to grant a certain amount of power or land to individuals whom they personally liked, but Richard took this to an extreme, overlooking and alienating senior nobles like his uncle, Thomas of Woodstock, who felt excluded from the king's patronage and trust. Two men particularly enjoyed his favour, William de la Pole and Robert de Vere, earl of Oxford. De la Pole was made chancellor in 1383 and became the earl of Suffolk in 1385, both honours being criticised by contemporary commentators. De Vere, despite being widely disliked, received even greater royal generosity, with a new rank of 'marquess' being created for him and also being made duke of Ireland in 1386, a rank that gave him the same status as the king's uncles.

Richard's methods and his new advisers were criticised on a number of grounds. Firstly, the level of the king's financial generosity to them was disproportionate and unsustainable, leading to royal debt. The Commons in parliament regarded this as galling when they were being asked to vote through continuing high levels of taxation to sustain the war with France, a war that was proving unsuccessful for the English in the 1380s. Tension increased as the king and his circle did not seem to be personally committed to the war; the fact that the king had spent much of his childhood in France, being known as 'Richard of Bordeaux' before he became king in 1377, fuelled suspicion of pro-French leanings. In addition, Richard never showed either the military capability or the interest of his father and grandfather. Throughout his life there was hostility to the fact that Richard did not, as was traditionally expected, lead many military expeditions himself. In addition, de la Pole advocated negotiating for peace with France, but whatever the practical merits of this policy it did nothing to enhance Richard's reputation as a warrior and particularly angered the king's uncles. His first campaign, designed to display his coming of age as a warrior and monarch, occurred in 1385, when Richard led forces to Scotland. The king refused, however, to fight beyond Edinburgh and the expedition ended badly, with a bitter quarrel between Richard and his uncle, John of Gaunt. This incident contributed to Gaunt's growing feeling of alienation from the king and suspicion that he was being deliberately excluded from power by Richard and de Vere. The breach was dangerous, given that Gaunt was the most senior noble in the realm and an extremely experienced politician and warrior. In 1386, he left England to pursue his claims towards the **Castilian** throne.

The 'Wonderful Parliament' of 1386 and its consequences

Gaunt's departure and a strong threat of invasion from France led to the first major challenge to Richard's leadership, during the '**Wonderful Parliament**' of 1386. Such was de la Pole's unpopularity that parliament demanded he was removed from office before it would grant taxation for the defence of the realm, a request that Richard scornfully and high-handedly denied, refusing even to discuss the matter. This led to a dramatic meeting at Eltham between Richard and a number of leading noblemen who warned him that, if he refused to attend parliament, it could dissolve itself after 40 days and no taxation would be forthcoming to help the country prepare to defend itself against the French threat. Richard, outraged by this attack on his royal prerogative, foolishly threatened to seek help from the French to deal with his disobedient subjects. In retaliation, Thomas of Woodstock and Thomas Arundel, the Bishop of Ely, reminded Richard that the nobles could, by common consent, depose a king who alienated his people, with the gruesome fate of the king's own great-grandfather, Edward II, providing an example. The warning was enough; Richard met with parliament and was forced to watch as his favourite was impeached, although the king refused to allow de la Pole's imprisonment. To Richard's fury, parliament also demanded an inquiry into royal finances by a commission appointed for a year to control the Exchequer and the **Great and Privy Seals**.

EXTEND YOUR KNOWLEDGE

What happened to Edward II and why was it significant in the context of Richard II's reign?
King Edward II (r. 1307–27) was the great-grandfather of Richard II. He was an extremely unpopular leader, partly because of his disastrous military career; he was famous for leading the English to defeat against the Scots in 1314 at the Battle of Bannockburn. He also, however, alienated many nobles because of his dependence upon favourites, notably Piers Gaveston, Hugh Despenser the Elder and Hugh Despenser the Younger (the Despensers were father and son). These men were regarded as abusing positions of trust to gain an unfair share of royal patronage, and blocking advice from other sources. The Despensers in particular were also regarded as taking part in a number of illegal acts regarding the seizure of property, especially from wealthy widows. Edward was also widely suspected of having homosexual relations with Gaveston and Despenser the Younger, which at the time was regarded as extremely scandalous.

Edward's wife, Isabella of France, became estranged from her husband and brought the couple's son and heir to the throne, Prince Edward (the future Edward III), to France in 1325. She then refused to bring the boy home and, with the assistance of her lover, Roger Mortimer, she led an invasion against her husband in late 1326. In this, she gained significant support from many English noblemen. Edward II was forced to abdicate and was then murdered, according to tradition, by having a red-hot poker pushed into his anus.

Although Edward II's fate was historically significant in relation to Richard II's position during 1386, there was one important difference: Edward II had a son and legitimate heir. So in January 1327, the throne passed to the new Edward III. The king's deposition, therefore, could be presented as Edward II resigning the throne in favour of his son. Richard II, however, was childless, and so in the 1380s and 1390s, the nobility were struggling with a problem of who could legitimately take the throne if the king were deposed.

Richard's anger at these infringements on his royal prerogative can hardly be overestimated and, throughout the year that followed, he began to move around the country, partially to avoid the commission into royal finances, but also to test the country's loyalty and to raise troops to defend himself and his favourites. He made de Vere justice of Chester and this was the beginning of Richard's particular association with this area, which he looked to for personal military support. He also sought legal advice, clearly seeking to be able to punish those who had attacked him during the Wonderful Parliament of 1386 as traitors to the crown.

ACTIVITY
KNOWLEDGE CHECK

The long-term causes of Richard II's usurpation
1 Make two lists, one of all the successes and strengths of Richard's reign to 1386, and one of all its failures and weaknesses.

2 In your view, what was the most significant factor in damaging Richard's reputation during the 'Wonderful Parliament' of 1386? Give reasons for your answer.

Richard's opponents clearly knew the danger of their position and presented the king with an appeal for five of his favourites, including de la Pole and de Vere, to be tried for treason. The men making these complaints became known as the '**lords appellant**' and included Thomas of Woodstock and, most significantly, Henry Bolingbroke, earl of Derby, who was the only son of John of Gaunt and Richard II's cousin. Richard's supporters from Chester, led by de Vere, were intercepted by the king's

KEY TERMS

Great Seal
A device used with wax to seal important state documents, to show they had the approval of the king.

Privy Seal
The king's personal seal, used to validate legal documents.

KEY TERM

Lords appellant
Five nobles who led accusations of treason against a number of the king's favourites in 1386. They were: Thomas of Woodstock, duke of Gloucester (1355–97), youngest son of Edward III and uncle of Richard II; Richard Fitzalan, earl of Arundel (1346–97); Thomas Beauchamp, earl of Warwick (c1339–1401); Henry Bolingbroke (1366–1413), earl of Derby, the king's first cousin; and Thomas Mowbray, earl of Nottingham (1366–99). They went on to lead troops against an army led by Robert de Vere, one of the king's favourites, winning a battle against him in 1387 at Radcot Bridge. The following year in parliament, they were joined by other nobles in bringing charges of treason against a number of royal favourites. The most historically significant lord appellant was Henry Bolingbroke, who later went on to depose Richard II and become King Henry IV.

opponents at Radcot Bridge in Oxfordshire and a battle was fought there. De Vere's troops were defeated, and de la Pole and de Vere fled abroad. This placed Richard entirely at the mercy of his critics and the king was obliged to attend the '**Merciless Parliament**' of 1388, where his favourites were put on trial for treason. Both de la Pole and de Vere were sentenced to death in their absence, while other supporters of Richard, such as his former tutor Simon Burley, were immediately executed. Richard never forgave their deaths or his humiliation at his enemies' hands. Bolingbroke's involvement in this act of opposition meant that Richard always subsequently distrusted and disliked him.

SOURCE

A description of the lords appellant entering the 'Merciless Parliament' of 1388 by Thomas Favent, a cleric and civil servant living in London in the late 14th century, taken from a short chronicle he wrote focusing on the parliaments of 1386–88.

Since Lent was thought to be a suitable and acceptable time to punish and correct the criminals according to their deserts, a great parliament was held on 2 February as follows: all the men of both estates, the nobles and distinguished men of the kingdom, met in the White Hall at Westminster.

The five prosecuting peers [i.e. the lords appellant], whose integrity was justly famed throughout the land, and who had been endowed with constant good fortune, entered the hall with a large crowd of followers, clothed in gold and linking their arms together; and when they saw the king they bowed down in unison and greeted him. The hall was crowded with people that even the corners were full.

... Then, after silence had been ordered, these peers put forward written articles of accusation on the subject of the act of treason. Geoffrey Martin, the crown clerk, stood in the middle of parliament and for two hours hurriedly read through these articles. Many people's hearts were stirred by the horrific content of the articles. Many had faces swollen with weeping, and tears were rolling down their cheeks.

After the articles had been read, the prosecutors appealed to the king to pass sentence of a just and appropriate kind, on the evidence of their allegations and proofs, so that the execution of the defendants could take place. King Richard promised to do this.

... Finally, on 11 February, when no evidence could be alleged on behalf of the absent men, John Devereux, the court steward, representing the king, pronounced that the Archbishop of York, the duke of Ireland, the earl of Suffolk and Robert Tresilian should be brought to Tyburn, there to be hanged forthwith on the gallows, and that all their goods should be confiscated, so that their heirs might not be able to enjoy them.

In the short term, the consequences of the 'Merciless Parliament' of 1388 for Bolingbroke were limited by the return of Gaunt to England in 1389. Richard received Gaunt warmly and appears to have relied on his advice at this stage in his reign. As well as bringing a level of political stability to the kingdom, Gaunt provided his son with the funds to travel and Bolingbroke spent considerable time travelling, both on pilgrimage and participating in tournaments. He gained an international reputation as a warrior through these events, returning to England in 1392. On his return to England, Bolingbroke took up a place at court alongside his father, John of Gaunt, serving in the Lords in various parliaments and advising the king in the great councils.

Richard II and the problems of the royal succession

By 1394, Gaunt's influence over Richard began to decline and Gaunt and Bolingbroke seem to have become concerned about the king's attitude towards their family and inheritance. A key factor in this underlying tension was the king's lack of an heir, as his marriage to Anne of Bohemia, who died in 1394, was childless. This kept the succession uncertain: strictly speaking, the king's heir was Roger Mortimer, earl of March, who was the grandson of Lionel of Antwerp, who had been the second-eldest son of King Edward III. Gaunt, however, also had a significant claim, as he was the third son of Edward III. In practical terms, Gaunt was also the stronger candidate, with very great wealth and military support at his disposal formed mainly through his estates held in his position as the duke of Lancaster. In these circumstances, Gaunt and his son Henry Bolingbroke were a potential threat to Richard's power.

The obvious political solution in these circumstances was for Richard II to remarry after Anne of Bohemia's death and try to father an heir quickly. This, however, the king seemed unwilling to do, possibly for personal reasons. He appears to have been completely faithful to his queen during her lifetime and deeply upset by her death; indeed, on hearing the news of her death in June 1394, Richard apparently flew into a rage of bitter grief and ordered that the palace in which she had died, at Sheen in Richmond, London, should be burned to the ground. Some historians have argued that the death of Queen Anne may have had a significant impact on Richard's mental stability and that after 1394 his outlook towards the nobility became more suspicious and tyrannical.

Whatever the truth of this suggestion, it is clear that Richard was not keen to engage in a physical relationship or to father an heir. This, combined with his increasingly pro-French outlook in regard to foreign policy, meant that in 1396 he agreed to marry Isabella, daughter of the French King Charles VI. This match was controversial as Isabella was only seven years old, so the marriage would remain **unconsummated** until she reached puberty (usually around 13 years), meaning that the king could not have a legitimate heir for at least another seven years. The marriage was also a sign of Richard's pro-French leanings, which were regarded as suspiciously unpatriotic by many at court. This pro-peace stance was increased as he realised that, in order to fight a foreign war, he would need the agreement of parliament for taxation and he was suspicious of this institution since the 'Merciless Parliament' of 1388. His marriage to Isabella was, therefore, an important step towards reducing hostilities with France and the marriage agreement was accompanied by a 28-year truce.

SOURCE 2 The Westminster Portrait of Richard II, which hangs in Westminster Abbey. Quite literally larger than life, the painting was probably created in the mid-1390s.

KEY TERM

Unconsummated
If a marriage is consummated, it means sexual intercourse has taken place, and this makes the marriage vows binding in the eyes of the Roman Catholic Church. An unconsummated marriage is one where intercourse has not yet taken place. It was fairly commonplace for aristocratic, medieval marriages to be arranged when one or both parties were a child. Therefore, such marriages remained unconsummated and the couple often lived separately until they came of age. Legally, this was considered to be aged 12 for girls and 14 for boys, although in reality sometimes couples waited until later, particularly until the girl had reached puberty.

SOURCE 3

An account by chronicler Thomas Walsingham of the first meeting between Richard II and his child-bride, Isabella of France, which took place in 1396. Walsingham was a monk at the Abbey of St Albans, which allowed him to be well informed of gossip from the royal court. He was a contemporary of the events he describes.

On Saturday 28 October, the kings of England and France met at Guisnes to discuss certain articles of their treaty, after which they swore on the Holy Gospels to observe what had been agreed. Then King Richard invited King Charles to dine with him on the following day.

On the Monday, the king of France came to the king of England's pavilion. Isabella, the daughter of the king of France, she who is now queen of England, was then conducted to the pavilion, and King Charles presented her to our king, who took her by the hand and kissed her, thanking her father for so noble and welcome a gift. Richard went on to declare that he was receiving her according to the conditions agreed between the kings, so that through the relationship thus established both monarchs could live in peace and tranquillity, and could secure a proper state of harmony between their two kingdoms for ever, and that no more Christian blood would be shed, as was all too likely to happen if this alliance were not made here and now.

The new queen was entrusted to the care of the duchesses of Lancaster and Gloucester and the countesses of Huntingdon and Stafford, and of other noblewomen who were there. They conducted her to Calais, accompanied by a large escort of men and horses, and twelve carriages full of noblewomen and ladies-in-waiting.

[After the feast] The king of England set the king of France on his way, and finally they shook hands and parted company. King Charles rode to Ardres, while King Richard proceeded to Calais, where he married Isabella, the daughter of the king of France, a little girl of seven or eight years.

This meeting of the two kings was a great occasion, marked by heavy expenditure on gifts. Quite apart from the presents which he gave to King Charles and to the other French magnates, which cost in excess of ten thousand marks, King Richard spent, so it was said, more than thirty thousand marks. Soon afterwards, he returned safely to England with his new wife.

The 'tyranny' of Richard II, 1397–99

The influential historian T.F. Tout argued that Richard's desire for the French match was selfishly motivated. According to this view, the king not only wanted freedom from taxation (and therefore the scrutiny of parliament) but more sinisterly, that Richard sought foreign armed support to subdue his own subjects. There are two key pieces of evidence to support this opinion: firstly, that in the crisis of 1386 the king had threatened to request French assistance against those who rebelled against him and, secondly, that during 1394–96 when negotiations for the marriage with Isabella of France were taking place, Richard specifically ordered his ambassadors to ensure a promise of French assistance against his own subjects should they rebel against him. Certainly, such a clause indicates the insecurity of Richard's position and his suspicions of the nobility.

The king's unease appears to have grown into paranoia and, in July 1397, he ordered three of the five lords appellant, the earls of Gloucester, Warwick and Arundel, to be arrested and tried for treason. The motivation for this attack is unclear: Richard may have believed the three men were going to plot against him and so had them arrested in a pre-emptive strike. Certainly, Gloucester especially had been highly critical of his marriage and treaty with France. Nonetheless, most contemporary English chroniclers regarded the move as revenge for Radcot Bridge. Interestingly, however, Bolingbroke and his father were not attacked and they both allied themselves firmly with the king during these trials, presumably in an effort to consolidate their own position. Gaunt presided over the trials in parliament, while his son allegedly gave evidence against his former ally, Arundel, who was executed. Gloucester, meanwhile, died at Calais, probably having been murdered while Warwick was imprisoned. Richard's anger did not openly show itself against Bolingbroke, however, who was made duke of Hereford in addition to his other titles, but there is evidence of growing anxiety at court generally, and for Bolingbroke in particular, that Richard was becoming increasingly tyrannical in his rule. Particularly frightening, according to chroniclers Adam Usk and the Monk of Evesham, was Richard's use of a private retinue of 700 archers from Cheshire, 300 of whom formed the king's personal bodyguard. These archers were used to surround parliament in September 1397 to ensure the conviction of the lords appellant.

SOURCE
4
The Wilton Diptych, painted c1396, which was probably commissioned by Richard II as his private altarpiece. He is shown on the left panel, kneeling before the baby Jesus, the Blessed Virgin Mary and angels, one of whom appears to be handing him the English flag of St George topped by a small orb. Magnification has shown this orb to depict a tiny island, probably intended to represent England. The men standing near to Richard are (from left to right) St Edmund, a former English king and a martyr, St Edward the Confessor, another English king, and St John the Baptist. The detail of the heraldry in the paintings is highly significant, and includes Richard wearing a tiny brooch with his own badge of the white hart and a collar displaying images of broomcods (a type of plant), which was a symbol of the French king, suggesting the portrait dates from the time of Richard's marriage to Isabella. The angels wear similar heraldry. The king's arms also appear on the panel behind the Virgin and Child.

SOURCE 5

From the chronicles of Thomas Walsingham, writing about Richard II's style of governance in 1397.

Richard was so puffed up... that from...[1397] onwards he began to behave even more loftily than usual, to impoverish the common people and to borrow large sums of money from every available source. He carried this to such extremes that throughout the realm no... individual known to be wealthy could avoid loaning money to the king.

... But the king's scheming behaviour soon threw all this into confusion when, without warning, he had his uncle, the duke of Gloucester, arrested... and... thrown into prison. Richard also invited the earl of Warwick to a banquet, and on that very day had him arrested and imprisoned likewise, after pretending to be well disposed to the earl and even having promised to be a gracious lord and true friend to him in the future.

Furthermore, Richard used deceitful promises to win over the earl of Arundel, who was powerful enough to have saved himself and freed his friends Gloucester and Warwick; when the earl submitted peacefully, the king dispatched him to imprisonment... Fearful lest the common people should be in uproar about the detention of these noblemen, the king put out a proclamation across the kingdom that these men had not been arrested on account of past misdeeds, but for new crimes against the king, which would be explained fully in the next parliament. Events proved the proclamation to have been wholly untrue.

... On 21 September, judgement was given against [the] earl of Arundel, whose claims and demands for pardon, both under the terms of the charters and as granted to him personally by the king, were unavailing. He was condemned to drawing, hanging, disembowelling, burning of his entrails, decapitation and quartering.

The king, of his grace, reduced this sentence to one of beheading only, which Arundel suffered soon afterwards. The earl's countenance never faltered, nor when he was awaiting judgement, nor when he received his terrible sentence, nor when he was taken from the place of his trial to the place of his execution, nor when he knelt and stretched out his neck for the sword. He grew no more pale than he would have done on receiving an invitation to a feast. He was led to the scaffold by a savage crowd of Cheshire men, armed with axes, bows and arrows.

A Level Exam-Style Question Section A

Study Source 5 before you answer this question.

Assess the value of the source for revealing the character of Richard II and the reasons for his deposition in 1399.

Explain your answer, using the source, the information given about its origin and your own knowledge about the historical context. (20 marks)

Tip

Ensure you consider not only the significance of the lords appellant, but also factors such as Richard's use of a private bodyguard of men from Cheshire.

SOURCE 6

A description of the behaviour of Thomas, duke of Gloucester in 1397 and his attitude towards Richard II's foreign policy. Gloucester was one of the lords appellant who Richard arrested. This was written by the chronicler Jean Froissart, who spent most of his life living in both England and France. He was in England towards the end of Richard II's reign. During the 1400s he wrote his main work, the *Chroniques*, which focus on the story of Henry Bolingbroke's usurpation of the throne. He was not in England for all the events he describes, but he was familiar with a number of the leading political figures of the time.

Now I must speak of [Thomas] the Duke of Gloucester... [who] had a knight with him called Sir John Lackinghay... to whom he confided his feelings in these words:

"If I were believed I should be the first to renew the wars and put a stop to the wrongs the French have done us, and still daily do, and all because of our own foolish slothfulness, particularly the slothfulness of our leader the king, my nephew, who will now ally himself by marriage to the French... this is hardly a sign that he wants war... he cares for nothing but for meat and drink... and dallying with the ladies: that's no life for the brave man who should want to seek honour and glory in battle. I well remember my last campaign in France. I think I had two thousand spears and eight thousand archers with me. We cut right through the realm of France... and found no one who dared to come out and fight us..."

"Yet, things cannot go on like this...[continued the Duke] the king is imposing heavy taxes on merchants and they grow discontented... there may soon be a rebellion in the realm...The people are beginning to grumble and say that they will bear this no longer...To put a stop to popular rumblings he says that once there is truce with France, he will lead an expedition into Ireland and thus employ his warriors and archers there. Yet he has been there before and gained but a small victory, for Ireland is hardly a place to provide either a great conquest or a great profit. The people there are rude and nasty and the land itself is poor and inhabitable..."

Thus... the Duke of Gloucester spoke unwise words like these... He had begun to so hate the king that he could find nothing good to say of him. Though, along with his brother the Duke of Lancaster, he was one of the greatest men in England, he barely took an interest in the government of the realm. Even when the king sent for him, he went only at his own pleasure, and sometimes not at all. Even when he did go, he was the last to arrive and the first to depart. When sitting in council, he would be displeased if his opinion was not accepted immediately and unconditionally, and would leave soon after.

A Level Exam-Style Question Section A

Study Source 6 before you answer this question.

Assess the value of the source for revealing the character of Thomas, duke of Gloucester and the reasons for the downfall of Richard II.

Explain your answer, using the source, the information given about its origin and your own knowledge about the historical context. (20 marks)

Tip

Ensure you consider not only Gloucester's treatment at the hands of Richard II in the late 1390s, but also his attitude towards the other lords appellant, especially Bolingbroke, and the king's leadership style more generally.

ACTIVITY
KNOWLEDGE CHECK

Richard II and the lords appellant

Read Source 6 and answer the following questions. Write in your own words throughout – do not include lengthy quotations from the source.

1 According to the source, what were Gloucester's main grudges against Richard II?

2 What impression is given of Gloucester's character?

3 What impression is given of Richard's character?

4 Based on Froissart's background and your own knowledge, how reliable do you think this account of Gloucester's character is?

5 What happened to Gloucester later in 1397 and why was this event so significant in relation to Richard's downfall in 1399?

Certainly, Bolingbroke seems to have become increasingly afraid of the king, begging pardon once again for his role in the events of 1387 and securing a promise from the king that he would not seize Lancastrian territories. He also hosted lavish entertainments for Richard at his own expense. Matters came to a head in late 1397, when Bolingbroke became embroiled in a quarrel with his former co-appellant, Thomas Mowbray, now duke of Norfolk. Although the king initially requested the disagreement be settled by combat, in 1398 Richard instead exiled both parties – Bolingbroke for ten years and Mowbray for life.

Initially, Richard's attitude towards Bolingbroke seemed to be relatively benevolent. He exiled him for a fixed period only, placed no limits on the countries he could travel to, gave him 1,000 marks towards his costs and, most importantly of all, presented him with letters permitting him to obtain any inheritance that came to him during his exile. This goodwill proved short lived, however: John of Gaunt died on 3 February 1399 and two days after his funeral Bolingbroke was disinherited. This decision was a major breach of custom and gave Bolingbroke an overwhelming motivation to make a serious military challenge. By May, Henry made a formal alliance with Louis, the duke of Orléans and the French king's brother, both men agreeing to support each other militarily.

EXTEND YOUR KNOWLEDGE

Thomas Walsingham (c 1340–1422), chronicler, and the historical significance of his writing
The writings of Thomas Walsingham are one of the most important sources for the reigns of Richard II and Henry IV. Walsingham probably studied at the University of Oxford in the 1370s, and joined the Abbey of St Albans as a monk at some point prior to 1390, holding senior positions there. He wrote on a range of subjects, including spirituality, music, classical literature and ancient Greek history.

His most significant works, however, were chronicles, which combined history with the retelling of contemporary or near-contemporary events. The Abbey of St Albans had a long tradition of this type of writing and Walsingham was clearly influenced by earlier writers of this kind. His main work was his *Chronica majora*, which he began in 1376, but he also wrote a number of other similar historical compositions.

St Albans in this period was an important place and this ensured that Walsingham was able to hear all the latest gossip from the royal court and from London. According to his modern biographer, John Taylor, Walsingham had a particular bias against foreigners and the lower classes of society.

Nonetheless, his writing is a very helpful and significant source for Richard II's reign, providing detailed and sometimes eye-witness accounts of key events such as the 1381 Peasants' Revolt. His writing and its various revisions also reveals a great deal about changing attitudes towards key political figures of the period. For example, the original version of the *Chronica majora* contained heavy criticism of John of Gaunt, the duke of Lancaster, but this was re-edited in the 1390s as Walsingham became more favourable to the Lancastrian house and more critical of Richard II.

Richard, however, appears to have been relatively unconcerned with the threat posed by Bolingbroke, the angry new duke of Lancaster. This was in part because of the truce with France, which should have prohibited any French support of an attack on his realm. In late May 1399, therefore, the king departed to lead an expedition to Ireland to suppress ongoing rebellion there. Unknown to Richard, however, the political situation in France and Burgundy shifted at this crucial time, with Henry's new ally, the duke of Orléans, gaining increasing influence over the mentally unstable French king, Charles VI. Bolingbroke was therefore permitted the freedom to arrange an invasion of England, and Orléans may have secretly assisted him in this endeavour.

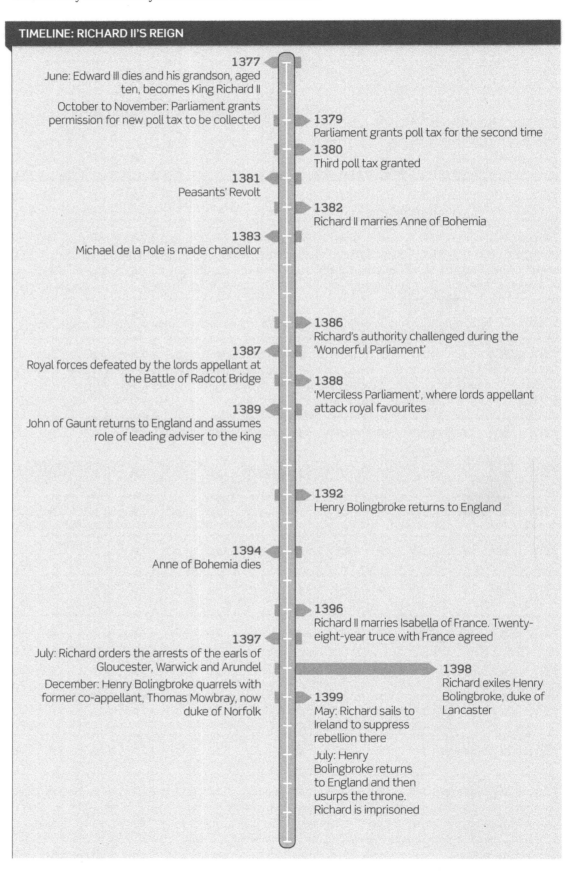

TIMELINE: RICHARD II'S REIGN

1377
June: Edward III dies and his grandson, aged ten, becomes King Richard II

October to November: Parliament grants permission for new poll tax to be collected

1379
Parliament grants poll tax for the second time

1380
Third poll tax granted

1381
Peasants' Revolt

1382
Richard II marries Anne of Bohemia

1383
Michael de la Pole is made chancellor

1386
Richard's authority challenged during the 'Wonderful Parliament'

1387
Royal forces defeated by the lords appellant at the Battle of Radcot Bridge

1388
'Merciless Parliament', where lords appellant attack royal favourites

1389
John of Gaunt returns to England and assumes role of leading adviser to the king

1392
Henry Bolingbroke returns to England

1394
Anne of Bohemia dies

1396
Richard II marries Isabella of France. Twenty-eight-year truce with France agreed

1397
July: Richard orders the arrests of the earls of Gloucester, Warwick and Arundel

December: Henry Bolingbroke quarrels with former co-appellant, Thomas Mowbray, now duke of Norfolk

1398
Richard exiles Henry Bolingbroke, duke of Lancaster

1399
May: Richard sails to Ireland to suppress rebellion there

July: Henry Bolingbroke returns to England and then usurps the throne. Richard is imprisoned

In early July 1399, Henry landed in the Humber estuary (in East Yorkshire) and was supported by many of his Lancashire retainers, as well as the earls of Northumberland and Westmorland and his lifelong friend, Archbishop Arundel. Bolingbroke should have been opposed by the duke of York, who had been appointed as Protector of the Realm in the king's absence, but York decided instead to support Henry, probably being significantly influenced by the fact that the bulk of Richard's military support was with him in Ireland. Richard also made a significant error in not returning to England straight away when he heard of the invasion on around 10 July, delaying his return until around 23 July. It is unclear if Richard was deliberately advised not to return by a disloyal earl of Albemarle, who may have wanted Henry to gain the throne, or if the delay was simply the result of difficulties in assembling his army. Whatever the cause, it was to prove disastrous for Richard. By the time he reached Wales, his troops began to desert as they learned of Bolingbroke's growing popularity and York's defection, and Henry strengthened his own position by seizing the king's treasure which was stored at Holt Castle in Wales. In an increasingly desperate situation, Richard sent the duke of Exeter and the earl of Surrey to reason with Henry, but Bolingbroke arrested them both. Eventually, the earl of Northumberland, acting on Henry's behalf, met with the king and negotiated that Richard would meet with his rebellious cousin at Flint Castle, although exactly what was promised to Richard in these negotiations remains unclear. On around 16 August, Bolingbroke and Richard met at Flint and, from this time onwards, Richard remained a prisoner at Bolingbroke's hands. On 19 August, **writs** for a parliament were issued in Richard's name and this parliament assembled on 30 September 1399. Richard was brought to London and imprisoned in the Tower.

KEY TERM

Writ
A legally binding, written command from an authority, such as the king or parliament. In this context, the writ was in effect a summons to attend parliament.

Why was Bolingbroke able to seize power in 1399?

Initially when Bolingbroke invaded, he claimed that he was simply seeking to regain his Lancastrian lands. Certainly, Richard's action in disinheriting Bolingbroke was widely criticised both within England and on the continent, so Bolingbroke could have been fairly certain of reasonable levels of support in his endeavours. It remains unclear whether this was ever his only aim, or how quickly this motivation changed to one of seeking to depose the king. His motivations remain unclear and it is possible revenge for his treatment was one factor. He must also have been very aware of the risk of leaving Richard in power to take revenge upon him later, as had occurred with the other lords appellant in 1397. More surprising than Bolingbroke wanting the throne, however, was the fact that so many others were willing to support his claim. Certainly, Henry was very warmly received in many areas, and he may well have been an opportunist who exploited this in order to further his dynastic ambitions. Richard's absence in Ireland was undoubtedly a crucial factor in this, particularly as he was accompanied by many of his leading supporters, including his formidable Cheshire retinue.

Nonetheless, the fact that even the duke of York, Protector of the Realm, was willing to support a usurper rather than the anointed king is a damning indictment of Richard's unpopularity among many noblemen, who were doubtless frightened by the king's growing aloofness and apparent desire to avenge himself on those guilty of past affronts. Historians such as Nigel Saul and Caroline Barron have particularly emphasised the significance of the king's increasingly tyrannical behaviour in relation to property ownership, with Richard's decision to disinherit Bolingbroke being seen as the crowning example of his willingness to ignore convention and legal restraint to seize a noble's land without just cause.

EXTRACT

1 From N. Saul, *Richard II*, Yale University Press (1999). Here, Professor Saul discusses the motivations for the decision of Henry Bolingbroke, duke of Lancaster, to seize the crown.

Just when the duke became committed to his new course is hard to say. It was not until 10 September that he openly signalled his ambition… But the general drift of his thinking was probably known to his supporters well before then. The reasons for his change of mind can only be surmised. Doubtless he had been encouraged by the warmth of his reception and the rapid triumph of his cause: his ambition may have been fed by the heady brew of popular favour. But it is also likely that to some extent he was acting defensively. He knew Richard to be vengeful and untrustworthy. Barely a couple of years before, he had witnessed the terrible punishment the king had inflicted upon the former Appellant lords for challenging the prerogative and executing his friends. There was no guarantee that if he were left on the throne he would not inflict similar punishment again. In all probability it was self-preservation rather than vaulting ambition that was the main spur to his action. But whatever the balance of motives in his mind, the illegality of the duke's intended course was clear. The duke was only too conscious of this himself. That was why he ordered the searches of the chronicles; he wanted his agents to come up with suitable precedents for his actions. His aim was to make a wholly illegitimate act appear as nearly legitimate as possible.

ACTIVITY
KNOWLEDGE CHECK

Henry Bolingbroke's motivations and justification for seizing the throne

Read Extract 1 carefully and answer the following questions:

1 According to Saul, what were the reasons for Bolingbroke's decision to seize the throne from Richard? Ensure you write in your own words rather than quoting directly from the text.

2 What other motivations, not mentioned in the extract, may Bolingbroke have had for his actions?

3 Do you think Saul's view that Richard was 'vengeful and untrustworthy' is justified? Write your answer in a paragraph, providing plenty of detailed evidence to support your view.

4 Saul refers to the 'terrible punishment… inflicted upon the former Appellant lords'. Make notes on this topic using these headings:

   a) Reasons for Richard's resentment of the appellants.

   b) Action taken against the appellants in 1397.

   c) Bolingbroke's reasons for fearing Richard and wanting revenge.

Write details under each heading in chronological order and include dates for all the key events.

HOW SIGNIFICANT WAS BOLINGBROKE'S USURPATION OF THE THRONE IN RELATION TO THE PROBLEMS OF HIS EARLY REIGN?

Henry IV and the problems arising from his behaviour in 1399

Bolingbroke met with relatively little military resistance as he took the throne, but he was well aware that retaining a secure hold on the crown was going to be much more difficult. In his first parliament as Henry IV, it was claimed that Richard had voluntarily resigned the throne when a delegation of nobles had approached him on the issue and explained to him that he could not rule because of his 'incapacity and insufficiency' to be king. In this rather implausible explanation, Richard gave up his throne 'willingly, as it appeared, and with a cheerful face', admitting that he was 'utterly inadequate and unequal to the rule and government of the said realms and dominions… and, on account of my notorious faults, I deserve to be deposed from them.' He then expressed a hope that Henry Bolingbroke should become the next king, placing his own gold ring on the finger of the duke.

Accusations against Richard II

EXTRACT

From A. Weir, *Lancaster and York: the Wars of the Roses* (1996). Historian Alison Weir discusses how Henry Bolingbroke, duke of Lancaster, justified his decision to seize the crown.

> Richard was by no means willing to give up the throne, and Bolingbroke knew it… Knowing that his [Bolingbroke's] title was precarious, the official line was to be that Richard's misgovernment justified his deposition. The laws of succession were best left out of it.

Clearly, this amicable arrangement is extremely unlikely and, instead, other sources of varying reliability suggest that Richard was either furious or heartbroken by his forced abdication. The widespread knowledge that Richard, despite Henry's claims of voluntary abdication, had in fact been forcibly removed from the throne was a serious problem for the stability of the new king's reign. Therefore, it was very important that the new regime carefully stage managed and legally supported the takeover in the broadest possible terms. The chronicler Adam of Usk is an important source of information about how the new Lancastrian regime justified Henry's seizure of power. He was an academic and lawyer, who

was probably a member of the Archbishop of Arundel's entourage until Arundel went into exile with Henry Bolingbroke in 1398. Upon invasion, Usk supported the Lancastrian side and was part of a committee that Henry appointed to determine legal justifications for the change in ruler. According to this account, the committee justified the deposition on the wide-ranging grounds of Richard's immoral rule, citing offences including sacrilege, perjury, sodomy, incompetence, lack of ability and greed. This, according to the committee, meant that the deposition was permitted by canon law, because of the immorality of Richard's rule. Accordingly, 39 accusations against Richard were read out at Henry IV's first parliament, which provided a comprehensive attack on government during the reign and included the following charges:

- The imposition of weighty and unnecessary taxes, which were not used for the common good, but for Richard's personal advantage.

- Richard's treatment of the lords appellant, with particular emphasis on the fact that he had previously pardoned their offences, but nonetheless had continued to harbour resentment towards them, culminating in his actions in 1397.

- The unlawful and violent behaviour of Richard's Cheshire retinue, which the king did nothing to restrain despite complaints.

- The unjust and unmerciful treatment of Henry, duke of Lancaster, especially while in exile.

- Royal intervention in the selection of local officers, such as sheriffs, and parliamentary representatives in the counties, and changing the traditional oaths of such officers, to make them more personally accountable to the king.

- Failing to pay back loans.

- Infringements on the rights of the Church, including requiring financial payments and interfering in cases in the ecclesiastical courts.

- Richard claiming that he personally made the law, rather than upholding the traditional laws of the realm.

- Using false accusations of treason as a method of raising money.

- Ignoring the advice of the council, and maintaining an arrogant attitude when nobles advised him so that they were 'frequently rebuked and reprimanded, suddenly and so bitterly that they did not dare to speak the truth in giving their advice on the welfare of the king and the kingdom.'

- Removing the crown jewels from England and taking them to Ireland when he went on campaign there.

- Seizing land from his subjects without good reason, and imprisoning them without fair trial.

Perhaps the charge that best captured the reason for Richard's downfall, however, was the view that he was so changeable that no one could trust him (see Source 7). While the accusations against Richard are clearly written by those very hostile to him and with the agenda of placing Henry on the throne, it seems fairly clear that leaving his subjects in a state of continual uncertainty was a defining characteristic of the reign and that this engendered terror and dislike among many of his leading subjects, contributing substantially to his downfall.

EXTRACT

3 From E. Hallam (ed.), *The Chronicles of the Wars of the Roses* (1988). The author discusses how Henry Bolingbroke, duke of Lancaster, justified the seizure of the crown to parliament.

[For Henry IV] it was necessary only to justify the revolution [of 1399] by discrediting Richard's regime. A list of crimes was patched together and proclaimed before parliament.

SOURCE

7 From the records of the first parliament of Henry IV, 1399, this gives details of some of the complaints against Richard II. Although this is a formal document and provides a fairly accurate account of what occurred in parliament, it should be borne in mind that the accusations against Richard listed here were shaped by Henry and his advisers, and so served the new regime's political agenda.

Also, the same king wishing not to observe or protect the just laws and customs of his realm, but to do whatever appealed to his desires according to the impulse of his will, at times, when the laws of his realm had been explained and declared to him by the justices and others of his council, and when they asked that he should do justice according to those laws, he frequently said expressly, with a stern and forbidding countenance, that his laws were in his mouth, or sometimes in his breast: and that he alone could alter and create the laws of his realm. And, seduced by that opinion, he did not allow justice to be done to a great number of his lieges, but through threats and terror forced a great number to cease from the pursuit of common justice.

... Also, the same king was accustomed almost continually to be so changeable and dissembling in his words and writings, and altogether contrary to himself, especially in writing to the pope and to kings, and to other lords outside the realm and within it, and also to other subjects of his, that almost no living person who knew what sort of person he was, could or wished to trust him. Rather he was thought to be so untrustworthy and inconstant that it became a disgrace, not only to his person, but also to his whole realm, and especially among foreigners throughout the whole world who learnt of it.

Also, although the lands and tenements, goods and chattels of any free man, by the laws of the kingdom in use for all time past, should not be seized unless they are forfeit; nevertheless the said king, proposing and endeavouring to undermine the laws of this kind, in the presence of very many lords and others of the community of the realm frequently said and declared that the life of any of his lieges, and his lands, tenements, goods and chattels, were his at his will, without any forfeiture: which is utterly against the laws and customs of his aforesaid realm.

A Level Exam-Style Question Section A

Study Source 7 before you answer this question.

Assess the value of the source for revealing the failings of Richard II as a monarch and the reasons for Henry IV's successful usurpation of the throne in 1399.

Explain your answer, using the source, the information given about its origin and your own knowledge about the historical context. (20 marks)

Tip

Ensure you consider not only the significance of Richard II's failings mentioned in the source, but also factors that are not touched on here.

The comprehensive critique of Richard's rule was probably a political necessity in the tense situation of 1399; in essence, it was important that there was overwhelming reason to remove the monarch, as such a course of action challenged the fundamental idea that the hereditary monarchy was ordained by God. Nonetheless, it cast a long shadow over the reign of Bolingbroke and his heir, as it provided a very public precedent for a king to be removed because he was unpopular and incompetent. The unspoken implication, therefore, was that from now on a king's conduct lay open to the criticism and potential judgement of his subjects. To some extent, this was not a new concept, as in 1327 Edward II had been deposed and murdered by his opponents, but an important difference was that, unlike Edward, in 1399 Richard II had no son to take his place. This breached the tradition of the throne passing from father to son or grandson, as Bolingbroke was only King Richard's cousin and not the only claimant to the throne. Therefore, it was now clear to all nobles that an unpopular king could be ousted by an 'over-mighty subject' provided he had sufficient military support.

Justifications for Henry Bolingbroke becoming king

In the circumstances, a great deal of thought clearly went into deciding how Henry IV should officially justify his seizure of the throne. In his first parliament, he simply stated that 'I am descended by right line of the blood from the good lord King Henry the third, and through that right that God in his grace has sent me, with the help of my kin and of my friends in recovering it; which realm was at the point of ruin for lack of governance and destruction of the good laws.' The reference to his royal lineage was deliberately vague, as his credentials in this regard were shaky. In fact, by right of **primogeniture**, arguably Edmund Mortimer, fifth earl of March and seventh earl of Ulster was next in line to the throne, as he was the great-grandson of King Edward III's eldest surviving son, Lionel of Antwerp (see Figure 3.1 on page 78). Mortimer's claim was somewhat weakened by the fact that he inherited through the female line (it was his grandmother, Philippa, who was of royal blood), but there were precedents for this type of inheritance on the continent and so Mortimer was, legally speaking, a potential threat to Henry's claim. In practice, this danger was considerably lessened by the fact that in 1399 Mortimer was only eight years old. Unsurprisingly, many preferred to support Henry because he was an adult male, a proven warrior and had a substantial retinue, rather than entrust the fate of the nation to another child-king. Indeed, Henry's reference to the 'help of my kin and my friends' in his parliamentary statement was a thinly veiled reference to his strong military support. Nonetheless, this was a dangerous way to claim the throne; in essence, from 1399 Henry made kingship legally conditional on competence and military might.

KEY TERM

Primogeniture
The right of the firstborn male to inherit the family title or estate, in preference to other siblings. If the firstborn male died before his father, these rights then passed to his eldest son or grandson, depending on survival.

Edmund Mortimer's claim to the throne

Edmund Mortimer was the eldest son of Roger Mortimer, fourth earl of March (1374–98), and Eleanor (d. 1405), daughter of Thomas Holland, earl of Kent. His claim to the throne was that his paternal grandmother, Philippa, was the daughter of Lionel of Antwerp, duke of Clarence. Lionel had been the second son of King Edward III to survive into adulthood. His elder brother, Edward, the Black Prince, died in 1376 and it was the Black Prince's son who became King Richard II, according to the laws of primogeniture. When Richard was deposed, it was arguably Lionel's heir, Edmund Mortimer, who should have taken the throne and not Bolingbroke, who was the son of John of Gaunt, Lionel's younger brother.

EXTRACT

4 Historian Professor Saul discusses Bolingbroke's claim to the throne. From N. Saul, *Richard II* (1997).

Henry's claim, when it was eventually framed, bore all the hallmarks of a compromise. There was a vestigial reference to the conquest and to the need to reform the realm, but the main argument was an hereditary one… By the later fourteenth century it was becoming common for the private estates of the nobility to descend in the male line rather than through the heir general, and Henry may have been implying that it was appropriate for the crown to do the same. Three-quarters of a century earlier the French monarchy had successfully applied this doctrine on the extinction of the direct line of the Capetians [who were the French ruling dynasty in the early fourteenth century]. It could [also] be argued that Henry was only following continental practice by doing the same.

Because of his youth, Edmund Mortimer, earl of March, could not himself take any active role in rebellion, but Henry was aware that there were others who would be willing to use him as a figurehead for revolt. He was a particular risk because the Mortimer family were one of the most powerful marcher families and had considerable support from Wales as they were descended from Llywelyn ab Iorwerth, the 13th-century prince of Gwynedd. This threat was made greater as, in the early 15th century, Wales was a hotbed of insurrection against the English crown. Consequently, Henry kept a close eye on the boy, making both Edmund and his brother Roger royal wards and ensuring they lived mainly at Windsor Castle. In 1402, when the king went to fight in Wales, the youths were moved to Berkhamsted Castle and placed under the supervision of a loyal Lancastrian, Sir Hugh Waterton. In this, Henry proved to be a leader of some foresight as in the same year the boys' uncle, Sir Edmund (IV) Mortimer, was captured by the Welsh prince and rebel leader Owain Glyndwr and he switched his loyalty to the Welsh, in December, announcing that his nephew was in fact Richard II's rightful heir and that Henry IV had no claim to the throne.

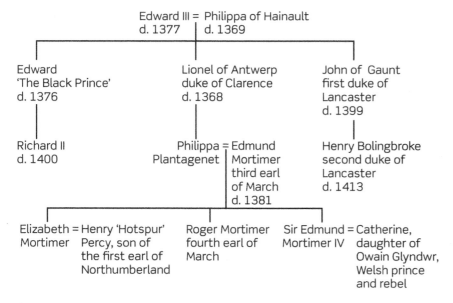

Figure 3.1 Family tree showing the various claims to the crown of Richard II, Henry Bolingbroke (later Henry IV), and members of the Mortimer family.

The strength of argument

This exercise is designed to help you consider the value of secondary extracts and how to analyse the evidence and arguments you are presented with by different historians.

Answer the following:

1 Read Extract 2.

 a) What is weak about this historian's claim?

 b) What could be added to make it stronger?

2 Read Extract 3.

 a) Is this an argument? If yes, what makes it one?

 b) How might this argument be strengthened?

3 Read Extract 4.

 a) How has Saul expanded his explanation to make his argument stronger?

 b) Can you explain why this is the strongest claim of the three extracts?

4 What elements make a strong historical claim?

The first stirrings of revolt and the death of Richard in 1400

Henry was crowned on 13 October with a full, traditional ceremony at Westminster Abbey, and quickly followed this by ensuring that his eldest son, also Henry, was invested as the Prince of Wales to secure the succession. This guarantee of an heir was an important method of strengthening his claim to provide the realm with newfound stability. He also sought to break away from Richard's more unpopular policies by revoking the decisions taken by the 1397–98 parliament and restoring those of 1386. No doubt in a bid for popularity, it was also in this first parliament that Henry promised that, owing to his extensive private landholdings, he would be able to 'live of his own' and only request taxation in times of war. This financial undertaking was a clear reference to Richard's frequent and very unpopular requests for taxation and a recognition of parliament's frequent criticism of royal expenditure. This promise was one which caused problems later for Henry (see Chapter 2, page 52), but at the time it was politically very useful and in the short term increased political support for the new king.

Recognising that a lack of mercy had been one of the key criticisms of Richard, Henry wisely sought conciliation with Richard II's erstwhile supporters, showing them clemency provided they showed a willingness to support the new regime. This was expedient as it ensured greater administrative and political stability at a time of turmoil and prevented a widespread backlash against the usurper early in his reign. Nonetheless, Henry's takeover was not universally welcomed and in January 1400 the '**Epiphany Rising**' took place, when a number of diehard Ricardians, notably the earls of Huntingdon, Kent and Salisbury, and Sir Thomas Despenser, planned a conspiracy to murder Henry and his sons during the traditional Christmas revelry at Windsor. Significantly, however, the plot failed. This was in part because Henry was forewarned and so had time to escape with his family to London. More significantly, however, the plan did not gain popular support; indeed, a number of the rebels were killed by local people before they could be found and executed. This indicates that while Bolingbroke's criticisms of Richard were clearly exaggerated in 1399, there was nonetheless a genuine and widespread dislike of the deposed king which increased Henry's stability on the throne.

The leaders of the 1400 rebellion all died, but their actions may have sealed the fate of Richard, who was by now imprisoned in Pontefract Castle on Henry's Lancastrian estates. While the previous king lived, it was clear that he would always provide a focal point of rebellion for those dissatisfied with Henry IV and, in February 1400, he conveniently died. The exact cause is unclear, with some contemporaries claiming he committed suicide by refusing all food and drink. The more likely explanation, however, is that he was murdered on Henry's orders. Certainly, the new regime recognised the importance of publicising his death to prevent pretenders causing unrest by claiming the throne

KEY TERM

Epiphany Rising
The Epiphany is a Roman Catholic feast day, held annually on 6 January (sometimes also known as 'Twelfth Night' or the 'Twelfth Day of Christmas'). It celebrates the arrival of the Three Magi (Wise Men) who visited the baby Jesus and brought gifts. This day was traditionally a time of great celebration in medieval England and it would have been celebrated lavishly by the royal court. The Epiphany Rising refers to a revolt which occurred in January 1400 against Henry IV. Rebels apparently planned to use the traditional court entertainments of the Christmas period as a cover for their activities.

and so the body was brought to London with the face displayed to prevent rumours of a substitution. He was then buried honourably, although not in the tomb he had designed for himself in Westminster Abbey.

Overall, Henry IV faced considerable difficulties at the start of his reign, which were mainly due to the legally dubious nature of his claim to the throne. He overcame them with a powerful combination of political skill and ruthlessness. He was helped by the evident unpopularity of Richard II, but was careful to emphasise the problems of the previous reign and to apparently make speedy attempts to remedy his predecessors' more controversial decisions, notably in the 1397–98 parliament. He quelled the first rebellion against him in early 1400 through a combination of good information and swift military skill. He also showed an understanding of the importance of propaganda in his speedy investiture of the new Prince of Wales and his display of Richard's body in February. Whether or not he arranged Richard's murder in 1400, no one could be in any doubt that this was a leader who was able and willing to act decisively against his enemies. Nonetheless, unlike his predecessor, he appeared also capable of mercy and conciliation; indeed, his rather rash financial promises were to become a hostage to fortune in later years. In the early stages of his reign, therefore, he kept the throne because Richard II had been extremely unpopular and Henry was politically militarily astute enough to capitalise on this advantage and not to alienate too many people. He was also greatly assisted in this as his only real rival claimant was an eight-year-old boy.

ACTIVITY
KNOWLEDGE CHECK

The deposition of Richard II and the claim of Henry IV

1 Write a list, in order of significance, of the key failings and problems of Richard II's reign. Colour-code this list into long-term, short-term and immediate causes. Add a key.

2 At which point in Richard II's reign was he most secure on the throne? Write a paragraph explaining your answer.

3 Write a paragraph explaining the strengths and weaknesses of Henry Bolingbroke's claim to the throne and why he was able to gain enough support to claim the crown.

TO WHAT EXTENT WAS THE LANCASTRIAN MONARCHY SECURE BY 1405?

The challenges from the Percies and Owain Glyndwr

Owain Glyndwr and the Welsh rebellion

Anglo-Welsh relations at the beginning of the 15th century were particularly hostile and formed the most serious threat to Henry IV's early reign. The Welsh were led by Owain Glyndwr, who had native Welsh origins, but also family connections via marriage to leading Anglo-Welsh families from the border region. In September 1400, Glyndwr led a rebellion that began at Glyndyfrdwy, which, according to later legal charges, elevated Owain to the status of a prince. He plotted the death of Henry IV and the destruction of the Lancastrian regime, and demanded the total obliteration of the English language in Wales. Glyndwr and his small army attacked and burned the town of Ruthin, which was part of the territory of Lord Grey of Ruthin, with whom Owain had a dispute. Within a week, however, Glyndwr's forces had been overwhelmed by troops raised by the loyal Lancastrian, Hugh Burnell. This occurred before the king, who had gone north in response to a threat from Scotland, could arrive. Henry therefore left his 13-year-old son, the Prince of Wales, in nominal charge of securing Wales, with Sir Henry Percy (known as 'Hotspur'), the earl of Northumberland's eldest son, as the real military commander.

EXTEND YOUR KNOWLEDGE

Henry Percy's nickname

Sir Henry Percy (1364–1403) was the son of the first earl of Northumberland. During the 1380s especially, he became renowned as a very able warrior and military commander. His reputation was particularly enhanced by his victories on the Scottish border. The Scots gave him the nickname 'Hotspur' in tribute to his willingness to attack and the speed with which his troops advanced.

Welsh resistance continued throughout the early 1400s, with Glyndwr and his supporters adopting **guerrilla tactics** against the English. The threat from Wales was mounting, with reports in early 1401 that those of Welsh origins living in England were returning home to prepare for war, including labourers and students at the universities of Oxford and Cambridge. Concerned by news from Wales, King Henry returned there in the late summer/autumn of 1401, but was unable to bring Glyndwr to open battle. In 1402, Glyndwr captured Edmund Mortimer IV, the uncle of the young earl of March, the alternative heir to Richard II. During his captivity, Mortimer switched loyalties to support the Welsh rebels, publicly proclaiming that his nephew was the rightful King of England and not Henry IV. The situation was sufficiently serious that, in September 1402, parliament enacted a series of statutes forbidding the sale of food supplies or armour to Wales and prohibiting public meetings, the bearing of arms, the keeping of castles or the holding of office by Welsh men or those married to Welsh women, especially any who showed allegiance to the 'traitor' Owain Glyndwr.

KEY TERM

Guerrilla tactics
Strategies that tend to be employed by smaller, more irregular armies against larger and more conventional troops. Methods of attack and defence are usually small scale and depend upon a good knowledge of the local terrain. They also make strong use of the element of surprise, and frequently include the use of ambush and trickery. Although tactics of this kind have been in use for millennia, and were clearly evident during the Middle Ages, it is important to note that the term 'guerrilla' was coined later and was first used in relation to campaigns by the Spanish and Portuguese against the French during the Peninsular War (1808-14).

SOURCE

This is the only surviving example of the royal Great Seal of Owain Glyndwr, which was attached to his 1404 treaty with Charles VI of France. It displays workmanship of a very high standard and was possibly made in France. On one side, Glyndwr is depicted enthroned holding a sceptre and under a canopy, but not wearing a crown. On the reverse, Owain is depicted as a warrior on horseback, with a crown on his helmet and on the horse's head. The writing, now damaged, is presumed to read 'Owain, by the grace of God, Prince of Wales'.

Hotspur's rebellion in 1403

Matters were made more dangerous for Henry IV by two additional factors. The first was the threat from Scotland, which persisted throughout the early years of the 15th century, and the second was the actions of members of the Percy family. As the earls of Northumberland, the Percies had been dissatisfied with Richard II's treatment of them, particularly in relation to the award of border offices, and so initially lent their support to Henry IV's regime. For this, they were lavishly rewarded and, by 1402, the eldest Percy son, Hotspur, had obtained numerous territories and responsibilities in the border areas of both Wales and Scotland. These grants, according to the historian Simon Walker, provided Hotspur with an almost complete monopoly on military and political power in North Wales and the East March, which were areas crucial to the ongoing security of the Lancastrian regime. Despite this display of royal confidence in him, however, Percy was becoming increasingly discontent with the Lancastrian regime. The exact cause of this dissatisfaction is unclear, but some possible motives were as follows:

- In September 1402, the earl of Northumberland and Hotspur fought alongside George, earl of Dunbar, a prominent Scottish magnate who had defected to the English two years earlier. Together, they won a significant victory over the Scots at Homildon Hill, making a number of important captures. Subsequently, however, there was a dispute between the Percies and Henry IV as a result of this battle, as the king ordered that no prisoners could be ransomed without his explicit permission. The Percies regarded this as unwarranted interference in their affairs and, although the earl of Northumberland eventually handed his prisoners over to the king, Hotspur did not. It has been suggested by some scholars that this significant military victory made Henry IV jealous, as it contrasted with his own lack of success in war.

- There were financial disagreements with the crown. In particular, the Percies wanted the king to pay money due to them for military service more promptly, as they felt this would assist them in their campaigns in Scotland especially. The earl of Northumberland and his son both wrote a number of letters to Henry IV complaining of their treatment, although the historian J.M.W. Bean has argued that in fact these grievances were unjustified.

- Hotspur's wife was Elizabeth Mortimer and she was the aunt of the young Edmund Mortimer, earl of March, who had a claim to the throne which rivalled that of Henry IV. Certainly, this made the king more suspicious of Hotspur and may have contributed to the growing rift between the monarch and the Percies.

- The situation in Wales was extremely fraught in the early 1400s, placing Hotspur under military and financial strain. He wished to negotiate a settlement with the Welsh, partly so the Percies could focus their resources more on war with Scotland, but the king would not compromise on the issue.

- In 1402, the Welsh captured Hotspur's brother-in-law, Sir Edmund Mortimer IV, uncle of the young earl of March who was a key rival to Henry IV for the throne. The king, probably with very good reason, argued that Mortimer IV was a traitor and refused to allow the Percies to negotiate for him to be freed by payment of a ransom. In addition, Henry IV seized Mortimer's goods and this matter caused considerable tension between the king and the Percies, which was increased in November 1402 when the prisoner married Glyndwr's daughter with great celebration.

- In April 1403, the Prince of Wales was placed in charge of the newly united military command in Wales. This reduced Hotspur's power in the area, as he held significant offices in North Wales. Another member of the Percy family, the earl of Northumberland's brother, Thomas, earl of Worcester, was given a leading position within the prince's household, but both Thomas and his nephew seem to have become increasingly frustrated by royal policy in Wales.

- There are some suggestions that Hotspur rebelled as he wished to claim the crown for himself; certainly Henry IV accused him of this and Hotspur's soldiers, during the battle against Henry IV that followed in 1403, are recorded as crying out 'Henry Percy King'.

In 1403, therefore, Hotspur rebelled and was joined in this by his uncle, the earl of Worcester. In Cheshire, they issued proclamations against Henry IV, claiming their allegiance to Richard II. The rebels fought against the royal army at Shrewsbury and were defeated, and Hotspur was killed on the battlefield, being buried only after the body had been publicly displayed on the king's orders, to prevent later claims that he was still alive.

EXTEND YOUR KNOWLEDGE

George, earl of Dunbar, also known as the earl of March

George, earl of Dunbar (born c1336; died between 1416 and 1423) was a magnate controlling large estates in the East Scottish march as well as having territorial claims elsewhere within Scotland. In the 1360s and 1370s he was very influential in re-establishing Scottish control around Berwick and was frequently engaged in attacks on the English border during the last quarter of the 14th century.

During the 1390s, his daughter Elizabeth formed a relationship with David Stewart, earl of Carrick, who was heir to the Scottish throne. The king, Robert III, however, opposed this match and in 1400 Stewart rejected Elizabeth and instead married Mary Douglas, a woman whose family were Dunbar's key political and military rivals.

As a result of this insult, Dunbar defected to the new English king, Henry IV, in 1400. This led to considerable internal political and military unrest in Scotland and he was an important asset for the English against the Scots, being a very able military commander, as indicated by the victory at Homildon Hill, which was a campaign largely based on Dunbar's suggested tactics.

The influence of relations with Scotland and France

As for any usurper, a key factor in securing Henry IV's throne was establishing international recognition of his right to rule. Given that Richard II had been decidedly pro-French and was married to a daughter of the king of France, it was unsurprising that Anglo-French relations were particularly difficult in the early 15th century. Although the duke of Orléans had lent tacit support to Bolingbroke when he invaded in 1399, his motivations were primarily to cause difficulties for England. He was no doubt horrified when Henry successfully took the throne from Richard, leaving England with a considerably more experienced military leader as king. Consequently, the duke of Orléans made things as difficult as possible for Henry IV. Strictly speaking, after Richard's death, the young **dowager** queen should have been returned to the French court with all her valuable dowry, but the negotiations for this were hostile and in 1401 she was returned without any of the wealth she had brought with her on her marriage. Subsequently, the duke of Orléans endeavoured to increase Henry IV's embarrassment as much as possible, challenging him to armed combat on two occasions during 1402–3, which Henry declined on the grounds that Orléans was not a worthy opponent because of his lower rank.

Hostilities between the two nations were also increased by the status of the Duchy of Aquitaine. This is a region that lies in modern-day France, mainly in the area of Gascony. In the 12th and 13th centuries, the people in this area were in general loyal to the Angevin royal family (notably Henry II, Richard I and John I), who also ruled England between 1154 and 1216. King John's successor, Henry III, however, had to give up many of his family's claims in France in 1259. As part of peace negotiations with the French king, he formally surrendered a considerable amount of the Angevin territory and agreed to keep the title of duke of Aquitaine as a vassal of the French crown. In 1337, however, Edward III renewed the English monarchy's claim to this area of France and refused to undertake an **act of homage** to the French king, thus beginning the Hundred Years War. Subsequently, the territorial claims of England and France in this area were hotly disputed and this friction was increased in the early 15th century by the fact that Richard II, who had been born in Bordeaux, was very popular in Aquitaine, while Henry IV was not. In what was probably a deliberate insult to the English, therefore, in 1401 Charles VI granted Aquitaine to his heir, the **Dauphin** Louis. This triggered a serious outbreak of piracy on both sides in the Channel, which neither king sought to curb, while the English sent a fleet to Aquitaine in 1402, although this was intercepted by the French. Financially, the hostilities in Aquitaine were extremely damaging to Henry IV. The cost of defence of the region was significant, but probably more significant was the negative impact that the widespread piracy had on trade. In 1405, for example, the Hanseatic League placed significant trade restrictions on the English doing business in the Baltic on the grounds of English involvement in piracy.

The French at this time were supported by their traditional allies against England, the Scots, which made the threat from the northern border all the greater for the new Lancastrian regime. The Channel became increasingly dangerous because of piracy and in 1403 French troops invaded Aquitaine, forcing the English army there into retreat. Henry IV displayed his wisdom in dealing with the nobility of the area, however, successfully mollifying them to the extent that the central area of Gascony remained loyal to the English crown. Nonetheless, it was a period of great tension, with two French naval attacks on the English south coast in 1404. Parliament heavily criticised the inadequate defences, which were linked to the mismanagement of royal finance as a result of the extravagance of the king's household.

At the very outset of his reign, Henry IV appears to have sought a more peaceful relationship with Scotland, presumably as he was very aware of his own weak position both domestically and abroad. The King of Scots, Robert III, however refused to recognise the legality of the usurpation and made a number of raids on the northern counties of England. On 10 November 1399, therefore, Henry informed parliament that he would wage war against Scotland, and in early 1400 wrote to Robert III and other lords demanding that they performed an act of homage to him as their 'good lord.'

KEY TERMS

Dowager
A widow who retains certain rights or a title from her deceased husband. A dowager queen, therefore, is a term used to refer to the king's widow.

Act of homage
An action undertaken by a vassal to show loyalty and humility before his lord.

Dauphin
Title of the heir to the French throne.

Unsurprisingly, the Scots did not comply and in August Henry invaded with an army of more than 15,000 (unusually large for the time), and he was obliged to borrow money in order to support them, which was risky given his fragile political and financial situation at the time. Militarily, however, he was assisted by the defection of George, earl of Dunbar (see page 82). In the event, the English met with very little resistance and reached Leith (near Edinburgh), where there were various diplomatic exchanges with Robert III's envoys, but no decisions were reached and by the end of the month the English army returned home having gained little. It is unclear why Henry did not seek more decisive action, but it is likely that he was concerned about the safety of the English throne and did not wish to be away for too long a period at this early stage in his reign. Indeed, as he returned with his army from Scotland, he learned of Owain Glyndwr's rebellion in Wales and travelled quickly to put down this more serious threat.

SOURCE

9 This is a tomb with a likeness of Henry IV. It was created at some point between c1408 and 1427, as tomb effigies were sometimes created prior to the death of the person they were for. Henry IV was buried, according to his wishes, in Canterbury Cathedral and this life-size likeness was placed on his tomb on the instructions of his widow, Joan, the dowager queen.

Poor relations with Scotland continued for the rest of the reign, with various attempts at diplomacy, chequered with border raids and bursts of fighting. It was not until 1402 that more decisive action was taken by the English, when the earl of Northumberland, George of Dunbar and Henry Hotspur defeated a Scottish raiding force at Homildon Hill, taking various important captives, including four Scottish earls. Paradoxically, however, this incident was to cause problems for Henry IV's security, as the ransoming of captives proved a matter of contention between the Percies and the Lancastrian king, being a factor in causing Hotspur's rebellion in 1403 (see pages 81–82). Henry IV himself never fought in Scotland after his abortive mission of 1400, as he was first preoccupied with the threat from Wales, and later became too ill.

Scrope's rebellion and the breakdown in Henry IV's health

The financial burden of defence and the perceived financial mismanagement of the king's government seem to have been the primary causes for a rebellion involving Richard Scrope, the Archbishop of York, as well as a number of noblemen such as the earl of Northumberland, the earl marshal Thomas Mowbray and Lord Bardolf in 1405 (see pages 52). The revolt was put down effectively, and Scrope was executed in June of that year on Henry's orders, an event which was widely criticised at the time. This criticism was partly on the grounds of the archbishop's popularity, according to the admittedly pro-clerical chronicler, Thomas Walsingham. More important, however, was the fact that it was extremely unconventional for a senior clergyman to be executed. Significantly, Henry's old friend, Thomas Arundel, tried to intercede for Scrope and was assured that his fellow priest would not be executed, but the king then betrayed this trust and had the archbishop killed anyway, despite the chief justice refusing to act in the matter. According to historians A.L. Brown and Henry Summerson, this action was uncharacteristic of the king, and they argue that this action was a result of the strain the king was under at the time. Whatever the cause of Henry's actions, for many moralists the almost immediate decline of the king's health, which began within days of the execution, was a sign of divine retribution for the death.

ACTIVITY
KNOWLEDGE CHECK

Threats to the Lancastrian regime, 1399–1405

1 Which factor(s) do you think was (or were) most decisive in causing Hotspur to rebel against Henry IV in 1403? Write a paragraph giving an explanation of your reasoning.

2 In your opinion, was Henry IV wise or foolish to order the death of Archbishop Scrope in 1405? Explain your answer using plenty of detailed evidence of how this action impacted upon the security of the Lancastrian regime.

3 Why do you think Hotspur's death was considered more acceptable than Scrope's by the wider population?

How did Henry IV survive the threats to his regime?

By late 1405, then, Henry IV was in a difficult position. The cost of defending his realm on so many fronts, Welsh, Scottish and French, was extremely high. The parliaments of 1404–5 became particularly hostile towards his government and the ongoing need for heavy taxation to meet these threats. His enemies were also assisting each other materially in a way that was very dangerous for England. In 1405, for example, the French sent 2,500 troops to support Welsh forces led by Glyndwr against the Lancastrian king. Nonetheless, despite a breakdown in his health and numerous threats to his throne, Henry remained king until his death from natural causes in 1413. This success was largely the result of a range of strategies he adopted to secure his throne throughout the reign. One important factor was his significant use of international diplomacy, especially in relation to marriage. Important events included the following:

- The marriage in 1402 of his daughter, Blanche, to Ludwig, the eldest son of Rupert, **Count Palatine of the Rhine** and **King of the Romans**, which gave Henry IV an important ally in a strategically important location in relation to France.

- The marriage of another daughter, Philippa, to the king of Norway, Sweden and Denmark in 1406. This gave him important support in his relationships with the Hanseatic League.

- His own marriage to Joan of Brittany, the widow of the duke of Brittany and daughter of Charles II of Navarre. This marriage, which occurred in 1402, created an alliance with Brittany, an area which throughout the 14th and 15th centuries declared its independence from the kingdom of France. Ultimately, Henry's hopes that the Bretons would support him against the French were disappointed, but, in the short term, the match must have had influence on the French and strengthened Henry's hand.

- Informal alliances formed with the king of Portugal in 1400 and the king of Castile in c1402 by inviting them to become members of the Order of the Garter. This was a chivalric organisation founded in 1348 by King Edward III and was an attempt to recreate the legendary ideal of King Arthur and the Knights of the Round Table. In essence, important individuals both from within England and from the continent were invited to join as a mark of their status and military prowess. This organisation had considerable international status during the 15th century, and the granting of membership was used as an important diplomatic tool by English kings in the late medieval period.

These alliances were undoubtedly influential, but most probably the most significant factor in ensuring Henry's security was the removal of alternative claimants to the throne. Whether or not Henry had Richard murdered, there can be little doubt that the former king's death was extremely convenient for his successor. Similarly, Henry was astute enough to keep the young earl of March closely guarded to prevent attempts to kidnap him and use the child as the figurehead of a rebellion against Lancastrian rule. He also successfully put down Hotspur's rebellion in 1403, literally killing any hope of a revival in opposition from the Percy quarter. By 1405, it can be argued, Henry was king largely because there were no viable alternative options and he had an adult male heir who was clearly militarily able, which was important for the future security of the realm.

> **A Level Exam-Style Question Section B**
>
> 'Richard II lost his throne because of his pro-French sentiments, whereas Henry IV maintained his government mainly because of his hostility towards France.'
>
> How far do you agree with this statement? (20 marks)
>
> **Tip**
>
> *Consider a range of factors that led to Richard's downfall, including his attitude towards noble landholding, not just his foreign policy.*

> **KEY TERMS**
>
> **Count Palatine of the Rhine**
> This title was held by a prince of the Holy Roman Empire who held an area of land (called a palatinate) on either side of the River Rhine, with a capital in Heidelberg (in modern-day Germany).
>
> **King of the Romans**
> This title was used by the heir apparent to the throne of the Holy Roman Empire.

> **A Level Exam-Style Question Section B**
>
> How important were Henry IV's efforts to secure international diplomacy for the stability of his reign up to 1405? (20 marks)
>
> **Tip**
>
> *Consider not only Henry IV's marriage, but the matches made for his daughters, as well as his use of the Order of the Garter. Remember, 'importance' will be assessed by a comparison with other factors.*

Conclusion

The collapse of Richard II's rule and the relatively small level of support given to the anointed king are indicative of the essential fragility of the concept of personal, hereditary kingship in the later Middle Ages. While virtually all contemporary commentators accept that having a king was necessary for the political system to function, the success of Bolingbroke's *coup d'état* in 1399 indicated that, for a king to keep the throne, it was necessary for him to function predominantly within the framework of established tradition and the law. When the stability of land ownership, in

A Level Exam-Style Question Section B

How significant was the challenge posed by Henry Percy's rebellion in 1403 to the stability of the Lancastrian regime? (20 marks)

Tip

Make sure you discuss alternative events of the early reign that might be equally, if not more, significant, such as hostility from France and Scotland, or Scrope's rebellion.

particular, was threatened, then the nobility's loyalty to the king became much less marked. This is not to say that Richard was cast aside without misgivings, and certainly Henry faced considerable threats in the first six years of his reign. Crucially, however, he established himself as the only viable option as leader; he was an adult male, he had a significant claim to the throne, and he was an able military commander with significant support from his Lancastrian retinue. Major opponents to the Lancastrian regime also usually ended up dead, notably Richard II, Henry Percy and Archbishop Scrope, although Henry cannot be seen as fully responsible for all their untimely ends. His financial situation was undoubtedly precarious because of the high military costs of hostilities from the Welsh, Scottish and French. It was, however, less hazardous than it could have been because of the significant income he gained personally from the Duchy of Lancaster. The Welsh and Scottish threats may also, surprisingly, have assisted him to some extent; many people must have been aware that, if England descended into internal rebellion or civil war, there were enemies close by who were all too ready to take advantage of the situation. Henry's other great advantage was his offspring, most notably Henry, Prince of Wales, who by 1405 had reached manhood and had already proven himself an able fighter and leader. While the king and his eldest son had a very fraught relationship, there can be little doubt that the presence of an able future king reassured the nobility, making the Lancastrians much more secure.

ACTIVITY
SUMMARY

Was Richard II entirely responsible for his own downfall?

1 Copy and complete this table.

Date	Event	Evidence that Richard II caused his own downfall	Evidence that others caused Richard II's downfall
1377–81	The king's minority	Richard cannot be held responsible for decisions taken at this time, as he was a child and not in control.	Richard's government was unpopular at this time, imposing heavy taxes and faring badly in the war against France.
1381	Peasants' Revolt	Richard improved the situation in the short term, by bravely meeting the rebel leader, Wat Tyler, and getting the crowds to return home.	The rebels blamed the king's 'evil councillors' (leading nobles who advised the king) for ruling the country badly. After the rebellion, these leading figures encouraged Richard to punish the rebels, which may have increased cross-class resentment.
1386	'Wonderful Parliament'		
1388	'Merciless Parliament'		
1397	Richard arrests the duke of Gloucester and the earls of Arundel and Warwick and they are either tried in parliament or die beforehand.		
1399	John of Gaunt dies and his son, Henry Bolingbroke, is disinherited.		
Summer 1399	Henry Bolingbroke invades England and Richard is imprisoned in Pontefract Castle.		

2 Using the information in your table, together with any further research you have done in relation to this topic, write an answer to the question: 'Was Richard II entirely responsible for his own downfall?' Remember to include detailed knowledge to support your argument and to structure it in paragraphs.

Why was Henry IV successful in maintaining the Lancastrian regime to 1405?

3 What were the key justifications Henry Bolingbroke used to support his usurpation of the throne in parliament?

4 a) List all the threats Henry IV faced to the security of his throne up to 1405.

   b) Colour-code these threats into three categories:

   i) Threats from foreign enemies (in this context, this includes Wales and Scotland).

   ii) Financial difficulties.

   iii) Threats from internal rebellion.

   c) For each of these threats, try to find at least one way in which Henry IV dealt with the problem.

The crises of 1399–1405

 WIDER READING

Bremner, I. 'The Reign of Richard II, 1377 to 1399', BBC History (2011). Available online at www.bbc.co.uk/history/british/middle_ages/richardii_reign_01.shtml#fourteen

Cavendish, R. 'Archbishop Scrope and Thomas Mowbray Executed', *History Today* 55:6 (2005). Available online at www.historytoday.com/richard-cavendish/archbishop-scrope-and-thomas-mowbray-executed#sthash.yttHtDew.dpuf

Hughes, J. 'Richard II: King of the White Hart', *History Today*, 62:12 (2012). Available online at www.historytoday.com/jonathan-hughes/richard-ii-king-white-hart

Mortimer, I. *The Fears of Henry IV: The Life of England's Self-Made King*, Vintage (2008)

Saul, N. *Richard II*, Yale University Press (1999)

Saul, N. 'Richard II: Author of his own Downfall?', *History Today*, 49 (1999). Available online at www.historytoday.com/nigel-saul/richard-ii-author-his-own-downfall

Saul, N. 'Richard II and the Crisis of Authority', *BBC History* (2011). Available online at www.bbc.co.uk/history/british/middle_ages/richardii_crisis_01.shtml

Stratford, J. 'Richard II's Treasure: the riches of a medieval king' (2007). Available online at www.history.ac.uk/richardII

Tuck, A. 'Richard II (1367–1400)', *Oxford Dictionary of National Biography*, Oxford University Press (2004). Online edn, Jan 2009 www.oxforddnb.com/view/article/23499

3.4

Henry V and the conquest of France, 1413–21

KEY QUESTIONS

- What was the significance of renewing war with France and the campaign of 1415?
- How important was the challenge from Lollardy and the royal response to heresy?
- Why was Henry V so successful in his foreign policy and what were the consequences of this success?

INTRODUCTION

Henry V is perhaps the most famous of the 'good' late medieval kings. For many contemporary and later writers, he was seen to exemplify two key qualities of a monarch: he was a very able military commander and warrior, and he was pious. His orthodox religious outlook was put to the test early in his reign, when he faced a rebellion inspired by a **heretical** group known as the Lollards, which he suppressed with great firmness. Henry has been immortalised thanks particularly to Shakespeare's depiction of him as the wild young man 'Prince Hal' in the plays *Henry IV Part 1* and *Henry IV Part 2,* who then becomes a mature and serious leader and military commander on his accession to the throne in the next play of the series, *Henry V.* Whatever the accuracy of this dramatisation, there is little doubt that Henry V was phenomenally successful in the Hundred Years War against France, winning a number of highly significant victories, including the Battle of Agincourt and the Siege of Harfleur in 1415. These and other victories led to the Treaty of Troyes (1420), a highly advantageous agreement from the English point of view that made Henry heir to the throne of France. This was a title that passed to his infant son when the king died unexpectedly in 1422. Henry V's French conquests were to shape much of the reign of his son, Henry VI, and the later loss of his territorial gains was highly significant in causing the outbreak of the Wars of the Roses in the 1450s.

KEY TERM

Heretical
In the context of medieval England, heretical beliefs are those that disagree with the established beliefs of the Roman Catholic Church.

WHAT WAS THE SIGNIFICANCE OF RENEWING WAR WITH FRANCE AND THE CAMPAIGN OF 1415?

The significance of renewing the war with France

Henry V's military and political experience prior to becoming king in 1413
Aged 26 when he came to the throne, Henry V's prowess as a fighter owed much to the time in his teens spent in Wales, where he was frequently engaged in battles against the Welsh. He also

1415 – July: Southampton Plot against Henry V fails
August: Henry V invades France
October: English victory at the Battle of Agincourt

1413 – March: Henry IV dies and his son becomes Henry V

1412	1413	1414	1415	1416	1417

1414 – January: Oldcastle leads Lollardy rebellion against the king
April: Parliament passes Statute against Lollards and strengthens legislation against rioting

1416 – August: English make alliance against French with Sigismund, King of the Romans

1417 – August: Henry again invades France
Late: Oldcastle captured, tried and executed

Portrait of Henry V by an unknown artist, painted at some point between 1504 and 1520. It was part of a series of historical portraits of monarchs commissioned either by Henry VII or Henry VIII.

partly ruled in place of the king up until 1411, with parliamentary approval. This group, which included Thomas Arundel, Archbishop of Canterbury, had some success in controlling the crown's finances, and this improved relations with the Commons in parliament especially during much of the rest of Henry IV's reign. Nonetheless, Henry's time as Prince of Wales and heir apparent was not an entirely glorious one. There was a serious breach between Henry IV and his son in 1411, perhaps following a suggestion from the prince's supporters, the Beauforts, that the king should abdicate in favour of his son. There were also differences over foreign policy. Certainly, Henry IV seems to have become angry and resentful concerning his son's use of royal power at this time. From 1411 to 1412, Prince Henry was very publicly excluded from political influence, which was a serious humiliation for him. In September, however, there was a public reconciliation between the two men and, when Henry IV lay dying in March 1413, he gave his blessing and advice to his eldest son and heir.

Background to the 1415 invasion of France

The Hundred Years War began in 1337 during the reign of the English King Edward III, but hostilities had substantially reduced during the reign of Richard II, who adopted a pro-French stance and confirmed this by his second marriage to a French princess. Conflict resumed under Henry IV, with significant levels of piracy on both sides in the Channel, French naval attacks on the south coast of England and land fighting, particularly in the area of Aquitaine. Henry IV's ill-health after 1406, together with financial difficulties and threats from both Wales and Scotland, meant that English royal focus on France during the later years of his reign was relatively muted and the English lost control of some important French territories.

Henry V was keen to regain a number of these losses. Early in his reign, he sent ambassadors to the French king, claiming all territories that were historically regarded as English, or that had been handed over in the 1360 **Treaty of Brétigny** signed by Edward III of England and John II of France. Henry V also asked for the hand of Catherine of Valois, the youngest daughter of the king of France, in marriage, accompanied by a large dowry. These demands were rejected by the French and a number of contemporary accounts describe how French ambassadors

led troops in 1403 against his former ally, Henry Hotspur, who rebelled against the Lancastrian regime, and fought on during the battle despite being wounded in the face. After Henry IV's descent into illness in 1405, his son gained an increasingly important role in governing the realm as part of a council that

---

1418 - July: Siege of Rouen (Norman capital) begins

1420 - May: Treaty of Troyes
June: Henry V marries French king's daughter, Catherine of Valois

1422 - 31 August: Henry V dies. His son, a nine-month-old infant, becomes Henry VI of England.
October: Charles VI, King of France, dies. Henry VI now also becomes King of France.

| 1418 | 1419 | 1420 | 1421 | 1422 | 1423 |

1419 - January: Rouen surrenders
September: John, duke of Burgundy murdered at Montereau

1421 - December: Henry V and Catherine have a son, Prince Henry

and/or the dauphin deliberately chose to insult the English king by sending a box of tennis balls to the royal court, on the grounds that, because of his youth, the king needed toys to play with. In response, Henry prepared a large invasion force during 1414–15.

EXTEND YOUR KNOWLEDGE

Catherine of Valois
Catherine was the daughter of Charles VI of France and Isabella of Bavaria. Little is known of her childhood, although it was probably unhappy as her father suffered from bouts of insanity. Her mother, Isabella, therefore periodically ruled as regent, with varying levels of success. The queen was rumoured to have rejected her daughter and to have taken a number of lovers, although these tales should be treated with caution.

The suggestion of marriage to Henry, Prince of Wales (later Henry V) first occurred in 1409, but the match did not take place until June 1420 following the Treaty of Troyes. Catherine gave birth to Prince Henry in December 1421. By 1422, however, she had been widowed and her infant son became king of England. When her father, Charles VI, died six weeks later the baby inherited the French throne as well. This necessitated two minority councils and resulted in major constitutional crises in both realms.

As a widow, Catherine continued to live in England and her political role mainly involved accompanying her child to various important functions. By 1425, there were scandalous rumours of an affair with Edmund Beaufort, nephew of the chancellor, Bishop Henry Beaufort. Parliament acted against the match in 1427-28, passing legislation which forbade marriage to a queen without consent of the monarch. Despite this, Catherine did secretly marry again, without royal consent. Her husband was Owen Tudor, a Welsh squire considered highly unsuitable in terms of wealth and rank. In 1485, their grandson usurped the throne and became Henry VII, the first Tudor monarch.

Henry's decision to invade France was no doubt spurred on by the fact that Charles VI, who had ruled France since 1380, suffered from an ongoing mental health problem that caused periods of complete incapacitation. Therefore, various royal princes ruled in his place and this caused significant political divisions in the government that Henry hoped to exploit. It should not be assumed that Henry desired a renewal of the Hundred Years War right from the beginning of the reign, but he took a number of diplomatic measures between 1413 and 1415 to isolate France. He may well have regarded attack as an opportunity to prove his worth as a monarch and to silence those who had criticised him while he was Prince of Wales or who continued to regard the Lancastrians as usurpers.

EXTRACT

1 From A. Curry, *Agincourt: A New History* (2006). This is an academic study of the Battle of Agincourt.

The impression one gets is that Prince Henry was 'a rebel without a cause'. The stories of a misspent youth have never been proved, but nor have they been disproved. A lack of application may therefore be a further factor contributing to his reputation towards the end of his father's reign. From his own perspective, he had not been given the role he felt was rightly his. As Prince of Wales he had military experience, but this consisted of small-scale, inconclusive campaigns against guerrillas, the uncertainty of garrisoning, and the constant strain of underfunding. He had not been allowed to flex his muscles against the French, a proper enemy, and he had lost face at home and abroad in his diplomatic and military plans. Furthermore, he had come to adulthood in an atmosphere of fear and insecurity. [During Hotspur Percy's rebellion] in 1403, he had fought against men who had been his friends and mentors. Even in 1412, he suspected men of plotting to prevent his inheritance of the crown. These experiences coloured his own approach to kingship and fanned his ambitions to prove himself and to prove his critics wrong. He was desperate for fame and success and would stop at nothing to achieve it.

Diplomacy and preparations for war, 1413–15

Thanks to his considerable military experience as Prince of Wales, Henry V was already a formidable army commander when he came to the throne. He was also politically astute, using carefully planned diplomatic tactics to secure his kingdom as well as to isolate France:

- He adopted a conciliatory attitude towards the Welsh, investigating complaints of oppression by royal officials there and issuing pardons to some former rebels. This made attacks on the Welsh border less likely in his absence, and also meant that some Welshmen were prepared to fight in the army against the French.

- Early in the reign, Henry took measures to rehabilitate the Percy family, who had fallen from favour during Henry IV's reign owing to Hotspur's rebellion in 1403. The king organised for Hotspur's heir (also called Henry Percy), who was living in **honourable captivity** in Scotland, to return to England and be permitted to inherit his family's substantial estates mainly in Yorkshire, Northumberland and Cumberland, as well as his grandfather's title of earl of Northumberland. Prior to Hotspur's rebellion, the earls of Northumberland had traditionally held responsibility for protecting the border with Scotland and Percy's reinstatement provided greater security in northern areas for England.

- Henry held King James I of Scotland prisoner as he had been captured in 1406 by the English. To some extent this reduced incursions on the northern border. This was particularly important, as France was an ally of Scotland.

- In January 1414, Henry agreed a ten-year truce with the duke of Brittany. Although the king of France theoretically ruled over Brittany, in reality the real power there was the duke. Henry could therefore exploit this truce in order to isolate France and to help prevent Bretons coming to the aid of the French king when he led an invasion there the following year.

SOURCE

2

From a chronicle written by the monk John Streeche and compiled shortly after 1422. It describes the English ambassadors' visit to France early in Henry V's reign. Throughout, Streeche takes a very patriotic and pro-Henrician stance. There are varying accounts of the incident involving the famous French gift of tennis balls to Henry V detailed here. Almost all, however, emphasise that the gift was a calculated insult to Henry and it has been argued (notably by Shakespeare) that this was designed to refer to his supposedly irresponsible and wayward behaviour as Prince of Wales.

King Henry, conspicuous for the nobility of his character, in the second year of his reign sent to France certain ambassadors in state, fittingly caparisoned: a bishop, two learned doctors, and two knights. They met with the king of France and his council to request that a marriage be solemnly celebrated between Henry, king of England, and the noble lady Catherine, daughter of the king of France; but they had only a brief discussion without reaching any conclusion consistent with the honour or convenience of our king, so they returned home. For these Frenchmen, puffed up with pride and lacking in foresight, hurling mocking words at the ambassadors of the king of England, foolishly said to them that as Henry was only a young man, they would send to him little tennis balls to play with and soft cushions to rest on until he should have grown to a man's strength.

When the king of England heard these words he was greatly moved and troubled in spirit; but he addressed these short, wise and honest words to those standing round him: 'If God wills, and if my life shall be prolonged with health, in a few months I shall play with such balls in the Frenchmen's courtyards that they will lose the game eventually, and for their game win nothing but grief. And if they shall sleep too long on their cushions in their chambers, I will wake them from their slumbers at dawn by beating down their doors.'

ACTIVITY
KNOWLEDGE CHECK

Henry V and relations with the French

1 Make two lists: one of Henry V's military experience by the time he came to the throne in 1413; and one of his political experience.

2 Read Source 2. Why do you think some chroniclers and later writers (notably Shakespeare) placed so much emphasis on the alleged diplomatic incident when the French sent Henry tennis balls?

In 1415, Henry faced the most serious domestic threat to his throne in the form of the Southampton Plot. This was led by the earl of Cambridge, Baron Scrope and Sir Thomas Grey, who plotted together to kill the king and put Edmund Mortimer, earl of March on the throne instead (see Chapter 1, page 16). This plot certainly involved Scottish and Welsh rebels, as well as Lollards. It was rumoured to have been partially funded by the French in the hope of heading off the projected English invasion. Henry was informed of the plot by Mortimer himself, and so was able to deal with the rebellion swiftly and ruthlessly, meaning that the execution of the rebels provided a chilling warning to other would-be dissidents. The possibility of French support for the rebellion may also have increased the king's determination to pursue his aggressive foreign policy towards France. The planned invasion went ahead in the late summer.

The campaign of 1415

The exact size of Henry's army has been debated, with estimates ranging from around 10,500 to 12,000 fighting men, who were transported in a fleet of ships. His troops began by surrounding the port of Harfleur both by land and sea and placing it under siege. The French initially resisted strongly, but surrendered on 22 September. Although victorious, the English suffered losses not only to the fighting but also because of an outbreak of dysentery among their troops. Henry arranged for the English wounded and sick to be shipped home and he left a large English garrison in charge, to

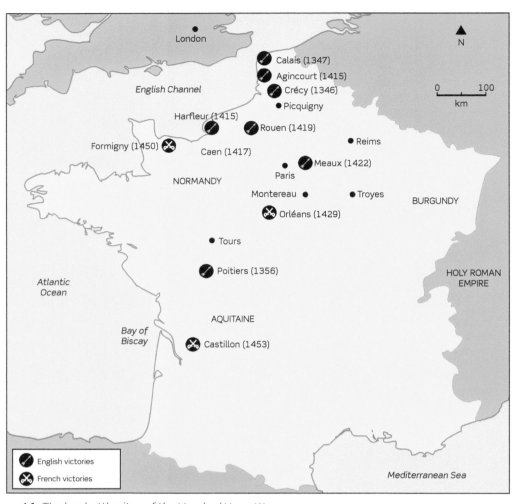

Figure 4.1   The key battle sites of the Hundred Years War.

defend the town against any further attack or resistance. Following this, he led the remainder of his army to Calais, where substantial English garrisons were based.

Henry's decision to march his troops to Calais is a subject of scholarly controversy. Some argue that the king's tactics were foolhardy as his soldiers had to undertake the long journey when they were exhausted. There was also the difficulty that the English would need to cross the River Somme and the French had taken a number of precautions against this. Firstly, the French organised a large army, possibly as many as 6,000 men, to wait at the most obvious ford at Blanchetaque, forcing Henry's troops to march upstream towards Amiens. Secondly, all bridges and crossing points were defended or blocked. Thirdly, the French army tracked their enemy's progress upstream and mirrored it on the other side of the river, which meant that if the English did cross, they were likely to be attacked while still wading through water. Realising the problem, Henry pushed his troops hard and gained half a day's march on the French, finding a causeway (exact location unknown) that had not been protected with stakes like the others, although it had been broken and so required the English army to rebuild it using materials to hand, which was a risky enterprise. Nonetheless, Henry's gamble paid off and by 19 October 1415 the English army had crossed the Somme. This was particularly beneficial as by this stage the possible crossing points in the river had become more frequent, and so the French army had to divide into small groups to protect them all, which meant that they were unable to quickly repel the English. A combination of Henry's determination and quick thinking, together with good fortune, therefore assisted the English at this point. Despite this, English victory was by no means assured. As quickly as possible the French massed their army and the Battle of Agincourt took place on 25 October.

On the day of battle, Henry and members of his household took the central fighting position, while Edward, duke of York and Thomas, Baron Camoys commanded troops to the right and left, respectively. One of the significant features of the composition of the English army in 1415 was the high proportion of archers, trained in the use of the **longbow**, compared to **men-at-arms**. On leaving England, 80 percent of the army were archers and by the time it fought at Agincourt in October, when the army had experienced significant losses because of injuries and disease, the proportion of archers was even higher. Some archers were stationed in front of the men-at-arms to protect them, but most were placed on the sides and were protected by sharp stakes. In addition, a group of highly skilled archers were sent secretly behind enemy lines to attack from the rear. The French, a significantly larger force, drew up their army into three divisions, with the first two divisions on foot and the third mounted. They decided to fight in close formation, a choice of tactic which proved disastrous as the battlefield was relatively narrow, meaning that the French were grouped too tightly and so had difficulty in fighting effectively. Wearing heavy armour on foot was also problematic as the ground was muddy, making it difficult for them to move quickly.

SOURCE 3

A 15th-century illustration of the Battle of Agincourt from the St Albans Chronicle, written by Thomas Walsingham a monk from the Abbey of St Albans (see Chapter 3, page 73). This copy of the manuscript was written in English but illustrated by Flemish craftsmen. Flanders was a major centre of fashionable manuscript decoration in the period.

As battle commenced, the English shot arrows into the French line, provoking some small French cavalry charges at the archers at the sides of the English formation, but these attacks were hampered by the use of stakes protecting the English troops. As the French carried out their main, frontal attack, the English line quickly recovered and the French got into difficulties both because of over-crowding in the line and the highly effective use of bowshot by the English, which killed and wounded many, throwing the enemy into confusion.

The presence of the French cavalry at the back of their formation also hindered their own troops who wished to fall back. English archers, once they had run out of arrows, were ordered to engage in hand-to-hand combat with the enemy. This proved highly successful because they were very lightly armed compared to their adversaries, and so could move much faster.

Towards the end of the battle, Henry feared that the rear of his army was being attacked and that French reinforcements were going to arrive. He therefore ordered that all enemies taken prisoner during the battle should be immediately killed to prevent them giving any assistance to the enemy. For contemporaries, this decision was the most controversial aspect of the battle; taking prisoners was an established military practice in this period and, in particular, it was customary for high-status noblemen to be kept alive if possible, as they could then be used as political hostages and to obtain diplomatic favours in the negotiation of peace, or to gain substantial ransoms. According to the Burgundian chronicler, Jean de Waurin (who was an eye-witness to the battle), many English soldiers were unwilling to kill their prisoners because they did not wish to forfeit the ransom. There was also some criticism of the morality of the order.

EXTEND YOUR KNOWLEDGE

Agincourt and national identity
Before setting out to France, Henry gathered troops for his army from his own and other nobles' retinues, as was usual. All those in the English army, however, had to obey a similar code of discipline and their unity of purpose was represented in the fact that every soldier was required to wear the red cross of St George on his front and back.

KEY TERM

Vanguard
The foremost part of an advancing army or navy.

In the event, the rumoured French reinforcements did not arrive and the English victory was complete. Henry's army sustained relatively few losses, probably in the region of one to three hundred, although there were two high-profile deaths, namely Edward, duke of York (the king's cousin who had led the **vanguard**), and Michael de la Pole, the third earl of Suffolk. The latter had only succeeded to the title weeks before, his father having died at the Siege of Harfleur. The French, by contrast, suffered an extremely heavy death toll. Exact figures are difficult to come by, but they clearly lost thousands of men. The number of nobles who were killed was unusually high owing to Henry's decision to kill those taken prisoner, including 11 magnates, 120 barons and around 1,500 knights. Nonetheless, the massacre of prisoners was not as complete as some chroniclers were to claim, as key figures such as the royal dukes of Orléans and Bourbon were taken alive.

The victory at Agincourt was to ensure Henry V's reputation as a great military leader, both for contemporaries and for subsequent generations. The battle remains the most famous conflict of the Hundred Years War and is sometimes cited as a factor in shaping patriotic English national identity. At the heart of this was the idea that the English were greatly outnumbered, but won against the odds, routing a numerically superior French army because of greater courage, ingenuity and more inspirational leadership. This image of a victorious underdog was first created by medieval English chroniclers, who were overwhelmed by joy at the success and provided highly coloured, one-sided accounts of the battle. In the *St Albans Chronicle* by Thomas Walsingham, for example, a French army of 140,000 faced 8,000 English troops. Such dramatic tales were highly advantageous to Henry V, who depicted his victory as a sign from God that he was not only the rightful King of England, but also had divine approval for his claims in France. These claims were seized upon by later writers, notably Shakespeare; in the play *Henry V* the king heroically dismisses concerns that the English army is too small when speaking to his troops: 'The fewer men, the greater share of honor… We few, we happy few, we band of brothers' (*Henry V*, Act IV, Scene III). Estimates by the historian Anne Curry place the figures at 9,000 English troops versus c12,000 French, statistics highlighting that the victory was certainly surprising, but not as astonishing as earlier accounts would have us believe. Nonetheless, the English faced substantial disadvantages (see Figure 4.2). In the final analysis, it would seem that victory had a great deal to do with Henry's able leadership and the commitment and skill of his men; it was not simply the result of French misfortune or military ineptitude.

ACTIVITY
KNOWLEDGE CHECK

Preparations for war and victories at Harfleur and Agincourt

1 Write a paragraph explaining Henry V's motivations for invading France, explaining which you think was the most significant factor and why.

2 Read Extract 1 (page 90) and compare it to the paragraph you have just written as your answer to Question 1. Is your opinion and that of Professor Curry similar or different? List the ways in which you agree and the ways in which you do not.

3 Read Figure 4.2 outlining the advantages and disadvantages faced by the English army in 1415. Use this to create your own table showing the advantages and disadvantages faced by the French.

Advantages	Disadvantages
• Troops had very recent fighting experience and had survived Harfleur. • Henry V was an inspirational leader, who was good at uniting his forces around him. • The French had a number of commanders, and so lacked the same unity of purpose and leadership that the English had. The French king did not lead the army as he was suffering from ill-health. • Had excellent, well-disciplined archers and the battle plan made strong use of the longbow, placing French troops under continuing heavy fire. • It rained the night before, making the recently ploughed field that separated the two armies very soft underfoot. Henry goaded the French to attack via a charge, which became very difficult for them as it was hard to charge across the mud. • As the French crossed the battlefield through mud, they were struck by arrows, with many being wounded or killed. This caused panic and French soldiers broke rank, which caused disarray in the lines of troops behind them.	• Were very tired after the trip across the Channel and from fighting in the Siege of Harfleur. • Had lost a considerable number of men at Harfleur, not only to battle, but also to dysentery. • Owing to the long march and the fact that little time was allowed for **pillaging** from local villages, it is likely that the English army lacked food by the time they reached Agincourt, • Had a smaller fighting force than the French, although estimates as to the exact difference in size vary considerably. • Had, according to English sources, initially less confidence than the French army because of exhaustion and their smaller numbers. • The French had the prospect of a force coming to relieve them, which the English did not. This meant that any French soldiers taken prisoner by the English were a potential threat, as they might fight against their captors if reinforcements arrived.

Figure 4.2 Advantages and disadvantages faced by the English at the Battle of Agincourt in 1415.

KEY TERM

Pillaging
Looting or plundering; the practice of armies taking food or other goods from the areas they attack or pass through, particularly on their way to and from battle. Often how commanders rewarded and fed their troops.

SOURCE

A description of the Battle of Agincourt by Jean de Waurin. Waurin was from Burgundy and related to a number of the leading noble and influential families there. As a 15 year old, he was in the French camp during the Battle of Agincourt and so was an eye-witness to the fighting. Later in the Hundred Years War, he fought on the side of the English in three battles and he was part of the pro-English faction in the court of the duke of Burgundy. This description is taken from his multi-volume work, the *Collection of the chronicles and ancient histories of Great Britain, now called England*, begun in the mid-1440s and finished in the 1470s. The manuscript was predominantly a collection of the writings of other people, and he was inclined to copy the work of others even when he had personal involvement with the event.

[The]… French had drawn up their battle formations between two small woods, one close to Agincourt, the other by Tramecourt. The place itself was narrow, [thus] greatly favouring the English, while acting very much against the French interest; for the said French had spent all the night on horseback in the rain; their pages, grooms and many others, while exercising their horses, had turned up the earth which had become very soft, so that only with some difficulty could the horses pick their hoofs up from the ground. In addition, the French themselves were so burdened with armour that they could hardly bear it nor move forward…. Together, this weight of armour and the softness of the sodden earth, as has been said, held them almost immobile, so that it was only with the greatest difficulty that they lifted their weapons; to crown all these mischiefs was the fact that not a few [of the French] were worn out by hunger and lack of sleep… Quite a number [of the French leaders]… commanded archers and crossbowmen, but they would not let them use their weapons since the ground was so confined, and there was really only sufficient room for the men-at-arms.

… The king of England ordered… his archers in front of the two wings… and exhorted all his men to fight well and with vigour in his name against the French, so as to secure and save their very lives… Thereupon the English archers… began with vigour to shoot arrows upon the French; the majority of these archers had no armour but were only wearing doublets…with hatchets and axes or, in some cases, large swords hanging from their belts; some of them went barefooted and with nothing on their heads.

The French… drew themselves into rank. The constable, the marshal, the admirals and the other princes strongly admonished their men to fight bravely and valiantly against the English… but the French soon put their heads down… such was the effectiveness of the English arrows, which fell so thick and fast that no man dared to uncover himself nor even to look up… Many of the French were… wounded by the arrows. When they finally reached the English they were… so tightly packed together that they could not raise their arms to strike their enemies, except those who were out in front.

A Level Exam-Style Question Section A

Study Source 4 before you answer this question.

Assess the value of the source for judging how far English victory at Agincourt was the result of the superiority of Henry V's tactics and leadership.

Explain your answer, using the source, the information given about its origin and your own knowledge about the historical context. (20 marks)

Tip

Discuss the reliability of Jean de Waurin's evidence especially carefully in this question, making sure you understand the relationship between the medieval dukes of Burgundy and the king of France before you begin writing.

KEY TERMS

Royal entry [to a town or city]
Medieval monarchs or members of the royal family making a formal entrance via an elaborate procession to an urban centre they were visiting.

Sacraments
In the Roman Catholic Church, sacraments are seven visible rituals which are regarded as revealing and communicating God's grace to believers. The sacraments are: Baptism, Penance, the Eucharist, Confirmation, Marriage, Holy Orders (i.e. the process of becoming a priest, deacon, monk or nun) and the Anointing of the Sick.

Eucharist
'Eucharist' means 'thanksgiving' and is often used interchangeably with the terms 'Mass' or 'Holy Communion'. The celebration of the Eucharist culminates in the priest consecrating (blessing) the bread and wine at the altar, replicating the actions of Jesus at the Last Supper. At the point of consecration, Catholics believe that the bread and wine become the Body and Blood of Christ while retaining the appearance of bread and wine. This spiritual transformation is called transubstantiation. Catholics are obliged to attend the Eucharist every Sunday and on certain other important dates in the Christian calendar, such as Christmas Day.

Penance
Also commonly called Confession and, in more recent times, Reconciliation. During this sacrament a penitent believer confesses his or her sins to a priest, offers a prayer of apology to God, and promises not to sin again. The priest then provides absolution, which is a pronouncement that confers God's forgiveness upon the penitent. The priest may also set a penance to be completed afterwards, for example prayer, fasting or giving money to the poor.

The significance of the 1415 French campaign

Following the English victory at Agincourt, Henry marched his army to Calais, where they then returned across the Channel and proceeded to London. The enthusiasm with which Henry was greeted when he arrived in the capital on 23 November can hardly be overstated and his victory was celebrated by a very carefully stage-managed formal '**royal entry**' to London, involving a large procession, pageants and feasting. According to the *Gesta Henri Quinti*, throughout these celebrations the king appeared detached from the celebrations, a fact the chronicler attributes to his great spirituality. This account provides an example of how chroniclers from the time were almost universal in their praise for the king as a result of his military success.

Henry's victory also brought his reign much greater political stability; his success against the odds was interpreted by many as a sign from God that he was the rightful king and a strong military defender was always far more popular domestically. On a practical level, the victory in France considerably reduced the threat of a French invasion (which had been significant during the reign of Richard II) and of French naval raids on the south coast (a feature of Henry IV's time in power). The fact that Henry was so clearly an excellent defender of the realm meant that parliament was much more willing to provide him with financial assistance. Indeed, modern scholars working on the parliament records for this year regard it as the briefest and least controversial parliament of the century. Before Henry had even arrived home from Agincourt, parliament had met and decided to grant him very generous revenue from taxation, with little requested in return, a rare luxury for a monarch in this period. This was an indication that for much of Henry's reign, parliament was very generous in funding his military campaigns, which assisted him as he prepared for further attacks on France. In addition, following his spectacular success in 1415, there was considerable public support for these endeavours.

HOW IMPORTANT WAS THE CHALLENGE FROM LOLLARDY AND THE ROYAL RESPONSE TO HERESY?

Lollardy and Lollards

In late medieval England, the only established and permitted Christian faith was that of the Roman Catholic Church. A priest and Oxford academic theologian called John Wycliffe had entered into royal service at some time in the 1370s, and appears to have developed an association with John of Gaunt, the duke of Lancaster (Henry V's grandfather). In 1377, Wycliffe was summoned to appear before the Archbishop of Canterbury and other bishops in London, having been charged with teaching on a number of religious matters in a way that contravened official Church teaching. Gaunt supported Wycliffe in this meeting against the senior prelates and the outcome of the event is unclear. Later in the same year, however, Wycliffe's teachings were publicly condemned by Pope Gregory XI, who criticised a number of the views expressed in Wycliffe's theological writings and ordered that the University of Oxford and a number of English bishops should investigate the case, although Oxford in particular proved very hostile to any sanctions made against their scholar. Wycliffe's theology contravened traditional Church teaching in a number of ways, particularly in relation to Church wealth and taxation, and the authority of the pope, and the role of the priest in **sacraments** of the **Eucharist** and **Penance**. Probably thanks to the influential support of Gaunt, Wycliffe himself seems to have escaped substantial punishment or persecution, dying of natural causes in 1384.

Wycliffe had a number of followers at Oxford, but his views quickly spread much more widely across the country, to an audience that crossed the range of social classes. These followers were known as 'Lollards' and they were noted particularly for translating the scriptures into English (at this time, the vast majority of biblical texts were in Latin). Lollardy persisted after Wycliffe's death, as evidenced by the production of English Bibles. A number of these manuscripts were of very high quality, which indicates that the movement had supporters in the higher ranks of society (see Source 5). The contemporary usage of the term 'Lollard' (meaning 'mumbler') is somewhat problematic; it tended

SOURCE 5 This is a section from one of the copies of the Bible in English made by Lollard groups during the late medieval period. The manuscript and its illumination are of high quality. It dates from the first quarter of the 15th century.

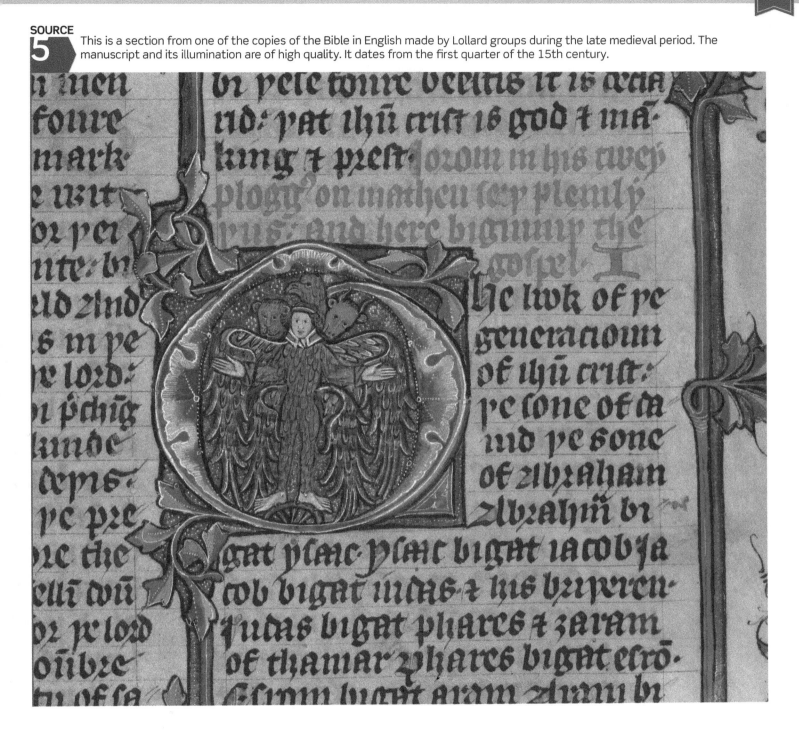

to be used broadly in relation to anyone expressing **anticlerical views**, when in fact not all such commentary was truly heretical. (Heresy, in this context, is strictly speaking a rebuttal of the official approved teaching of the Roman Catholic Church, not merely any criticism of clerics. Contemporaries did not always make this distinction, however.) Additionally, as Lollardy spread, it developed some aspects that were not precisely linked to Wycliffe's writings, although most of the views the group shared had this common heritage.

KEY TERM

Anticlerical views
Criticism of the Roman Catholic clergy, usually in relation to vices such as perceived greed, laziness, sexual immorality or worldliness. This was widespread in the late medieval period. It is important to note that, while anticlerical sentiments could encourage people to adopt Lollard views, not all those who criticised the clergy were in fact criticising Church teaching, rather how some priests were interpreting (or ignoring) it.

Approved teaching of the Roman Catholic Church	Wycliffe views
Doctrine of transubstantiation: the belief that, during the celebration of the Eucharist, the bread and wine used become the Body and Blood of Christ when they are consecrated by the priest.	Argued that no such transformation took place based on the priest's words, with many claiming that transubstantiation could be performed by any good Christian, while some others argued that the role of the bread and wine during services was symbolic only.
Role of the priest in persona Christi *(in the person of Christ) when celebrating the sacraments:* the belief that the priest is Christ himself during sacraments such as when he speaks the words of the consecration of the Eucharist or forgives sin during Confession.	Claimed that the priest remained an ordinary man on all such occasions. Others argued that many of the sacraments, including oral confession, were unnecessary.
Wealth of the Church: Church argued that it could as an institution hold property and wealth.	Argued that the Church should not hold property and wealth.
Temporal (secular) roles of the clergy: the Church allowed priests to hold secular roles, such as being a political adviser to the king or acting as a clerk in the Chancery.	Claimed that priests should not take on 'worldly' roles, but should confine themselves exclusively to spiritual matters.
Use of Latin: all services, prayers and religious texts, including the Bible, were in Latin, the official language of the Catholic Church.	Wanted the Bible written in English and, during Lollard services, great emphasis was placed on reading scripture in English.
Role of the pope as Supreme Head of the Church on earth: the belief that Jesus' disciple, Peter, was the first pope and that subsequent popes are Peter's successors. This teaching stated that (a) the role of pope as leader of the Church is instituted by Christ; and (b) the pope – Peter and his successors – has been invested with the authority to define religious and moral teaching on earth.	Lollards argued that the Church in Rome was corrupt and that the pope should not be regarded as the Head of the Church. This had important financial implications in terms of whether taxes should be paid to the Church in Rome or not, something that had always been a sensitive political issue in England.
Purgatory and prayers/good works for the dead: the Church taught that after death a person's soul could arrive at one of three destinations: Heaven, for those who were in perfect union with God while alive, having fully repented any sins; Hell, for those who were unrepentant; and **Purgatory**, for those who died in friendship with God but who needed to be purified of their sins before entering Heaven. It was taught that people could reduce the amount of time they spent in purgatory by leaving money for charitable works in their wills, or by organising for prayers and Masses to be said for their souls after death.	Claimed that no charitable works or prayers after death had any effect on the destination of souls. Some Lollards also argued that Purgatory did not exist.

Figure 4.3 Orthodox versus Lollard views on key theological issues.

KEY TERM

Purgatory
According to the Catholic Church, after death, souls requiring additional cleansing from sin prior to admission into Heaven go to a place called Purgatory. Here purification is carried out. In the medieval period it was widely believed that this took the form of harsh punishment, notably burning in fire. This teaching, however, was positive in the sense that souls only spent time in Purgatory temporarily, before reaching Heaven.

ACTIVITY
KNOWLEDGE CHECK

John Wycliffe and Lollardy
1 Summarise Wycliffe's background in two sentences.
2 Read the table in Figure 4.3 outlining core Lollard beliefs. Which views do you think were likely to be most popular in the 15th century and least popular? Give reasons for your answer.

The royal response to heresy

John Wycliffe himself had received tacit support from Henry V's grandfather, John of Gaunt, who particularly used Wycliffe's talent for theology to help argue that England should not send money to the pope in Rome, something that had always been politically controversial. The teaching that the pope was not all-powerful, and that kings therefore might not be bound by his decisions, was obviously also useful for monarchs in Europe from time to time. Nonetheless, it was virtually unheard of for any late medieval monarch to support heretical groups openly and the key reasons for this were threefold. Firstly, English kings at this time took a vow at their coronation to protect the Church, and there was a strong contemporary expectation that the king should support the clergy and show himself to be pious. Secondly, the pope in Rome had enormous moral authority in this period and for a king to openly ally himself with those condemned by the Church would be tantamount to political suicide, as the pope could impose an **interdict** that prevented people within the country from receiving certain sacraments of the Church. This made kings highly unpopular and also allowed would-be rebels to claim they were acting with God's blessing in attacking the monarch. Thirdly, the role of the king was regarded in part as a religious one. The coronation ceremony was conducted in a Church and the king took his vows before God. He was anointed with holy oil and blessed by the clergy, who emphasised that this role was divinely ordained. The Church, therefore, though a powerful potential critic of a king, was also a very potent ally and to rebel against God's chosen king was depicted as sinful by **orthodox** clerics.

John Oldcastle and his rebellion against the crown

Sir John Oldcastle had been a campaigner on the Lancastrian side during the rebellion of Glyndwr and had been militarily and politically active in the border area during the 1400s, serving under the future Henry V. In c1408, he made an advantageous marriage which gave him territorial interests in Norfolk, Wiltshire, Northamptonshire, London and Kent. The exact origins of his unorthodox religious beliefs are unclear, but Herefordshire, the county where he grew up, as well as the Welsh Marches were noted for the prevalence of heresy. His strongly unorthodox views were evident in 1410, when he wrote congratulating two individuals in Bohemia who had launched strong opposition to the clergy there. He was called to parliament as a member of the Lords in the same year and was probably responsible for some of the anticlerical legislation proposed at this session. Petitions at this parliament included a request to modify and limit the statute against heretics, making it much harder to prosecute them, and also a proposal to confiscate some Church property. While neither bill was passed, these suggestions caused serious alarm to Archbishop Arundel.

As Archbishop of Canterbury, Arundel had responsibility for ensuring that Catholics within England remained faithful to the official teaching of the Church in Rome. He therefore began a campaign against heresy following the 1410 parliament. For example, on 1 March he ordered the retrial of John Badby of Evesham, who had been imprisoned for extreme heretical views the previous year, and Badby was publicly burned four days later at Smithfield when he refused to **recant**. Henry, then Prince of Wales, showed his support for the action by personally attending the execution, along with his brother, Prince John, and the duke of York. Soon afterwards, a number of Lollards in London were arrested. Arundel's hostility to Oldcastle in particular became evident in April 1410 when the archbishop lodged a complaint against Oldcastle's chaplain, whom he accused of teaching heretical views in various churches in the locality of the Hoo Peninsula. Arundel initially ordered both the chaplain and the churches involved to be placed under interdict, but quickly relented. It is possible that Arundel's lenience in this case was owing to Oldcastle's long-standing association and friendship with the Prince of Wales. Henry appears to have still trusted Oldcastle in military matters, sending him to Burgundy to lead an expedition against the duke of Orléans' troops in 1411, and this may have been a deliberate tactic on the prince's part to ensure Oldcastle was absent from parliament that year and so could not get himself into further trouble.

Arundel seems to have kept Oldcastle's behaviour under close scrutiny in 1413: another of his chaplains, John Lay, was questioned by the archbishop and in May a raid on the workshop of a London illuminator discovered a heretical book owned by Oldcastle himself. By this time, Henry was king and initially seemed keen to protect his former comrade-in-arms, but by August he gave Arundel permission to prosecute. The ecclesiastical court found him guilty. Henry requested that he be given 40 days in the Tower as an opportunity to repent. Oldcastle, however, escaped from prison in October with the help of other Lollards and began to plot against the king.

In January 1414, he led a group of religious dissidents to St Giles' Fields, just north of London. The plan appears to have centred on disguising a number of the conspirators as actors and thus entering Eltham Palace, where the royal family were celebrating the Epiphany (see Chapter 3, page 79). Oldcastle's precise motives for rebellion against Henry V were unclear, but it would appear that his unorthodox religious views were a crucial factor in pushing him towards treason. The rather unlikely aim of the plot, therefore, seemed to be to kidnap the king and force him either to accept Lollard views or to murder him so that Oldcastle could rule in his place. Oldcastle's impression of Henry's traditional religious views was supported by the king's rejection of Lollard-inspired petitions at the 1410 parliament, as well as Henry's willingness to support and witness the burning of the heretic John Badby of Evesham in the same year.

The short-term significance of the rebellion

Clearly Oldcastle's rebellion was concerning for Henry V and his government: it was headed by a former close associate of the king and it occurred early in the reign before the king had time to consolidate his position. Arundel was keen to use Oldcastle's prosecution for heresy as a high-profile example to prevent Lollardy posing a more serious threat to the Church in England, although Henry initially showed inclination to shield his former friend somewhat from the full rigours of the law. This may well have occurred because Henry had a sense of loyalty to the memory of their earlier comradeship in Wales and also out of respect for Oldcastle's abilities as a fighter.

Nonetheless, by escaping from the Tower and plotting against the king, the Lollard knight placed himself in an exceedingly dangerous position. The rebellion itself can be regarded as an early example of Henry's decisiveness and suitability for kingship. The king made careful use of spies and intelligence networks and on 5 January rewards were granted to two men for informing Henry of the plot. This advance notice ensured that the disguised actors were easily captured and the king then proceeded to St Giles' Fields, where the rebel troops were surrounded and overpowered quickly and decisively. This swift action improved Henry's reputation for omniscience and power.

The size and significance of the rebellion is difficult to gauge owing to discrepancies in the primary source material. There were rumours of the involvement of 25,000 Lollards, which some chronicle accounts repeat, but it seems that this was an exaggeration, with only 220 people definitely being known to be involved. Sixty-nine insurgents were convicted of treason, of whom 31 were hanged the next day, with a further seven being both hanged (for treason) and simultaneously burned (for heresy). Oldcastle himself escaped and remained on the run for nearly four years. According to historian C.T. Allmand, despite a number of rebels being executed, Oldcastle's rebellion was not in fact a particularly significant threat to Henry V. Certainly, there is some truth in this view; the plot was ill-conceived and Oldcastle was unlikely to ever receive widespread support. Nonetheless, it is clear that there was contemporary concern about the domestic security of the realm, especially as Henry was about to embark on an invasion of France. This is evidenced by the records of the parliament that was held in Leicester in April 1414, which focused

EXTEND YOUR KNOWLEDGE

Analysing the chronicle accounts of Oldcastle's rebellion
Most contemporary chroniclers regard Oldcastle's rising as highly significant. This is an advantage for historians, as they provide detailed and lengthy accounts of the event. This focus, however, should not be regarded as an indication that the event was enormously politically important for Henry V. Virtually all the chronicles were written by orthodox monks or priests in the Catholic Church, such as Thomas Walsingham, who were utterly opposed to Lollardy. This makes it likely that they place great emphasis on the size and threat of the uprising, as from the perspective of orthodox clerics it was of considerable religious significance.

This is illustrated in the *Gesta Henrici Quinti* ('Deeds of Henry V'), written by an unknown English priest attached to the royal court. The unknown author was clearly well informed and was with the king on the day of the Lollard rising of 1414. He chose this event very deliberately to begin his chronicle, using Henry's victory over the conspirators to prove that God favoured the king, and, by implication, that the Lancastrian dynasty was legitimate. In part, then, the emphasis on the Lollard revolt in this text was a literary device designed to highlight Henry V's role as a virtuous monarch, a point emphasised by the frequent biblical references throughout the text. Indeed, it would appear that the author of the *Gesta* had connections with Archbishop Arundel himself.

on how to combat heresy and lawlessness. Here the 'Statute of Lollards' was enacted, which increased the role of the secular authorities in the investigation and prosecution of heresy. The key terms were as follows:

- All the crown's officers of the judiciary, and especially local Justices of the Peace (JPs), were responsible for providing the Church with more active support in searching out and tackling Lollardy.
- All those convicted of heresy who were handed over to the secular judicial system for execution would also forfeit all their property and movable goods to the crown.

The increased involvement of the state in prosecuting heresy indicates the clear concern that religious dissent was associated with treason. The confiscation of property and goods for convicted heretics not only increased potential income for the crown, but also provided an additional deterrent for would-be Lollards, as it could lead to their family losing position or, in the case of the less socially exalted, even becoming destitute if conviction occurred.

In addition to the Statute of Lollards, the 1411 Statute of Riots was strengthened. This was a piece of legislation designed to give the chancellor and the court of the King's Bench greater powers to take action against criminals who had escaped justice because of failures by local sheriffs and JPs. In particular, a commission of enquiry was introduced, which meant that the personnel of the King's Bench travelled through the country dealing with a backlog of cases. Fines for rioting were also increased.

The long-term significance of the rebellion

After his escape on 6 January 1414, Oldcastle's activities are unclear, with rumours of sightings in different parts of the

In what circumstances were heretics burned alive?
The late medieval punishment for heretics was to be tied to a stake and burned alive, a fate of almost unimaginable horror that has understandably frightened and fascinated people through history. This was the same penalty that could be used against those accused of witchcraft, although it must be emphasised that it is a popular misconception that witch burnings were a routine part of everyday life in medieval England. In reality, such events were rare in the 14th and 15th centuries (the execution of Joan of Arc on charges of heresy and witchcraft being a famous exception), although it became more common in the 16th century.

The burning of heretics was specified in the parliamentary legislation of 1401. Owing to the brutality of the punishment, it was used only as a last resort, in cases of recidivism, that is, when someone had been proven to be a heretic, had been given an opportunity to repent, and had voluntarily chosen to remain loyal to their unorthodox beliefs. Those convicted of heresy were, on a first offence, subject to a variety of punishments, which could include public acts of penance such as public confession in Church, wearing distinctive clothing, whipping or carrying a faggot (a bundle of twigs) through the streets as a sign that should they return to heresy they would be burned.

While heresy trials were heard by the ecclesiastical courts, after conviction the Church handed them over to the secular authorities if execution was deemed necessary, as technically the Church courts could not be involved in ordering the shedding of blood. The temporal as well as the spiritual authorities, therefore, had to agree to the punishment. The case of John Oldcastle was, of course, more complex as he was not only a heretic but also a traitor against the king, the latter also being an offence that warranted the death penalty (usually by hanging).

country. He appears to have inspired loyalty in his friends, as a number of individuals helped him practically during this time, at considerable personal risk. While he was on the run, he may well have endeavoured to conspire with enemies of England, including the Scots and the Welsh, which potentially made him more of a threat to Henry. Nonetheless, there is no direct evidence linking Oldcastle to any further Lollard rebellions, although it is clear that some with unorthodox religious views were at this time dissatisfied with Henry V's government. This was shown most dangerously in 1415, when many Lollards supported a more serious challenge to the king's authority made by the Southampton Plot, led by Richard, earl of Cambridge, Henry Scrope, baron Scrope of Masham, and Sir Thomas Grey. This was more of a threat as it had support from Scottish and Welsh rebels, the earl of Northumberland and his men, and possibly also the French king, who was seeking to divert Henry's attention from the planned invasion of France. Again, however, Henry swiftly defeated the plot (see Chapter 1, page 16), and set sail for France as planned. While this departure may have seemed foolhardy given the obvious domestic unease, it was a gamble that paid off for the king. Henry's personal authority and popularity was massively boosted after the successful French campaigns of 1415, meaning that any attempts to conspire against the king would be regarded very unsympathetically by most people. Indeed, it is notable that one friend who sheltered Oldcastle in August 1415 was pardoned the offence, but another accused in October 1416 was executed, perhaps reflecting a growing feeling of patriotism and loyalty

within the country to Henry V after the Battle of Agincourt. After 1415, there was no further serious rebellion against Henry V, despite his frequent absences from England while fighting in the Hundred Years War.

How significant was the challenge posed by John Oldcastle's rebellion in 1414 to the government of Henry V? (20 marks)

Tip

Ensure that you consider the threat posed by Oldcastle's rebellion in the context of Henry V's imminent departure to France.

What happened to John Oldcastle?

When he was finally captured in 1417 in Montgomeryshire, Oldcastle was probably returning from North Wales, where he is likely to have been meeting with Gruffydd, son of his former nemesis, Owain Glyndwr. This danger should not be exaggerated, as by conspiring with his country's enemies, he lost respect and support within England. Once captured, Oldcastle faced trial in a parliament deeply hostile to the traitor. By this stage, he appears to have lost all sense of personal caution and preached a sermon to the assembled lords, declaring his loyalty to Richard II, whom he claimed was the rightful king and was still alive in Scotland. This speech was the immediate trigger that led to his conviction for treason and execution, and is an important reminder that he was killed as much for his political as his religious loyalties. He was sentenced and then immediately returned to the Tower, where he was dragged through the streets of London to St Giles' Fields, then suspended by an iron chain and finally hanged and burnt simultaneously. His last words, spoken to the knight who lit the fire, were that he would rise again on the third day, a scriptural reference to the **Resurrection** of Christ.

Resurrection
The core Christian belief that Jesus Christ died and three days later rose from the dead, appearing to his disciples on various occasions before ascending to Heaven.

Study Source 6 before answering this question.

Assess the value of the source for assessing the political significance of Oldcastle's 1414 rebellion.

Explain your answer, using the source, the information given about its origin and your own knowledge about the historical context. (20 marks)

Tip

Ensure you answer the question by focusing on the political consequences of the rebellion in terms of national security and the stability of the Lancastrian regime, rather than spending too much time discussing the origins of Lollardy.

SOURCE

6

From the chronicle of Tito Livio dei Frulovisi, *The Life of Henry the Fifth*. Tito Livio was an Italian, who arrived in England in the 1430s and wrote a posthumous account of Henry V's life in c1437. This work was commissioned by Humphrey, duke of Gloucester, who was Henry V's younger brother. Gloucester requested that the work be written after Henry V's death for the purpose of encouraging the new king, Henry VI, to take an interest in war with France.

In the year 1413, on 4 April, the prince who was at that time twenty-six years old was crowned and anointed as Henry V, with all the pomp and ceremony that was customary.

... Then, when affairs had been properly settled in Ireland, Scotland and Wales, Henry decided to win back the kingdom of France which belonged to him by birthright. First, however, he sought advice in all the schools and universities from men learned in divine and human law whether he might justly ask without fear of wrongdoing to seek to gain the crown of France by force of arms. Without exception they all agreed he might pursue this plan.

In the mean time, the heroic King Henry V was concentrating all his resources on preparations for war. His first battle, however, was with heretics and others who were straying from the true doctrines of the Church. For there were at that time in England two knights, Sir John Oldcastle, whom the king himself, before his coronation, had dismissed from his retinue and sent away on account of his heretical views, and Sir John Acton, who was the leader of a sect devoted to a wicked superstition. These men, together with a vast band of followers of similar persuasion, made war against the priests, the Church, the king and the entire kingdom.

The king was at Eltham for the feast of Epiphany when he first heard news of this dreadful crime. He was told that the rebels had already gathered in a field not far from Westminster. The good king, making no public mention of this matter, at once made his way quietly to his palace at Westminster. He summoned thither a large number of men-at-arms who made an assault on the heretics and overcame them almost without a struggle.

The rebels were seized and put to death. The king's men crucified their captives, except for the leaders who were kept in chains for many days and afflicted with the torture they deserved. Thus the first great victory of the prince was gained for Christ and God's Church against evil heretics.

ACTIVITY
KNOWLEDGE CHECK

Analysing contemporary attitudes towards Oldcastle's rebellion and its significance

1 Create a 'Wanted' poster for Sir John Oldcastle in 1417, explaining in detail what his offences were and why Henry V was justified in feeling personally betrayed by this knight.

2 Imagine you are a traditional and orthodox cleric in 1414, and are horrified by Oldcastle's recent rebellion and the growth of Lollardy. Write a letter to Henry V, explaining in detail why this form of heresy is a particular threat to the stability of the monarchy.

3 Make two lists, one of the strengths and the other of the weaknesses of the primary source material that survives for Oldcastle's rebellion.

4 Read Source 6. Tito Livio was a lay person (i.e. he was not a member of the clergy). Why does this make his account potentially particularly valuable in the context of Oldcastle's rebellion?

5 How well informed was Tito Livio on the events of 1414? In your answer, consider the origin, purpose and content of Source 6.

6 Which aspects of Source 6 are likely to be inaccurate, based on your own knowledge of the event?

7 What image is given of Henry V's character in Source 6 and why? Include short, relevant quotations from Source 6 in your answer, as well as considering the source's origin and purpose.

WHY WAS HENRY V SO SUCCESSFUL IN HIS FOREIGN POLICY AND WHAT WERE THE CONSEQUENCES OF THIS SUCCESS?

The importance of the Burgundian Alliance of 1419

The Duchy of Burgundy was a territory between the Saône and Loire rivers, south of Troyes and north of Lyon. In 1361, it passed into the hands of the Valois dynasty, at the time the kings of France.

TIMELINE: THE INVOLVEMENT OF THE DUKES OF BURGUNDY IN THE HUNDRED YEARS WAR

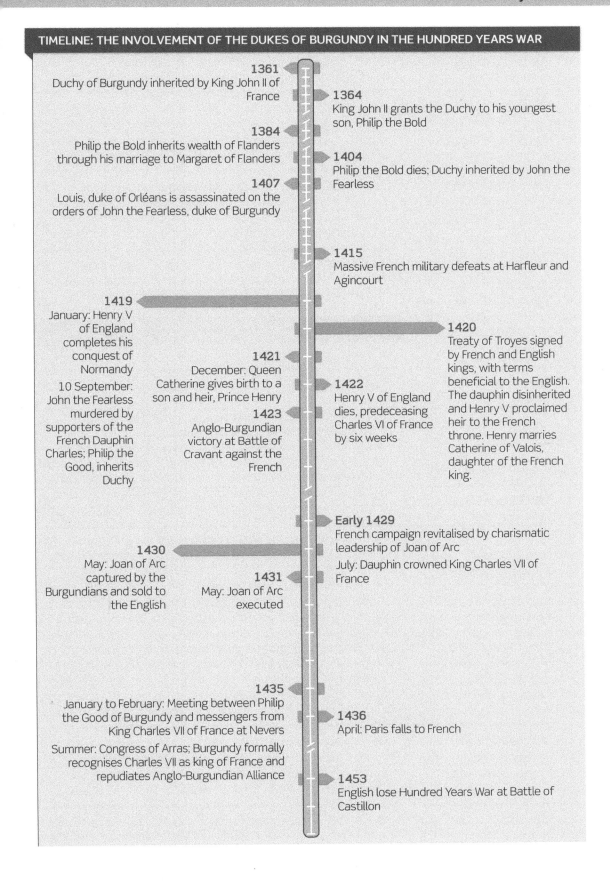

1361
Duchy of Burgundy inherited by King John II of France

1364
King John II grants the Duchy to his youngest son, Philip the Bold

1384
Philip the Bold inherits wealth of Flanders through his marriage to Margaret of Flanders

1404
Philip the Bold dies; Duchy inherited by John the Fearless

1407
Louis, duke of Orléans is assassinated on the orders of John the Fearless, duke of Burgundy

1415
Massive French military defeats at Harfleur and Agincourt

1419
January: Henry V of England completes his conquest of Normandy

10 September: John the Fearless murdered by supporters of the French Dauphin Charles; Philip the Good, inherits Duchy

1420
Treaty of Troyes signed by French and English kings, with terms beneficial to the English. The dauphin disinherited and Henry V proclaimed heir to the French throne. Henry marries Catherine of Valois, daughter of the French king.

1421
December: Queen Catherine gives birth to a son and heir, Prince Henry

1422
Henry V of England dies, predeceasing Charles VI of France by six weeks

1423
Anglo-Burgundian victory at Battle of Cravant against the French

Early 1429
French campaign revitalised by charismatic leadership of Joan of Arc

July: Dauphin crowned King Charles VII of France

1430
May: Joan of Arc captured by the Burgundians and sold to the English

1431
May: Joan of Arc executed

1435
January to February: Meeting between Philip the Good of Burgundy and messengers from King Charles VII of France at Nevers

Summer: Congress of Arras; Burgundy formally recognises Charles VII as king of France and repudiates Anglo-Burgundian Alliance

1436
April: Paris falls to French

1453
English lose Hundred Years War at Battle of Castillon

In 1364, King John II of France granted the Duchy of Burgundy to his youngest son, Philip the Bold. The power of the Duchy was enhanced greatly by Philip's marriage to Margaret, daughter of the count of Flanders, an exceptionally wealthy heiress. When the count died in 1384, therefore, Philip inherited the wealth of Flanders making his territories and power roughly equal to that of the kingdom of France. Later dukes also made highly advantageous marriages, strengthening the power of the region. Consequently, the Duchy's support became an important factor in the Hundred Years War and during the 14th century this allegiance was with the French. However, this altered at various points in the 15th century, which was an important factor in the outcome of battles during the rest of the Hundred Years War.

From 1392 onwards, King Charles VI of France became a serious political problem for his country, as he began to suffer from repeated and prolonged bouts of insanity that seriously impaired the smooth running of government. This crisis led to various dukes, notably those of Burgundy and Orléans, running their own areas as independent states and vying with each other for control at the French court. A particularly bitter struggle developed in the early 15th century between John, duke of Burgundy (Charles VI's nephew) and Louis, duke of Orléans (Charles VI's younger brother), the latter effectively being regent in France at the time. In 1407, matters reached a head and Duke John arranged the murder of the duke of Orléans, who was brutally killed by a group of paid assassins. This led to massive tension between the Burgundians and the supporters of Orléans, called the Armagnacs. Although there was a formal reconciliation between Duke John and Louis' heir, in reality the two men were now at loggerheads and Henry V of England chose to exploit this situation once he came to the throne in 1413, planning an invasion of France in part assuming that the divisions in the French camp would ensure that his enemy was unable to present a united response to the English assault.

Between 1417 and 1419, Henry V conquered Normandy (see page 105) and on 19 January 1419 he was the clear victor, having captured Rouen, the castle that was traditionally held by the dukes of Normandy. To consolidate this victory, he began diplomatic overtures towards both the French royal court and the Burgundians. He was greatly assisted in his negotiations by serious domestic problems faced by the French government as, at this time, Charles VI was incapacitated and there was considerable friction at court between Queen Isabella and the Dauphin Charles, with both seeking to control the kingdom. The duke of Burgundy, meanwhile, resented French claims of sovereignty over his Duchy. Fortunately for Henry, there was deep-seated distrust between the dauphin (who was supported by the Armagnacs) and the Burgundians. This hostility was dramatically increased on 10 September 1419 when the various French parties agreed to meet at Montereau to discuss possible ways to deal with the English. This meeting, however, ended in disaster when John the Fearless was murdered by the Armagnacs in revenge for the 1407 killing of Louis, duke of Orléans. This fresh assassination was carried out by two of the dauphin's men and very possibly with his full knowledge and agreement. Therefore, Duke John's heir, Philip the Good, immediately broke off any negotiations with the dauphin and instead formed an alliance with the English.

The Anglo-Burgundian alliance was crucial to the continuing success of Henry V's conquest of France. Firstly, preventing a French–Burgundian alliance was important because if these two states had united they would have been a formidable force and could have driven the English out of Normandy. Secondly, it meant that Philip the Good supported Queen Isabella's faction in the French court. This group was much more inclined to come to terms with the English and accept a treaty and marriage between Henry V and the French princess, Catherine of Valois. This was crucial as it would unite the English and French crowns and would disinherit the Dauphin Charles, making Henry **regent** and heir to the French throne. This Treaty of Troyes was signed in 1420. To cement the alliance with the Burgundians, Henry agreed to assist Philip the Good in waging war against the Armagnacs, which was to be part of his revenge for the murder of John the Fearless. This agreement was obviously advantageous to the English, as it was clear that Henry would face a considerable challenge to his authority in France from those who wished to see the dauphin crowned.

> **KEY TERM**
>
> **Regent**
> An individual who rules in the place of the monarch if they are a child or are incapacitated.

Henry V's death in 1422 was a serious blow to English unity and strength, particularly as his heir was the infant Henry VI. Nonetheless, the Anglo-Burgundian alliance survived. It met its first major military challenge in 1423 at the Battle of Cravant, when it fought the dauphin's forces who were invading Burgundy. The alliance was successful, despite being significantly outnumbered. Despite this victory, however, the two armies rarely fought alongside in the years that followed, instead tending to operate in separate battles. Nonetheless, the alliance was initially successful in the war against the French Armagnacs during the 1420s, but this altered in 1429 when the French gained new charismatic leadership from Joan of Arc, a peasant girl who convinced the dauphin that she was destined by God to lead his armies to victory. With her guidance, he was crowned King Charles VII of France in Reims and presented a much more serious challenge. From this point on, Duke Philip of Burgundy began to engage in short, regional truces with the dauphin that increased military pressure on the English. The alliance then came under increasing strain in 1434 when Pope Eugenius IV granted formal recognition to Charles VII's kingship. According to the historian A. Compton Reeves, by mid-1434 Duke Philip was seriously contemplating breaking the alliance when the moment was advantageous. In early 1435, Philip met messengers for King Charles at Nevers and came to a preliminary peace agreement with the French. This was formalised in the summer at the Congress of Arras, to which delegates from the English government and the pope were invited, although the English ambassadors withdrew part way through negotiations in protest at the demands of the French that Henry VI should abandon his claim to the French throne. Duke Philip gained considerable territory from the French crown in return for his change of allegiance. This was a critical blow for English hopes of consolidating a dual English and French monarchy, as evidenced by the fall of Paris to the French in April 1436.

1 Create bullet point notes under these headings:

   a) Causes of the Anglo-Burgundian alliance of 1419.

   b) Significance of Philip the Good in the Hundred Years War from 1407 to 1436.

2 Create a 'living graph' with the title 'Changing significance of the threat to the English from Charles Valois (the dauphin and then the French king) in the period 1407–36'. The horizontal axis should have the dates, ranging from 1407 to 1436, while the vertical axis should be scaled from 1 at the bottom to 10 at the top and be labelled 'Threat to English from Charles (VII)'. Label each significant event on the graph with a short note explaining why it had an impact on the political or military situation in the Hundred Years War.

The significance of the conquest of Normandy and the Treaty of Troyes, 1417–20

The military campaign, 1417–19

Following Henry V's spectacular victories in the campaign of 1415, the English government was keen to secure more territory in France. Initially, Henry attempted to obtain territory in Normandy by placing diplomatic pressure on the French, but failed, and so in August 1417 he again led his army to France. He now aimed at the conquest of Normandy and prepared carefully to engage in siege warfare against the heavily fortified French towns, bringing with him several canons as well as an army of c10,500 soldiers. The campaign was well funded, partly through heavy taxation voted through in 1415–16 by grateful and patriotic parliaments and partly via loans. Consequently, the English were a formidable threat and after landing at the Seine estuary on 1 August the army headed straight to Caen, which fell in September after a bitterly fought siege.

Following this, Henry and his lieutenant Richard Beauchamp, earl of Warwick, led a series of assaults on key towns such as Alençon and Domfront while Humphrey, duke of Gloucester, the king's brother, besieged Cherbourg, finally starving it into surrender in autumn 1418. Henry was also careful to set up new administration in Caen to consolidate his control, something which was a recurring theme in the aftermath of his conquests. The king then seized Pont-de-l'Arche on 20 July 1418, a strategic location just a few miles from Rouen, upstream on the River Seine. Rouen was significant as it was the capital of Normandy and through his victories thus far, Henry had cut off any possible support from Paris. He then besieged Rouen from late July to January 1419, the people there enduring extraordinary hunger and hardship in this time. The English fined Rouen heavily, the sum being equivalent to £50,000, which the city took many years to pay. They were also required to recognise Henry as their feudal lord and he took possession of the castle, which was politically significant as it was traditionally held by the duke of Normandy.

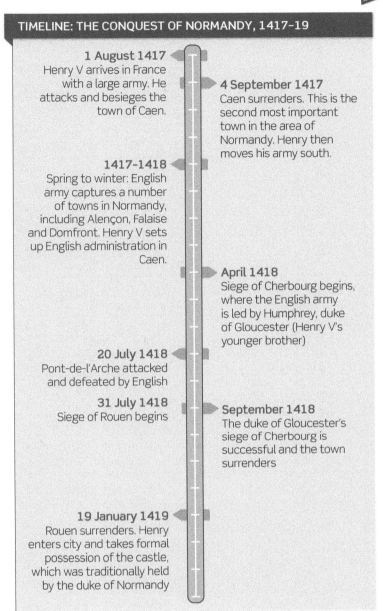

TIMELINE: THE CONQUEST OF NORMANDY, 1417–19

1 August 1417
Henry V arrives in France with a large army. He attacks and besieges the town of Caen.

4 September 1417
Caen surrenders. This is the second most important town in the area of Normandy. Henry then moves his army south.

1417–1418
Spring to winter: English army captures a number of towns in Normandy, including Alençon, Falaise and Domfront. Henry V sets up English administration in Caen.

April 1418
Siege of Cherbourg begins, where the English army is led by Humphrey, duke of Gloucester (Henry V's younger brother)

20 July 1418
Pont-de-l'Arche attacked and defeated by English

31 July 1418
Siege of Rouen begins

September 1418
The duke of Gloucester's siege of Cherbourg is successful and the town surrenders

19 January 1419
Rouen surrenders. Henry enters city and takes formal possession of the castle, which was traditionally held by the duke of Normandy

The impact and cost of success

Henry's victory was devastating for the French and was all the more serious as it had, in part, occurred because the English had been able to take advantage of the ongoing tension between the Burgundians and the Armagnacs which was running high in this period. Henry cleverly manipulated this situation, increasing the distrust between the two factions by negotiating first with one and then the other. The assassination of John the Fearless, duke of Burgundy on 10 September 1419, however, was to prove decisive in securing the Burgundians change of allegiance away from the French towards the English. Taking advantage of this, Henry renewed his demand for the French crown and a marriage with the French princess, Catherine of Valois. On 21 May 1420, Henry V and Charles VI signed the Treaty of Troyes, with the marriage taking place on 2 June. The key terms of the agreement and their significance are outlined in Figure 4.4.

Key terms of the Treaty of Troyes	Political significance
Henry to be recognised as the heir to the French throne until Charles VI died.	This disinherited the Dauphin, Charles, who would not accept this agreement and declared his intention of fighting to make good his claim to the throne. He had significant support from the Armagnac faction and was regarded in the South of France especially as the rightful heir to the throne. Unexpectedly, Henry V predeceased Charles by six weeks, which meant that he was never crowned King of France. This weakened the claim of his son and heir, Henry.
Henry to marry Catherine of Valois.	As any child would be closely related to both English and French monarchs, this would strengthen the Lancastrian dynasty's claim to be rulers of both England and France. A son, Prince Henry (later Henry VI), was born to the couple in 1421. The fact that Henry V died unexpectedly in 1422, however, meant that a baby inherited both crowns. Both countries, therefore, had to be governed by minority councils and this was particularly problematic in France, given that the country was in reality still at war about who should be king.
Until Charles' death, Henry would rule as regent of France, observing French laws and customs and assisted by a council of French noblemen.	Henry was regarded by a significant section of the French nobility as a usurper and so considerable friction developed regarding the governance of French territories.
Normandy was to be regarded as separate from France until Charles VI died, but to be reunited with the kingdom of France when Henry became king.	Henry focused on developing new administrations in his conquered territories and making substantial grants of land there to both his English supporters and to key members of the Norman nobility, whom he wished to conciliate. These grants of land to English nobles meant that many wealthy men in England had a vested interest in ensuring that English holdings in France were maintained. This meant that during Henry VI's reign there were key figures, such as Humphrey, duke of Gloucester, who wished to avoid making territorial concessions to the French.
The English and Burgundians agreed to work together to prevent the dauphin and his supporters challenging the treaty.	During much of the 1420s, this alliance successfully prevented the dauphin seizing power. Henry and the duke of Burgundy fought together in 1420 to consolidate the treaty, taking Sens and Montereau, both towns allied to the dauphin's cause. Consequently, by December 1420 Henry was able to enter Paris and have his French claims publicly acknowledged. The dauphin subsequently sought to invade Burgundy, but was repelled by combined Anglo-Burgundian troops at the Battle of Cravant in 1423. Although the alliance was less secure by the late 1420s, the Burgundians were responsible for the capture of Joan of Arc and it was not until their allegiance changed in 1435 that English fortunes in the Hundred Years War were truly reversed.

Figure 4.4 Terms of the 1420 Treaty of Troyes and their significance.

In addition to the political consequences of the conquest of Normandy in France, Henry V's military campaigns were to have an important impact on English domestic policy. In order to fund the 1417 invasion, parliament had voted through a package of heavy taxation. A number of loans were also used to support the military. Although the general euphoria of 1415 gained Henry great goodwill, these costs were to become politically significant in the longer term, as they placed considerable strain on crown finances. Further taxation and loans were therefore necessary as the war continued and, once the Treaty of Troyes was signed, it became evident in December 1420 that the English parliament did not wish to continue to fund an apparently never-ending conflict that was increasingly being perceived as a French civil war, not simply an English conquest. This reluctance to fund campaigns in France was starting to prove evident in the later parliaments of Henry V's reign, and provoked growing concern about royal finances.

The English parliament's insistence, however, that the king's French conquests should fund further military endeavours was unrealistic; French towns and trade had been badly damaged by the war. Gascony's wine exports, for example, were very substantially disrupted, causing significant economic problems for the region, as well as damaging English interests in Bristol, as this port was heavily involved in the shipping of this product. Large sections of the French population, too, had been displaced and poor weather affected the harvest of 1420, meaning many died of starvation in the following year.

In response to these problems, Henry sought to consolidate his control over France by settling Englishmen there and making them grants of land and titles, often in return requiring military service. According to C.T. Allmand, this appears to have provided improved stability in Normandy. In addition, Henry instituted considerable financial reforms in France in an attempt to remedy its economic difficulties, but these had not had time to reach fruition when he died unexpectedly in 1422.

Henry V, therefore, left his baby son with a complex legacy of a great military reputation to live up to, financial difficulties, and the leadership of two countries, one of which (France) was already in the grip of civil war. The growing lack of English enthusiasm for war, together with its high costs to the English taxpayer and the social and economic difficulties in France has led many historians to argue that the Treaty of Troyes was doomed to failure, and created an impossible situation for Henry V's heir. While C.T. Allmand has suggested that this interpretation is too gloomy, and that in fact contemporaries regarded Troyes as a workable arrangement for much of the 1420s, this view appears less plausible in light of the growing financial burden created by Henry V's conquests and the weakened royal financial situation.

THINKING HISTORICALLY   Change (8a, b & c) (I)

Imposing realities

The shape of history is imposed by historians viewing events with the benefit of hindsight. Therefore, people who lived through the 'history' did not always perceive the patterns that later historians identify. For example, some people living through the Hundred Years War may have understood that great change was taking place, but they would not have been able to understand the massive economic, social and political consequences of events such as the Treaty of Troyes.

Answer the following:

1 Explain why the conversation in the cartoon above would not have happened.

2 Explain why someone living in the 1420s would have been unable to make a judgement about the length or the historical significance of the Hundred Years War.

3 Who living at the present time might regard the conquest of Normandy as an important event?

4 What does this cartoon tell us about the structure of history as we understand it?

Thomas Walsingham describes the death of Henry V and gives his opinion on Henry's character, probably writing at the time of, or very close to, the actual event. Walsingham was a monk, mainly based at the Abbey of St Albans, and did not travel to France during this period, although he appears to have been well informed about many important political events.

In the course of a lengthy illness, which he had contracted as a result of long and excessive labours, the king suffered from an acute fever, with violent dysentery, which so consumed his strength that the doctors dared not to give him internal medicine and despaired of his life.

Seeing that his death was approaching, the king called together his dukes and others who were able to be present, to represent the kingdoms of England and France and the duchy of Normandy. He made wise arrangements, wrote his will and provided for his debts to be paid from his treasuries and numerous jewels.

After taking Holy Communion and the other sacraments that were the duty of a Christian, in true penitence, proper faith, certain hope, perfect charity and right remembrance, he gave up his soul to his creator on the last day of August, after he had reigned for nine years, five months and fourteen days.

King Henry V left no one like him among Christian kings or princes: his death, not only by his subjects in England and France, but in the whole of Christendom, was deservedly mourned.

He was pious in soul, taciturn and discreet in his speech, far-seeing in counsel, prudent in judgement, modest in appearance, magnanimous in his actions, firm in business, persistent in pilgrimages and generous in alms; devoted to God and supportive and respectful of the prelates and ministers of the church; war-like, distinguished and fortunate, he had won victories in all his military engagements. He was generous in constructing buildings and founding monasteries, munificent in his gifts, and above all pursued and attacked enemies of the faith and the Church.

… All the French who had experienced the English king's just and prudent rule, after such a turbulent and dishonest tyranny, mourned for him with great lamentations. The people of Paris and Rouen, who honoured Henry's body in lawful funeral rites and gave him manifold offerings to the best of their powers, offered huge sums of gold to have his body buried in France as a sign of their respect and as a unique way of consoling themselves.

ACTIVITY
KNOWLEDGE CHECK

Henry V's death and legacy according to Thomas Walsingham

Read Source 7.

1 Write down five words that do *not* appear in the source to describe Henry V's character as Walsingham saw it.

2 Why did Thomas Walsingham choose to emphasise Henry's piety in this passage? List as many reasons as you can think of, explaining each one fully.

3 Why is there an emphasis in this source on the reaction of the people of France to Henry's death?

4 How plausible do you think this account of Henry's character is? Refer to the origin, purpose and content of the source, as well as your own knowledge.

A Level Exam-Style Question Section B

'Henry V's main aims throughout his life were the same as his father's.'

To what extent do you agree with this statement? (20 marks)

Tip

Note that this question refers to Henry V's life, not his reign; in other words, it is asking you to not only discuss the time when he was king, but also his actions and personality while he was Prince of Wales.

ACTIVITY
SUMMARY

The significance of renewing war with France and the campaign of 1415

1 Write notes explaining how Henry prepared for war with France in 1415 under these headings:

   a) International diplomacy.

   b) Maintaining law and order at home.

   c) Financing the army.

The Lollard threat and the royal response

2 Create a timeline of events from 1400 to 1417, giving details of Oldcastle's association with the Lancastrian regime, his rebellion and its aftermath.

3 What was the significance of the royal response to the Lollard revolt of 1414? Write a paragraph answering this question, outlining what Henry V and parliament did, and explaining which of these actions was the most important.

Henry V's military campaigns against France and reasons for their success

4 To what extent was Henry V responsible for victory at Agincourt? Write a paragraph answering this question, giving detailed evidence to support your opinions.

5 Write out the key terms of the Treaty of Troyes (1420) and next to each term write down the potential problems that this would cause.

WIDER READING

The Agincourt 600 website provides a number of easily accessible and valuable articles on the battle and its aftermath: www.agincourt600.com

Allmand, C.T. *Henry V*, Yale University Press (1997)

Allmand, C.T. *The Hundred Years War: England and France at War c.1300–c.1450*, Cambridge University Press (1988)

Barker, J. *Agincourt: The King, the Campaign, the Battle*, Abacus (2006)

Cavendish, R. 'Joan of Arc born at Domremy', *History Today*, 62:1 (2012)

Cavendish, R. 'The Duke of Orléans is ambushed', *History Today*, 57:11 (2007)

Curry, A. *1451 Agincourt: A New History*, The History Press (2006)

Curry, A. *Essential Histories: The Hundred Years War*, Osprey (2002)

Curry, A. *The Battle of Agincourt: Sources and Interpretations*, Boydell (2009)

Given-Wilson, C. *Chronicles: The Writing of History in Medieval England*, Hambledon Continuum (2004)

Hudson, A. and Kenny, A. 'Wyclif [Wycliffe], John [called Doctor Evangelicus] (d. 1384), theologian, philosopher and religious reformer', *Oxford Dictionary of National Biography*, Oxford University Press (2004). Available online at: www.oxforddnb.com/view/article/30122

Kightly, C. 'OLDCASTLE, Sir John (c.1370–1417), of Almeley, Herefs. and Cobham, Kent' in Roskell, J.S., Clark, L. and Rawcliffe, C. (ed) *The History of Parliament: the House of Commons 1386–1421*, Boydell and Brewer (1993). Available online at: www.historyofparliamentonline.org/volume/1386-1421/member/oldcastle-sir-john-1370-1417

3.5 Renewed crises and challenges, c1449–61

- To what extent did key personalities of Henry VI's reign affect the governance of England from 1449 to 1461?
- Why did a rebellion occur in England in 1450 and what was its significance?
- Which leading member of the Yorkist faction was the most responsible for Henry VI's downfall?

INTRODUCTION

In a century noted for the eccentricity of its politics, the reign of Henry VI arguably ranks as the most bizarre and disastrous period. He inherited the throne in 1422, aged nine months, and, according to the historian K.B. McFarlane, 'in Henry VI second childhood succeeded [the] first without the usual interval'. Henry's youth created the need for a council to govern in his name throughout his minority but, much to the concern of the nobility, as the king reached the age of maturity, he appeared unwilling or unable to take on the responsibility of government. Clearly mentally unstable, Henry developed into a man who was easy to manipulate, apparently at times incapable of making firm decisions and an indifferent warrior. The contrast with his father could hardly have been more complete. In these circumstances, it is unsurprising that those close to the king, notably his wife Margaret of Anjou and a number of noblemen, were to gain increasing influence over Henry and that this was liable to become unpopular. This discontent most dramatically demonstrated itself firstly, in 1450, during a popular uprising led by a man called Jack Cade, which was in part a response to the disastrous losses in France, and, secondly, in the outbreak of a series of violent conflicts often described as 'the Wars of the Roses', which included the 1461 Battle of Towton. This was the bloodiest conflict ever to be fought on English soil, leading to thousands of deaths and the emergence of a new royal dynasty – the House of York.

TO WHAT EXTENT DID KEY PERSONALITIES OF HENRY VI'S REIGN AFFECT THE GOVERNANCE OF ENGLAND FROM 1449 TO 1461?

The personality of Henry VI

Owing to the deaths of Henry V and Charles VI in 1422, Henry VI inherited the titles of the English and French thrones. During his childhood, however, both countries needed to be governed by

1450 – English loses Gascony and Normandy. Duke of Suffolk murdered.
June: Act of Resumption
Summer: Jack Cade's rebellion

1453 – 17 July: English defeated at the Battle of Castillon and lose all territory in France except Calais. Duke of Somerset arrested.
August: Henry VI suffers total mental collapse
13 October: Henry VI and Margaret of Anjou have a son, Prince Edward

1450	1451	1452	1453	1454	1455

1451 – Parliamentary bill requesting Richard of York recognised as heir presumptive. Bill rejected and MP imprisoned.

1452 – Richard, duke of York meets royal forces at Dartford

1454 – March: Duke of York made Protector of the Realm
December: Henry VI recovers and reverses some arrests made by the duke of York

1455 – May: First Battle of St Albans. York victorious.

separate councils of adult noblemen, who would make decisions in place of the king. Unsurprisingly, this made Henry's reign in both countries politically vulnerable. Given this, many hoped that the young king would prove himself to be an active and decisive ruler. These expectations were to be unrealised. Usually, a monarch was deemed to have reached the **age of majority** at around 14 or 15 years and so it is often from c1437 that Henry's adult reign is dated. In reality, however, it is unclear exactly when, if ever, the king took over genuine control from his advisers.

KEY TERM

Age of majority
The age at which someone is considered to have reached adulthood and, in this case, is able to take on their inheritance as ruler.

EXTEND YOUR KNOWLEDGE

The situation in England and France during the minority of Henry VI

The size of the territory conquered by Henry V made it difficult to govern effectively from across the Channel and the French were understandably unenthusiastic about paying taxes to the English crown. The dauphin also became increasingly determined to regain his inheritance, which had been lost through the 1420 Treaty of Troyes. When French military morale was revived through the endeavours of Joan of Arc in 1429, therefore, he was crowned as Charles VII, King of France. English dominance in France was severely weakened in 1435 by the breakdown in the Anglo-Burgundian alliance, as the duke of Burgundy signed a new agreement with Charles VII called the Treaty of Arras. In the following year, the French recaptured Paris. By the 1440s, the ongoing expense of war and its apparent futility had disillusioned a number of leading English noblemen as to the desirability of maintaining Henry V's territorial gains in France.

Henry VI: saint or sinner?

The majority of contemporary and modern commentators agree that Henry VI was a disastrous king, being militarily inept, physically and mentally feeble, indecisive, easily influenced and a poor judge of character. It became increasingly evident during the reign that Henry had very little military interest or capability and did not take any active role in leading his men into battle. He had inherited none of his father's charisma or authority over men and seemed to be very easily influenced by others, something that was heavily criticised by contemporary commentators. It was also noted that he was often poorly dressed (very unusual in a king) and appeared to take little interest in the normal noble pursuits of the day, such as hunting, feasting, jousting, sports or fashion. While these matters might initially appear unimportant to a modern audience, for contemporaries it was considered extremely worrying that the king did not behave according to the social norms of his class. The fact that Henry dressed unimpressively in public was also problematic as sumptuous clothing was considered an important display of wealth, status and power both at home and in terms of diplomatic negotiation with foreign nations. Henry's lack of the usual royal extravagances of luxury clothes and jewels highlighted the uncomfortable truth that the royal finances were in a poor state. Henry V had spent a great deal of money on war and left his son with little hard cash, and Henry VI was so ineffective and unimpressive a ruler that he found it difficult to persuade people to give him credit or to support him with taxation.

There have been different interpretations of the reasons for this inability to govern effectively. Some contemporaries argued that Henry made a poor ruler because he was unconcerned with worldly matters as he was intensely spiritual. The king appears to have been personally devout, and spent a considerable amount of time in prayer. His interest in the Church was evidenced by the fact that he personally set up two institutions for educating future priests: Eton (founded in 1440) and King's College, Cambridge (founded in 1441). The main contemporary source for this assessment of Henry's character was a work by John Blacman, called the *Compilation of the Meekness and Good Life of Henry VI*. Blacman had the advantage of knowing the king personally between 1444 and 1461, and also used a number of eye-witness testimonies to the king's behaviour during the period 1461–71 from individuals such as Bishop Waynflete and the royal chaplain, William Kymberley. Nonetheless, the accuracy of his assessment of Henry VI's character can be questioned. Blacman was himself a priest and relied for much of his evidence on other priests, making a bias towards spiritual concerns almost inevitable. Indeed, a focus on the world to come was something Blacman was particularly admiring of, as he himself had previously written a devotional work on the importance of

1458 – March: 'Loveday', public display of reconciliation between Lancastrians and Yorkists, ordered by Henry VI

1460 – June to July: Battle of Northampton. Henry VI captured.

October: York enters parliament seeking throne but is denied. Act of Accord passed, making York heir apparent.

December: Battle of Wakefield. Richard of York killed.

| 1457 | 1458 | 1459 | 1460 | 1461 | 1462 |

1459 – Autumn: Battles of Blore Heath and Ludford. Yorkists flee the country.

November: 'Parliament of Devils'. York, Warwick and Salisbury convicted of treason and sentenced to death in their absence.

1461 – March: Battle of Towton. Yorkists victorious. Henry VI, Margaret of Anjou and Prince Edward flee. Edward of York proclaimed King Edward IV.

abandoning unspiritual matters and focusing entirely upon Christ. He regarded many of Henry's political failings as spiritual virtues, for example regarding his disregard for personal display through clothing as a sign of his devotion to God.

EXTRACT

1 Historian Colin Richmond provides an assessment of the limitation of the medieval political system when dealing with a deeply inept monarch. From the *Oxford Dictionary of National Biography* (2008).

The speed with which the English were removed from Normandy in 1449–50, after an occupation of thirty years, followed by the equally dramatic extinction of four centuries of English rule in Gascony, had a traumatic impact. Who was responsible for so great a disaster? The answer late twentieth-century historians wholeheartedly agree upon was not available to mid-fifteenth-century politicians, or at any rate was not pronounceable by them. To stand up in parliament and say it was all the fault of Henry VI was not only impossible because political courtesy forbade it; because political rhetoric did not include it, it was not even contemplated. Politicians had been thinking that the king was an ass ever since Henry had first demonstrated his asininity over a decade previously, but the current vocabulary of politics did not enable them to give such a thought expression.

In 1471, Henry died in the Tower of London, probably as a result of murder by supporters of the Yorkist usurper, Edward IV. After this, a religious cult developed around Henry. It was claimed that people who prayed to Henry after he had died had miracles performed for them, which according to the Catholic Church is a sign of sainthood. For obvious reasons, Edward IV sought to suppress such claims, which were probably inspired not only by popular devotional practice of the day, but also by Lancastrian supporters who wished to cause political problems for Edward IV.

When the Yorkists lost power in 1485 and Henry Tudor came to the throne, the political landscape changed again. The Tudor claim was via the Lancastrian line, and so Henry VII had an interest in promoting the sainthood of his uncle, Henry VI. Consequently, at the end of the 15th century Henry VI's reputation was rehabilitated and the **hagiography** of his life developed substantially, building on the work of John Blacman. This was part of the Tudors' official campaign to have Henry VI **canonised** as a saint by the pope in Rome. Although ultimately unsuccessful, this campaign was to have a considerable influence on later interpretations of Henry VI's reign, the most famous being William Shakespeare's depiction of him as a devout and peace-loving man, who was religious but unsuited to the role of king.

KEY TERMS

Hagiography
The biography of a saint, holy man/woman or ecclesiastical leader. In the medieval context, it tends to focus on the miracles performed by a particular individual, who is considered a saint by the Roman Catholic Church. These sources can contain valuable information, but are necessarily one-sided in their views, and so need careful analysis in order to be used profitably.

Canonise
The official process by the Roman Catholic Church by which certain individuals are recognised as saints after their death. As well as living a particularly holy life, the person to be canonised as a saint must have performed recognised miracles after death for those who pray to them.

EXTEND YOUR KNOWLEDGE

The cult of Henry VI
Tudor propaganda supported the 'cult' of Henry VI. Henry's body was buried in St George's Chapel in Windsor, and large numbers of people began to visit the grave seeking miracle cures. Henry VII sought to capitalise on this and made plans to move the tomb to Westminster Abbey, although this did not occur. Nonetheless, many Londoners seem to have been enthusiastic about the cult of Henry VI, as evidenced by archaeological finds. These include around 500 pilgrim souvenirs, which were usually small, mass-produced badges purchased after visiting the tomb. There are a number of late 15th- and early 16th-century accounts of miracle cures, particularly for children.

While Tudor propaganda was clearly massively influential, it is important to note that Henry VII built on popular interest and enthusiasm for the 'martyred' king, rather than creating it entirely. There are accounts of people seeking cures via the intervention of Henry VI from the reign of Edward IV onwards.

Unsurprisingly, over the centuries most modern scholars have disagreed with this saintly interpretation of Henry VI's personality. The influential historian John Watts, for example, has argued that Henry was an exceptionally ineffective and inane king, who can be considered more as a vacuum than a personality. Watts argues that Henry's helplessness presented the ruling elite with a considerable political problem. Indeed, his argument highlights the level of respect for hereditary monarchy and the political status quo among the nobility generally, but suggests that the medieval system of government simply could not function for a long period of time without an active monarch, which is why the country eventually descended into civil war. Other scholars, however, attribute more personality to Henry, albeit a very flawed one. Bertram Wolffe, for example, has emphasised that Henry VI was a far more morally imperfect character than traditionally believed, who did play some active role in government. To a certain extent, he is supported in these views by Ralph Griffiths, who emphasises that Henry was not totally uninvolved in government, at least prior to his breakdown in 1453.

While historians like Wolffe and Griffiths are critical of Henry VI, they have recognised that he faced considerable difficulties in his reign, which would have severely tested a much more-able man. These problems are important to consider when evaluating the king's personality and are listed below:

- Henry VI followed an exceptionally successful father, Henry V, who had unusually high levels of military success against France and political authority at home. For both contemporaries and later commentators, the contrast between the two monarchs increased the impression of the inadequacy of Henry VI.

- The Treaty of Troyes (1420) left Henry VI with an extremely complex legacy, leaving him as monarch of both England and France. In France, the situation was made especially fraught by the fact that many people did not accept his claim to the throne, instead supporting the claim of the dauphin (later crowned Charles VII).

- Henry V's military campaigns had been very expensive and so his heir inherited a difficult financial situation. Even at the end of Henry V's reign, parliament was beginning to complain about the costs of maintaining English claims in France, so it is unsurprising these problems intensified quickly after 1422.

- Henry VI inherited the English throne at the age of nine months, and the French throne six weeks later. In both his realms, therefore, there had to be governance by a minority council for a long time before he came of age (usually around 15 years in this period). The nobles governing in the young king's name in both countries disagreed on important points of policy and in England there was extreme hostility between some of the king's main councillors. Henry VI, therefore, never had a living example of how a monarch should manage advisers, nor was he ever accustomed to seeing a court functioning normally.

EXTEND YOUR KNOWLEDGE

Kings and the medieval age of majority

Although aristocratic boys were deemed to have reached their majority at around 15 years, as they could be married at this time, in reality this was still a very young age to manage the political complexities of ruling a kingdom. Even extremely active and able monarchs, therefore, such as the 14th-century King Edward III, did not really take control until the age of 17. It is therefore highly unlikely that any youthful monarch would be completely in charge until their later teens. In Henry VI's case, some contemporary assessments indicate that he was never truly able to take political control. This makes it hard to judge how much involvement he had in decision making, although once he was an adult king he was legally responsible for the actions of his government. When reaching an assessment of Henry's personality, therefore, historians generally focus on the period from the late 1430s to 1453, as this is the period when the king was adult and had not suffered a complete mental collapse.

In addition to these circumstantial difficulties, Henry suffered from a hereditary mental illness that had also afflicted his maternal grandfather, King Charles VI of France. This appears to have been a lifelong problem, with a number of contemporary commentators suggesting that the king was a 'fool' or 'idiot', and that he never really fully took control from his advisers, even as an adult. In the 1450s, his health deteriorated and he suffered periodically from complete mental collapse, which left him unable to respond to any stimulus, sometimes for over a year. These bouts of insanity caused political crises and left the king severely weakened in authority even when he regained some of his faculties.

ACTIVITY
KNOWLEDGE CHECK

The personality of Henry VI

1 Create lists under these headings:

   a) Arguments and evidence that Henry VI was deeply religious, but impractical

   b) Arguments that Henry VI was entirely inactive

   c) Arguments that Henry VI had some active role in politics in the 1440s and 1450s.

   Give as much detail as you can.

2 Summarise the key personality flaws of Henry VI in no more than 20 words.

The personality and influence of Margaret of Anjou

In contrast to the apparent saintly imbecility of Henry, his wife Margaret stands out in contemporary literature as an unusually ferocious and vengeful woman. Before assessing the queen's character, however, it is important to understand the controversy that surrounded her betrothal to Henry, as it explains why she was regarded from the outset of her marriage with great hostility by English commentators.

Following considerable struggle in France in the early 1440s and a number of English defeats by 1444, a group of Henry VI's closest advisers had lost their enthusiasm for continued hostilities. At the forefront of the movement towards negotiated peace were Edmund Beaufort, duke of Somerset, and William de la Pole, duke of Suffolk. To this end, Suffolk arranged a two-year truce with France in 1444 at Tours. This was extremely controversial, not least as the king's uncle and heir presumptive, Gloucester, strongly favoured continued military endeavours in France. The key terms of the agreement at Tours were as follows:

- Henry VI was to marry Margaret of Anjou, the niece of Charles VII of France.

- No dowry was to be provided for Margaret, as was customary, and the English had to pay for the entire cost of the wedding, which involved a very substantial financial outlay. This especially infuriated Gloucester.

- England was to surrender the area of Maine to France at the end of the truce. It was recognised that this concession would be extremely unpopular in England, as the territory was valuable and had been hard won. Therefore, this element of the arrangement was kept secret, with the intention of only making it public when lasting peace had been secured.

In 1445, therefore, when the 15-year-old Margaret became queen she entered a royal court where a number of noblemen, notably Humphrey of Gloucester, were actively opposed to her marriage and the treaty it sealed, regarding it as highly dishonourable and unpatriotic. Consequently, she was naturally inclined to seek support and friends in the more pro-peace faction at court, led by Somerset and Suffolk. This helped to confirm her reputation as a queen who promoted factionalism and who interfered in politics.

The long-standing image of Margaret as a vicious, strident and domineering woman is partly the result of the prejudices of medieval English chroniclers, who were extremely hostile towards her on the grounds of her nationality and sex. Misogynistic attitudes towards women exercising authority generally, and particularly over their husbands or in political matters, were widespread and there is a considerable body of literature and legislation in this period that sought to limit the role of women and ensure they remained subordinate to men in general and their husbands in particular. Foreign queens, too, were often in an exceedingly difficult position with regard to their loyalties; on one hand, a woman was supposed to support her husband and her adopted country, while on the other, she was expected and trained by her own family and court to act effectively as an envoy abroad after her marriage, promoting the interests of her place of birth.

SOURCE 1

This passage from Aristotle's famous work, *The Politics and the Constitution of Athens*, was written in the 4th century BC. It discusses the perceived problem of women having a role in government and having too much influence over husbands who were political leaders. Aristotle's works were highly influential throughout the medieval period.

In those states in which the condition of women is bad, half the city may be considered as having no laws. And this is what actually happened in Sparta [an ancient Greek state]; the legislator wanted to make the whole state hardy, and he has carried out his intention in the case of men, but he has neglected the women, who live in every sort of intemperance and luxury. The consequence is that in such a state wealth is too highly valued, especially if the citizens fall under the dominion of their wives... What difference does it make whether women rule, or the rulers are ruled by women? The result is the same... The influence of... women has been most mischievous... We are... considering what is right and wrong, and the disorder of women... not only gives an air of indecorum to the constitution considered in itself, but tends in a measure to foster avarice.

Therefore, a French woman acting as the power behind the throne was unlikely to be popular in England in the 15th century, during one of the most violent and fraught periods of the Hundred Years War.

Nonetheless, like most others of noble birth in the court of Henry VI, Margaret cannot be acquitted of self-interest and factionalism. She actively opposed York and, later, Warwick, and from 1453 onwards clearly sought to control the king, seeking the regency for herself. Her protectiveness towards her young son and his claim as heir presumptive was understandable, but it is not clear whether, before the late 1450s, York was actually seeking to replace the young prince in the line of succession: he did agree to make a number of submissions and oaths of loyalty to the child. It is true, also, that Lancastrian troops became notorious for looting, murder and riot after victories on the battlefield, and this was an important factor in Henry VI's waning support – from Londoners especially. Margaret also encouraged her husband to agree to vengeful acts, notably the complete disinheriting of the heirs of York, Salisbury and Warwick at the 1459 'Parliament of Devils' (see Chapter 2, page 54), which again increased tensions between the two sides. All in all, the Shakespearean image of Margaret as the 'She-Wolf of France' reflects 15th- and 16th-century prejudices against a foreign queen, but most likely encapsulates some of the reality of her personality and behaviour.

The impact of Henry VI and Margaret of Anjou on the governance of England, 1449–61

The period 1449–61 was a particularly disastrous one in English history and the personalities of Henry and Margaret were significant in shaping this time. An area where Margaret was alleged to have considerable influence was in the important relationship between the king and Richard, duke of York. York was a key figure in this period; indeed, from the death of Humphrey, duke of Gloucester in 1447 until the birth of Prince Edward in

SOURCE 2

This is a fairly common image found in medieval art. It shows a woman beating a man (probably her husband) with her distaff, a type of spindle for weaving regarded at the time as a symbol of the female domestic role. The pictures were apparently designed to satirise women who exercised control over their husbands, and the men who allowed them to do so.

1453 he was heir apparent to the throne. According to chroniclers such as Jean de Waurin, Margaret deliberately sought to isolate York and to stop him having a say in government, as she favoured his enemies at court, Somerset and Suffolk. Contemporary historians attribute Margaret's actions largely to her desire to discourage English attacks on France, with accusations that she used her influence to have York removed from his post as military commander in France, in favour of Somerset. The fact that Somerset then went on to preside over a series of devastating defeats for England in the Hundred Years War lent weight to the widespread suspicion that she was deliberately excluding York to further pro-French policy in government, although these allegations were probably exaggerated in the extreme.

Margaret's influence over the English surrender of Maine

In March 1448, Maine had been surrendered to France as agreed under the terms of the Treaty of Tours. This was massively unpopular in the country at large and Henry appeared reluctant to make the final handover, but he was placed under considerable pressure from the French king's envoys as well as from his wife. In this matter, Margaret was in fact behaving as might be expected; her marriage to Henry had occurred to confirm the Treaty of Tours, and it was considered usual for a foreign queen to use her position effectively as an ambassador for the country of her birth. Indeed, had Margaret not sought to persuade Henry to keep to the terms of the treaty, she would have been betraying her own family in France in a very unusual way. Nonetheless, contemporary English chroniclers were highly critical of this action, because of the unpopularity of the surrender, alleging that she tormented the malleable king day and night with her continual nagging on the subject. This undoubtedly added considerably to her unpopularity. The extent to which Margaret was really responsible for the handover remains a moot point, as historians are divided on how far Henry VI was an active force in the 1440s, with some, like John Watts and Christine Carpenter, arguing that the king was an entirely negligible force with no will of his own. It must be emphasised, however, that Margaret was not alone in pushing for an acceptance of the treaty, as Somerset and Suffolk also backed the agreement.

Nonetheless, it is clear that Margaret was firmly allied to the faction at court led by the dukes of Somerset and Suffolk and, as news of defeats in France continued between 1450 and 1453, her popularity suffered accordingly. Her childless state was also a cause of criticism until 1453, when she fell pregnant and in October gave birth to a male heir, Prince Edward. Although this should have been a cause of great rejoicing, the occasion was marred by the fact that by this time Henry VI had fallen into a type of coma and was unable to recognise the child (see Chapter 2, page 57).

Henry's mental incapacity was a major challenge for the medieval political system, as well as for Margaret personally. There was clear tension over who should govern in Henry's stead. The queen apparently argued that she should be made regent, although official records of this request do not survive and so our knowledge of her exact demands are dependent on a piece of private correspondence recalling the events of parliament. Her suggestion that she should govern were opposed by parliament, no doubt on the grounds both of her sex and nationality, as well as her allegiance to the unpopular Somerset faction. In March 1454, York was instead appointed and this was a worrying development for Margaret, who feared that he would take advantage of the situation to try to disinherit her baby son. York placed Somerset in prison during his period as Protector and Defender of the Realm, further isolating the queen and ensuring she felt extremely vulnerable.

Henry VI's recovery during Christmas 1454 must have come as a great relief to Margaret, both for personal and political reasons. In February 1455, Richard of York was formally relieved of his duties as Protector of the Realm. Quickly, the factions allied to Somerset and the queen were rejuvenated and the first blows of civil war came in May 1455 at the First Battle of St Albans, where York, supported by the Nevilles, took up arms against Henry VI, Somerset and the Percies. This battle was a resounding victory for the **Yorkists**, with Somerset being killed and branded a traitor. The winners also captured the king and escorted him to London. Richard and his supporters emphasised heavily in their subsequent publicity that the Yorkists were loyal subjects who only wished to rid the king of 'evil councillors'. A carefully stage-managed ceremony took place on 25 May at St Paul's Cathedral, whereby Henry was reinstated as king and the Yorkists took vows of loyalty to him, but it was clear that Richard's supporters now intended to control the feeble monarch. Therefore, key political appointments were given to supporters of Richard, including the significant military role of Captain of Calais being granted to Richard Neville, earl of Warwick. The parliament of July was supportive of these measures and by November 1455, as Henry's health again deteriorated, York was reinstated as Protector of the Realm.

Throughout all of this, Margaret of Anjou remained hostile to York and contemporaries argued that she sought to undermine his position as far as possible. In this she was aided by the fact that Richard lacked determination in his actions; as the historian Anthony Pollard has pointed out, during his periods of political ascendancy York often failed to consolidate his position entirely and in 1455 he did not completely rid the royal government of the queen's **Lancastrian** supporters. By February 1456, this group ensured that Richard of York was removed from his role as Protector of the Realm. Margaret seems to have been a particular focus for the heirs of those who had supported and died for Henry VI at the First Battle of St Albans. There was an attempt at reconciliation between the two sides, however, in 1458, when a public ceremony of reconciliation was organised in London, called 'Loveday'. During this, the capital's inhabitants were treated to the rather odd sight of the queen walking arm-in-arm with York and the earl of Salisbury walking with the new duke of Somerset (son and heir of the Somerset killed at the First Battle of St Albans). The participants then attended a religious ceremony at St Paul's in an attempt to show contrition and a love of peace. This has been viewed by most historians as occurring at the king's instigation and being a reflection of his spiritual, unworldly and rather impractical outlook on medieval politics. Certainly the professed reconciliation was short lived and the two sides were soon preparing again for battle, with the king's forces marching against York at Ludford Bridge (Shropshire) in October 1459. Learning of the size of the army opposing him, York and his allies fled in the middle of the night and went into exile.

KEY TERMS

Yorkist
A person who supported Richard, duke of York, and later his son and heir Edward, earl of March who later became King Edward IV.

Lancastrian
A person who supported the Lancastrian king Henry VI and Margaret of Anjou. Yorkists and Lancastrians were the two sides in the Wars of the Roses.

When assessing Margaret's role in the politics of 1456–59, it is important to take into consideration these three difficulties with the source material and subsequent interpretations of her actions:

- The 15th-century English chronicle accounts are all hostile to her, and make considerable play of her 'unnatural' desire to rule over her husband. Many of these sources were written to support Yorkist claims to the throne after 1461 and need to be treated with considerable caution, but have nonetheless been highly influential for many historians making judgements about the period.

- It can be argued that it is highly unlikely that Margaret alone could have affected any key change in government policy, however weak her husband, as she herself did not command military support. Instead, she provided a useful focal point for those who wished to oppose York.

- There is some historical debate about whether she genuinely wished to make peace with Richard. Traditionally, they have been regarded as sworn enemies, but more recent research has suggested that she in fact tried to present herself in the traditional female role of peacemaker to gain support and that the 1458 'Loveday' processions in fact took place at her instigation as much as Henry's.

Whatever the queen's involvement in Loveday, by 1459 the two sides were fiercely opposed once more. Initially, the Lancastrians appeared in the ascendancy and, when York fled to Ireland in the autumn, the subsequent parliament at Coventry, packed with Lancastrian supporters, was vicious in its revenge against York, Warwick and Salisbury. Named the 'Parliament of Devils', this meeting condemned the leading Yorkists to death in their absence and also completely disinherited them and their heirs. The harshness of the action has often been laid at the door of the queen, with historians such as John A. Wagner viewing the parliament as her act of personal vengeance. It should be borne in mind, however, that if this was the case, she certainly had enthusiastic support from a large following. The session also included all the lords recognising Prince Edward as Henry VI's heir and taking a solemn oath of loyalty to him.

The severity of the action at Coventry was to backfire, making Yorkists eager to regain control in England. York gained considerable military support in Ireland and made plans for a coordinated attack on England with his eldest son, Edward of March and the earl of Warwick. Warwick was an especially important ally given that he commanded very high levels of military support. Warwick and Edward therefore invaded in June 1460, landing in Kent, and were highly successful, defeating Lancastrian forces marshalled by Prince Edward and the queen at the Battle of Northampton on 10 July. They professed loyalty to Henry and claimed only to wish to rid him of evil councillors. For reasons which remain obscure, however, York did not join his allies until September. Significantly, he then quickly began to claim the throne for himself, and while negotiations with parliament were underway Margaret and Prince Edward regrouped with their forces in Yorkshire and planned their next assault. Doubtless much to the dismay of the queen and Prince, parliament agreed to an

Act of Accord in 1460, which disinherited the prince and made Richard the king's heir instead. In response, a large Lancastrian force surprised the duke of York at Sandal Castle and killed him on 30 December. To mock his claims to the throne, they cut off his head and displayed it on the walls of the city of York, wearing a paper crown.

The queen's victory was to prove short lived, however. Yorkist forces were now led by the determined son and heir of Richard, Edward of March. There were a series of battles in 1461 (see Figure 5.1), but the decisive victory for the Yorkists came at the Battle of Towton on 29 March. This led to Edward of March being declared King Edward IV, while Henry VI, Margaret of Anjou and Prince Edward were forced to flee to Scotland.

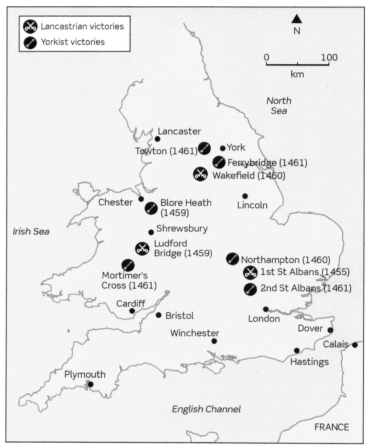

Figure 5.1 Key battles of the first phase of the Wars of the Roses, 1455–61.

Interpreting the personality of Margaret of Anjou

1 Read Source 3. What impression does it give of Margaret of Anjou? How justified is Waurin in his opinion of her?

2 With a partner or as a group, debate the statement: 'Margaret of Anjou was more a victim of circumstance than a perpetrator of hate'.

SOURCE 3

From *The Recueil des croniques et anchiennes istoires de la Grant Bretaigne, a present nomme Engleterre* ('Collection of the chronicles and ancient histories of Great Britain, now called England') by Jean de Waurin. Waurin was related to a number of influential figures at the court of Philip the Good, duke of Burgundy. He had fought on the English side in some battles of the Hundred Years War as part of the Anglo-Burgundian alliance, but his military career ended in 1436. He wrote his chronicle from the mid-1440s until at least 1471 (he died in 1473/4). The work is largely based on other chronicles and histories, which he copied from other authors, and this tendency is evident even when he describes events that he personally witnessed. Here, Waurin describes the duke of York, Margaret of Anjou and Henry.

The very noble duke of York, governor general of the duchy of Normandy and consequently of all the conquered territories, had been appointed to this post by Henry V.

York's duty was to guard and protect this country from the French, our enemies, and during his time in office, he governed admirably and had many honourable and notable successes over the French in different places and in various ways.

Everything he did was highly commendable, not only for himself, but also for the honour and furtherance of the crown of England, and for the exaltation of his master the king, whom he served with due reverence and loyalty, as all noble hearts should serve their sovereign lords.

Nevertheless, in spite of all these qualities, envy, which never dies and is the enemy of all virtue and nobility, reared its head amongst the princes and barons of the kingdom of England, and was directed at the duke of York, who was gaining in honour and prosperity. What is more, he prospered far too much for the liking of those who did not devote themselves loyally to the benefit of the king and his country.

Above all, envy prompted the duke of Somerset, who despised the duke of York and who found a way to harm him. He was well liked by the queen of England, Margaret of Anjou, daughter of Rene, duke of Anjou, and the king of France's niece.

She worked on King Henry, her husband, on the advice and support of the duke of Somerset and other lords and barons of his following, such that the duke of York was recalled from France to England. There he was totally stripped of his authority to govern Normandy, which he had done well and for some time, and despite his having acted commendably throughout the whole English conquest of France.

In York's place, the duke of Somerset was appointed due to the solicitation and exhortation of the said queen and of some of the barons who, at that time, were in positions of power in the kingdom.

It must be pointed out that this change and others that took place in the kingdom were due to the simple-mindedness of the king, who was neither intelligent enough nor experienced enough to manage a kingdom such as England, which had been further enlarged by the conquest of Normandy and other areas of France.

A Level Exam-Style Question Section A

Study Source 3 before you answer this question.

Assess the value of the source for revealing the characters of Henry VI and Margaret of Anjou and the reasons for the downfall of the duke of York.

Explain your answer, using the source, the information given about its origin and your own knowledge about the historical context. (20 marks)

Tip

Make sure you cover both the characters of the king and queen, as well as considering the reasons for York's downfall; it is a common error to focus too much on only one of the key components.

THINKING HISTORICALLY   Cause and consequence (6c)

Connections

Work in groups or individually and answer the following:

1 Read Source 1 (page 114). How are Aristotle's beliefs about women exercising power and influence in government similar to criticisms of Queen Margaret in the 15th century?

2 Look at Source 2 (page 114).

   a) Why is the artist depicting a woman beating her husband? Is he criticising the woman in this image?

   b) How is this image similar to the views expressed by those criticising Margaret of Anjou?

3 Read Source 3. What long-standing ideas about women (for example from classical authors like Aristotle) was Waurin influenced by when writing this account of the queen's behaviour?

4 Why it is important for historians to see these links across time and be able to explain how causal factors can influence situations much later in time?

The duke of Suffolk's downfall in 1450

William de la Pole, duke of Suffolk, had been active as a soldier in the Hundred Years War under Henry V, participating in the Siege of Harfleur, the Battle of Agincourt and the Siege of Rouen. In 1430, he made an advantageous marriage to Alice Chaucer, dowager countess of Salisbury, who was related to the Beauforts. Partially through this alliance, Suffolk rose in political prominence and became a leading adviser to the king during the late 1430s and 1440s, alongside his ally, Edmund Beaufort, duke of Somerset.

By 1450, Suffolk was extremely unpopular, both with the duke of York and among the population at large, for the following reasons:

- He had negotiated the truce at Tours in 1444, which was regarded as shameful because the marriage of Henry to the dowerless Margaret of Anjou was unpopular and the surrender of Maine was seen as unpatriotic.

- In 1449, he was a key advocate of the English attack on Fougères, which triggered Charles VII's retaliatory attacks on Normandy and resulted in massive English defeats. In addition to national humiliation, the loss of Normandy meant that a number of noble families in England lost valuable lands, including Richard of York.

- He was a leading member of Henry VI's government, which was in serious financial difficulty, and there was widespread suspicion of financial mismanagement of the taxes raised for the war in France. It has been estimated that, by 1450, the crown owed around £370,000, an amount equivalent to about £168 million today. York was one of the crown's main creditors, being owed more than £38,000 by this time (about £17 million today). The crown's continued failure to repay York for money he had expended on the country's behalf in France was a major area of contention between the government and the duke and, by the time he left for Ireland in 1449, Richard had been obliged to sell some of his manors as well as one of his most precious family jewels, a collar decorated with white roses (a symbol of the House of York) regarded after the crown jewels as the most valuable treasure in England.

- He was widely regarded as manipulating the king's weak and indecisive personality for his own ends, using his influence to ensure he was given the lion's share of **royal patronage**. Suffolk gained valuable land in the form of the lordship of Guînes (in northern France), was made great steward of England in 1445 and gained other very valuable offices during the 1440s, including the post of chamberlain of England in 1447.

- In 1449–50, Suffolk was accused by the Commons in parliament of arranging a marriage between his son and Margaret Beaufort, Somerset's niece, in order to strengthen his own family's claim to the throne. Owing to the fact that Suffolk was descended from Edward III, this match would have put Suffolk in a very powerful position indeed, allowing him to use his son to challenge Richard of York for the throne of England when Henry VI died. It is unclear if this accusation was justified, but the suspicion of it certainly damaged Suffolk's reputation further.

Complaints against Suffolk therefore encapsulated all that was reprehensible about Henry VI's government: it was financially unsound and corrupt, it was regarded as unpatriotic and militarily weak, especially in relation to the war with France, and the king was regarded as so easily manipulated that he did not recognise potential challenges to his own authority. Suffolk's involvement in the marriage of Henry to Margaret was particularly damaging as much of the anti-French hostility in England during the 1440s and 1450s focused on the queen.

How did Suffolk die?

Given the loss of France, the national desire for a scapegoat and Suffolk's unpopularity, it is unsurprising that he was targeted in the heated parliament of 1450, when he was imprisoned in the Tower on a charge of treason. The Commons in parliament were very hostile to Suffolk, as was the population at large, but Henry VI was reluctant to condemn his former favourite and cleared him of all charges. In order to save Suffolk from further reprisals, however, Henry agreed to banish the duke for five years, beginning on 1 May 1450. Concern for de la Pole's well-being was well founded, as on 19 March he had to be escorted from Westminster at night for his own protection, because an angry mob threatened to lynch him. News of his release increased public hostility, as he remained at his own manor of East Thorp, in Suffolk, for six weeks. During this time, parliament reopened and there were continued calls for the duke's execution. In this atmosphere of hostility, Suffolk left for the **Low Countries** with a small group of loyal retainers. He was intercepted, however, by a **privateering** ship called the *Nicholas of the Tower* and was taken prisoner by its crew. A mock trial followed, the sailors claiming the right to act for the public good. Suffolk was beheaded on 2 May 1450.

What was the significance of Suffolk's downfall for the authority of Henry VI?

Suffolk's unpopularity and his apparent influence over the king were extremely damaging for Henry VI's reputation as a ruler; for contemporaries, it was a clear example of an 'over-mighty subject' controlling an 'under-mighty monarch'. (These terms are discussed in Chapter 1, page 16.) While in the official parliamentary records it was Suffolk who was criticised for being an evil and malicious councillor, it is virtually certain that Henry himself was a subject of popular criticism for allowing the situation to become so uncontrolled. Indeed, there is some evidence that in this period people were prosecuted for complaining about the weakness of the king, for instance describing him as an 'idiot', 'child' or 'fool'.

The growing lack of respect for Henry was shown most dramatically in Suffolk's **judicial murder**, which was a very public affront to the authority of the king. The sailors' claim to be acting for the public good was especially embarrassing for the government, with its clear implication that the king and his advisers were not caring for the realm in the way that they should have done.

> ### KEY TERM
>
> **Judicial murder**
> When a murder takes place, but the killers claim to be acting in a lawful way, often carrying out a mock trial and/or putting the person to death in a way that mirrors executions by the government. In the case of the duke of Suffolk, for example, the victim was beheaded because that was the established punishment for people of noble birth who were executed on the orders of the king.

ACTIVITY
KNOWLEDGE CHECK

The governance of England in the 1440s and 1450s

1 Write down five words to describe each of the following personalities:

   a) Henry VI.

   b) Margaret of Anjou.

   c) The duke of Suffolk.

2 Write a list of causes of Suffolk's unpopularity by 1450. Start with the most significant cause and end with the least significant. Then write a paragraph explaining your decisions.

3 Create a Venn diagram (three overlapping circles) with the following labels:

   a) Unpopularity of Henry VI.

   b) Unpopularity of the queen.

   c) Unpopularity of Suffolk.

   In each circle, write as many causes of criticism for each of these individuals as possible.

WHY DID A REBELLION OCCUR IN ENGLAND IN 1450 AND WHAT WAS ITS SIGNIFICANCE?

The reasons for Cade's rebellion

From May to July 1450, there was a popular and widespread rebellion against Henry VI's government under the leadership of a man called Jack Cade. Little is known about Cade's identity and personal motivations for leading the revolt, but it is likely that he was not of particularly high social standing. He was popularly known as 'the Captain of Kent', indicating the loyal following he developed in that part of the country. He also used the alias of John Mortimer during the summer of 1450, possibly a name chosen in the hope of falsely giving the impression he was a family connection of Richard, duke of York, whose mother had been a Mortimer before her marriage. While the rebels showed support for York and wished for him to take what they argued was his rightful place on the royal council, the causes of the uprising were far more complex and numerous than this motivation alone.

The revolt started in Kent, partly as a result of local grievances against two powerful men in that region, Lord Saye and William Crowmer. Crowmer was the local sheriff and noted for his corruption, while Saye was a man of greater national significance, being the king's treasurer, but also held a local reputation for violence and avarice. A key trigger of the revolt apparently occurred when the corpse of the murdered duke of Suffolk was washed up on the shore in Kent (see pages 118–119) and there were rumours that Saye and Crowmer had threatened widespread destruction in the region in revenge for the attack, although there was in fact no evidence to suggest that the people of the area were complicit in the murder. Whether or not such threats were ever made, many people locally clearly believed them, causing an open rebellion against the government. The fact that the inhabitants of Kent feared these men enough to take the dangerous course of action indicates the very poor level of law and order maintained in the area and the widespread assumption that powerful supporters of Suffolk habitually acted outside the law without redress from the king.

The unpopularity of Henry's government was such that the uprising swiftly spread from Kent to Surrey, Sussex, Middlesex and Essex. Although not personally led by Cade, there were other risings and riots that occurred at the same time in the Midlands, the South and the West, which appear to have been inspired by the widespread insurrection in the South. On 29 June in Wiltshire, for example, Bishop Aiscough of Salisbury, the king's confessor and a leading adviser during many of the unpopular decisions of the 1440s, was dragged from his church during Mass and brutally hacked to death by a mob.

In addition to concerns about law and order, Cade's rebels were also motivated by complaints regarding high taxation to fund the spectacularly unsuccessful war with France. Major English defeats had occurred in 1449–50 that ultimately resulted in the loss of Normandy in the summer of 1450. There was widespread public dissatisfaction with how Henry's government had handled the crisis, with Somerset being particularly blamed as he was in charge of English military operations in France. In addition, Somerset and Suffolk, as well as a number of the king's other leading advisers, were widely suspected of taking advantage of the weakness of the king to obtain an unjustified proportion of royal patronage in the form of land, honour and money. Saye appears to have been particularly unpopular as, firstly, he had become extremely wealthy and powerful under Henry VI and, secondly, he was the king's treasurer (see pages 12–13) at a time when it was widely suspected that financial corruption in government had led to the misuse of taxes intended for the defence of France, thereby contributing to England's defeat in Normandy.

In the early stages of the revolt, most rebels were craftsmen, peasants and some lesser gentry, including many who were prominent and respectable figures in local village life. This indicates that the rebellion was mainly supported by those with a stake in society, who had much to lose by taking illegal action, suggesting that Henry's government was considered completely intolerable by large sections of society. Such rebels were doubtless motivated in part at least by financial problems, which included disruption to trade and a fall in cloth and wool prices that caused a notable decline in income for textile workers and sheep farmers, who made up a significant proportion of the population in the South East.

The events of Cade's rebellion

The rebels marched on London and set up camp just outside the city, at Blackheath on 11 June. Initially, Henry sent a delegation led by Archbishop Stafford and Cardinal Kemp to try and calm the situation, but this was rejected by Cade and so the king marched against the rebels on 13 June, only to find the camp deserted. Later in the month, however, near Sevenoaks, the rebels ambushed a group of the king's men, killing Sir Humphrey Stafford and William Stafford. This was an important act of defiance to Henry's authority and the situation was then made

worse for the government when there was mutiny in the ranks of the royal army, with some of the king's former soldiers rampaging around London attacking the property of those they claimed were 'enemies of the realm'. In an attempt to appease the mob, Henry ordered the arrest of Lord Saye and had him placed in the Tower.

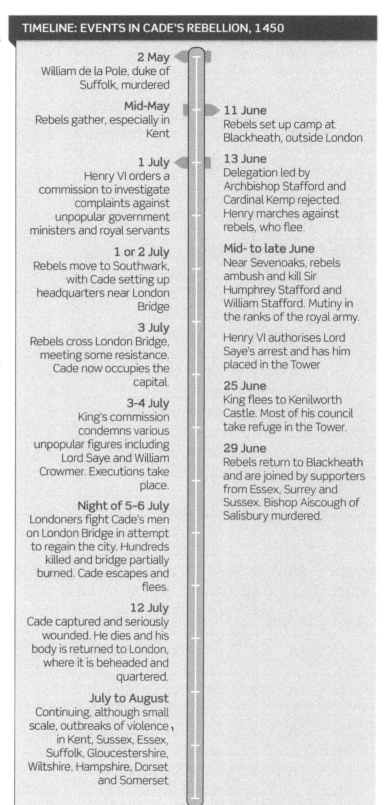

TIMELINE: EVENTS IN CADE'S REBELLION, 1450

2 May
William de la Pole, duke of Suffolk, murdered

Mid-May
Rebels gather, especially in Kent

1 July
Henry VI orders a commission to investigate complaints against unpopular government ministers and royal servants

1 or 2 July
Rebels move to Southwark, with Cade setting up headquarters near London Bridge

3 July
Rebels cross London Bridge, meeting some resistance. Cade now occupies the capital.

3–4 July
King's commission condemns various unpopular figures including Lord Saye and William Crowmer. Executions take place.

Night of 5–6 July
Londoners fight Cade's men on London Bridge in attempt to regain the city. Hundreds killed and bridge partially burned. Cade escapes and flees.

12 July
Cade captured and seriously wounded. He dies and his body is returned to London, where it is beheaded and quartered.

July to August
Continuing, although small scale, outbreaks of violence in Kent, Sussex, Essex, Suffolk, Gloucestershire, Wiltshire, Hampshire, Dorset and Somerset

11 June
Rebels set up camp at Blackheath, outside London

13 June
Delegation led by Archbishop Stafford and Cardinal Kemp rejected. Henry marches against rebels, who flee.

Mid- to late June
Near Sevenoaks, rebels ambush and kill Sir Humphrey Stafford and William Stafford. Mutiny in the ranks of the royal army.

Henry VI authorises Lord Saye's arrest and has him placed in the Tower

25 June
King flees to Kenilworth Castle. Most of his council take refuge in the Tower.

29 June
Rebels return to Blackheath and are joined by supporters from Essex, Surrey and Sussex. Bishop Aiscough of Salisbury murdered.

While not all accusations were true, there certainly had been considerable financial mismanagement in the government in this period and Saye had clearly profited in a very unscrupulous manner during his time of influence with Henry VI.

During mid- to late June, the situation in the South East worsened considerably, with rebels gaining more support. On 25 June, therefore, the king fled to Kenilworth Castle in Warwickshire, while most of his council took refuge in the Tower of London for their own safety. Heartened by their opponents' apparent cowardice, Cade's supporters returned to Blackheath four days later, after which they briefly took and controlled the capital, ordering and carrying out the execution of Lord Saye. Horrified by the situation unfolding, Henry again sought to address the rebels' grievances by ordering a commission to investigate their complaints. By this time, the ranks of Cade's 'army' had been increased by some retainers of the king and his nobles who decided to betray their masters and support the cause. This group, of course, included many men who had fought in the English army in France and were bitter about recent defeats in Normandy, indicating how far Henry VI's government had alienated its own supporters. This rise in numbers also made the rebellion a far more serious threat to law and order, as the men were seasoned veterans, accustomed to looting, which was a mainstay of warfare in the period. Medieval chronicles are notoriously unreliable concerning statistics, but the fact that one contemporary believed Cade's 'army' to be 46,000 strong indicates the perceived danger of the threat, if not the precise figures.

SOURCE 4

The Burgundian chronicler, Jean de Waurin, gives an account of Cade's rebellion, focusing here on the events of 4 July, when Lord Saye was condemned to be executed by the king's commission. According to Waurin, Cade agreed to allow Saye to see a priest but, after the beheading at Cheapside, took vengeance on the corpse.

He despoiled the body of Lord Say and, having tied his feet to his own saddle, dragged him naked, with his arms outstretched, out of Newgate and thence through the Old Bailey, through Ludgate into Watlin Street and thence through Candlewick Street to the bridge. There Jack Cade circled a great stone, beating it with his sword. He put the three heads [of three 'traitors' who had been executed, including Saye] on a tower and dragged the headless corpse of Lord Saye to St Thomas's hospital in Southwark.

In the end, however, it was the prevalence of violence by rebels in the capital that lost the insurgents the crucial support of the Londoners, despite many being deeply unhappy with Henry's government and the country's financial situation. Henry's weakness was shown again, however, on the night of the 5–6 July when it was Londoners, not the king and his nobility, who fought Cade's army on London Bridge, there defeating the rebels decisively.

Grievances of the rebels

The rebels produced a document listing their grievances and presented it to the king, and copies of this manuscript circulated in the south of England (see Source 5). They were keen to emphasise their loyalty to Henry VI himself, adopting the traditional medieval rhetoric that they criticised only the king's

'evil councillors'. Abuses by the king's advisers bore the brunt of the criticism, with Suffolk's supporters at court being described as greedy, jealous and malicious. It would be unduly naïve to assume, however, that Cade's supporters genuinely regarded Henry himself as an unproblematic ruler. A close reading of the text indicates the popular unease with Henry as king and his unpredictable personality, which was too easily influenced by advisers who sought deliberately to mislead him. Comments on Henry's lack of ability and discernment are necessarily veiled to avoid charges of treason, but there is a clear implication throughout the document that the king was a poor judge of character.

SOURCE 5

The rebels' petitions to the king, 1450.

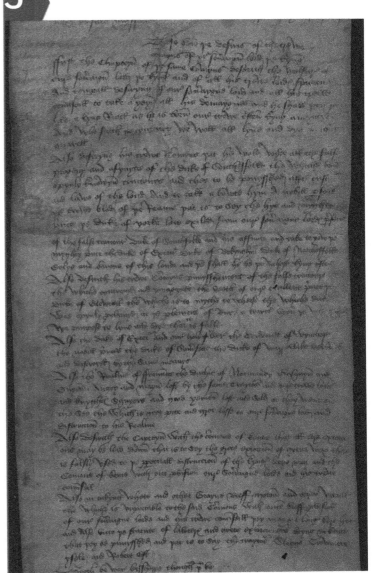

The core complaints of the rebels appear to have fallen into these categories:

- That Richard, duke of York had been excluded from government by a group of the king's less-able and less-honourable favourites, who had slandered York to the king. The rebels also wanted the duke of Exeter, the duke of Buckingham and the duke of Norfolk to form part of Henry's royal council, to ensure that the king received a range of good advice.

- That the king was surrounded by 'evil councillors', in particular Lord Saye, the king's treasurer, Lord Dudley, a diplomat and royal councillor, and Bishop Aiscough of Salisbury. It is notable that many of those targeted had had some involvement with negotiating the truce of Tours in 1444 and the marriage of Henry VI to Margaret of Anjou: Bishop Aiscough, for example, officiated at the wedding itself. There was clearly much anger concerning the loss of French territory, which was directly attributed to the mismanagement of the group surrounding the king (including the recently killed duke of Suffolk).

- That there should be access to the king for the purposes of petitioning and obtaining justice, and that currently a small group was controlling this access for its own purposes.

- That the country was bankrupt and that the government was persisting in financial corruption and mismanagement.

- A breakdown in respect for the law among the nobility and encouraging of Henry to take tyrannical and unlawful decisions. It is clear from the tone of the petitions that rebels were particularly concerned about land and goods being seized unlawfully.

- That there was misgovernment and corruption among royal law enforcement officers in Kent especially.

- That there was a need for law and order to be restored in many areas, that the courts needed to be fair, and that bribery and corruption needed to be stopped.

SOURCE

 A series of extracts from Jack Cade's complaints on behalf of the rebels to the king, 1450. Each complaint is against the king's favourites and leading advisers at court (often referred to as 'they' in the text). The text has been modernised by H. Carrel.

Item. They [i.e. the King's advisers] say that our sovereign is above his laws to his pleasure, and he may make the law and break it as he pleases, without any distinction. The contrary is true, or else he should not have sworn to keep it...

Item. It is to be remedied that the false traitors will suffer no man to come into the king's presence for any reason without bribes where none ought to be demanded. Any man should be able to come to [the king] to ask him grace or judgment in such case as the king may give.

Item. They say that whoever the king decides shall be [considered a] traitor, and whom he wills shall not...

Item. The law serves of nought else in these days but for to do wrong, for nothing is spread almost but false matters by colour of the law for reward, dread and favour and so no remedy is had in the Court of Equity in any way.

Item. We say our sovereign lord may understand that his false council has lost his law, his merchandise is lost, his common people is destroyed, the sea is lost, France is lost, the king himself is so set that he may not pay for his meat nor drink, and he owes more than ever any King of England ought, for daily his traitors about him where anything should come to him by his laws, quickly they take it from him.

Item. They take gentlemen's goods and lands in Kent and call them rioters, and traitors and the king's enemies, but [in reality] they shall be found the king's true liege [loyal] men and best friends with the help of Jesus, to whom we cry day and night with many thousand more that God of His grace and righteousness shall take vengeance and destroy the false governors of his realm that has brought us to naught and into much sorrow and misery.

Item. We will that all men know we blame not all the lords, nor all those that are about the king's person, nor all gentlemen nor yeomen, nor all men of law, nor all bishops, nor all priests, but all such as may be found guilty by just and true inquiry and by the law.

Item. His true commons desire that the king will remove from him all the false... supporters of the Duke of Suffolk and to take about his noble person his true blood of his royal realm, that is to say, the high and mighty prince the Duke of York, exiled from our sovereign lord's person by the noising [malicious rumours] of the false traitor, the Duke of Suffolk, and his affinity. Also to take about his person the mighty prince, the Duke of Exeter, the Duke of Buckingham, the Duke of Norfolk, and his true earls and barons of his land, and he shall be the richest king Christian.

Historiographical debate concerning the king's advisers of the 1440s

Among modern historians, this image of the overwhelming personal greed of leading noblemen has become somewhat unfashionable, being regarded as a rather outdated image of the causes of the Wars of the Roses. John Watts and Christine Carpenter, for example, have emphasised that the medieval political system could not function long term without an active king and that, in fact, given this, many leading noblemen showed considerable restraint and concern for the public good during the long and dysfunctional reign of Henry VI.

This alternative perspective is certainly very valuable and it is important that we are not unduly influenced by the demands of the rebels who were, in part at least, by early July 1450, a mob who were engaged in murder and looting. It is essential to remember that Suffolk and his supporters had the unenviable task of trying to manage two countries, a war and a mentally unstable king, so failure and unpopularity was arguably inevitable.

Nonetheless, it is essential that, in trying to shift the historical view of the period away from an image of personality politics and violent feud, we do not exonerate all politicians in this period. Certainly, Suffolk and Somerset had a difficult task and certainly warmongers such as Humphrey of Gloucester were unrealistic in their demands for continued warfare. However, the exclusion of York from the hub of royal influence and power to Ireland was a demotion, and was seen as such by the Commons. Additionally, greed was quite clearly a major factor influencing many surrounding the king in the 1440s, and the parliamentary move in 1449–50 to the Act of Resumption provides evidence of this.

Aftermath of the rebellion

Initially the king made promises of clemency to the rebels, presumably partly in the hope of encouraging the crowds to disperse. As pockets of resistance continued around the country, however, a firmer line was taken: in 1451, Henry toured areas of unrest to enforce law and order, witnessing a significant number of executions of rebels personally. Cade was mortally wounded during his capture on 12 July, dying shortly afterwards, and his body was returned to London where it met the traitor's fate of being beheaded and quartered. His head was then boiled until only the skull remained, before being placed on a spike and publicly displayed.

The significance of Cade's rebellion

Although Cade's rebellion was suppressed and Cade killed, there were a number of factors that made it politically damaging for Henry VI. The most obvious was that the king himself did not choose to face the rebels. This was a marked contrast to the daring actions of the 14-year-old Richard II in 1381, who met with the rebels and personally witnessed the death of the uprising's leader, Wat Tyler. The revolt also provided evidence of a serious breakdown in law and order. Suffolk's murder had shown that the king's favour was no protection against attack and Cade's

rebellion reiterated this point with, for example, the brutal attack on Bishop Aiscough. Importantly, the rebels' hold on the capital and the extent of the uprising obliged Henry to agree to a royal commission to examine their complaints, and to try and execute his own advisers effectively on the orders of the insurgents. Jean de Waurin's graphic and terrifying description of Jack Cade's treatment of the corpse of Lord Saye (see Source 4) demonstrates the extent to which the king and his government had lost authority; the body being treated thus was, after all, that of the treasurer of England, one of the most senior political figures in the country, as well as a personal friend of Henry VI.

The events of 1381 certainly provided a precedent for such attacks, but the extent of the rebellion and its violence towards those in power was unusual and demonstrated widespread popular resentment towards the government and its policies, as well as the personalities in power. It is also notable that it was largely the Londoners themselves, led by the mayor and civic government, who battled the rebels on London Bridge and succeeded in ejecting them from the capital, rather than royal forces. The Londoners' motivation seems primarily to have been a desire to prevent the rebels looting or resorting to other forms of violence, as earlier on in the rebellion there is evidence that there was some popular support within the capital for Cade's 'army'. The removal of the insurgents from the capital, therefore, arguably owed more to Londoners' self-interest and desire to protect their own livelihoods than it did to loyalty to the king's government. Perhaps the most significant element of Cade's rebellion and demands, however, were the references made in the petitions to Richard, duke of York. Although York himself was in Ireland at the time of the uprising, the use of his name by the rebels and the widespread unrest were to spark the duke's growing involvement in domestic politics in a radical and unsettling manner.

Nonetheless, the significance of Cade's rebellion should not be overstated. The fact that the duke of York was not present, still being in Ireland, made the situation considerably less politically dangerous for Henry VI. Medieval society was so conservative about status and rank that it was highly unlikely that a man of Jack Cade's lowly origins would have been successful in seizing real power for long from the anointed king. The fact that the rebels were opposed by Londoners was also significant – the capital was crucial in making and breaking political rulers, as the city held the key government offices and was the financial centre of the country. It is also notable that the key tangible legal change that occurred after the revolt was an Act of Resumption, which was passed by parliament in 1450. This allowed the crown to recover most of the land granted by Henry VI to his favourites during the 1440s. Certainly the decision was a major humiliation for the king and was carried out partly to appease public opinion, as well as to resolve the increasingly desperate position of royal finances. It should be noted, however, that this Act cannot be only regarded as a response to the violence of Cade's rebellion, as the Commons were already petitioning for it when events of the rebellion interrupted the parliamentary session.

Cade's rebellion and its aftermath

1 Read Source 6 listing rebels' complaints. For each complaint, write down the extent to which you think the rebels were justified in their demands, using your own knowledge of Henry VI's reign up to the summer of 1450.

2 Write a paragraph summarising the key events of Cade's rebellion and its immediate aftermath, from May to August 1450.

3 Write a list of the key consequences of Cade's rebellion, in order of political significance.

A Level Exam-Style Question Section B

'Cade's rebellion in 1450 was much less significant in the politics of the 1450s than the personal dislike between the duke of York and the duke of Somerset.'

How far do you agree with this statement? (20 marks)

Tip

Make sure that, throughout your answer, you focus on analysing the consequences and significance of these two factors, rather than simply describing the rebellion and/or the rivalry between York and Somerset.

WHICH LEADING MEMBER OF THE YORKIST FACTION WAS THE MOST RESPONSIBLE FOR HENRY VI'S DOWNFALL?

The importance of the duke of York's First Protectorate

The period 1449–53 was one of disaster for the English in the Hundred Years War. In 1450, the valuable area of Normandy was lost and 1451–52 saw considerable losses in Gascony. The English finally lost the war on 17 July 1453, when their commander John Talbot was killed at the Battle of Castillon and his army heavily defeated. Quickly, the French took Bordeaux and drove the English out of France completely, except in Calais. News of this military disaster appears to have caused Henry VI to suffer a complete mental breakdown. The exact form of the king's illness is unknown, but it reduced him to a totally helpless state. For 17 months, Henry was apparently incapable of recognising or responding to anyone, or understanding what was said to him. A number of pages and grooms needed to be with him at all times to feed him and support him from room to room at Windsor Castle, where he remained under the care of doctors, supervised by the council, for his period of incapacity.

The question of who should rule in Henry's place was fraught and made more politically sensitive in October 1453 by the birth of Henry's son and heir, Prince Edward. At a meeting of the great council in November 1453, Somerset was accused by the duke of Norfolk, Richard of York's long-standing supporter, of treason on the grounds of his poor military leadership of the Hundred Years

War. In a weaker position because of Henry's illness, Somerset was arrested and imprisoned in the Tower. According to some surviving correspondence from those attending parliament in 1454, Margaret of Anjou attempted to be declared regent and to exclude York from consideration but, given his seniority in terms of wealth and lineage, this was an unrealistic move. In late March 1454, York was declared Defender and Protector of the Realm by parliament.

EXTEND YOUR KNOWLEDGE

York's career prior to 1454
From 1440 to 1445, York was heavily involved in the defence of Lancastrian France, being Henry VI's military commander there. He was then replaced in this post by his enemy the duke of Somerset and instead posted as lieutenant of Ireland. It is highly likely that York regarded this move as a demotion. Somerset then presided over massive English defeats in France during 1449–50, which helped to trigger Cade's rebellion.

In September 1450, in the aftermath of revolt, York returned from Ireland, possibly motivated by the fact that Somerset had also returned to England and had established himself as the king's leading adviser. On landing in Wales York travelled to London, backed by an army of 3,000 retainers. He presented a series of bills to the king, outlining his complaints. This was clearly an attack upon the king's leading ministers, notably Somerset, and one that was to cause an irreconcilable breach between the two men. York arrived at the parliament of November 1450 with an intimidating force and ensured that Somerset was imprisoned in the Tower.

Subsequently, the duke's campaign for reform lost momentum and there was little real change in the structure of the king's government. By Christmas, Somerset was released and the lords showed greater loyalty to Henry VI than to York. In 1452, York grew increasingly frustrated with the lack of change and Somerset's growing ascendancy at court, particularly when Somerset was made Captain of Calais, a role which gave him command of a large army and demonstrated clearly Henry's ongoing military trust in the man who many, notably York, blamed for the loss of Normandy. In 1452, therefore, Richard took up arms against the king and met the royal forces at Dartford in Kent. The duke was supported by the earl of Devon and Lord Cobham, but most of the powerful nobility, including the duke of Buckingham and the Neville earls of Salisbury and Warwick, remained loyal to Henry. York was obliged to submit to the king and make a public and humiliating apology in St Paul's Cathedral, taking an oath of future loyalty to the king. Soon afterwards, Margaret of Anjou's pregnancy was announced, damaging York's claim to be heir presumptive to the throne.

York's period as Protector has received considerable attention from historians because they view it with the benefit of hindsight, and know that in 1460 the duke was to attempt to usurp the throne. There has therefore been debate about whether York was aiming to seize the crown from this early stage, or whether this ambition grew later as the political situation in England deteriorated. Certainly, 1454 was an opportunity for the duke to indicate if he was a plausible alternative to Henry VI. According to John Watts, the duke's leadership during his First Protectorate demonstrated statesman-like qualities that showed his willingness to govern in a just and non-partisan manner. One pro-Yorkist chronicler wrote that the period of his Protectorate was one of excellent governance for England, reducing much of the disorder that had afflicted the country. Richard was willing to declare openly his loyalty to the infant Prince Edward as heir to the throne. While Protector, Richard also surrounded himself with advisers who held a range of opinions, and that was a statesmanlike act. Nonetheless, it is clear that the duke was not trusted by the nobility as a whole and that there was real unease about supporting York to take crucial decisions in the absence of an effective monarch. It is notable, for example, that despite his unpopularity in the country at large, Somerset remained in prison but untried throughout the period of Henry's illness, indicating that York did not have enough backing to ensure a conviction by the Lords in a trial. This suggests that the nobility as a whole were uneasy about York's suitability as an alternative ruler.

Nonetheless, for Margaret of Anjou and Somerset, it must have been deeply concerning that York now had the backing of the powerful Neville family, who had switched their allegiance in October 1453, partly because of a land dispute with the duke of Somerset over the lordship of Glamorgan. York therefore began his Protectorate by appointing Richard Neville, earl of Salisbury as chancellor. This partisan move may have been politically essential for York in the circumstances, but it somewhat undermines John Watts' claims that the duke acted entirely in the public interest. Certainly, it was an appointment that enraged the Nevilles' main rivals in the North, the Percies. The Percies were backed by Henry Holand, duke of Exeter, and Lord Egremont. By May, Lord Egremont, the duke of Exeter and other rebels were attempting to gain support in Yorkshire, Lancashire and Cheshire for an armed rebellion against the new Protectorate. On 19 May 1454, York led a strong military force, backed by Lord Cromwell, against the rebels and his opponents were forced to flee. Nonetheless, it proved difficult to implement legal redress against the rebels as local law officers could find themselves at risk when trying to make arrests in the Percy strongholds of the North. By July, however, York managed to capture Exeter and to imprison him in Pontefract Castle, although there was a recurrence of Neville–Percy violence in the autumn of 1454, around Stamford Bridge.

The end of the First Protectorate
Henry VI's recovery from his illness in the Christmas of 1454 meant that York's stance against Exeter was undermined. The vulnerable and weak-willed King Henry, always easily influenced, was quickly persuaded to release a number of those made prisoners during York's Protectorate, including the duke of Exeter and the duke of Somerset. Somerset was completely exonerated from the treason charges by Henry and resumed a leading position in the king's government. On 9 February 1455, York resigned as Protector and a court faction around Margaret of Anjou and Somerset regained power.

The immediate political significance of the Protectorate was weakened by its brevity and the fact that Henry VI reversed so many of York's decisions almost as soon as he recovered his wits. This undermined York publicly and was probably a key factor in increasing his desire for greater control within government. The period is useful, however, in providing a snapshot of how the duke would seek to govern if he were king and it is fair to state that he dealt reasonably well with the manifold problems that Henry's poor leadership had created. Although he did not have widespread support from the nobility at this stage, the most significant aspect of the Protectorate was the consolidation of his alliance with the powerful Nevilles, who were to go on to support the Yorkist cause over the next decade.

ACTIVITY
KNOWLEDGE CHECK

York's First Protectorate

1 Create a table below showing York's achievements and failings during his First Protectorate. Make sure you consider political appointments, treatment of enemies, and military action against rebels.

2 What is Waurin's view of Richard of York (Source 3 on page 117)? Based on your own knowledge, how accurate is this assessment of his military and political ability?

York's growing ambitions, 1454–60
The extent of the king's recovery remained doubtful, however, and there were constant rumours concerning his health and competence. York and his supporters were incensed by the return of Somerset, as well as fearful of potential reprisals by their enemies. In April, therefore, they left the king's court without permission and on 22 May 1455 the two sides met at the First Battle of St Albans, a conflict which is often regarded as the first real battle of the Wars of the Roses. Here, the Yorkists were victorious against an army led (in theory at least) by Henry VI; Somerset was killed, as was Richard Neville's old rival, Henry Percy, earl of Northumberland. Shockingly, the king himself was wounded in the neck during the battle, highlighting both the political and physical danger the monarch was in at this time. Henry's other leading supporter, the duke of Buckingham, was wounded in the face. Henry was captured by the Yorkists but, in a deliberate show of loyalty to the king, the Yorkist lords made a display of submitting to the monarch on their knees and begging his forgiveness for their actions, emphasising that they only wished to attack 'traitors' to the realm. The point that the duke of York and his supporters wished to make was that they were loyal subjects, who were seeking only to help the king to govern well and justly. Nonetheless, the underlying threat to the Lancastrian regime was very clear; indeed, during a public reconciliation ceremony between Henry and York, when the two men entered London together, Henry received his crown from York's hands during a service at St Paul's Cathedral. The implications of this ceremony were designed to be clear: York could give Henry the crown, and he could also take it away.

York's Second Protectorate
In the short term, York's victory at St Albans placed him back at the heart of political power and, in November 1455, this role was formalised when the duke was once again made Defender and Protector of the Realm on the grounds that Henry was not well enough to discharge his duties personally. Prince Edward's position as heir to the throne was also emphasised. There is some evidence to suggest that Henry suffered another breakdown in his health, requiring a Protector to be appointed, although there has been considerable scholarly discussion about the truth of this, with some

TIMELINE: RICHARD, DUKE OF YORK'S INVOLVEMENT IN DOMESTIC POLITICS, 1450–60

1450

May to July: Jack Cade's rebellion

September: York returns to England from Ireland. Heads to London with an armed force of c3,000 men.

1453

July: Major defeat for English at the Battle of Castillon. French forces drive the English out of France, with the exception of Calais.

October: Margaret of Anjou gives birth to Prince Edward, son and heir of Henry VI

1454

March: York declared to be Defender and Protector of the Realm by parliament

Winter 1454–55: Henry VI recovers his health. Somerset is released from prison and returns to a prominent position in the king's government.

August: Henry VI has complete mental breakdown and is incapable of governing

November: The duke of Somerset is charged with treason by the Council and imprisoned in the Tower without trial

1455

February: York resigns as Protector of the Realm

April: York and his supporters leave the royal court without permission

1456

January: Earl of Warwick made Captain of Calais

February: York resigns as Protector

May: Yorkist victory at the First Battle of St Albans. The duke of Somerset is killed.

November: York made Defender and Protector of the Realm for the second time

1458

March: 'Loveday' reconciliation in London

1459

June to October: Henry VI convinced that the Yorkists are plotting to seize the throne. Battles of Blore Heath and the 'rout' of Ludford Bridge drive Yorkists abroad.

1460

June to July: Yorkist 'invasion' and the Battle of Northampton. Henry VI captured, Buckingham killed and queen and Prince Edward escape.

September: York returns to England

October: York enters parliament and seeks to claim throne. Instead, Act of Accord passed making York heir apparent.

December: Battle of Wakefield; York and his second son, Edmund of Rutland, killed

November: Lancastrians take revenge on their enemies at the 'Parliament of Devils'

historians arguing that York exaggerated the king's ill-health to justify a seizure of power. This is unlikely, however, given that other lords and parliament would have had to agree to the decision.

York's main gain from the Second Protectorate was the new prominence it gave Richard Neville, earl of Warwick. He had played a significant role in securing York's victory during the battle, possibly being responsible personally for the death of Somerset. Afterwards, Warwick increasingly began to take pre-eminence over his own father, becoming, according to A.J. Pollard, York's right-hand man. As part of his reward for his service to the Yorkist cause, he was granted the Captaincy of Calais, a post that had previously, and controversially, been held by Somerset. This significant military role gave Warwick an important powerbase during the late 1450s, which he was to use to great effect in his support of the Yorkist cause.

Throughout the Second Protectorate, York faced determined opposition from the queen, who was enraged by York's power and the perceived threat to the dynastic claims of her young son. A significant section of the nobility also remained uncertain about the growing power of York and was unwilling to give the duke unqualified backing. Some of the nobility were also fearful of the fact that York might have given in to pressure from the Commons in parliament to agree to an Act of Resumption, taking back into crown ownership lands that had been granted all too freely to them by Henry VI. As a result, in February 1456, York was removed as Protector although he continued to play a significant role in the king's council.

York develops his powerbase

Rather unsurprisingly, the period of 1456–59 was one of political unease, with the 'Loveday' celebrations of 1458 (see page 115) being a public attempt to reconcile factional differences that had been so clearly demonstrated at the Battle of St Albans. This demonstration of harmony, however, was short lived and, in 1459, Henry VI was convinced by Margaret of Anjou, her new ally Humphrey Stafford, duke of Buckingham and sons of those killed at the Battle of St Albans that York was plotting to seize the throne. In June, therefore, the Great Council met at Coventry, and it is notable that at this meeting only Lancastrians were present. Here, it was decided to accuse the Yorkist leaders of treason, and Buckingham raised an army to defeat York and his supporters. York remained in the Welsh Marches at this stage, awaiting military support from the Nevilles. This aid was intercepted, however, by Lancastrian troops, although the commander chosen by the queen, Lord Audley, was killed during the fighting at Blore Heath. Nonetheless, the Yorkists were in a difficult military position and they fled rather than face Henry VI and his Lancastrian supporters at Ludford Bridge in October 1459. York and his second son sailed to Ireland, while Salisbury, Warwick and York's eldest son, Edward, earl of March, fled to Calais.

Flushed with victory, the Lancastrians now sought to ensure that they avenged themselves fully upon their Yorkist enemies during the so-called 'Parliament of Devils', held in Coventry in November 1459. Warwick, Salisbury and York were convicted of treason in their absence, sentenced to death and had their lands and goods seized. Unusually, this parliament also ordered that the heirs of the traitors were not permitted to inherit **entailed estates**, a measure that was widely regarded as an unjust breach of custom and was no doubt an important influence in encouraging the Yorkists to seek redress.

The 'Yorkist invasion' of 1460

While in exile, the Yorkists sought to build up resources and influence to enable them to return to England in force. It is clear that they wished to rid Henry VI of his 'evil councillors', but it remains uncertain if York was plotting to seize the throne at this stage. Despite his 'traitor' status, the duke negotiated with Anglo-Irish political leaders while in Ireland and granted them considerable, unprecedented levels of political recognition and autonomy at the Drogheda parliament of 1460. In return, the duke gained a large number of archers and other resources to assist with his attack. Probably more significant in what was to be the Yorkists' next success, however, was Warwick's influence in Calais and the town's important strategic location. Aside from providing them with considerable numbers of armed troops and a base to operate from on the Channel, Warwick was also able to raise money via piracy, mainly against the French. This increased his popular standing in England, especially

Entailed estate
A legal term referring to property that has a pre-ordered line of succession. In other words, an individual cannot leave the land to whomever he wishes in his will; instead, it is already decided that the land will, for example, pass to the eldest son of each generation.

in the capital where there was much disquiet regarding a slump in trade and government policies that appeared to favour foreign merchants over English citizens. The careful use of propaganda by the Yorkists meant that in June, when Salisbury, Warwick and March landed in Sandwich in Kent, they received considerable support, particularly (and rather unsurprisingly) in Kent, the former seat of Cade's rebellion, as well as in London.

In these circumstances, it was predictable that the Yorkists would be victorious when they met royalist forces at the Battle of Northampton on 10 July 1460; the king was captured and Buckingham killed, with the queen escaping to the North with Prince Edward. Rather more surprising was the reaction of the duke of York, who had remained in Ireland and did not return until around 9 September. The reason for this delay in joining his allies has never been clearly established. It is evident that he soon began to display the trappings of monarchy and, on 10 October, provocatively entered parliament and laid his hand on the empty throne, apparently seeking to claim the crown. Significantly, however, he was not supported in this by the lords and it appears to have taken the Nevilles themselves by surprise, as they had continued to assert their loyalty to Henry VI and enmity only towards his councillors. It is evident that many nobles were in an extremely difficult position, as they were unwilling to support either side unequivocally. Consequently, an uneasy compromise was reached in October 1460, called the Act of Accord, which made Henry VI king for life but disinherited his son and heir, Prince Edward, granting the throne instead to the duke of York and his heirs upon Henry's death. This would have effectively ended the Lancastrian dynasty.

Parallels between this Act and the 1420 Treaty of Troyes were evident (see Chapter 4, page 106). Prince Edward, the disinherited heir, was only seven years old at the time, but the queen and his supporters sent a document in his name to the city of London, asserting Lancastrian rights and denouncing York as a traitor. The Lancastrian forces also regrouped. On 30 December, York was attacked by a large Lancastrian force and, in the subsequent Battle of Wakefield, both he and his second son, Edmund of Rutland, were killed. Salisbury was captured and afterwards executed. As a warning to others, York was posthumously beheaded as a traitor and his head was displayed on the walls of the city of York wearing a paper crown.

The reasons for the triumph of Edward IV in 1461: the Battle of Towton, March 1461

The Lancastrian victory was to prove short lived, in part because Londoners were reluctant to support Margaret owing to the reputation of her forces for looting. In addition, York's eldest son, Edward, earl of March took on the leadership of the Yorkist forces. Only 19 at the time, Edward was nonetheless a formidable military tactician and was determined to avenge the deaths of his father and brother. On 2 February 1461, he had tackled Lancastrian forces led by Jasper Tudor and defeated them at the Battle of Mortimer's Cross. The Yorkists faced a setback, however, on 17 February at the Second Battle of St Albans. Errors in information about the Lancastrians' movements meant that the earl of Warwick was taken by surprise and his army had to retreat, and Henry VI, who had been in Warwick's custody, was recaptured by the Lancastrians and returned to the queen's side. Fortunately for Warwick and Edward, however, Londoners refused to open the city gates to Lancastrian forces and so the Yorkists were able to regain the initiative. In March, Edward arrived in London and was proclaimed King Edward IV. Edward's usurpation was predictably controversial and, before his coronation ceremony could be arranged, he moved north to tackle gathering Lancastrian forces in what was to be one of the most famous battles of the Wars of the Roses, at Towton on Palm Sunday, 29 March 1461.

Towton was significant in the sheer size of the armies involved, with historian Charles Ross estimating that, of English and Welsh men aged between 16 and 60, one-tenth were involved in this battle. Archaeological evidence suggests that the two sides also appear to have been exceptionally brutal towards each other (see Source 7), reflecting the bitterness of the civil war thus far and the success of propaganda campaigns on both sides, which had depicted the enemy in inhuman terms. Warwick, in particular, had depicted the Lancastrians as bent on rape and pillage, which no doubt made the Yorkists all the more determined to gain victory. Indeed, at Towton, according to rumour, Warwick sent away his horse before fighting began to indicate his willingness to fight with his men to the death. He could certainly have expected no mercy from Margaret of Anjou and her supporters in the event of failure.

The Yorkist victory has been viewed by some historians as rather surprising, as the Lancastrians held the higher position on the field and were well supplied by the local region. In addition, Henry VI received significant support from at least 18 nobles, including Exeter, Somerset, Northumberland, Devon and Wiltshire, as well as a number of Yorkshire gentry figures such as Sir William Plumpton, a level of support that outnumbered that of Edward IV. The weather, however, proved a major disadvantage for them, as the wind was behind the Yorkist longbowmen, meaning their arrows travelled further into the enemy line, while the Lancastrian archers' shots fell short. The Yorkists' archers were also particularly well commanded by Edward IV's maternal uncle, William Neville, Lord Fauconberg, who ordered his troops to collect the arrows fired short by the Lancastrians and use them against the enemy. This tactic proved so devastating that the Lancastrians were unable to hold their superior position and were forced to charge in an attempt to end the slaughter by engaging in hand-to-hand combat.

Henry and Margaret of Anjou's army was blinded by both arrows and sleet as it charged. Although medieval chroniclers are very prone to exaggerating battle statistics, it is evident that the Lancastrians suffered very heavy losses, and although they fought on for a number of hours, they were further damaged by the arrival on the Yorkist side of reinforcements led by the duke of Norfolk. Norfolk was a close associate of Edward IV and his involvement at Towton was probably decisive in bringing the new king to victory. As the Lancastrians began to flee the field, many were drowned trying to cross the River Cock, which was fast flowing and swollen owing to the recent rain and snow, making it extremely dangerous; so many bodies piled up in the river that they created a dam, and others tried to flee across the corpses to safety.

SOURCE

7

The skull of someone killed at the Battle of Towton. The severity of the injuries highlight the brutality of the fighting.

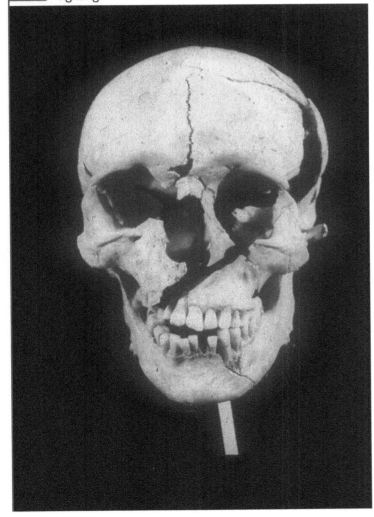

During the battle, a number of leading Lancastrian supporters were killed, including Northumberland, Welles and Dacre, and others, such as Devon and Wiltshire were executed afterwards. This decimated the support of Henry VI and Margaret. The only drawback as far as Edward was concerned was that Henry VI, Margaret of Anjou and Prince Edward managed to escape to Scotland, but their military support was virtually destroyed.

The importance of the earl of Warwick

It is evident that the ultimate victory of the Yorkist cause in 1461 was largely owed to the work and resources of the earl of Warwick. He was an extremely wealthy man and his ability to support the Yorkist cause in the period of 1459–61 was significantly enhanced by his Captaincy of Calais, a role that had been granted to him by Richard of York during his Second Protectorate. This role gave him command of the only significant regular army in the country and he used the heavily fortified town of Calais as his base from 1456 to 1460. As the only remaining English holding in France after 1453, it was also of considerable importance in terms of publicity for Warwick and he proved extremely adept at manipulating rumour to support the Yorkist cause and tarnish the reputation of the queen in particular. For example, in 1457, when the French attacked Sandwich in Kent to try to cut off English supply lines to Calais, Warwick insinuated that Margaret herself had encouraged the attack to help the French. During periods when the government was unable or unwilling to pay the garrison at Calais, Warwick engaged in well-publicised acts of piracy against foreign sailors in order to fund his troops, attacks which gained him considerable popular support in England. In 1458, he was authorised by the crown to use his position as Captain of Calais to negotiate with Charles VII of France and Philip the Good of Burgundy and he maintained these lines of communication even after he had been dubbed a traitor at the Coventry parliament of 1459. He therefore was important in secretly gaining some international support for the Yorkist cause, and ensuring that figures such as the duke of Burgundy did not intervene to support Henry VI.

Warwick's enormous wealth and power, as well as his experience as a leader of men and as a military tactician, were of great benefit to the young Edward IV, and his role in bringing the earl of March to the throne was one of the factors that has led to him being described as a 'kingmaker'. In return, Warwick would now expect great favour and great influence in the running of the country, to be, in contemporary terminology, 'an over-mighty subject', who could sway the king easily. The next political test for England was to be the battle of wills between Edward IV and his former loyal supporter.

A Level Exam-Style Question Section B

How significant was English military failure in France to the downfall of Henry VI and the Lancastrian cause in 1461?

(20 marks)

Tip

In your response, not only discuss Henry VI's military losses but also consider alternative factors that might have played a part in his downfall, such as the key personalities of the reign.

ACTIVITY
KNOWLEDGE CHECK

Causes of Yorkist victory at Towton, 1461

1 Create a spider diagram of all the ways in which the earl of Warwick aided Edward IV to the throne.

2 List all the weaknesses of Henry VI's government between 1454 and 1461 that aided the Yorkists in being able to claim the throne. Colour-code the list to show avoidable and unavoidable errors.

ACTIVITY
SUMMARY

The influence of key personalities on the politics of 1449–60

1 Draw and complete a table charting the key achievements and failures of Henry VI, Margaret of Anjou, the duke of Suffolk, the duke of Somerset, the duke of York and the earl of Warwick. How reliable is the available source material when assessing their characters?

2 On a piece of A3 paper, create a timeline that covers the key battles of the period 1449–61, including details of why each battle was significant (especially which key figures were killed/taken prisoner/escaped). Draw a red rose by battles that were victories for the Lancastrians and a white rose by battles that were a victory for the Yorkists.

WIDER READING

Castor, H. *She-Wolves: The Women Who Ruled England Before Elizabeth*, Faber & Faber (2011). Only the chapter on Margaret of Anjou is relevant.

Dockray, K. *Henry VI, Margaret of Anjou and the Wars of the Roses: A Source Book*, Sutton Publishing (2000)

Griffiths, R.A. 'Henry VI (1421–1471)', *Oxford Dictionary of National Biography*, Oxford University Press (2004). Online edn, May 2015, www.oxforddnb.com/view/article/12953

Pollard, A.J. 'Neville, Richard, sixteenth earl of Warwick and sixth earl of Salisbury [*called* the Kingmaker] (1428–1471)', *Oxford Dictionary of National Biography*, Oxford University Press (2004). Online edn, Jan 2008, www.oxforddnb.com/view/article/19955

Rawcliffe, C. 'The insanity of Henry VI', The Historical Association (1996)

Watts, J. 'Richard of York, third duke of York (1411–1460)', *Oxford Dictionary of National Biography*, Oxford University Press (2004). Online edn, May 2011, www.oxforddnb.com/view/article/23503

Watts, J. *Henry VI and the Politics of Kingship*, Cambridge University Press (1999)

Wolffe, B. *Henry VI*, Yale University Press (2001)

3.6 The Yorkists divided, 1478–85

KEY QUESTIONS

- How significant were tensions in the Yorkist camp in the late 1470s and early 1480s?
- How effective was Richard III as a monarch?
- Which factors were most important in supporting Henry Tudor's seizure of power in 1485?

INTRODUCTION

The 1470s and 1480s are undoubtedly the most famous period of the Wars of the Roses. Above all, popular conceptions of the period have focused on the personalities of Edward IV and his two brothers, George, duke of Clarence and Richard, duke of Gloucester (later Richard III). Clarence and Gloucester were frequently at loggerheads, rivalling each other for favours from the king and in the matter of marriage; indeed, according to rumour, Clarence was so keen to prevent Richard making an advantageous marriage at one stage that he disguised Anne Neville, the prospective bride, as a kitchen maid to prevent Richard meeting her. Political tensions were also increased by the rise in power of the Woodville family, thanks to Elizabeth's advantageous marriage to Edward IV, and the increasing dominance of this group around the heir to the throne, the young Prince Edward. Steeped in a love of power, and most exhibiting an extremely ruthless streak, the characters of this period are fascinating; indeed, they have formed the basis of numerous literary creations, including the well-known Shakespeare plays *Henry VI, Part III* and *Richard III*, as well as popular historical novels by Philippa Gregory, such as *The Red Queen* and *The White Queen*. While these imaginative accounts of the period undoubtedly have many merits, it must be said that the second reign of Edward IV and the seizure of the throne by his brother is a tale where facts are even more gripping than fiction. Clarence's continued disloyalty and troublemaking led to his judicial murder in 1478, on the orders of his brother, Edward IV. According to legend, he was drowned at the Tower of London in a butt of wine. The king himself died of natural causes unexpectedly in 1483, precipitating a major political crisis. His son and heir, Prince Edward, was only 13 and he and his younger brother, Richard of Shrewsbury, were swiftly removed from the care of the Woodvilles and placed in the Tower on Gloucester's orders, never to be seen again, while their uncle became King Richard III. The disappearance of the boys has been a topic of speculation and controversy ever since, as has the personality and political ability of the new king. The suspicion that he was a child-murderer damaged Richard's reputation at the time and was an important factor in increasing support for an alternative king, Henry Tudor, who invaded England from exile in France in 1485 and was victorious at the Battle of Bosworth. Henry VII was crowned; the Tudor dynasty had begun.

1478 – February: Clarence is privately executed in the Tower

1483 – 9 April: Edward IV dies at Westminster.

May: Richard of Gloucester and Edward V enter London together. Edward V is housed in the Tower of London.

Gloucester named as Protector.

13 June: Gloucester arrests a number of Edward IV's leading allies at a council meeting.

26 June: Richard of Gloucester proclaims himself King Richard III

1478	1483 April	1483 May	1483 June	1483 July	1483 August

1483 – Late April: Richard of Gloucester, supported by an armed retinue, intercepts Edward V's party at Stony Stratford and arrests members of the young king's household.

Edward V's proposed coronation delayed.

Queen Elizabeth Woodville seeks sanctuary at Westminster Abbey with her second son, Richard.

6 July: Coronation of Richard III

Late July: Plot to free princes in the Tower uncovered. Those involved put on trial and found guilty.

Summer: Princes in the Tower disappear and are assumed dead

HOW SIGNIFICANT WERE TENSIONS IN THE YORKIST CAMP IN THE LATE 1470S AND EARLY 1480S?

Edward IV and the breach with the earl of Warwick

After the Yorkist victory at the Battle of Towton on 29 March 1461, Edward IV was swiftly crowned king. Initially, he was highly dependent upon the earl of Warwick, who helped him defend the northern border against attack from the Scots, supported by Lancastrian dissidents in exile there. In return, the king lavished land, favours and status upon the earl. Warwick was a major power behind the throne in the early 1460s and engaged in important diplomatic missions on behalf of the king. Various foreign commentators noted in their correspondence how influential Warwick appeared to be at court, depicting him as an 'over-mighty subject' in their letters. Such observers, however, were unaware of growing tension by 1464 between Edward and Warwick and were therefore shocked when this disagreement was played out in an embarrassingly public manner over the matter of the king's marriage. In 1464, for over a year Warwick had been engaged in seeking to arrange a match between Edward and the French king's sister-in-law, Bona, daughter of the duke of Savoy. This match was designed to ensure peace between France and England, which was important for domestic security as France was the traditional ally of Scotland, where Henry VI, Margaret of Anjou and their son, Prince Edward, were in exile. Edward scuppered this arrangement in May 1464, however, by secretly marrying the highly unsuitable Elizabeth Woodville. Contemporaries viewed Elizabeth as unfit to be queen for the following reasons:

- She was English, and so the match brought no advantage in terms of foreign diplomacy.

- She was a member of the gentry and by royal standards relatively poor, so did not increase royal wealth.

- She was a widow with two children, when usually it was considered more appropriate for a king to marry a virgin.

- Her former husband, Sir John Grey, and her own family had all previously supported the Lancastrian cause.

- She came from a very large family, whom she encouraged Edward to reward lavishly. Her relatives soon became infamous for their greed in relation to royal patronage.

Edward kept his marriage to Elizabeth secret from all his advisers, including Warwick, until September 1464. This was deeply humiliating for the earl given his royal marriage negotiations with the French. It marked a turning point in the relationship between the two men, as Warwick was keen to promote good Anglo-French relations, but Edward now insisted on developing an alliance with the

1483 - Late September: Rebellion against Richard III in favour of Henry Tudor, supported by Duke of Buckingham

1484 - Autumn: Tudor flees from Brittany to France, where he gains support for his invasion of England from Charles VIII's minority council

1483 September	1483 October	1483 November	1483 December	1484	1485

Early November: Rebellion in Tudor's favour fails. Henry Tudor flees to Brittany.

1485 - 22 August: Battle of Bosworth. Richard III killed and Henry Tudor takes throne as King Henry VII.

dukes of Burgundy, who were enemies of the French. Warwick was also alienated by Edward's favour towards the Woodville family, most notably Elizabeth's father, Richard. Queen Elizabeth was anxious to marry her numerous relatives advantageously and to block profitable matches by other members of the nobility. In particular, she encouraged the king to oppose a marriage between Warwick's eldest daughter, Isabel Neville, to the king's brother, George, duke of Clarence.

From 1467 onwards, Warwick was probably shifting his allegiance towards the Lancastrian cause. Certainly the French believed that he was now moving to support Margaret of Anjou and, in the winter of 1467, he remained absent from Edward IV's court, instead basing himself in Yorkshire. At this time, Edward was planning an invasion of France and Louis XI responded by encouraging as much civil strife in England as possible. In this, he was aided by the fact that there was considerable dissatisfaction among the nobility at this time concerning Edward's generosity towards his Woodville relations.

Warwick took his revenge against Edward in 1469 when he set sail for Calais. There, the earl arranged the marriage of his daughter Isabel to George, duke of Clarence, a match that took place on 11 July. Subsequently, Warwick and Clarence jointly published criticisms of Edward's government, and especially the power of Richard Woodville. Warwick's supporters successfully fought the king's forces at the Battle of Edgecote on 26 July 1469 and the king was later captured and imprisoned. Warwick may have wished to depose Edward, but the extent of disorder in the country was so great that the earl was forced to come to terms with the king and release him.

This situation was untenable in the long term. Warwick had been flagrantly disloyal and it was a matter of time until the situation flared again. There was obviously some attempt at reconciliation and making government more acceptable to the earl, but Warwick clearly felt insecure and fled to the court of Louis XI. Here the wily French king, remarkably, managed to reconcile two former arch-enemies: Warwick and Margaret of Anjou. To seal the pact, the Lancastrian heir, Prince Edward, was married to Warwick's younger daughter, Anne Neville. Warwick agreed to restore Henry VI to the throne. In autumn 1470, the earl invaded England, Edward IV was forced to flee, and Henry VI was reinstated.

Henry VI's readeption was unsurprisingly short lived, with Edward IV reinvading England and landing in the Humber in March 1471, supported by Burgundian troops. Quickly, Clarence betrayed Warwick and instead returned to his brother's side, a highly significant blow to the earl's cause. By 11 April, the reunited Yorkists had seized Henry VI and, on 14 April, they forced the Lancastrian king to come with them to face Warwick's forces at the Battle of Barnet, in order to create confusion and conflicting loyalties in the enemy's troops. Warwick was defeated and killed as he fled the field. Henry VI was imprisoned in the Tower of London and Edward IV returned as a victorious king. The Yorkist success was confirmed on 4 May when, at the Battle of Tewkesbury, the Lancastrian Prince Edward was killed and Margaret of Anjou captured. Henry VI died two weeks later in the Tower, probably having been murdered on Edward's orders.

SOURCE

1 Manuscript drawing of Richard Neville, sixteenth earl of Warwick's family tree, including his wife, Anne, and their descendants, including their daughter Isabel and her husband, George, duke of Clarence, brother of Edward IV.

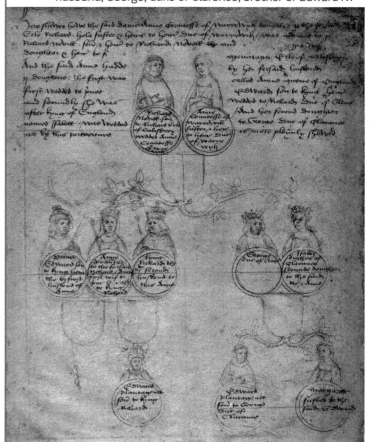

The rift between Edward IV and the earl of Warwick was clearly highly significant in undermining the security of the new Yorkist regime in the 1460s. In the matter of his marriage especially, Edward showed a disregard for the opinion of his closest adviser that was probably deliberately insulting, and the whole incident may well have been deliberately designed by the king to prove to Warwick that Edward would not be dictated to by a subject. Warwick's ambition was so great that there was a certain inevitability about a breach between the two men. Nonetheless Edward adopted a high-risk strategy in this matter and nearly lost his throne as a result. In the end, however, it worked out well for Edward; when he returned to the throne in 1471, overall, he was in a much stronger position:

- Henry VI and his son, Prince Edward, were dead, so there was no figurehead around to provoke a possible rebellion. With both her husband and son dead, Margaret of Anjou became a politically negligible figure who could command little support and who, in any case, spent much of the 1470s under guard before she was returned to France and was obliged to live largely on the charity of the French king, Louis XI.

- Richard Neville, earl of Warwick, had been killed, so the threat from this quarter no longer existed.

TIMELINE: KEY EVENTS IN EDWARD IV'S FIRST REIGN AND THE READEPTION OF HENRY VI

29 March 1461
Battle of Towton – a decisive Yorkist victory.
Edward IV becomes king.

May 1464
Edward IV secretly marries Elizabeth Woodville

September 1464
Edward IV's marriage announced to his
advisers, including the earl of Warwick

11 July 1469
Isabel Neville (daughter of Warwick) marries
George, duke of Clarence (brother of Edward IV)
in Calais

Late August/September 1469
Growing disorder in the North leads to
Edward IV's release

26 July 1469
Battle of Edgecote – victory for Warwick's
supporters

Late July 1469
Edward IV captured and imprisoned by Warwick

April 1470
Warwick flees to France

22 July 1470
Warwick formally reconciled to House of
Lancaster and Margaret of Anjou

13 September 1470
Warwick's invasion
force lands in England

25 July 1470
Warwick's daughter, Anne Neville, betrothed to
Lancastrian Prince Edward

2 October 1470
Edward IV flees to
the Netherlands.
Henry VI reinstated
by Warwick.

14 March 1471
Edward IV invades England

3 April 1471
Duke of Clarence betrays Warwick and instead
supports his brother Edward IV

4 May 1471
Battle of Tewkesbury. Yorkist victory. Edward,
Prince of Wales killed.

14 April 1471
Battle of Barnet. Yorkist victory

21 May 1471
Henry VI dies in Tower of London

- The death of Henry and his son meant that Edward IV was able to become reconciled to some previously staunch Lancastrian supporters, such as Sir Richard Tunstall, because they no longer had a surviving monarch who required their loyalty. Edward was careful to ensure that such men were found a place in the new regime so that they did not become disaffected. Only a few diehard Lancastrians who would not accept Edward as monarch, such as Jasper Tudor, his nephew Henry and John de Vere, earl of Oxford, remained excluded from the royal court and lost their estates, but at this stage they were unable to gain substantial support for a large-scale rebellion against the Yorkist king. De Vere did attempt an invasion with French assistance in 1473, but this was a failure and served to underline that Edward was now an established monarch.

Royal patronage and the quarrel of Clarence and Gloucester

The downfall of Warwick and some other supporters of Henry VI gave Edward a large amount of territory to redistribute. This had to be done with care, as the king needed to avoid creating more 'over-mighty subjects' while also creating loyalty and control. In this, Edward was only partially successful. He concentrated most of the wealth and power in the hands of members of his own family, with his two brothers being the main beneficiaries of this generosity. Gloucester, who had always been loyal to the king, gained all of Warwick's confiscated properties in the North and was given the leadership of the 'Council of the North', a body based in the city of York that had responsibility for the maintenance of law and order and defence in the region, especially against the Scots. Clarence, despite his betrayal, was forgiven and restored to all his properties, as well as being granted all Warwick's southern estates and lands confiscated from the Courtenay family in Devon. In order to try to restore order in the North, however, the king required Clarence to give up his properties so that they could be returned to the Percy family in an attempt to win support for the regime in the troublesome North. This angered Clarence and, in an attempt to satisfy him, the king gave him the earldom of Richmond, which had belonged to Henry Tudor (who was currently disinherited and in exile along with his diehard Lancastrian uncle, Jasper Tudor), but had initially been granted to Gloucester. This was just one of the factors that created resentment between the two brothers, and led to rivalry that lasted until Clarence's dramatic fall from royal favour and murder in 1478.

The main area of tension was surrounding the prospect of a marriage between Gloucester and Anne Neville, younger daughter of the deceased earl of Warwick. The daughter of the wealthiest and most influential peer in the country by the end of the 1460s, it was always anticipated that Anne would make a politically valuable match. There is evidence that, during Edward IV's first reign, her father was anxious to marry both his daughters to the king's brothers – Isabel to Clarence and Anne to Gloucester. Edward, however, forbade both marriages, presumably as he did not want to concentrate even more power in Warwick's hands. When Warwick and Clarence rebelled in 1469, therefore, Clarence

had married Isabel in an act of defiance against the king. To complete the bargain, the 14-year-old Anne was married to the young Lancastrian, Prince Edward. In the context of the time, both Anne and Edward were considered of age; the marriage was clearly consummated (see page 69) and considered valid. When Prince Edward was killed in May 1471, the widowed Anne was therefore technically the dowager Princess of Wales but, in reality, her power and influence were almost non-existent. She was brought from Tewkesbury into the household of the duke of Clarence and she appears to have lived there for some months, although we have little evidence about what happened to her during this period. For at least part of the time, she was concealed by Clarence to prevent her marriage to Gloucester. In the early 1470s, however, Richard removed her from Clarence's care, apparently with her consent.

The date of the marriage between Anne and Richard is unknown, but it probably occurred at some point between February and March 1472. The consequences were significant, as the quarrel between Gloucester and Clarence was embarrassing for the king. Eventually a settlement was reached that was, according to historian Charles Ross, designed to flatter Clarence's ego. Clarence was compensated by being created earl of Warwick and Salisbury, as well as being given considerable further estates in Essex and the Midlands, a townhouse in London and being made Great Chamberlain of England, a role that had previously been held by his brother, Richard, who was obliged to resign in his sibling's favour. In March 1472, a provisional agreement about the division of the Neville sisters' inheritance was made by parliament and this was enforced by two Acts of parliament

Figure 6.1 Richard of Gloucester's landholdings in the North of England by 1483.

in 1474–75, giving the two women (and thereby their husbands) half the inheritance each, in the process disinheriting a number of other claimants, including Isabel and Anne's mother, the dowager Countess of Warwick. These arrangements demonstrated the ruthlessness of the York brothers in relation to property, but more importantly also indicated that in the first half of the decade, Edward IV was still very inclined to capitulate to Clarence's demands. The marriage of Richard to Anne Neville was also to have significant long-term consequences, as it gave Richard of Gloucester increased control and wealth in the North especially. It was in this area that he built up a substantial powerbase and where he appears to have developed considerable popularity, being regarded as a good lord to his men and an able warrior.

The reasons for the attainder and murder of George, duke of Clarence in 1478

Clarence's wife, Isabel, did not enjoy her inheritance for long. In October 1476, she gave birth to a second son, but both she and the baby died within months. Clarence's reaction to his bereavement was bizarre, lending some weight to the theory of historian J.R. Lander that the duke suffered from mental instability. On one hand, he quickly sought to capitalise politically on his new status as a widower, seeking a marriage with Mary, the daughter of Duke Charles of Burgundy. Edward would not permit the match, as the dukes of Burgundy were extremely wealthy and powerful, as well as having a claim to the English throne. It is understandable that Edward was suspicious of Clarence given his treacherous history and was unwilling to give him the potential motivation and resources to rebel against him. Clarence, however, was furious and allegedly spread rumours that the king was illegitimate, a serious charge that would invalidate Edward's right to the throne. As relations between the two siblings deteriorated, Edward also blocked a proposed second match for Clarence, this time to the sister of the king of Scotland. During this period, Clarence rarely attended court and appeared reluctant to consume food or drink when in the king's house, presumably as he wished to give the impression he feared poison. This was embarrassing for the king, and also damaging to the queen, as there was a well-established enmity between Clarence and Elizabeth and the duke's actions encouraged rumours that he feared the Woodvilles were plotting against him.

Despite his apparently business-like approach to remarriage, Clarence appeared distressed by Isabel's death, taking care over his late wife's funeral arrangements. His behaviour at this time became paranoid and, in April 1477, he seized Isabel's former servant, a woman called Ankarette Twynho, from her home in Somerset and brought her by force to Warwick. There, Clarence accused the unfortunate woman of poisoning the duchess and terrorised a jury and the local JPs into passing a guilty verdict. In a clear miscarriage of justice, Ankarette was hanged on 15 April, in an act widely regarded as that of an 'over-mighty subject' abusing the judicial process for his own ends. Clarence's motivations are unclear; it has been suggested that he was seeking to imply either the king or queen was responsible for ordering

his wife's death, but he never made such an accusation clear. Regardless, his behaviour certainly gave Edward a perfect cause for attacking the duke, under the cloak of protecting the common people from acts of barbarity.

Edward was extremely angry with Clarence and during April and May he appears to have been seeking evidence of his brother's treachery. An opportunity came when an Oxford astronomer called Dr John Stacey was arrested on the grounds that he had used magic with ill intent. Under torture, Stacey confessed to working with a member of Clarence's household, Thomas Burdett, to predict the early deaths of the king and his eldest son. In a staged trial, the men were found guilty, with Burdett also being convicted of inciting rebellion against Edward IV. They were hanged in London on 19 May. Enraged by the death of a member of his household, Clarence interrupted a council meeting at Westminster and ensured that Burdett and Stacey's final declarations of innocence were read out. Edward at this time was at Windsor, but when he returned he personally charged the duke, in the presence of witnesses, of having violated the laws of the realm and of interference with the judicial system, presumably references to the judicial murder of Ankarette Twynho. Clarence was imprisoned in the Tower and kept there until he was tried by parliament in January 1478 on charges of treason.

SOURCE 2

The charge presented to parliament in January 1478 by King Edward IV against his brother, George, duke of Clarence, on the grounds of high treason.

The king is mindful of the many conspiracies against him which he has repressed in the past, and although many of the rebels and traitors have been punished as an example to others yet, as a merciful prince, he spared not only the rank and file but also some of the movers and stirrers of such treasons. Notwithstanding, a conspiracy against him, the queen, their son and heir and a great part of the nobility of the land has recently come to his knowledge, which treason is more heinous and unnatural than any previous one because it originates from the king's brother the duke of Clarence, whom the king had always loved and generously rewarded. In spite of this, the duke grievously offended the king in the past, procuring his exile from the realm and labouring parliament to exclude him and his heirs from the crown. All of which the king forgave, but the duke continued to conspire against him, intending his destruction by both internal and external forces. He sought to turn his subjects against him by saying that Thomas Burdet was falsely put to death and that the king resorted to necromancy. He also said that the king was a bastard, not fit to reign, and made men take oaths of allegiance to him without excepting their loyalty to the king. He accused the king of taking his livelihood from him, and intending his destruction. He secured an exemplification under the great seal of an agreement made between him and Queen Margaret promising him the crown if Henry VI's line failed. He planned to send his son and heir abroad to win support, bringing a false child to Warwick castle in his place. He planned to raise war against the king within England and made men promise to be ready at an hour's notice. The duke has thus shown himself incorrigible and to pardon him would threaten the common weal [i.e. the common good], which the king is bound to maintain.

By the advice and assent of the lords and commons the king ordains that the duke be convicted of high treason and forfeit his estate as duke and all the lands he holds by the king's grant.

Edward's behaviour towards his brother in 1478 demonstrated considerable ruthlessness, which was at odds with his previously lenient attitude towards Clarence; it appears the king had reached the limit of his endurance with the duke. The *Crowland Chronicle* emphasised that, as soon as Edward heard of Clarence's public protestation of the innocence of Burdett, he began to recall the duke's various other past misdemeanours and decided to take decisive action. The chronicler is clearly of the view that Clarence's fate was sealed from this point on, implying that the outcome of Clarence's trial was a foregone conclusion. This is supported by the fact that it was Edward himself who brought the accusations against his sibling, and that no one spoke in the duke's defence (see Sources 2 and 3). Some contemporaries, however, argued that Edward was encouraged into this decision to destroy Clarence by Queen Elizabeth and her family, who allegedly regarded Clarence as a potential threat to the succession of the young Edward, Prince of Wales. Certainly, some of the case against the duke was apparently prepared by members of the Woodville family, and Gloucester was granted a number of Clarence's properties and titles in anticipation of the outcome of the trial, presumably to ensure he did not cause any dispute regarding his brother's downfall. Nonetheless, contemporary accusations against the queen should be treated with caution, as her family were very unpopular and most of the claims in this regard seem to have been based on rumour. In addition, while Gloucester undoubtedly benefited from his brother's death, there is no evidence aside from this to support the Tudor view that he deliberately engineered the quarrel and trial.

SOURCE

The *Crowland Chronicle* describes the trial in parliament of George, duke of Clarence in 1478. The *Crowland Chronicle* is a very long manuscript spanning a number of decades, written by more than one author.

The mind hesitates to relate the events that followed in the next parliament, for the dispute between two brothers of such stature was so sad a spectacle. No one argued against the duke except the king [who accused him of high treason], and no one replied to the king except the duke. Several persons, however, were brought forward and it was not clear to many whether they were appearing as accusers or witnesses. The two functions conflict when performed by the same person in the same case. The duke dismissed all the charges with a total denial, offering to defend his case in single combat if this was admissible.

Why dwell on all of this? The members of parliament considered that the information they had heard was sufficient, and they passed judgement against him. The sentence was pronounced by Henry, duke of Buckingham, who had been appointed steward of England for this occasion. The execution was postponed for a long time, until the speaker of the commons came with his colleagues to the house of lords to make a new request to finish the matter. As a result, whatever was the method of execution, it was indeed concluded – but would that this were the end of the misfortunes – in secret in the Tower of London within a few days.

Whoever was the key driving force in overthrowing Clarence's power, there is certainly some indication that Edward IV had difficulty in passing a death sentence on his brother. The *Crowland Chronicle* highlights that the sentence was passed by the duke of Buckingham, not the king himself, and there was a delay in carrying out the execution, which had to be requested again by the Speaker of the Commons. The manner in which Clarence died has been subject to some controversy; he was certainly killed in secret in the Tower of London on 18 February 1478. According to two contemporaries, Dominic Mancini and Jean de Roye, he was killed by being drowned in a butt of wine instead of being beheaded, as would have been usual. No official records exist to support this claim, which was repeated by Tudor propagandists (most famously Shakespeare) seeking to emphasise the drama and savagery of the Yorkist regime. Nonetheless, no other method of execution is detailed in any contemporary source.

ACTIVITY
KNOWLEDGE CHECK

Quarrel between Clarence and Gloucester

1 Make a list of the causes of Clarence's downfall in 1478, in order of significance.

2 Read Source 3. Create and complete a table, outlining the strengths and weaknesses of the source as evidence of Clarence's treacherous personality. Consider not only the content of the source, but also its provenance and historical context.

3 How strong is the evidence to support Clarence dying by being drowned in a butt of wine? Summarise your view in three sentences.

Clarence's death was a mixed blessing for Edward IV in terms of the security of his reign. On one hand, organising the death of one's own brother, whatever the provocation, was viewed as unnatural and was criticised by contemporaries on moral grounds. In addition, many were clearly sceptical about the fairness of the trial in 1478, which was highly politicised. However, it is true that Clarence's earlier behaviour in Edward's reign, notably his betrayal in 1469–70, would have provided legal justification for a treason charge had the king not decided to pardon him at that time. According to the *Crowland Chronicle*, the trial and death of Clarence led many to distrust and fear the king, implying that Edward was now regarded as something of a tyrant who would stop at nothing to quell opposition. Nonetheless, the chronicler's evidence in this passage is contradictory. On one hand, he claims people stopped supporting the king, but on the other, he writes that Edward posted 'the more trustworthy of his servants in all parts of the kingdom to guard castles, manors, forests and parklands' so that 'no threat could be made anywhere in the land however secretly by any man, whatever his rank, without his being immediately confronted with it'. Clearly, even according to this rather hostile account, Edward was able to maintain the loyalty of at least his key supporters, who acted to maintain control over the rest of the population. There is evidence to support the *Crowland Chronicle*'s claim that Edward relied heavily on loyal Yorkists. During his second reign, he developed the role of regional councils under the leadership of trusted supporters to help him control different areas in the country, a process that he had begun in his first reign, but which continued in the 1470s. The most well known of these was the Council of the North and he placed his brother, Gloucester, in the leading role, substantially increasing the duke's territorial holdings and providing him with growing dominance in the area.

A Level Exam-Style Question Section B

How significant was the challenge posed by George, duke of Clarence to Edward IV in the 1470s? (20 marks)

Tip

Although you will need to mention Clarence's earlier history of rebellion, focus predominantly upon his actions during Edward's second reign.

The impact of Edward's early death in 1483

During Easter 1483, Edward IV became suddenly ill and he died on 9 April at Westminster. There are conflicting contemporary accounts of the cause, but most agree that he died of natural causes in his early forties. His death was unexpected as he was ill for only ten days. In addition to his religious preparations, Edward added various **codicils** to his will in this time. Rather surprisingly, he did not make clear provision for how the succession should occur, namely whether his young son should be crowned immediately, and assisted as a minor to rule with the help of the royal council, or whether a Protector should be appointed to govern the realm in his stead until he came of age.

KEY TERM

Codicil
An addition or postscript to a legal document, such as a will.

Edward's death created a political crisis. The heir to the throne was his eldest son, also called Edward, and at that time only 12 years old. Given the catastrophic reign of Henry VI, the dangers of a child-king were well known. It was also of considerable concern that the queen's unpopular family had a high level of involvement with, and influence over, the new boy-king. Prince Edward had, for example, lived for many years at Ludlow in a household presided over by Queen Elizabeth's brother, Anthony Woodville, and was there at the time of his father's death. Therefore, when Richard of Gloucester decided to declare himself Protector on 4 May, he did not meet with opposition from the royal council, many of whom viewed him as the obvious candidate for such a role, as Edward's only surviving brother.

Richard of Gloucester's behaviour between Edward IV's death in April and July 1483 continues to be the subject of intense controversy, as during this period he seized the throne from his young nephew. This was surprising, as he had always appeared loyal to his brother the king. Richard's motivations doubtless included personal ambition for the crown, but may also have been motivated by concern for his own and the realm's safety if the young Edward V was allowed to rule under the influence of the Woodville family.

KEY TERM

Sanctuary
In the medieval period, all churches offered 'sanctuary', that is, immunity from arrest for 40 days for those fleeing the law. It was considered a particularly serious sin to attack, arrest or kill someone while they were in a church during this period of sanctuary. Certain important churches and abbeys offered sanctuary for longer periods, or even indefinitely, and sometimes had small communities of offenders living within their precincts.

On hearing news of his father's death, the new king, Edward V, travelled with his entourage from Ludlow towards London to prepare for his coronation. During this journey, he was intercepted at Stony Stratford by Gloucester and his retinue, who had travelled from the North apparently for this express purpose. Richard arrested the leading members of the Prince's household and the dowager queen's family, including Anthony Woodville, Sir Richard Grey (the queen's son by her first marriage) and Sir Thomas Vaughan. Clearly fearful, Elizabeth Woodville sought **sanctuary** at Westminster Abbey with her younger son, Richard.

Richard of Gloucester and Edward entered London on 4 May, and Richard was named Protector. The Woodvilles were unpopular and there does not seem to have been widespread opposition to Richard taking on the role, with some in the royal council perhaps being relieved that the queen's family would not maintain their strong influence over the boys. Nonetheless, it would be inaccurate to suggest Richard had overwhelming support. It is significant, for example, that, despite dislike of the Woodvilles among the nobility, Richard was unable to secure the execution of a number of leading members of the queen's family on the grounds of treason. At this stage, Richard's seizure of the throne was not inevitable in the eyes of contemporaries; indeed, the unwillingness to execute even unpopular members of the Woodville family suggests that many were afraid to declare their allegiance to Richard against the queen too openly, in case the situation changed later. The young Edward V was housed in the Tower of London. The choice of abode for the young king did not immediately cause alarm, as it was the traditional palace where monarchs stayed prior to coronation, but it had the highest levels of royal security and so prevented any Woodville supporters reaching the boy.

During May and June of 1483, the coronation was repeatedly delayed on Richard's orders, although the royal council met on 9 June to discuss the costs of Edward's crowning ceremonies, indicating that they still regarded this event as imminent. During June, Richard requested armed reinforcements against the dowager queen and her supporters, and tension between the two groups was heightened when a number of Edward IV's supporters, including Lord Stanley, the Bishop of Ely and the Archbishop of York, were arrested during a council meeting on the orders of Richard. It is probable that these men were seized because they were likely to oppose Richard's usurpation of the throne.

On 13 June, one of Edward IV's greatest friends, William, Lord Hastings, was executed by the Protector, after a hastily arranged trial. This execution was deplored by many who saw it as unjustified. Indeed, Rosemary Horrox has put forward the hypothesis that Hastings may have been killed as he refused to support Richard's bid to overthrow Edward V, a claim that is entirely plausible, although it cannot be supported by anything other than circumstantial evidence.

Somewhat surprisingly, at this stage, Elizabeth Woodville agreed to release her second son, Richard of York, from sanctuary at Westminster to attend his brother's coronation. The fact that she required the reassurance of both the Archbishop of Canterbury and the Bishop of Lincoln beforehand, however, was an indication of her unease. Both children were now housed together in the Tower and immediately after Richard of York's release from sanctuary, Gloucester delayed the coronation again, until 9 November. The timing of this postponement was highly significant and probably suggests that Gloucester had plans to seize power.

By late June, two of Gloucester's supporters, Dr Ralph Shaw and the duke of Buckingham, had given public statements supporting his claim to the throne. According to the chronicler Dominic Mancini, this focused initially on claims that Edward IV was himself illegitimate, but later claimed that the boys were born out of wedlock, on the grounds that Edward IV's marriage to Elizabeth Woodville was invalid because Edward had already been **precontracted** to another woman.

SOURCE 4

John Rous's description of the seizure of Edward and members of his household at Stony Stratford by Gloucester. Rous was a chaplain in the service of the earls of Warwick. Between c1480 and 1486, he wrote a work called *Historia regum Anglie* [A History of the Kings of England], which was originally intended for Edward IV. The work, however, was not completed until 1486, by which time Richard III had both gained and lost the throne and Henry VII was in power. Therefore, the work was altered and rededicated to the new Tudor king, making various unflattering references to Richard III.

Richard, duke of Gloucester, brother of the deceased king and by his ordinance protector of England, came upon him with a strong force at Stony Stratford and took the new king his nephew into his governance by right of his protectorship. The rest, namely Anthony, Earl Rivers [i.e. Anthony Woodville], elder brother of the queen and the new king's uncle, Richard Grey, [half-] brother of the king on his mother's side, and Sir Thomas Vaughan were forthwith arrested, and imprisoned at Pontefract, where shortly afterwards they were unjustly put to death. And so the new king was separated from his loyal servants and was received like an innocent lamb into the hands of wolves.

... Shortly after, Rivers, Grey and Vaughan were cruelly killed at Pontefract, lamented by almost all. Anthony Woodville, Earl Rivers, was found to be wearing, at the time of his death, the **hair shirt** which he had long been in the habit of wearing against his bare flesh. These lords were condemned to death by the earl of Northumberland on the false charge that they had in fact plotted the death of Richard, duke of Gloucester, at that time protector of the kingdom of England; and, for a thing they had never contemplated, the innocent humbly and peaceably submitted to a cruel fate from their enemies' butchers. The consecrated hair shirt of Earl Anthony was long after hung before the image of the Blessed Mary the Virgin at the Carmelite Friars at Doncaster.

On 25 June, Anthony Woodville, Richard Grey and Thomas Vaughan were executed at Pontefract in the presence of Richard's army and the following day Richard of Gloucester declared himself King Richard III of England. He was crowned on 6 July in Westminster Abbey. The claim that the boys were illegitimate was later to be made again formally in Richard's first parliament after he seized the throne.

ACTIVITY
KNOWLEDGE CHECK

Richard III's seizure of power

1 Create and complete a table of two columns, labelled:

   a) Arguments that Richard III should take the throne in 1483.

   b) Arguments that Richard III should not take the throne in 1483.

   Include factors such as the views of the royal council and previous experience of child-kings.

2 Draw up a timeline or flowchart of events from Edward IV's death in April 1483 to King Richard's coronation in July. Then highlight any factors that were likely to make Richard of Gloucester unpopular, and in each case make a note of which person/group they were likely to alienate.

3 Read Source 4. Is Rous's statement about Richard's role as Protector at this date accurate?

4 In the source, why is Rous's claim that Edward's servants were condemned on a 'false charge' significant in shaping an opinion of Richard of Gloucester's character?

5 Why does Rous emphasise Anthony Woodville's wearing of a hair shirt?

6 What impression is given of Richard III and the supporters of Edward IV in this passage? Why does Rous choose to emphasise the 'cruel fate' of Anthony Woodville, Richard Grey and Thomas Vaughan?

HOW EFFECTIVE WAS RICHARD III AS A MONARCH?

The significance of Richard's seizure of the throne in 1483

Richard III's seizure of power was significant mainly in terms of the impact it had upon his reputation, both at the time and after his death in 1485. Usurpers, such as Henry IV and Edward IV, had always been at a disadvantage in terms of the perceived legitimacy of their claim, which made them less stable on the throne. They were obliged to prove their worth to a greater degree than a king born to the role. It is hard to imagine a king as incompetent as Henry VI, for example, keeping the throne from 1422 to 1461 if he had usurped rather than inherited the throne. Nonetheless, as Henry IV and Edward IV had proved, usurpers could reign with some success and die of natural causes. Richard, however, held the throne only briefly, until 1485, and was killed in the Battle of Bosworth by an invading army led by Henry Tudor, a man with a relatively shaky claim to the throne. Richard's downfall was partly owing to military disaster on the battlefield, but also the fact that his support within the country as a whole was weakened by the perception that he had killed his nephews to gain the crown. This accusation of child-murder has never been proven, but it was widely suspected by contemporaries and has shaped perceptions of Richard III in subsequent centuries.

The most influential later interpretation of Richard was by William Shakespeare, who depicted him as thoroughly evil, cold-hearted, calculating and cruel in his play *Richard III*. In this dramatic interpretation, Richard is seen to have planned the downfall and death of not only his two nephews, the 'princes in the Tower', but also his brother Clarence, his wife Anne Neville and Edward IV's friend, William Lord Hastings. There can be little doubt that this play was influenced by sources written in the reign of his successor, Henry VII, which deliberately sought to blacken Richard's reputation to support the Tudor claim to the throne. There have more recently been strong attempts to rehabilitate the image of Richard, with the Richard III Society strongly arguing that he was innocent of the charges laid against him by his detractors. Modern historians have in general argued that Richard was responsible for the murder of his nephews, although this is still a highly contentious issue. Most scholars agree, however, that some of the accusations made against him have relatively little evidence to support them.

KEY TERM

Royal progress
A tour of the realm carried out by the monarch or a member of the immediate royal family. Such tours were designed to establish the king or queen's authority over the whole country.

The disappearance of the princes in the Tower

By 16 June 1483, both of Edward IV's male heirs were in the Tower of London and accounts of what happened thereafter are varied and controversial. In late July, while Richard was on **royal progress** in the North, he learned of a plot to free the boys from the Tower, which was unsuccessful. This may well have made him determined to kill his nephews, as potential rivals to his power. His brother, Edward IV, had acted in a similar way in May 1471 when Henry VI was murdered and this had made the Yorkist regime much more secure in the 1470s. Clear evidence for Richard as murderer, however, is not forthcoming, despite numerous accounts of events in the next few weeks. The only source actually written at the time of the usurpation was by Dominic Mancini, an Italian who visited London on a diplomatic mission in 1482, leaving shortly before Richard III's coronation in July 1483. He was therefore in the capital during the turbulent months that followed Edward IV's death and, as a foreigner, had the advantage of being able to express his opinions freely concerning the English monarchy, without fear of reprisals. He apparently wrote his account of what happened later in 1483, after he had left England, at the request of his patron, the Archbishop of Vienne. Mancini himself indicates that his account was imperfect, writing in the introduction that during his time in England he had not been able to obtain full information as to the reliability of his sources, and so his account lacked full and accurate detail. Historians such as Keith Dockray and Peter Hammond have questioned how much English Mancini may have spoken and where he gained his information from, although it does seem from the text that he was in contact with the boys' physician, Doctor Argentine, from whom he apparently gained information. Certainly, Mancini, like many chroniclers, was keen to tell a good story and his praise of the saintly behaviour as well as the extraordinary intelligence and charm of Edward may well be a rhetorical device, designed to contrast the dastardly behaviour of Richard of Gloucester (see Source 5). It is notable, however, that Mancini hesitates to state exactly what happened to the boys during the summer of 1483, stating that he is unable to be certain if Edward V was killed and by whom.

A Level Exam-Style Question Section A

Study Source 5 before you answer this question.

Assess the value of the source for revealing the character of Richard of Gloucester and the reasons for his successful usurpation of the throne in July 1483.

Explain your answer, using the source, the information given about its origin and your own knowledge about the historical context. (20 marks)

Tip

As well as assessing the provenance of the source, also consider the language Mancini uses and how the chronicle account is structured. It would also be worth considering the value of this source in light of the other available evidence.

SOURCE

An extract from Dominic Mancini's work, *The Usurpation of Richard III*, written in 1483.

Richard's actions up until now had given reason to think he was aiming for the crown. Yet some hope remained that this might not be his intention, for he had not yet gone so far as to lay claim to the throne itself. Indeed, he declared that he acted as he did only so that treason might be avenged and past wrongs righted. Moreover, all private deeds and official documents continued to bear the titles and name of Edward V.

However... the attendants who had previously ministered to the young king's needs were all kept from him. He and his brother were transferred to the inner chambers of the Tower proper.

Every day their appearances behind the bars and windows grew less frequent and eventually they ceased to appear altogether. The doctor, Argentine, was the only one of Edward's former retine who still attended him. He told how the young king, like a victim prepared for sacrifice, sought remission of his sins by daily confession and penance, believing death was close at hand... Such was the dignity of his person and charm of his visage that none who looked upon him was every weary of the sight. And after he disappeared, I saw many men moved to weeping and lamentation at the mention of his name. However, I have not yet been able to establish whether he was done away with and, if so, by what means.

Once Richard felt secure...he paraded himself with the intention that the people should see him and acclaim him – though he still pretended to no more than the title of protector... [H]e entertained large numbers of guests in his private apartments; yet, when he displayed himself in... London, almost no one came to watch. Rather... hoping he would be punished with a fate in accordance with his misdeeds, for his intentions were by now clear to all.

... For he had so corrupted the preachers of God's word that they did not blush to say in their sermons to the people, without the slightest regard for decency or religion, that King Edward IV's offspring should be disposed of at once, since he had no right to be king, and no more had they. For they claimed that Edward was conceived in adultery and bore no resemblance to the late duke of York [Edward IV's father], though he had been passed off as his son.

EXTRACT 1

C. Ross, *Richard III* (1999). Ross presents evidence to support the reliability of Mancini's account.

The importance of Mancini's narrative lies in the fact that he provides direct contemporary evidence that Richard's ruthless progress to the throne aroused widespread mistrust and dislike, to the extent that at least some of his subjects were willing to believe... that Richard had disposed of his nephews by violence. He had no good reason to invent this... story... Such stories cannot have been mere inventions of Tudor propagandists writing years after Richard's death. Recent attempts to discredit Mancini's testimony by presenting him as a prejudiced foreigner later corrupted by Tudor agents rests upon mere biased speculation and do not deserve serious consideration.

EXTRACT 2

C. Carpenter, *The Wars of the Roses: Politics and the Constitution in England, c.1437–1509* (1999). Carpenter expresses doubts as to the usefulness of Mancini's account of Richard of Gloucester's behaviour in the summer of 1483.

Mancini's 'Usurpation of Richard III' is, on the face of it, a straightforward account of events by an informed observer and it has in the past been treated as a reliable source. It is now apparent that Mancini was seriously handicapped not only by his ignorance of English and lack of access to high places, but also by a 'humanist' perspective which drove him to moralise and to find patterns in events which may not have been there. This is especially true of his account of the behaviour of Richard of Gloucester, which he made to look carefully planned.

THINKING HISTORICALLY   Evidence (6c)

Comparing and evaluating historians' arguments

Dominic Mancini's account of the usurpation of Richard III is unusual as he was present in London during the events in question and is the only primary source to be free of Tudor influence.

Read Source 5 and then consider the two historians' accounts of the value of Mancini's evidence and the events of 1483, provided in Extracts 1 and 2. Use these to answer the questions below:

1 Compare Extracts 1 and 2 and identify factual statements or claims that they both agree upon. Make a list of these points.

2 Look carefully at how the historians use language. Do they both use equally cautious language in making their claims or is one more confident and assertive than the other? Is one (or both) of the historians over-claiming?

3 Look back at Source 5. Do both historians appear to have made equally effective use of Mancini's evidence?

4 Are both of the historical accounts equally credible or are there reasons to prefer one account more than the other?

All other chronicle accounts of the fate of the princes are written after the death of Richard III, and are therefore potentially tainted with a desire to please Richard's enemy, Henry VII. Like Mancini, they also no doubt wished to tell a good story and this is a weakness of the chronicle genre as a source of evidence. An outline of the key early Tudor sources for the boys' fate is given below:

- The earliest Tudor source is found in the *Crowland Chronicle*, a very long manuscript written by more than one author. The section relating to Richard was written c1486 (early in Henry VII's reign) by an anonymous author, who seems to have been very well informed about the politics of the period and may have been either John Russell, Bishop of Lincoln, who was a royal councillor to Edward IV as well as chancellor during the reign of Richard III, or perhaps more plausibly one of his junior colleagues.

- One of the London chronicles suggests Henry Stafford, the duke of Buckingham, as the instigator of the murder (see Source 6). The author of this work is an unknown London citizen, probably writing in the early 16th century. This view is supported by two French contemporary commentators, Commines and Molinet, who claim that this was a widespread view at the

French royal court. It is possible Buckingham murdered the boys to advance his own claim to the throne, via his connection with the Beauforts. He probably felt less loyalty to the boys than others, as he appears to have not been a favourite of Edward IV; indeed, he seemingly had been excluded from court politics for much of his adult life, except on ceremonial occasions, despite having been married to Queen Elizabeth's sister, Katherine Woodville, since he was a child. Reasons for this apparent exclusion by Edward IV are unclear. After Edward's death, however, Buckingham was a major supporter of Richard of Gloucester as he journeyed to Stony Stratford to seize Prince Edward during the months which followed. On 10 May 1483, Richard, in his capacity of Protector of the Realm, granted Buckingham control of Wales and the Marches, as well as the right to raise troops in Shropshire, Herefordshire, Somerset, Wiltshire and Dorset. Following Hastings' death, he gained control in the North Midlands and was part of the group that negotiated with Elizabeth Woodville for the release of her second son from sanctuary. He also gave a speech to Londoners on 24 June 1483 at the Guildhall, promoting Gloucester's claim to the throne, although the text of the speech provided by Sir Thomas More in his *History of King Richard III* is fictional.

- Polydore Vergil was an Italian priest who lived for much of his life in England. He wrote a *History of England*, beginning the initial research in c1507 at the request of Henry VII, but the first version of the text seems to have been written in 1512–13, early in the reign of Henry VIII. He used a wide range of sources and, unusually for this period, often subjected them to considerable critical analysis. He argued that Richard initially ordered Robert Brakenbury, the lieutenant of the Tower of London, to murder the boys, but that Brakenbury could not bring himself to do so and then Richard turned instead to James Tyrell, who was a loyal member of Richard's retinue.

SOURCE 6

An anonymous early London chronicle that gives an account of the events of 1483.

This year [1483] King Edward V, late called the Prince of Wales, and Richard, duke of York, his brother, King Edward IV's sons, were put to death in the tower by the vise [advise/design] of the duke of Buckingham.

SOURCE 7

An account of the princes' death from Polydore Vergil's 'History of England', written c1512.

Richard, without the assent of the community... by the strength and determination of certain noblemen of his faction, seized the realm, contrary to the will of God and man... The heinous guilt of his wicked conscience did so frighten him that he lived in constant fear, for... he decided by death to dispatch his nephews, because as long as they lived he could never be out of danger; therefore he sent a warrant to Robert Brackenbury, lieutenant of the Tower of London, to organise their death... But the lieutenant of the Tower of London, after he received the king's horrible commission, was astonished by the cruelty... did therefore defer the deed in the hope that the king would spare his own blood, or their tender age, or alter that weighty decision. But any one of these considerations was far from taking place, seeing that [Richard's] mind remained immoveable... When King Richard realised that the lieutenant was delaying, he quickly gave the order of speeding the slaughter to another... James Tyrell, who, being forced to do the king's commandment, rode sorrowfully to London, and, to the worst example that has been almost ever heard of, murdered those babes of the royal line. This end had Prince Edward and Richard his brother, but with what kind of death these good children were executed is not certainly known. But King Richard, delivered by [their deaths] from his care and fear, kept the slaughter not long a secret, and, within a few days, allowed the rumour of their death to spread, with the intent (as we may well believe) that once the people realised there was no male issue of King Edward now left alive, they might with better mind and good will bear and sustain his government. But when the news of this notably foul deed was spread through the realm, so great a grief smote the hearts generally of all men, that they... wept everywhere and when the could weep no more, they cried out, 'Is there truly any man living so far in the enmity of God, so opposed to all that is holy and religious, so utterly an enemy to man, who would not have abhorred the evil of so foul a murder?' But especially the queen's and children's friends exclaimed against him, 'What will this man do to others who thus, without any reason, has killed his own relatives?'

A Level Exam-Style Question Section A

Study Source 7 before you answer this question.

Assess the value of the source for revealing the guilt or innocence of Richard III in relation to the disappearance of the princes in the Tower.

Explain your answer, using the source, the information given about its origin and your own knowledge about the historical context. (20 marks)

Tip

When writing your answer, remember to demonstrate your knowledge of the different primary sources available for this event and their strengths and weaknesses, while particularly analysing the source given.

- Sir Thomas More's *History of King Richard III* was written between c1513 and 1517, in the early years of the reign of his patron, Henry VIII. More was only six years old at the time of Richard's usurpation, and so he relied for much of his information on the testimony of John Morton, Archbishop of Canterbury, who was very hostile to Richard of Gloucester's assumption of power, having been imprisoned by him at the council meeting when Hastings was arrested. He also made use of Polydore Vergil's work. According to More's version (see Source 8), Richard decided to have the boys killed shortly after his coronation, in order to make his own hold on the throne more secure. The task was delegated to Sir James Tyrell, who employed two men to do the killing itself – Miles Forest, one of their guards, and John Dighton, Tyrell's horse-keeper. More claimed that the boys were smothered with pillows as they slept and that their bodies were buried at the foot of the stairs within the Tower of London.

SOURCE

An extract from Thomas More's *History of King Richard III,* written in the second decade of the 16th century, describing the murder of the princes in the Tower.

I shall rehearse you the sorrowful end of those babes [Edward and Richard], not after every way that I have heard, but after that way I have so heard by such men and by such means I think it were hard but it should be true.

King Richard, after his coronation, taking his way to Gloucester... devised as he rode to fulfil that thing which he before had intended. And for as much as his mind misgave him that, his nephews living, men would not reckon he could have right to the realm, he thought therefore without delay to be rid of them, as though the killing of his kinsmen could amend his cause and make him a kindly king.

... Sir James Tyrell devised that they should be murdered in their beds. To the execution whereof, he appointed Miles Forest, one of the four that kept them, a fellow hardened in murder before-time. To him, he joined one John Dighton, his own horsekeeper, a big broad, square, strong knave. Then, all the others being removed from them, this Miles Forest and John Dighton, about midnight (the innocent children lying in their beds) came into the chamber and suddenly lapped them up among the bedclothes, so bewrapped them and entangled them, keeping down by force the feather bed and pillows hard unto their mouths, that within a while, smothered and stifled, their breath failing, they gave up to God their innocent souls in to the joys of heaven, leaving to the tormentors their bodies dead in bed.

Which after that the wretches perceived, first by the struggling with the pains of death, and after long lying still, to be thoroughly dead; they laid their bodies naked out upon the bed, and fetched Sir James to see them. Who, upon the sight of them, caused those murderers to bury them at the stair foot, suitably deep in the ground, under a great heap of stones.

One factor which the Tudor sources unsurprisingly omit is that Henry VII had a motivation to arrange the death of the boys. He himself could not have perpetrated the crime as he was in exile in the summer of 1483, but obviously the murder of the children had the double effect of tarnishing Richard III's reputation and removing alternative claimants to the throne. Henry Tudor's mother, Lady Margaret Beaufort, was certainly extremely active in her son's cause and a consummate plotter, so the possibility of a conspiracy here deserves some consideration, but the evidence for such a plan is circumstantial only.

ACTIVITY
KNOWLEDGE CHECK

Richard III's seizure of power and his reign

Use index cards or pieces of A5 paper and write on each one the name of a core source for the usurpation of Richard III. As a minimum, include Dominic Mancini, Thomas More, Polydore Vergil, the *Crowland Chronicle* and the anonymous London chronicle.

On one side of the card/paper, write down in your own words what the source claims about who killed the princes in the Tower and any other significant claims they make about Richard III's character. Then, on the other side, write two lists: one of the value of the source (why it might give an accurate picture; where it is supported by other evidence; where it provides an insight into the matter which is unusual, etc.) and another of the weaknesses of the source as evidence (areas where it is factually inaccurate, where it is biased, or factors it is unable to comment on).

Richard's coronation and early reception as king

Richard was crowned on 6 July at Westminster, apparently without any protest concerning his usurpation. Indeed, at the feast after the crowning, the king's champion, as was traditional, rode into the banqueting hall and demanded if any questioned Richard III's right to the throne, and no noble raised an objection, although it may well have been an awkward moment. There was considerable continuity of government personnel in the first two months of the reign, suggesting that the new king was not particularly fearful of objections outside the immediate Woodville circle. In order to consolidate his power, King Richard and Queen Anne then toured the realm and were greeted in various cities with the normal lavish pageantry to celebrate the arrival of a new monarch. It was during this royal progress that news reached Richard of a conspiracy to free the princes. The figures involved were not politically significant, and so the plot was easily foiled.

The duke of Buckingham's rebellion

More serious was the next rebellion against Richard, which occurred in October and had the aim of placing Henry Tudor, the son of Lady Margaret Beaufort, on the throne. The fact that rebels now sought a different claimant to the throne from Edward V indicates that the boys were widely believed to be dead by the autumn of 1483, as otherwise opponents of Richard III would undoubtedly have been more inclined to support Edward IV's son. It also possibly lends some weight to the idea that Tudor may have been responsible for the boys' deaths in the first place. Henry Tudor's claim was based on his (illegitimate) descent from

the Lancastrian line, via the Beauforts, a somewhat shaky dynastic argument, but nonetheless offering a viable alternative to the reign of Richard III. Henry had been in exile in Brittany during the second reign of Edward IV and his mother was extremely active on his behalf in seeking support for his claim to the throne. Most significantly, Lady Margaret plotted with the dowager Queen Elizabeth to marry Henry to Elizabeth of York, the eldest daughter of Edward IV, a match that would have strengthened Henry's claim to the throne considerably and also gained him support, as such a marriage would unite the two sides – Yorkists and Lancastrians – thus potentially ending the Wars of the Roses. As a result of these activities, in October 1483 a series of rebellions broke out in the South of England, an area where Richard had considerably less influence and strength than in the North. Most dangerously of all for Richard, his former ally, the duke of Buckingham, betrayed him and decided to support Henry Tudor instead. Tudor and Buckingham were, in fact, cousins, which may have been a factor in this decision, or Buckingham may have had designs on the throne himself. Henry was proclaimed king by the rebels on 3 November, and he left Brittany with ships and finances to attempt invasion. He was, however, defeated, mainly by bad weather, as his fleet was scattered by a storm and he was unable to land safely in England as King Richard had been forewarned and placed soldiers along the Devon and Dorset coasts. Henry Tudor was therefore forced once again into exile in Brittany, where he was joined by a number of fellow rebels, including relatives of the Woodvilles and those who remained loyal to the memory of Edward IV.

Although the rebellion failed, it had a significant political impact for two key reasons. Firstly, it showed clearly that many of Edward IV's former servants and supporters did not favour rule by Richard III, as they were prepared to join the rebellion against him. This made the new king feel insecure and therefore when a number of these people lost their land when Richard punished the rebellion, he instead gave it to his own loyal retainers (usually from the North). While an understandable strategy, in the longer term this was to cause problems because the newcomers were often resented and so did not bolster royal authority in the way which had been hoped. Secondly, and perhaps most importantly, it advertised the fact that there was an alternative claimant to the throne. Therefore, Henry was joined in exile in Brittany by around 400 disaffected supporters of the former king, Edward IV, who now pledged loyalty to the Tudor claim. The threat from Tudor was increased when, by Christmas 1483, Henry had made public his intention of marrying Edward IV's eldest daughter, Elizabeth of York, in a match arranged by Henry's mother, Lady Margaret Beaufort, and the dowager queen, Elizabeth Woodville. The fact that such a marriage was contemplated by the Woodvilles shows that by this stage, they themselves believed the 'princes in the Tower' to be dead.

Edward IV and Richard III compared

Personality and family relations

In terms of personal authority and inspiring loyalty across the country, Edward IV in his second reign generally seems to have fared better than his successor. Other than Clarence's sedition, Edward in the 1470s faced no serious challenge to his power while he was living, and was at least partially successful in delegating authority to regional councils and to high-ranking, trusted Yorkist lieutenants in these areas. His decision to grant his brother Richard considerable power in the North provided loyal support during his reign, although it did undermine his son in 1483. Nonetheless, Edward's marriage and the dominance of the Woodvilles at court remained unpopular particularly among the nobility and he continued to behave extremely generously to his wife's family in the second reign, to a level which lost his wife considerable support after his death in 1483.

Richard as duke of Gloucester appears to have been held in high regard in many areas of the North especially, and there is anecdotal evidence of warm support for Richard as king from individuals who held him in high esteem, such as Thomas Langton, Bishop of St David's (see Source 10). Buckingham's rebellion illustrated, however, that after he usurped the throne, Richard III had serious problems with the loyalty of the southern counties. Obviously, this was a major weakness of his kingship and during a series of minor risings in 1484–85 he became increasingly dependent upon his own northern retinue to maintain power, which undermined him in his kingly role of impartial and 'good lord' to all.

SOURCE 9

Portrait of Richard III, c1516, by an unknown artist.

Richard' Rex Angli

SOURCE 10

Private letter from Thomas Langton, Bishop of St David's, to his friend the Prior of Christ Church, Canterbury, written in 1483, after Richard III was on the throne. Described as a royal chaplain during the reign of Edward IV, Langton was clearly in Richard's favour and as Protector, Gloucester secured for him the bishopric of St David's. Later, in 1485, Richard granted him a more valuable post in Salisbury. Here, Langton describes his early impressions of Richard as king.

He contents the people wherever he goes better than did any prince... I never liked the qualities of any prince as well as his; God has sent him to us for the welfare of us all.

It is evident that during Richard's brief reign, the threat of rebellion and a challenge to the throne was never far away. After the disappearance of the princes, this was mainly owing to the threat from Henry Tudor. The French government used Henry's claim to disadvantage Richard, placing him in a weak position politically. To combat this, as well as to reduce his financial difficulties, Richard agreed an Anglo-Scottish truce in 1484 that relieved pressure on the northern border. He also sought to improve relations with the Woodvilles. In response to this, Richard sought reconciliation with Elizabeth Woodville. On 1 March 1484, he finally persuaded the dowager queen and her daughters to leave the sanctuary of Westminster Abbey and promised to find the girls suitable husbands. In the circumstances, any relationship was predictably filled with suspicion, as evidenced by Richard needing to promise that their personal safety would be respected if they left sanctuary. Nonetheless, Richard was successful and so welcomed Elizabeth and her eldest daughter to court at Christmas that year. Indeed, such was the warmth of his welcome to his niece that he scandalised some observers, including the *Crowland* chronicler. Rumours were rife that he wished to marry the princess.

To some extent, then, both Edward IV and Richard III had political difficulties because of their relationships with women and the rumour and scandal mongering which could surround these. Edward had suffered setbacks, particularly in his first reign, because of his secret and unsuitable marriage to Elizabeth Woodville. Certainly, this had been a major contributor to the loss of the throne in 1470, but he was able to regain power owing to his own military ability and, above all, the inherent weakness of Henry VI. Edward was also strengthened in his position by the fact that he had two sons, indicating that his dynasty could continue.

Richard, on the other hand, was damaged domestically by the fact that his son died in 1484 and so he lacked an heir. The death of Queen Anne in 1485 caused further problems. There is evidence from London merchant records and the *Crowland Chronicle* that Richard was suspected of involvement in the death of his wife in order to be able to marry his niece, Elizabeth of York. This match would have enabled Richard to scupper a possible marriage between the princess and Henry Tudor. While probably an unjustified rumour, it is notable that the chronicle accounts claim the accusation alone weakened Richard's support in the North, as Anne Neville's family were held in very high esteem there because of her family's long association with the area. Indeed, so widespread was the whispered accusation that Richard was obliged to publicly declare both to the civic government of London and to the royal council that he grieved the death of Anne and that he had no desire to marry Elizabeth of York.

Royal finances

In terms of royal finance, it is clear that both Edward IV and Richard III were beset by problems. Under Henry VI, crown revenues had fallen and the problem was made substantially worse by the weak monarch's very tenuous understanding of the importance of the careful use of royal patronage. There was also a trade recession, and an extremely costly and ultimately ineffective campaign in France, which resulted in heavy and unpopular taxes. Edward needed to remedy these problems in his first reign, preferably without relying too heavily on taxation, which required the consent of parliament and was liable to be less forthcoming to a king who had recently usurped the throne. He did this, to a certain extent, by farming royal lands more efficiently, claiming customs (prior to 1465 without parliamentary permission to do so) and using revenue from lands that either were part of his own private inheritance from his father, or from estates gained by the crown from traitors to the Yorkist regime, that is, Lancastrians who had found themselves on the wrong side in the Wars of the Roses. Most controversially, however, Edward adopted a number of financial measures, some of which were of dubious legality. These measures included:

- obliging the clergy to pay a subsidy, nominally in response to Pope Pius' call for a crusade to be launched, although in reality the money went to the English crown

- re-issuing coinage, and devaluing the amount of gold and silver in the coins, to make a profit for the king

- borrowing money from wealthy subjects, in particular London merchants

- borrowing money from foreign bankers and merchants, notably the Italians

- tighter customs, controls

- the collection of forced gifts of money (called 'benevolences') from wealthier subjects (see Chapter 2, page 58).

However useful, none of these measures fully met Edward IV's costs, but he was greatly assisted financially in 1475 when he invaded France and negotiated the Treaty of Picquigny with the French king, gaining a pension of £10,000 per annum from the French government. This allowed him to live without needing to appeal to parliament for taxation in normal circumstances (i.e. when not at war). While this treaty was widely viewed as grasping and unpatriotic, it did clearly give Edward financial comfort and independence in the last eight years of his reign. Nonetheless, Edward had a large family to provide for, including his mother, the

queen, his brothers and children, which was a significant drain on his income. In terms of public relations, Edward was also often criticised for being extravagant with personal expenditure, and his wife Elizabeth Woodville was also regarded as mercenary.

Despite his brother's much emphasised greed, however, Richard III inherited a very empty royal treasury. Indeed, Richard was obliged to pay £800 out of his own pocket towards the expenses of the king's household in June, before he had taken the throne. In addition, his claim to the throne was shaky as a usurper and, quite possibly to ingratiate himself with parliament, he did not collect the taxes that had been granted to his brother by a previous session. In 1484, despite his weak financial position, he was careful not to make financial demands and had to agree to a petition from the Commons in parliament that his subjects should no longer be subject to benevolences (see Source 11). The tone of this petition reflects how very unpopular this form of money collection had been and indicates one of the weaknesses of Edward IV's reign. Nonetheless, this promise proved very difficult for Richard to keep, and in 1485, faced with invasion by Henry Tudor, he was obliged to request loans (rather than gifts) from his subjects, but the *Crowland Chronicle* expressed the view that these were benevolences by another name and that the loans would not be repaid.

A Level Exam-Style Question Section B

'Both Edward IV and Richard III faced rebellions during their reigns because of their usurpations of the crown.'

How far do you agree with this statement? (20 marks)

Tip

Remember to include information about both the reigns of Edward IV.

SOURCE

11   Petition from the Commons to Richard III in the parliament of 1484, requesting that 'benevolences' no longer be collected. The king agreed to this request.

The king, mindful that the commons of this his realm have been enslaved by intolerable charges and exactions as the result of new and unlawful inventions and inordinate covetousness, contrary to the law of this realm, and in particular by a new imposition called a benevolence, by which for several years the subjects and commons of this land, against their will and freedom, have paid great sums of money, to their almost complete destruction, as a result of which several worshipful men of this realm were compelled by necessity to break up their households and to live in great penury and wretchedness, their debts unpaid and their children unpreferred, and such memorials as they had ordained for the good of their souls were cancelled and annulled, to the great displeasure of God and to the destruction of this realm. Therefore the king wills that it be ordained, by the advice and assent of his lords spiritual and temporal and the commons assembled in this present parliament, and by authority of the same, that henceforth his subjects and the commonalty of this his realm shall in no way be burdened by any such charge, exaction or imposition called a benevolence or by similar charges, and the exactions called benevolences taken before this time shall not be taken as a precedent for making such or the same charge upon any of his said subjects of this realm in future, but shall be voided and annulled forever.

Military success and failures

In military terms, both Edward and Richard were able fighters and commanders. Edward was fortunate, however, that in the Battle of Tewkesbury of 1471 the Lancastrian Prince Edward was killed, which effectively ended immediate Lancastrian opposition to his rule. Although only in his late teens, the death of Prince Edward on the battlefield was considered honourable and so aroused none of the emotive response of the disappearance of the younger 'princes in the Tower', and so did not undermine Edward IV. In terms of foreign policy, Richard III's decision in 1484 to antagonise the French, Bretons and Scots through naval attacks was certainly unwise, as this lent Tudor international support at a crucial stage in his preparations for invasion (see below). This contrasted with Edward's much less warlike stance against the French in the early stages of his first reign, when he was largely preoccupied with dealing with domestic rebellions and threats on the northern border. Edward only became focused on a French invasion later, from 1468 onwards, and while his tax collections for this were a cause of unpopularity, this slower approach to war was less antagonistic to foreign powers at a time when he was seeking to establish his authority and support networks at home.

 THINKING HISTORICALLY   Interpretations (6a)

Ever-changing history

Our interpretations of the past change as we change. This may be because our social attitudes have changed over time, or perhaps because historians have constructed a different theory, or perhaps technology has allowed archaeologists to discover something new.

1 Work in pairs. Make a timeline that starts with the defeat of Richard III at the Battle of Bosworth and ends 50 years in the future. Construct reactions that illustrate the point that time changes history. In the future box, you can speculate on how people might react to Richard III's reign in 50 years' time. Below is an example.

1485	1500 (Henry VII's reign)	1590s (Elizabeth I on the throne)	1920s	1980s	2013 (Richard III's skeleton discovered)	2066
Defeat of Richard III by Henry Tudor.	Tudor supporter: 'A fantastic victory, which demonstrated it was God's will that he defeated the evil Richard III.' Ricardian supporter: 'A tragic defeat for a brave warrior, who was beset by problems and whose reign was cut short.'	Shakespeare fan: 'Richard III's reign was undoubtedly the worst part of the dreadful Wars of the Roses. He was a hideous, deformed, and evil man.' Tudor politician: 'Richard III had no heir. Civil war is dangerous for a country. How will we cope once the queen dies?'	Member of the Richard III Society: 'Richard III has had his reputation systematically and unfairly blackened by Tudor propagandists.' School textbook: 'Richard III's reign was the darkest period in the late Middle Ages, a period of witchcraft, child-murder and hatred.'	Member of the Richard III society: 'There is no evidence to support the view that Richard III was evil; this is as much Tudor propaganda as the claims he was a hunchback.' Academic historian: 'Richard III probably ordered the killing of the princes in the Tower, but there is no conclusive evidence and his reputation has undoubtedly been damaged by subsequent Tudor propaganda.'	Member of the Richard III society: 'The deformity of Richard III's spine might be proven, but Tudor accounts of his reign are still deeply unreliable.' Academic historian: 'The discovery of the deformed skeleton lends more credence to Tudor accounts of his appearance; can the same be true for his character as king?'	?

Answer the following questions.

2 Identify three factors that have affected how Richard III's personality and reign have been interpreted over time, or might affect their interpretation in the future.

3 If a historian was to write a book proposing a radically new interpretation of Richard III's reign, how might other historians react? What would affect their reaction?

4 How will the future change the past?

WHICH FACTORS WERE MOST IMPORTANT IN SUPPORTING HENRY TUDOR'S SEIZURE OF POWER IN 1485?

Henry Tudor and reasons for his success at the Battle of Bosworth: foreign aid and the role of the Stanleys

Beset by problems domestically, it is unsurprising that Richard III was concerned regarding the threat from Tudor. In order to quell this, in 1484 the king began to negotiate with Pierre Landais, treasurer to the duke of Britanny, for the handover of the troublesome rebels in exile. News of this plan reached Henry in the autumn, however, and he escaped to France, where the duke of Britanny allowed his supporters to join him. The king of France at this time was Charles VIII, who was in his early teens in 1485 and heavily influenced by his regents, his elder sister Anne and her husband, Pierre de Bourbon, lord of Beaujeu. The French government was anxious to assist Henry and to make as much trouble as possible for Richard III. Accordingly, they provided him with money, ships and supplies to launch an invasion, which headed to England in the summer of 1485. Henry landed in Wales, an area where he could rely on considerable support because of family connections, probably with between 2,000 and 4,000 troops (contemporary accounts vary considerably in their figures). His troops consisted of around 400 English exiles who opposed Richard, including significant nobles with experience of military command, such as John de Vere, the earl of Oxford. The bulk of the army were experienced French soldiers, with some Scottish fighters as well. Henry gathered more support as he marched across the country. Despite this, he had the smaller army, probably numbering around 5,000 on the eve of battle, compared to c12,000 of Richard's troops. Richard therefore had some justification for confidence as well as a strong motivation for success: defeating Tudor would also have removed a thorn in Richard's side, and provided clear evidence for doubters that he was a monarch chosen by God.

In supporting the Tudor cause, the French were undoubtedly trying to destabilise Richard III. During the winter of 1483–84, Richard had pursued an aggressive policy of naval attacks on Brittany, France and Scotland. This helps to explain why Tudor was able to gain some international support at this stage, which was to prove highly significant for his ultimate victory. Certainly, by early 1484, the French government was very concerned that Richard might try to invade France to take advantage of weakness caused by a child-king. Therefore, they encouraged the duke of Brittany to support a Tudor invasion by allowing Henry to organise troops there while in exile, renewing their alliance with Scotland.

Aware of the risk of a joint French–Scottish attack, as well as the threat from Tudor, Richard changed strategy in autumn 1484 and instead negotiated peace with the Scots at Nottingham in September, agreeing a three-year truce. He also sought to re-establish good relations with Brittany, but Henry Tudor fled from the duke of Brittany's court before he could be captured. Instead, Henry established himself in the court of the French king. Dramatically, in December 1484, Richard condemned the French support of Tudor and responded by renewing English claims to the French throne. This ensured that Charles VIII's government backed the Tudor invasion in the summer of 1485.

In the circumstances, Richard was highly aware of the prospect of invasion and had readied his forces. He was somewhat weakened, however, by inaccurate spy reports that informed him that Tudor would land on the south coast, when in fact he entered via Wales. This meant that Richard was less prepared and had to move his troops quickly, intercepting Henry's army at Leicester. The two sides fought on 22 August at the Battle of Bosworth, in Leicestershire.

Relatively little detail is known for certain about the battle as there are numerous discrepancies in the contemporary accounts. Ongoing archaeological projects into the site are currently showing that it involved the early use of gunpowder and firearms, indicating that it was a fight of considerable significance in relation to military technology. Contemporary commentators, however, focused much more on the personalities of the leading participants. It was noted, for example, that Henry Tudor's vanguard appears to have been particularly ably commanded by the earl of Oxford. It is also clear that the role of two men was considered particularly important: that of Henry Percy, earl of Northumberland and Thomas, Lord Stanley. Northumberland came to battle apparently in support of Richard III, but failed to engage his troops (who included a number of Richard's northern retinue) in the battle, thereby depriving the king of considerable support. It is possible that this was a deliberate ploy on his part, motivated by a calculation that Henry Tudor was likely to grant him more control in the North (the traditional area of dominance for his family) than Richard III had done in his reign. Indeed, some modern commentators have argued that he may have made a secret prior arrangement with Henry Tudor to act in this way. The idea of a secret pact is made less likely, however, by the fact that Northumberland was imprisoned briefly after the battle by the victorious new King Henry VII, and only released when it became clear that the Tudor regime could not hope to control the North without Northumberland's influence.

Even more significant to the outcome of the battle was Thomas, Lord Stanley, who had around 4,000 of Richard's 12,000 troops under his command. He was the second husband of Lady Margaret Beaufort, and so was Henry Tudor's stepfather. Despite his wife's obvious partisanship, according to historian Michael J. Bennett, Stanley appeared a stalwart of Richard III's regime. He had supported Richard in the aftermath of Buckingham's rebellion and replaced the disgraced duke as constable of England, although it is unclear if in reality he shared his wife's preference for a Tudor king. Certainly he was obliged by Richard to, in theory at least, act as his wife's gaoler and was charged with preventing her from engaging in any further political intrigue after her actions in 1483.

Richard III appears to have remained understandably doubtful of Stanley's loyalty and, as news reached the king of Henry's planned invasion, he immediately demanded that Stanley came to his side with his retinue. According to the *Crowland Chronicle*, Stanley avoided this requirement by claiming he was ill with sweating sickness, a much-feared form of epidemic disease in this period. The author of the same chronicle also claimed that Richard insisted that Stanley's eldest son, George, Lord Lestrange, remained as hostage to ensure his father's good behaviour during the invasion. Whatever the exact truth of this claim, Thomas Stanley and his brother, Sir William, both arrived at Bosworth. Thomas Stanley was careful to take no part in the fighting, hanging between the two armies and not taking a side. His brother, meanwhile, gave crucial support to Henry and this intervention led to a Tudor victory. It is plausible that this careful double game had been pre-planned between Henry and his stepfather, possibly at a secret meeting on 20 August. Certainly, Henry Tudor appeared very grateful to the Stanleys and confirmed Lord Thomas Stanley's role as Constable of the Realm in early 1486, as well as providing him with other titles and grants of land.

SOURCE 12

This section of the *Crowland Chronicle* describes Richard's preparations for fighting in August 1485, and the Battle of Bosworth itself. From Henry T. Riley (trans.), *Ingulph's Chronicle of the Abbey of Croyland* (1908).

At day-break… there were no chaplains present to perform Divine service on behalf of king Richard, nor any breakfast prepared to refresh [his] flagging spirits… besides which… he declared that during the night he had seen dreadful visions, and had imagined himself surrounded by a multitude of dæmons. He consequently presented a countenance which, always attenuated, was on this occasion more livid and ghastly than usual, and asserted that the issue of this day's battle, to whichever side the victory might be granted, would prove the utter destruction of the kingdom of England. He also declared that it was his intention, if he should prove the conqueror, to crush all the supporters of the opposite faction; while, at the same time, he predicted that his adversary would do the same towards well-wishers to his own party, in case the victory should fall to his lot…

A battle of the greatest severity now ensuing between the two sides, the earl of Richmond, together with his knights, made straight for king Richard; while the earl of Oxford, who was next in rank to him in the whole army and a most valiant soldier, drew up his forces, consisting of a large body of French and English troops, opposite the wing in which the duke of Norfolk had taken his position. In the part where the earl of Northumberland was posted, with a large and well-provided body of troops, there was no opposition made, as not a blow was given or received during the battle. At length a glorious victory was granted by heaven to the said earl of Richmond, now sole king, together with the crown, of exceeding value, which king Richard had previously worn on his head. For while fighting, and not in the act of flight, the said king Richard was pierced with numerous deadly wounds, and fell in the field like a brave and most valiant prince; upon which… many others, chiefly from the north, in whom king Richard put the greatest confidence, took flight without engaging; and there was left no part of the opposing army of sufficient importance or ability for the glorious conqueror Henry the Seventh to engage, and so add to his experience in battle.

Through this battle peace was obtained for the entire kingdom, and the body of the said king Richard being found among the dead… Many other insults were also heaped upon it, and, not exactly in accordance with the laws of humanity, a halter being thrown round the neck, it was carried to Leicester; while the new king also proceeded to that place, graced with the crown which he had so gloriously won.

In the event, the Battle of Bosworth was short lived, probably lasting two to three hours. Almost all chroniclers, even those hostile to Richard, note that Richard III fought bravely to the death, probably dying only right at the end of the fighting. This suggests that he was a formidable and determined warrior. The discovery of his remains in 2013 supports this view, as the body shows evidence of severe head injuries in evidence.

EXTEND YOUR KNOWLEDGE

Archaeological evidence for the death of Richard III

In 2013, a venture by the Richard III Society, the University of Leicester and Leicester City Council resulted in a major dig in Leicester to find a Franciscan priory called Greyfriars, where historical records indicated that Richard III had been buried after the Battle of Bosworth. The remains of Richard III were discovered. The skeleton showed severe injuries, particularly to the skull, but Jo Appleby from the University of Leicester has argued that only minor facial disfigurement was caused as Henry Tudor wished Richard to be identified to prevent any later claims that he had survived the battle.

It is clear from the bones that some of the injuries occurred when Richard was not wearing armour. It is likely that Richard was killed, then stripped of his armour and that some damage was then inflicted on the corpse post-mortem. This suggests that Richard's enemies engaged in some form of humiliation of the corpse.

Conclusion

Henry Tudor was in many respects an unlikely victor in 1485: he had spent much of his life in exile, and so was unable easily to build up a support base within England; his dynastic claim to the throne was tenuous; and an earlier attempt at invasion had been unsuccessful. Richard, on the other hand, had spent considerable time at the heart of royal power during the reign of Edward IV, and was exceptionally wealthy and influential in the North especially. Several factors undermined Richard III's reign, however, some of which went as far back as the Yorkist usurpations of 1461 and 1471. Although the second reign of Edward IV had appeared stable, there was latent disquiet from disaffected Lancastrian supporters, which was exacerbated by the power of the unpopular Woodvilles. In these circumstances, Richard's usurpation of the throne from his nephew caused further divisions in an already disunited realm. Crucially, it split the Yorkist supporters into those who favoured Edward IV and V, and those who wished to support Richard's claim to the throne. Whatever the truth of the situation, rumours that Richard had killed the boys, and the clear fact that he imprisoned them in order to seize the throne, was also morally unpalatable even to politically cynical 15th-century onlookers and made them less inclined to support him. While Richard's major support base in the North was valuable, he was not successful in securing the loyalty of the South during his short reign, which added to his vulnerability, as did his aggressive foreign policy in relation to the French which, with hindsight, proved unwise as it is unlikely Henry could have succeeded without military support from Charles VIII's government. In 1485, the shrewd and determined Henry Tudor proved able to take advantage of this situation to make his bid for power, and took full advantage of wavering loyalty towards Richard III from key figures such as Sir Thomas Stanley.

ACTIVITY
KNOWLEDGE CHECK

Henry VII and evaluating reasons for his success at the Battle of Bosworth

1 Create a table with two columns, labelled: 'Richard's strengths in 1485' and 'Richard's weaknesses in 1485'. Complete this in detail. Then highlight the two most significant weaknesses and write a paragraph explaining why they are particularly important.

2 With a partner, debate the statement: 'Richard III was defeated at Bosworth because of his failings in foreign policy, not his failings in domestic policy.'

3 Create a living graph of Henry VII's actions between 1483 and 1485. The bottom axis should give the dates and the vertical axis should give a scale of 1 to 5 and be labelled 'Henry Tudor's success'. Mark each key event on the graph with a small cross and label it, giving some detail of the event and why it was/was not significant to his claim to the throne.

ACTIVITY
SUMMARY

The second reign of Edward IV

1 Reread the information about Clarence's behaviour during Edward's second reign and the reasons for his downfall. Then use it to copy and complete this table (the first example has been completed for you):

Date	Event	Does this event indicate that Clarence was untrustworthy/plotting against the king?	How well did Edward handle this problem?
1471	Edward seeks to restore order in the North, so asks Clarence to give up his northern properties to the Percy family. This angered Clarence and in an attempt to satisfy him the king gave him the earldom of Richmond (originally belonging to the exiled Henry Tudor), but which had initially been granted to Gloucester.	It indicates Clarence was ungrateful to Edward, who had forgiven his earlier betrayal, and that strong rivalry existed between Clarence and Gloucester. Noblemen rarely wished to give up land or honours, however, so it is not evidence that Clarence was plotting at this stage.	He sought to placate Clarence at Gloucester's expense, which was likely to foster problems in the future. The proposal to return northern estates to the Percies was probably wise, but it would be better if this confusion had been avoided from the outset.

2 a) Write a list of the consequences of Clarence's downfall.

   b) Did Clarence's death make Edward IV more or less secure on the throne?

3 Write a list of reasons why some people would support Richard of Gloucester's bid to be Protector of the Realm in 1483.

4 Draw a mind map of the difficulties Richard III faced as king during his reign. Colour-code his problems into these categories:

   a) Financial problems.

   b) Domestic political problems.

   c) International political problems. (Include Scotland here.)

   Where possible, in a different colour, add information about how Richard tried to resolve these threats.

5 To what extent was Henry Tudor's success at the Battle of Bosworth a result of his own ability, and to what extent was it a result of Richard III's unpopularity?

WIDER READING

Buckley, R. and Morris, M. *Richard III: The King under the Car Park: The Story of the Search for England's Last Plantagenet King,* University of Leicester School of Archaeology and Ancient History (2013)

Chrimes, S.B. *Henry VII,* Yale University Press (1999)

Cooper, S. 'Putting Richard III on trial', *History Today* 63:11 (2013)

Cunningham, C. *Henry VII,* Routledge (2007)

Dockray, K. and Hammond, P. *Richard III: From Contemporary Chronicles, Letters and Records,* Fonthill Media (2013)

Gunn, S.J. 'Henry VII (1457-1509)', *Oxford Dictionary of National Biography,* Oxford University Press (2004). Online edn, Jan 2008 www.oxforddnb.com/view/article/12954

Horrox, R. *Richard III: A Study in Service,* Cambridge University Press (1989)

Pollard, A.J. *Richard III and the Princes in the Tower,* Endeavour Press (1991)

Richmond, C. 'The Battle of Bosworth', *History Today,* 35:8 (1985)

3.7

Henry VII: seizing the throne and trying to keep it, 1485–97

KEY QUESTIONS

- How successful were the methods Henry VII used to secure his hold on the throne?
- Who challenged Henry VII and how significant was this opposition?
- How serious were the tax rebellions of 1489 and 1497?

INTRODUCTION

Henry VII's reign and personality present historians with an intriguing range of contradictions: he had a very weak claim to the throne after a bloody civil war, yet died in his bed and founded a long-standing dynasty; he was noted for financial greed, yet was also famed for the lavishness of his hospitality and the splendour of his court; he married for political expediency and was known for his ruthlessness even with loyal supporters, but also was a faithful husband, a loving father and a man of considerable personal piety. Henry was an able politician and diplomat, engaging in important negotiations during his reign with the Netherlands, Scotland and France, while also subduing two popular anti-tax rebellions at home in 1489 and 1497. For all his successes, however, and the perceived stability of his reign, his reign was also seriously challenged twice by **pretenders**.

More illustrious members of the early Tudor court also had colourful personal histories: the new queen, Elizabeth of York, for example, was the daughter of Edward IV and Elizabeth Woodville. She hid in sanctuary with her mother in 1483 when her brothers were imprisoned. Later, she was allegedly courted by her own uncle, Richard III, probably in an attempt to break her projected alliance to Henry Tudor. Lady Margaret Beaufort, the king's mother, was another prominent figure who fought hard for her new-found role as a royal **matriarch**; she gave birth to Henry when she was only 13 and later plotted with his uncle, Jasper Tudor, to bring him to the throne.

Given the difficulties Henry had experienced in gaining power, it is unsurprising that he displayed considerable determination to hold onto the throne. As a usurper, he remained suspicious throughout his reign of possible challenges to his power. In his striving for security, he raised new figures to power, including the much disliked, rapacious lawyer, Edmund Dudley. Henry's reign certainly secured the kingdom for his heir, but it was also a time of suspicion, intrigue, espionage and counter-espionage, diplomacy and war. The death of the king's eldest son, Arthur, in 1502, shortly after Arthur's marriage to Katherine of Aragon, was a serious blow for Tudor dynastic claims and it was this family bereavement that gave Henry a new heir who was to change England even more than his father, the infamous Henry VIII.

KEY TERMS

Pretender
Someone who impersonates a more important figure, in this context in order to claim the throne.

Matriarch
A female head of a family, and indicates that this person exercised considerable personal authority over her children and grandchildren. The male equivalent is a patriarch.

1485 – August: Battle of Bosworth. Richard III killed and Henry Tudor becomes king.

1487 – February: Lambert Simnel appears in Ireland, claiming to be Edward, earl of Warwick. Receives support from some Irish earls and English Yorkists including the earl of Lincoln. Lincoln flees England.
June: Simnel, Lincoln and Lovell invade England and are defeated at Battle of Stoke by Henry VII

1495 – February: Sir William Stanley executed for treason
Mid- to late 1495: Warbeck attempts revolt in Ireland and invasion of England via sea

1485	1486	1487	1488	1489	1490	1491	1492	1493	1494	1495

1486 – January: Henry VII marries Elizabeth of York
March to April: Viscount Lovell and Humphrey Stafford of Grafton lead unsuccessful rebellion against Henry VII

1489 – April: Yorkshire rebellion against Henry VII, led by Sir John Egremont. Rebels defeated but Egremont escapes.

1491 – Perkin Warbeck visits Ireland and impersonates Edward IV's younger son, Richard of York

Early 1493 – Alleged conspiracy to support Warbeck's claim among senior members of the Tudor court discovered by Henry's spies

HOW SUCCESSFUL WERE THE METHODS HENRY VII USED TO SECURE HIS HOLD ON THE THRONE?

Claiming the throne and the significance of the marriage to Elizabeth of York

The late 14th and 15th centuries were a period when the laws governing the dynastic succession of the monarchy were severely tested, and Henry VII's accession to the throne was a prime example of this. The Tudor claim to the throne by right of birth was undoubtedly dubious; indeed, there were several alternative candidates for the crown with equally strong claims. Henry VII, however, had the decided advantage that he had won a decisive victory at the Battle of Bosworth in 1485, with Richard III being killed in the process. This was regarded by some as a sign of God's approval of the Tudor candidate. In the speech Henry gave to his first parliament in November 1485, therefore, he suggested that his claim was hereditary (and kept the details vague), but also by right of conquest (see Source 1). He also indicated that he would allow all those who were loyal to him to prosper. His claim, then, was one based as much on the fact he was an acceptable and practical option, as on any ideological underpinning. In these circumstances, Henry was understandably concerned about the strength of his hold on the throne and was anxious to consolidate his position as quickly as possible. To assist him in this endeavour, he cleverly dated his reign from 21 August, the day before the Battle of Bosworth, so that technically all those who had fought against him were traitors. This instantly put Yorkist supporters in a legally weak position and ensured that they were immediately made very aware of their need to please the new monarch.

SOURCE

Taken from the official records of the parliament of November 1485, the first meeting of Henry VII's reign. It describes how the new king met with the Commons and outlined by what right he claimed the throne.

The... lord king, addressing the aforesaid commons in person and demonstrating that his coming to the right and crown of England was as much by lawful title of inheritance as by the true judgment of God in giving him victory over his enemy in battle, announced that all his subjects, of whatever estate, degree or condition they might be, should have and hold to them and their heirs, all their lands, tenements, rents and hereditaments, and enjoy them, with the exception of such people as have offended his majesty, who should be punished in the court of the present parliament according to their desserts.

A key factor in stabilising the kingdom and consolidating Henry's claim on the throne would be his choice of bride. Before Bosworth, he had publicly pledged to marry Edward IV's eldest daughter and the sister of the 'princes in the Tower', Elizabeth of York. This match was potentially very advantageous for Henry as it would allow his heirs to claim the throne on both the Yorkist and Lancastrian side, effectively ending the Wars of the Roses. For Elizabeth, too, it was essential to

1496 – 24 February: Henry VII signs 'Magnus Intercursus' trade treaty with the Netherlands, forcing Margaret of Burgundy to end public opposition to the Tudor monarchy

September: Warbeck and James IV of Scotland jointly invade England across the northern border. English troops force Scottish army back.

1502 – Prince Arthur, heir to the Tudor throne, dies

| 1496 | 1497 | 1498 | 1499 | 1500 | 1501 | 1502 | 1503 | 1509 | 1510 |

1497 – May to June: Cornish rebellion

September: Warbeck arrives in England and unsuccessfully leads troops against the royal army. Truce agreed between England and Scotland.

1499 – November: Perkin Warbeck and Edward, earl of Warwick executed for treason

1501 – Prince Arthur marries Katherine of Aragon

1509 – Henry VII dies. His eldest surviving son becomes Henry VIII.

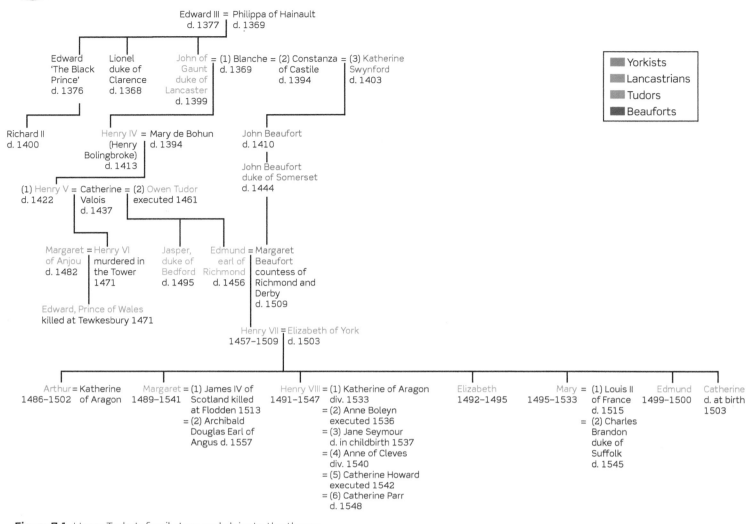

Figure 7.1 Henry Tudor's family tree and claim to the throne.

secure the safety of her remaining Woodville family and marry a man of royal status. This match was negotiated by the mothers of the bride and groom – respectively the dowager queen, Elizabeth Woodville, and Lady Margaret Beaufort – in the autumn of 1483, once it became widely assumed that the Yorkist princes were dead, making Henry Tudor's claim to the throne a viable possibility.

Once Henry became king, therefore, it was important he married Elizabeth; indeed, on 10 December 1485 parliament formally requested that he do so and he stated that this was his intention. Nonetheless, there were two important impediments to be overcome before the marriage could take place: the first was that Henry and Elizabeth were related because they were both great-great-grandchildren of John of Gaunt, the 14th-century duke of Lancaster. Therefore, they required a papal dispensation to marry. Secondly, at the instigation of Richard III, all the children of Edward IV and Elizabeth Woodville had been declared illegitimate, on the grounds that King Edward's marriage to his Woodville bride had never been valid because he had been pre-contracted to Lady Eleanor Butler (see Chapter 6, page 140).

The bastardisation of Edward IV's heirs and parliament's reversal of this

The parliamentary Act of early 1484 which **bastardised** the heirs of Edward IV had clearly been designed as a method of legalising his own usurpation of the throne. The parliamentary Act was politically motivated and had been primarily aimed at the princes. Nonetheless, it was a significant problem for Elizabeth of York too, as a young woman declared illegitimate by parliament could not hope to marry a king, nor would her children necessarily have a claim to the throne.

> **KEY TERM**
>
> **Bastardisation**
> A legal process, by which the children of a marriage that is later declared invalid are declared bastards (i.e. illegitimate offspring, conceived outside matrimony). In the medieval period, this would have meant they could not inherit a title or position from their father, and their inheritance of property and goods was also limited. Being considered illegitimate often carried a social stigma.

156

By mid-January 1485, however, parliament had agreed not merely to reverse the Act of Bastardisation, but unusually had ordered the record of such an Act and all copies of it to be burnt and completely destroyed, so that they would be totally removed from the formal record and memory. This extreme measure was an indication of Henry's insecurity at this early stage of his reign and the potential seriousness of the threat to the legitimisation of his heirs. Happily for Henry, however, a papal dispensation for the marriage was authorised and, two days later, on 18 January, the wedding celebrations took place.

EXTEND YOUR KNOWLEDGE

The pope's support of the new Tudor regime

A papal dispensation was required for the marriage of Henry VII and Elizabeth of York because they were both great-great-grandchildren of John of Gaunt, the 14th-century duke of Lancaster and uncle to King Richard II. In this matter, the Vatican appears to have been happy to support Henry VII's claim to the throne.

Pope Innocent VIII was probably influenced in Tudor's favour by Bishop John Morton, who visited Rome early in 1485, as well as by the Italian Giovanni Gigli, who at this time was living in England and was the Bishop of Worcester, with some involvement in the royal court. Gigli advised the pope in a letter that the marriage of Elizabeth of York and Henry VII would be very popular, as it was most beneficial for the kingdom as a whole.

In March, the pope officially confirmed Henry's marriage and his title as king. According to the document, this intervention from Innocent occurred entirely of the pope's own initiative and was not requested in any way by the king, although this level of disinterest seems rather implausible. Henry capitalised on this evidence of papal approval as much as he could by having the document copied into English and widely publicised.

How successful was Henry's marriage to Elizabeth of York?

Given the circumstances of their marriage, it was clearly a match made for reasons of political expediency rather than love, but nonetheless the union appears to have been content. Historian Alexander Grant has emphasised that Henry was very careful to ensure his wife and family did not attract negative attention and cause him any unpopularity, as had been the case when Edward IV married the unsuitable Elizabeth Woodville (see Chapter 6, page 133). Certainly, Henry benefited from having a smaller circle of both blood-relations and in-laws, so he was not required to support too many people. Perhaps also to ensure careful control of the king and queen, Henry VII's mother, Lady Margaret Beaufort, played a very high-profile role in the king's court and some commentators regarded her as dominating her daughter-in-law to an unusual degree. Certainly, the two ladies are often recorded as acting together or both being present in discussions. The main evidence for this comes from letters from Spanish ambassadors to the government of their own country, who were involved in the negotiation of a match between Prince Arthur and the Spanish princess, Katherine of Aragon, and so were keeping a close eye on matters at the English court. For example, the Spanish diplomat, Pedro de Ayala, felt that Henry VII was overly influenced by his mother and that Elizabeth of York resented this. There was also a comment from the same source

that Elizabeth was bullied by Margaret Beaufort and that therefore the Spanish royalty should make a fuss of the queen, as she would welcome this attention and so would favour the Spanish position. This evidence, however, should not be viewed as infallible, as foreign ambassadors did on occasion misread situations in court and it is also notable that Elizabeth must have had some influence over her husband if the Spanish felt it was worth cultivating her friendship. Nonetheless, there is some other evidence of tension in the relationship, most colourfully provided by a minor and rather disgruntled royal servant seeking favour, who commented that when he met Queen Elizabeth at Nottingham, she had spoken to him kindly, and he would have continued the conversation unless the king's mother, who he described as a whore, had not intervened.

EXTRACT

1 A. Grant, *Henry VII: The Importance of His Reign in English History* (1985). Here, the historian Alexander Grant compares Henry VII's reign to that of Edward IV.

> In Henry VII's reign things were completely different. Whereas, for example Edward IV's marriage to Elizabeth Woodville was a disastrous mistake, Henry VII's to Elizabeth of York was the most sensible marriage possible. It was designed to heal political divisions, and probably did so. But after it, the queen and her relatives (who could be called Woodvilles, since Elizabeth of York was the daughter of Elizabeth Woodville) were kept in the background, so far as politics were concerned. Woodville influence, or the influence of the queen's relatives, was no longer a factor in the England of Henry VII. Moreover, unlike Edward IV, Henry VII had no brothers to cause problems either during his reign or after his death... Over the reign as a whole, moreover, it is clear that the English nobility was not as impressive in numbers and (more importantly) in the extent of its possessions as under most of Henry's predecessors. The late medieval English nobility may not have killed itself off during the Wars of the Roses, but it had changed significantly by the end of the fifteenth-century. And if its members were neither so numerous nor so powerful as in the past, then they were unlikely to have posed such a potential threat to the king.

Whatever her relationship with Margaret Beaufort, Elizabeth of York, like her mother before her, was highly successful in a much-prized sphere of queenship: she was fertile and gave birth to a number of children, five of whom survived infancy. Helpfully, her first child was a boy, Arthur, providing Henry with a much-needed heir to help make his reign and dynasty more secure. Later, she had two other sons, Henry and Edmund. Of the three boys, however, only Henry grew to old age; the eldest brother, Arthur, predeceased his father and mother, dying in 1502, aged 15, shortly after his marriage to Katherine of Aragon. The loss of Prince Arthur was clearly a serious blow for his parents in personal as well as political terms. This is nicely illustrated by the account of John Leland, writing in the reign of Henry VIII, who described the scene when the royal couple were told of Arthur's death. According to this, Elizabeth comforted her husband, reminding him not only of their three surviving offspring, but also stating practically that they were young enough to have more children. Later, however, when she withdrew to her own room, she was overcome by weeping and her attendants discussed whether or not to send for the king to comfort her, because of her great distress.

Sadly for Henry and Elizabeth, their younger son, Edmund, died in childhood and, in 1503, Elizabeth herself died as a result of giving birth to a last baby girl, Katherine, who also did not survive. After 1503, therefore, Prince Henry was the sole male heir to the throne and, when his father died in 1509, he succeeded to the throne as part of a now-established royal dynasty.

ACTIVITY
KNOWLEDGE CHECK

Henry VII's claim to the throne and the significance of Henry's marriage to Elizabeth of York

1 In three sentences, summarise Henry VII's justification for claiming the throne.

2 List the advantages of the match with Elizabeth of York from the point of view of Henry VII.

3 Compile a list of problems/disadvantages of the marriage with Elizabeth of York for Henry VII, and also note how the king sought to resolve these problems.

4 In your view, which was more politically significant: the death of Prince Edward, son of King Richard III, or the death of Prince Arthur, son of Henry VII? Support your argument with evidence.

Living in fear and striving for security: the use of spies and bonds

In order to secure the throne for the Tudor dynasty he was creating, Henry used a number of methods to control the people of the realm, and the nobility in particular. This is a topic of considerable debate among historians, with the key areas of argument focusing on the claim of J.R. Green, writing in 1874, that Edward IV and Henry VII created a 'new monarchy', in other words, that these two kings substantially altered the role of a king and how the politics and the finances of the realm were managed. In particular, Green argued that these two reigns were notable for a shift towards a more tyrannical form of kingship. Subsequently, historians have tended to focus more on the role of Henry in this shift, rather than that of Edward IV, creating the idea of 1485 as a watershed in English history, with the Tudor regime being seen as bringing in a more modern form of government, with much tighter and effective controls over the nobility and over financial matters. The idea that Henry ruled in a very different way from his medieval predecessors was supported by a number of scholars, but later criticised in the 1950s by J.D. Mackie and G.R. Elton who, instead, emphasised a more gradual pace of change. In 1985, however, Alexander Grant argued that the death of Richard III in 1485 was a key turning point, as Henry VII subsequently created peace and stability, which was a real change from the strife of the Wars of the Roses. Here, Grant supports the very traditional assessment of Henry VII's reign as one where a successful monarch brought peace to England by ending the Wars of the Roses, a reasonable conclusion but one which benefits greatly from hindsight. While it is fairly easy for a modern scholar to argue that the Tudors were secure now we have evidence of the longevity of that dynasty, for those living through Henry VII's reign it is likely that the various rebellions, pretenders and other threats to the throne appeared to be serious threats to the country's stability and peace.

This famous portrait of Henry VII was painted in 1505 by an unknown artist from the Netherlands. According to the inscription, it was commissioned by Maximilian I, the Holy Roman Emperor and was probably painted as part of an unsuccessful negotiation for Henry to marry Maximilian's daughter, Margaret of Savoy, after the death of Elizabeth of York in 1503.

A Level Exam-Style Question Section A

Study Source 3 before you answer this question.

Assess the value of the source for revealing the character of Henry VII and the reasons for his successful control of the country until 1509.

Explain your answer, using the source, the information given about its origin and your own knowledge about the historical context. (20 marks)

Tip

Remember to structure your answer clearly, so each paragraph develops a new line of your argument. Focus on evaluating the reliability of Vergil's comments rather than simply describing what the source tells you.

SOURCE

In this section of Polydore Vergil's *History of England*, which was completed in 1513, the author evaluates the character and reign of Henry VII.

Henry reigned twenty-three years and seven months... He had eight children, four boys and as many girls. He left three surviving children, an only son Henry, prince of Wales, and two daughters; Margaret married to James King of Scotland and Mary betrothed to Charles, prince of Castile... His spirit was distinguished, wise and prudent; his mind was brave and resolute and never, even at moments of the greatest danger, deserted him. He had a most pertinacious [strong] memory. Withall he was not devoid of scholarship. In government he was shrewd and prudent, so that no one dared to get the better of him through deceit or guile. He was gracious and kind and was as attentive to his visitors as he was easy of access. His hospitality was splendidly generous; he was fond of having foreigners at his court and he freely conferred favours on them. But those of his subjects who were indebted to him or who did not pay him due honour or who were generous only with promises, he treated with harsh severity. He well knew how to maintain his royal majesty and all which appertains to kingship at every time and in every place. He was most fortunate in war, although he was constitutionally more inclined to peace than to war. He cherished justice above all things; as a result he vigorously punished violence, manslaughter and every other kind of wickedness whatsoever. Consequently he was greatly regretted on that account by all his subjects, who had been able to conduct their lives peaceably, far removed from the assaults and evil doing of scoundrels. He was the most ardent supporter of our faith, and daily participated with great piety in religious services. To those whom he considered to be worthy priests, he often secretly gave alms [charity] so that they should pray for his salvation... But all these virtues were obscured latterly only by avarice... This avarice is surely a bad enough vice in a private individual, whom it forever torments; in a monarch indeed it may be considered the worst vice, since it is harmful to everyone, and distorts those qualities of truthfulness, justice and integrity by which the state must be governed.

Henry's intelligence network

A feature of the early Tudor regime that has given rise to the image of Henry VII as a despotic ruler was his use of spies. It is important, however, to analyse carefully exactly how much of the Tudor use of an intelligence network was an innovation, as previous monarchs also made careful use of secret agents and informers in various guises. In the ideal of medieval kingship, the social structure itself formed a communication network between a monarch and his people: according to theory, nobles communicated with and advised the king about difficulties in the kingdom and the king used the nobility and gentry as a mouthpiece for proclaiming his will to the people. In reality, however, as the Wars of the Roses had dramatically shown, a monarch could not always trust the leading landowners of the day and all kings had relied to an extent on secret information to ensure that they were well informed of plots against them. The use of spies and scouts was particularly established prior to battle, to gain knowledge of the enemy's position, proposed tactics and strength. According to Christine de Pisan, a late medieval author writing about chivalry and battle, it was wise for a leader to send out spies discreetly, to ascertain his enemy's intentions. Indeed, so established was this procedure that often complex methods of counter-espionage and trails of false information were laid to deceive the spies of an enemy. For example, when the duke of Clarence and the earl of Warwick rebelled against

Edward IV in 1470, they deceived the king by sending him a series of letters, purportedly from his own spies, which gave false positions. In this regard, then, Henry VII behaved no differently from his predecessors in seeking sound information, for example in 1497, using scouts to keep him informed of the Cornish rebels' movements.

EXTRACT

From an article by I. Arthurson, 'Espionage and intelligence from the Wars of the Roses to the Reformation', *Nottingham Medieval Studies* v.35 (1991).

By 1450 the regular collection of military and diplomatic intelligence was a normal function of government. However the use of spies was undoubtedly stimulated by the civil wars. Henry VI, for example, paid informers for political intelligence in the mid-1450s. Recourse to espionage would have been second nature to many of the major protagonists at the opening of the Wars of the Roses as they were conversant with spying techniques employed in the closing stages of the Hundred Years War. While it is conventional to paint Henry VII as the greatest activist in diplomatic and political espionage, I would hesitate: Edward IV awaits exposure as a considerable spymaster. The exigencies of his first reign taught Edward IV the necessity for espionage. When Henry VI and his Queen fled to Scotland Edward built up the Douglases as an English party within Scotland and gave pensions to the bishops of St Andrews and Aberdeen. He also employed a Scottish merchant William Alaynson and his relations to supply him with political intelligence concerning his enemies; even to flush Henry VI out of Scotland. At the same time, in the early 1460s, since the Lancastrians threatened to ally with France, he conducted covert diplomacy on the continent. Four times in 1466 John Russell, future Lord Chancellor, 'exploratori' [*sic*], visited Burgundy. In that same year Edward sent outher 'exploratori', spies, to Cheshire to run the hapless Henry VI to ground. This they did, capturing him in Lancashire. Ultimately Edward's life depended on his spies. In 1470 he placed a man in his northern opponents' army. It was this man who warned him that his capture was imminent before he fled to Burgundy. All this cost money... in 1468 he spent £2210 9s 'on certain secret matters concerning the defence of the kingdom'.

Henry also behaved in typical fashion by ensuring he had good information from other royal courts. This was a wise precaution as foreign involvement, especially from France and Scotland, was an important factor in assisting a number of rebellions or invasions of England during the Wars of the Roses; indeed, Henry VII's own takeover had occurred largely as a result of foreign support. Many continental governments placed resident ambassadors in foreign royal courts, and these individuals kept their homeland closely informed of the latest gossip, news and information in order to inform diplomatic policy. The English used their only remaining French holding, Calais, to considerable effect as a base for espionage. In particular, it was useful when mobilising a spy network to gain information about the Scots, as France and Scotland had traditionally been allies against the English. Henry VII certainly paid his fair share of spies and informers, but the traditional view of him as greatly innovative in this regard is something of an exaggeration; it is quite clear that, during the Hundred Years War and then during the Wars of the Roses, all late medieval kings had made use of espionage. Even the unworldly Henry VI, for example, paid for political intelligence in the mid-1450s, while Edward IV paid Scottish informers during the 1460s to keep him informed of the movements of Henry VI and Margaret of Anjou, who had fled there. It was also thanks to Edward IV's spy network that Henry VI was ultimately captured in 1466. Henry VII also had a particular concern with the Low Countries as Margaret, dowager duchess of Burgundy, was Richard III's sister and a strong supporter of all Yorkist plotting against the Tudor regime. Therefore, Henry VII sought to infiltrate her court during the 1490s to obtain intelligence about plots against his throne from the dissidents gathered there. It is probable that Sir Richard Clifford, who informed Henry of the disloyalty of some at the English court, including Stanley, was in fact a double agent used by the king to secure information of possible traitors. Alexander Grant has also highlighted that this system of espionage was particularly successful in assisting Henry against Perkin Warbeck and Edward, earl of Warwick during the 1490s, allowing Henry to act while plans were still being made, rather than once they had developed.

Traditionally, Henry VII has been regarded as being unusually sophisticated in his deployment of spies. While this is rather inaccurate, as highlighted above, there were two areas of espionage in which the Tudor regime was innovative. Firstly, it was not until 1505 that **ciphers** were routinely used by the English government in their sensitive correspondence, although they had been used by some other European governments prior to this. Indeed, it was apparently Henry's Spanish daughter-in-law, Katherine of Aragon, who introduced ciphers to the English king. Secondly, and more significantly, he placed a great deal of financial pressure on the nobility to ensure they acted as informers, willing or otherwise. This use of bonds to gain information and secure loyalty was one of his least popular policies.

KEY TERM

Cipher (also cypher)
A type of code used to encrypt secret messages and make them difficult to read. Ciphers use letters, numbers or symbols to replace the original letters or numbers and a key is used to change the message back into an understandable form.

Henry's financial policies towards the nobility

Significantly, Henry developed the use of financial forms of coercion against the nobility to obtain intelligence. A number of historians, notably J.R. Lander and Michael Hicks, have placed emphasis on Henry's use of bonds and recognisances as a new and effective method of controlling the nobility and ensuring their loyalty. This policy has been largely responsible for a school of thought among some historians that Henry VII distrusted the nobility and sought to control them by fear rather than working with them more collaboratively, as was the medieval ideal. These bonds were payments to the crown by members of the nobility in return either for privileges or as fines, which were imposed upon those whose loyalty to the king was questionable or who were liable to quarrel violently with another noble family. The payment of bonds was not new, but Henry increased their use considerably and, during his reign, more than half the peerage was obliged to pay money to the crown as security for their good

behaviour, with some nobles being forced to agree to more than one bond. These payments were not always called in, but the nobles in question lived under continual threat of being forced to sacrifice huge amounts of money if they offended the king in any way. In addition, a noble could be made to pay an annual sum in lieu of the whole amount, so, in 1507, when Lord Abergavenny was fined the colossal sum of £70,000 and he was unable to pay, Henry instead agreed to receive payment of £500 per year for the next ten years, provided no disloyalty was suspected. In addition, some wealthy figures were obliged to sign bonds to guarantee the good behaviour of their poorer relations, which again bound more people to the king in financial terms. As Michael Hicks has succinctly highlighted, Henry's policy around bonds was a threat to anyone who might otherwise indulge in secrecy or criticisms of the royal family that would formerly not have been regarded as treasonous. 'Absolute obedience to, and dependence upon, the monarch himself became a defining feature of Henry's reign, a point nicely illustrated by the fact that, when even one of his trusted advisers, Sir Richard Empson, in 1507 was granted some local offices, Henry personally crossed out the term "for life" in the grant and instead replaced this with the words "during [the king's] pleasure".'

A key figure who was frequently linked to the formulation and exaction of Henry VII's more unpopular financial policies was Edmund Dudley, a lawyer who became president of the king's council in 1506. Dudley was disliked by many nobles because of his involvement in the use of bonds and recognisances, which effectively operated outside the law and allowed Henry to control and, in actuality, punish nobles without trial. Dudley's unpopularity was such that he was arrested and sent to the Tower only days after Henry VII died and, in 1510, was beheaded on the orders of Henry VIII. He was, according to S.J. Gunn, a convenient scapegoat and in fact the policy decisions were of the king's own making. During his arrest, Dudley revealingly commented that Henry VII was keen to make people feel insecure and dependent upon his good will, creating an image of a highly suspicious king. Alexander Grant has emphasised that the primary purpose of bonds and recognisances for Henry was not to gain large amounts of money, but rather to ensure monarchical control over the nobility; while Grant possibly underestimates Henry's desire for money in the royal coffers, he is correct in his argument that Henry equated financial security with power.

Henry was nowhere near as generous with the nobility as his predecessors had been; the days of 'over-mighty subjects' and 'under-mighty monarchs' were clearly over. In part, this was simply owing to the fact that he had a smaller family, but it is notable that he did not seek to increase the peerage substantially with new creations, and that he was very careful in how he distributed patronage. In addition, any nobles accused of treasonous plotting were treated very harshly, not only by the fact that many were executed even for relatively minor involvement in any conspiracy, but they also lost all their possessions, which meant that their heirs were disinherited and the family lost power and influence. Unlike his predecessors, Henry was disinclined to reverse these attainders and, if he did so, this was usually only to grant back part of the lands after large payments by the traitor's heirs. While a lack of mercy and avarice are not particularly attractive characteristics, and were certainly heavily criticised by some contemporaries, nonetheless this Tudor policy did ensure that no significant noble opponents, such as Warwick 'the kingmaker' or the infamous George, duke of Clarence, came to the fore during his reign. Instead, the main threats to his throne came from impostors, whom most historians argue were supported by Yorkist sympathisers, not because their false credentials were genuinely believed, but because it was tacitly acknowledged that the Tudor king would execute rivals – and, so, risking the life of a real alternative claimant to the throne was too dangerous at an early stage.

EXTRACT

3 M. Hicks, *Wars of the Roses* (2012). Here, the author evaluates the differences in approach to patronage between Henry VII and previous monarchs.

Henry VII's rule contrasted sharply with that of the usurpers Henry IV, Edward IV and Richard III, who had been bountiful to those who made them kings and thus gave them even more cause to back their title. These usurpers had created vested interests in the continuance of their regimes. Edward IV even admitted former Lancastrians to his Yorkist establishment. Henry VII was not a liberal patron and was much more sparing in his patronage. Although attainders against his supporters were reversed and lands restored, although offices had to be filled and were staffed with his supporters, he created very few titles and granted away relatively few estates, or indeed lands at all, from the substantial quantities in his hands. Patronage did not buy Henry the support of his subjects. Denying himself the carrot, Henry resorted to the big stick: to coercion... But such bullying could be counter-productive. Victims could justifiably be paranoid and think themselves victimized, and even be driven to extremes that they had never intended. That possibly is what befell Edmund de la Pole, whom Henry's cackhanded management made into an enemy and hence more dangerous than he needed to be.

THINKING HISTORICALLY   Change (8a, b & c) (II)

Judgements about change

If two professionals were asked to track a patient's health over time, one might approach this task by measuring heart rate, weight and cholesterol, while the other professional might assess the patient's mental well-being, relationships and ability to achieve their goals. Both are valid approaches, but result in different reports. What is true in this medical case is true in historical cases. Measuring change in something requires: (a) a concept of what is being assessed (e.g. 'What is "health"?', 'What is an "economy"?'); (b) judgements about how this should be measured; and (c) judgements about what denotes significant change from temporary and insignificant fluctuations.

Historians have differed in their accounts of political control in the 15th and 16th centuries and debated the appropriateness of the term 'new monarchy', coined by J.R. Green in 1874, to characterise the reigns of Edward IV and, more particularly, Henry VII.

Look at Extracts 1, 2 and 3 about the 'new monarchy' and then answer the questions below.

1 Do all three accounts agree that a 'new monarchy' developed in England under Henry VII?

2 Do all three accounts agree on the chronology of change? In other words, do they see change happening at the same time and at the same pace?

3 Do all three accounts agree in characterising change as follows?

  a) Rapid.

  b) Dramatic.

  c) Impacting on the nature of kingship as a whole.

4 Do the historians all think of the nature of the monarchy and power in the same way? For example, do they all focus on the importance of the king having the goodwill of his nobles?

5 Generalising from these examples, to what extent do historians' judgements about change depend upon what historians decide to look at and how they decide to measure change?

ACTIVITY
KNOWLEDGE CHECK

Henry VII's relationship with the nobility: the use of spies and bonds

1. In which ways did 15th-century kings use espionage to remain secure on the throne?
2. In which ways can Henry VII's use of spies be regarded as different from that of previous monarchs?
3. Write down five adjectives you would use to describe Henry VII's personality and style of kingship. For each one, justify your choice of word with two pieces of evidence. You may not use the same piece of evidence more than twice.
4. Summarise in two sentences the role bonds and recognisances played in Henry VII's kingship.
5. Write a paragraph summarising the role and political significance of Edmund Dudley, which includes these words (in any order):
   a) justified
   b) popularity
   c) Henry VIII
   d) law
   e) nobility.

WHO CHALLENGED HENRY VII AND HOW SIGNIFICANT WAS THIS OPPOSITION?

Lovell's rebellion, 1486

Given Henry's rather tenuous claim to the throne, it is unsurprising that there were a number of other potential claimants to the throne, as outlined in Figure 7.2.

It is notable that the first conspiracy Henry VII faced in 1486 did not involve any of these alternative claimants. It was led by Francis, Viscount Lovell, who had been a close associate and supporter of Richard III. Given his close relationship with Richard, and the fact he had fought against Henry at Bosworth, Lovell was attainted for treason in Henry's first parliament and fled with another opponent of the Tudor regime, Humphrey Stafford of Grafton (in Worcestershire). During March and April 1486, these men conspired to raise a rebellion against Henry, with Stafford inspiring insurrection in the West Midlands and Lovell in Yorkshire. There proved little appetite for further fighting in these areas, however, and crucially the major northern landholders failed to rally to Lovell and Stafford's cause. Consequently, when Henry arrived in York on 20 April, he discovered that the rebels had fled. Lovell headed to safety in Burgundy, where Margaret, the dowager duchess of Burgundy, sought to aid those causing trouble for the new Tudor regime.

The conspiracy of Lambert Simnel and the earl of Lincoln

During the 1480s, one of the most politically significant and discussed topics of the day was the fate of Edward IV's sons, the so-called 'princes in the Tower'. While most contemporary reports suggested that the boys had been killed on the orders of their uncle, Richard III, various other stories circulated, including the idea that one or both of the boys had escaped or that the younger boy, Richard of York, had been spirited out of the country by his supporters and his place had been taken by an impostor. Given this, it is unsurprising that, when Henry VII came to the throne, there was considerable speculation about the identity and fate of the young alternative claimant to the throne, the 12-year-old Edward, earl of Warwick, whom Henry placed in the Tower as soon as he acceded to the throne, to reduce the risk of a rebellion in his favour. In 1486, for example, there were reports that the boy had escaped and there were apparently also rumours that, before the boy's father, the duke of Clarence, was tried in 1478, he had arranged for the child to be sent to Ireland for safety and placed another child in his nursery instead. This confused conjecture provided plenty of fuel for a possible pretender to the throne to become the focus of a rebellion.

KEY TERM

Trade embargo
A government trading ban with a particular country or group.

Alternative claimant	Justification of claim	How serious was the threat from this individual?
Edward, earl of Warwick (often referred to as Edward of Warwick).	Son of George, duke of Clarence (Clarence was Edward IV's brother, who was executed in 1478).	He was only ten years old in 1485, but his Yorkist blood made him a serious candidate for the throne. His father had been attainted for treason, which normally would exclude someone from inheriting any titles/rights, but Henry VII could not easily use this justification as he himself had been attainted for treason under the Yorkists. Henry had him imprisoned in the Tower from 1485 for the rest of his life. In 1499, he was accused of plotting to escape and challenging the throne with the help of Perkin Warbeck, charges he admitted but which are generally believed to have been partly manufactured by Henry's intelligence network. He was beheaded in November 1499.
Pretenders to the throne, such as Lambert Simnel and Perkin Warbeck.	These youths in their own right had no real claim to the throne; however, manipulated, they claimed to be others with a strong bloodright. Simnel claimed to be Edward, earl of Warwick, and Perkin Warbeck claimed to be Edward IV's youngest son, Richard of York, whom some claimed had escaped from the Tower and was still alive.	Both were quite clearly pretenders, but nonetheless received significant support from those who disliked the Tudor regime. Clearly, the idea that one of the sons of the House of York had survived was a potent political weapon against Henry VII.
John II of Portugal.	Descended from John of Gaunt (uncle of Richard II) and his first wife, Blanche of Lancaster.	Claim weakened by the fact he was not English, and so was less likely to have support in England. Does not appear to have threatened Henry VII's rule.
John of Pontefract, also referred to as John of Gloucester (died around 1499).	Illegitimate son of Richard III.	Illegitimate children were usually barred from inheriting titles/position from their parents. However, normal rules of succession were seriously under threat at this time and Henry's own claim via the Beaufort line was partially dependent on a claim of illegitimacy (he was descended from the offspring of John of Gaunt and his mistress, Katherine Swynford. Although Gaunt later married Katherine and legitimised these children, not everyone accepted this as valid). Henry was clearly concerned about the threat from John of Pontefract and so had him imprisoned in the Tower of London, where he died.
John de la Pole, earl of Lincoln (d. 1487). (As there are a number of claimants with this surname, throughout he will be referred to as 'Lincoln' only.')	After Richard III's son died, Richard named Lincoln his successor. His mother was Elizabeth Plantagenet (d. 1503/4), the sister of Edward IV and Richard III.	Appeared loyal to Henry early in his reign and entered his service, so this initially reduced the threat from this quarter. In 1487, however, he fled Henry VII's court and joined Viscount Lovell in Flanders, where they were provided with military support by Margaret of Burgundy. He and Lovell based themselves for a while in Ireland and in May 1487 they crowned a pretender Lambert Simnel, claiming that he was the rightful claimant 'Edward VI'. Troops then invaded England in support of this claim, but were defeated at the Battle of Stoke, where the earl of Lincoln was killed during the fighting.
Edmund de la Pole, earl of Suffolk (d. 1513).	Third son of John de la Pole, second duke of Suffolk (d. 1492) and his wife, Elizabeth Plantagenet (d. 1503/4), a sister of Edward IV.	When Henry VII took the throne Edmund was too young to pose a serious threat in his own right, probably being aged only 12 or 13. As he grew up, he appeared to be in the favour of Queen Elizabeth, perhaps indicating his Yorkist leanings. He was placed under considerable financial pressure by Henry VII, and this may have contributed in 1499 to his flight to his aunt Margaret of Burgundy. Henry VII, however, negotiated Edmund's return by threatening the duke of Burgundy with a **trade embargo**. Henry again made Edmund's position financially humiliating and he fled the court again in 1501, this time to the court of Emperor Maximilian, from where he plotted invasion. Henry VII used his spy network successfully against Edmund and his supporters, however. Following negotiations, in 1506 Edmund was once again returned to Henry VII and this time imprisoned in the Tower. His position became extremely vulnerable, when his brother, Richard de la Pole, was recognised by the king of France as the rightful king of England in 1512. Once this became known, Edmund was executed and died on 4 May 1513.
Richard de la Pole, (d. 1525), sometimes after 1506 known as 'Blanche Rose' (meaning, 'The White Rose', the symbol of the House of York).	The fifth son of John de la Pole , second duke of Suffolk (d. 1492) and his wife, Elizabeth Plantagenet (d. 1503/4), a sister of Edward IV. He was the younger brother of John de la Pole, earl of Lincoln (d. 1487), and Edmund de la Pole, earl of Suffolk (d. 1513).	In 1501, he fled to the court of Emperor Maximilian abroad with his older brother Edmund (see above). Both men and their brother William were charged with treason by parliament in 1504. He later moved to Hungary and Henry VII tried, unsuccessfully, to negotiate with the king there for his return. He never posed a serious threat to Henry VII, but was later to cause problems for Henry VIII.

Figure 7.2 Potential claimants to the throne.

In February 1487, a boy who was really called Lambert Simnel appeared in Ireland and probably claimed to be Edward, earl of Warwick, although some sources suggest that he instead claimed to be Richard of York. Little is known of the real origins of Simnel, but they appear to have been humble and his father was probably an Oxford organ-maker or carpenter. He was apparently influenced by a priest called Simonds (first name uncertain) who later confessed to having organised the pretence, but there were more significant political supporters of the boy among diehard Yorkists, who wished to use the opportunity to cause trouble for Henry VII. The support Simnel gained from many in Ireland was also largely opportunistic, and included the backing of Thomas Fitzgerald, chancellor of Ireland, his brother, Gerald Fitzgerald, earl of Kildare and the king's deputy, and Walter Fitzsimons, the Archbishop of Dublin, reflecting considerable dissatisfaction in the Dublin area of Ireland at least, with the Tudor regime. This was possibly due to the fact that Edward IV's father, Richard of York, and brother, George, duke of Clarence, had previously been lieutenants in the country.

Henry acted quickly to limit the impact of Simnel's claims and the real earl of Warwick was taken from the Tower and paraded through the streets of London to prove publicly that he was in Henry's custody. This tactic backfired, however, as Warwick's first cousin and another claimant to the throne, John de la Pole, earl of Lincoln, declared that Simnel was the real Warwick and Henry's captive was the pretender. Lincoln then headed to Antwerp, where he stayed with Margaret of Burgundy, and she too gave her support to the Simnel conspiracy, including financial assistance. At the end of April, a group of prominent opponents to Henry VII, including Lincoln and Lovell, sailed to Ireland with a group of German mercenaries. Once they arrived, the boy was crowned as Edward VI in Dublin, a parliament was held in his name and new coins **minted** with his image upon them.

However farcical the pretence had at first seemed, the threat to Henry's hold on power was now significant. This was made evident on 4 June, when supporters of Simnel, including Lincoln, invaded England, backed by between 1,500 and 2,000 German mercenaries and c4,000 Irish light infantry. The Yorkist-inspired invasion received backing from some within England, including two Yorkshire magnates (both members of the Scrope family) and some Londoners, but this support was very limited and even places such as the city of York, which had strong ties to Richard III, remained loyal to the new Tudor regime. Henry defended his realm at the Battle of Stoke on 16 June 1487, and was aided in his victory by a strong strategic location, extremely effective archers and the fact that the Irish troops were poorly equipped. Lincoln was killed during the battle, while Lovell escaped and fled to Scotland. Simnel, meanwhile, was captured, although he was pardoned his offences (presumably because of his young age). According to at least two accounts, he was then employed in the king's household in the kitchens and Polydore Vergil claimed Simnel was later promoted to the role of falconer (that is, someone who cared for the king's hunting birds). Little else is known about him and he played no further role in the politics of the period.

KEY TERM

Minted
When a coin is created, it is described as being 'minted'. Coins are made in the Royal Mint.

ACTIVITY
KNOWLEDGE CHECK

Lambert Simnel and the security of the Tudor regime

1 Create a timeline of Lambert Simnel's rebellion against Henry VII, beginning in February 1487 and ending in June.

2 On your timeline, highlight the point at which you think Simnel posed the most serious threat to the king and explain why you have chosen this date.

3 Create two lists: one showing the factors and evidence that indicate that Simnel's rebellion was a genuine threat to Henry VII; and one showing the factors and evidence that support the view that it was not a matter of serious concern for the Tudor regime.

The conspiracy of Perkin Warbeck and Sir William Stanley

Ireland was to be a continuing thorn in Henry VII's side and it is notable that the next significant rebellion against him also began there, although there was considerable English involvement as well. In the early 1490s, an individual called Perkin Warbeck visited Cork in Ireland and while there was persuaded by Yorkist supporters to impersonate the younger of the princes in the Tower, Richard of York. Initially, this agenda received backing from Charles VIII of France, who wished to distract

Henry VII from defending Brittany against a French invasion, but, in November 1492, the two kings made a peace treaty and so Warbeck was forced to flee to Margaret of Burgundy, who pursued her own political agenda by confirming that he was really her nephew. In order to try to force Margaret to capitulate and disown Warbeck, Henry suspended English trade with the Netherlands, but this led to unemployment and riots in London and seemed only to stiffen Margaret's resolve. In the meantime, Warbeck managed to gain further international status by gaining the very public support of Maximilian, King of the Romans, whom he visited in 1493. He also, apparently, began to gain supporters who were close to Henry at the English court.

Henry VII used a complex network of spies to obtain important political information, so it is unclear exactly when he began to suspect a conspiracy. Whatever his suspicions, he had ample confirmation of them in the winter of 1494–95 when Sir Robert Clifford, who appears to have initially been one of Warbeck's secret supporters, leaked information and evidence about the plot to the king. Indeed, Clifford may have always been working for Henry, in the role of a double agent. Several senior figures in the English court were accused of taking part in a conspiracy to support Warbeck's claim. The most significant figure here was Sir William Stanley. In truth, it is unlikely Henry ever fully trusted Sir William, as the Stanleys as a family were notable for remaining ambivalent in their loyalties in battle until the last moment, so they could be sure of ending up on the winning side. Nonetheless, the betrayal must have been a blow to the king; Stanley was the chamberlain of England, so had a very high level of responsibility within the kingdom, and he was the brother of Henry's own stepfather, Sir Thomas Stanley. Most importantly of all, Stanley's support had been crucial to Henry at the Battle of Bosworth and according to one chronicle he was the person to present the crown of England to Henry on the battlefield. This made his disloyalty especially concerning, as he had a strong military power and could muster very large numbers of troops. These factors explain why Henry showed no mercy when he learned of Sir William's involvement in the plot and, in February 1495, he was tried and executed for treason.

EXTRACT

A. Grant, 'Henry VII: the importance of his reign in English history', Lancaster Pamphlets (1985). Modern historian Alexander Grant outlines his view of Henry VII's attitude towards the loyalty of key figures within his government, as well as emphasising the value of the Tudor intelligence service.

The most striking victim of Henry's 'intelligence service' was Sir William Stanley, the person who had brought the Stanley forces in on Henry's side at Bosworth. Sir William and his brother Thomas Lord Stanley had been well rewarded for that, and Sir William had become head of Henry's household (private staff and bodyguard). In 1494, however, he was named among those involved with Perkin Warbeck; and although all that he could be accused of was agreeing not to oppose Warbeck if Warbeck were the true son of Edward IV, that was enough to bring about his trial, conviction and execution in February 1495. Some historians have argued that Stanley – who did not have the benefit of hindsight – was simply taking out a sensible insurance against a further change of dynasty. But that misses the point. Henry VII, unlike his predecessors, was not prepared to tolerate Stanley ambivalence. The fact that he would not take the risk of a repetition of Sir William Stanley's treachery towards Richard III helps to explain why he succeeded in keeping the throne for his own dynasty. Stanley's lack of absolute loyalty would have been doubly alarming in view of the fact that the household provided the essential core of the royal army.

Despite Clifford's defection, in the spring and summer of 1495, Warbeck and his supporters led a rebellion against Henry in Ireland and, with the military and naval backing of the King of the Romans (see Chapter 3, page 85), attempted to invade England. This failed, but Warbeck discovered another enemy of Tudor England who would be happy to support his attempts to cause trouble for the regime, James IV of Scotland.

How and why did James IV of Scotland support Perkin Warbeck?

James IV came to the Scottish throne in 1488, aged 15, and royal policy was largely shaped by his advisers during his minority rule. It was not until 1495, when he was 22, that he assumed personal rule of the country and, at this time, he seems to have been very keen to make his mark on the international military scene. This helps to explain why, despite the misgivings of some of his advisers, in the winter of 1495–96, James decided to ally himself with Warbeck against the English king. The two men seem to have reached an agreement that they would jointly invade England, with Warbeck promising the Scots the border town of Berwick if he was successful with their support.

KEY TERM

Jousting
A medieval sport practised only by the noble and gentry classes. It involved mounted knights charging at each other with blunted lances, and trying to knock each other off their horses.

Berwick was a place claimed by both the Scots and the English in this period and was frequently a focus of fighting in Anglo-Scottish wars. In order to bolster Warbeck's public persona and emphasise his (alleged) royal status, on 13 January 1496, King James arranged for Warbeck to marry a distant relation – Lady Katherine Gordon, daughter of George, earl of Huntley – and further emphasised his approval of the match by taking part in the **jousting** that took place as part of the marriage celebrations. He also provided considerable military support for the English rebels and gave them the use of Falkland Palace in Scotland as a base from which to plot their next move.

SOURCE 4

Portrait of a man, said to be King James IV of Scotland, by an unknown artist of the Netherlandish School, painted between c1510 and 1520.

On 21 September, James and Warbeck invaded England, but Warbeck quickly withdrew when it became clear that he had little English support. James also had to withdraw after five days, when English troops forced the Scots back, although considerable damage was done to some English border property. In retaliation, Henry began to prepare a very large army to invade Scotland and, in November, declared war on James. Unfortunately for Henry, however, his planned attack was delayed because of a rebellion in Cornwall, giving the Scots time to prepare their defences. Aware of the danger he faced domestically, in 1497, Henry reopened peace negotiations with Scotland and sought an agreement to be sealed by the marriage of James to Henry's daughter, Margaret. To facilitate this, James removed one diplomatic obstacle to the match by sending Warbeck away to Ireland in July. Although the marriage between James and Margaret did not take place until 1503, a truce was agreed in September 1497 and this was later extended, giving a significant period of peace between the two nations.

The importance of Margaret of Burgundy

Margaret of Burgundy (also referred to as Margaret of York) was the sister of Edward IV and Richard III. In 1468, she married the powerful Charles, duke of Burgundy. The Burgundian court had been an important ally of the Yorkist kings, with Edward IV staying there during some of his time in exile and, for England, good relations with the duchy were important in terms of trade, as it was a key market for England's main export, woollen textiles. Charles died in 1477, and so Margaret was a dowager duchess, but nonetheless she still wielded considerable influence at the Burgundian court. It was, therefore, a predictable but significant problem for Henry VII that she refused to recognise his kingship and offered support to his opponents. Lovell found safe haven with her after his failed rebellion in 1486 and soon he was joined by another important figure fleeing from the Tudor regime – her nephew, John de la Pole, earl of Lincoln.

Margaret was to play an ongoing and significant role in assisting those causing difficulties for Henry VII, in particular by recognising the pretender Perkin Warbeck as her nephew in 1492. Her plotting was somewhat undermined by Henry's careful use of his intelligence networks, which infiltrated her court in the 1490s and resulted in the execution of alleged Yorkist sympathisers, such as Sir William Stanley, among the nobility in England. Nonetheless, it was clear that Margaret was a considerable thorn in the side of the Tudor regime until 1496. Henry's decision in 1493 to try to limit her influence by placing an embargo on trade with the Netherlands backfired spectacularly. As the Netherlands was such an important textile market for English goods, this measure caused rioting in the capital by unemployed cloth workers. Consequently, Margaret continued to work against the Tudor regime until 1496, when Henry finally managed to

SOURCE

5 Portrait of Margaret of Burgundy, painted c1468–80, possibly by Hugo van der Goes, held in the collections of the Louvre, Paris. Van der Goes was a Netherlandish painter based in Ghent, which was an important art centre in Europe in the 15th century.

create a new trading alliance with the Netherlands, called the 'Magnus Intercursus' or 'Great Intercourse'. This agreement obliged Margaret to bring her political manoeuvring to an end and provides evidence of how foreign trade diplomacy was important for ensuring domestic political stability in England in the late 15th century.

TIMELINE: MARGARET OF BURGUNDY'S POLITICAL INVOLVEMENT AGAINST HENRY VII

1485
Battle of Bosworth

April 1486
Lovell and Stafford rebel unsuccessfully against Henry VII and flee

May 1486
Lovell welcomed by Margaret to the Burgundian court

February 1487
Lambert Simnel claims to be Edward, earl of Warwick (son of Margaret's dead brother, George, duke of Clarence).

Earl of Lincoln flees England and meets with Margaret at Antwerp.

April 1487
Lincoln, Lovell and other prominent Lancastrians sail to Ireland to support Simnel. Margaret gives financial assistance.

1489
Tax rebellion in the North of England, led by Sir John Egremont. Egremont escapes and is sheltered by Margaret in Burgundy.

June 1487
Simnel, Lincoln and Lovell invade England. Defeated at the Battle of Stoke.

1491
Perkin Warbeck persuaded by Yorkists to impersonate Edward IV's younger son, Richard of York

November 1492
Warbeck flees to Margaret's court. Margaret claims that Warbeck is her nephew.

Early 1493
Alleged conspiracy to support Warbeck's claim by members of the Tudor court discovered by Henry's spies.

November 1494–95
Winter: Sir Robert Clifford betrays plot among Yorkists to Henry VII. A number of people arrested for treason.

May to June 1493
Henry appoints commissioners to investigate allegations of treason across the country. Some suspects, including Sir Robert Clifford, escape to Margaret's court.

February 1495
Sir William Stanley is tried and executed for treason.

Mid-late 1495: Warbeck tries to raise revolt in Ireland and to invade England. Margaret petitions Pope Alexander VI to remove the papal edict that anyone who revolts against Henry VII is liable to be excommunicated.

July 1493
Sir Edward Poynings and Dr William Warham sent by Henry to the Netherlands to denounce Warbeck as a pretender.

September 1493
Henry bans all English trade with the Netherlands

15 October 1493
Unemployed cloth workers riot in London about trade ban. Margaret helps Warbeck to gain the support of Maximilian, King of the Romans.

24 February 1496
Henry VII signs 'Magnus Intercursus' trade treaty with the Netherlands

Perkin Warbeck and the threat to the Tudor throne

1 Summarise the importance of each of these figures in Perkin Warbeck's rebellion, in under 20 words for each one. Remember to include dates in your answers:

a) Margaret of Burgundy.

b) Charles VIII of France.

c) James IV of Scotland.

d) Sir William Stanley.

e) Maximilian, King of the Romans.

2 Create a timeline of Perkin Warbeck's career as a pretender to the throne of England, starting in 1491 and ending with his death in 1499.

HOW SERIOUS WERE THE TAX REBELLIONS OF 1489 AND 1497?

The Yorkshire rebellion of 1489: causes, events and impact

Over the centuries, Henry VII has retained an unattractive reputation for avarice. One factor in establishing this was a rebellion against him in the North, following the announcement of a parliamentary tax of a 'tenth' to fund the defence of Brittany against French aggression. In order to try and persuade people to pay their taxes, Henry Percy, fourth earl of Northumberland made a speech to an angry crowd at Topcliffe, in Yorkshire, in which he attempted to explain the importance of the charges. He was, however, set upon by the mob and lynched. Hostility to the charge and to Northumberland was increased because of the following:

- Traditionally the North of England paid less tax for defence of the realm and wars on the continent because they were more directly engaged than the rest of the country in defending the border with Scotland. Henry, however, broke with this custom in 1489 and instead insisted upon the entire country paying a tenth. This provoked outcry in Yorkshire and Durham, with a widespread refusal to pay the tax.

- The North of England was where Richard III had most of his estates and where most of his loyal following had been based, so people may well have resented the Tudor regime more in this area.

- The earl of Northumberland's retinue had previously had Richard III as their 'good lord' (see Chapter 1, page 12). They failed to defend Percy against the mob and this may have been because they felt little loyalty towards him or to the new king, whereas they had supported Richard.

Percy's murder indicated a significant level of hostility towards the charges and to the reign of Henry VII. It was also a serious breakdown in law and order that undermined Henry's claims to have brought peace to the country. The murder was particularly shocking as the Percy family had a long tradition of governance in the North; he was a senior nobleman with particular responsibility for the Scottish Marches and the security of this sensitive area. It was a serious embarrassment to Henry VII, therefore, and Northumberland's death also potentially had important consequences for the security and stability of the region as his heir was a minor, leaving something of a power vacuum. Henry also was apparently concerned that the rising would develop from a tax revolt into a more general, pro-Yorkist rebellion and he was determined to crush it with a large force.

Aware of the seriousness of their actions, the rebels appear to have become anxious about the consequences of such a high-profile murder, particularly given the king's reputation for harshness. The fear that the king's reprisals would be felt across the area led to the insurrection escalating under the leadership of Sir John Egremont, a Yorkist sympathiser. The rebels declared that they would fight against the king's 'evil councillors' to defend their rights, leading a rebellion which, according to historian Anthony Goodman, was only briefly truly threatening to the crown. Henry himself accompanied the earl of Surrey to subdue the insurgents. The rebels, however, quickly lost their determination and fled, although some ringleaders were hanged at York. Egremont escaped and found refuge with Margaret of Burgundy, who was in Flanders at this time. Although the rebellion was fairly easily defeated, it was notable that Henry, despite all his desire for money, was careful in the future not to demand taxation against custom in the North. This placed a significant limitation on his military ambitions, and provides a reason for his more limited ambitions in the arena of foreign war during his reign. Indeed, the modern historian Christine Carpenter has argued that Henry VII's avaricious financial policies were often liable to backfire, and that Henry's keenness for money was counterproductive, as it in fact made his throne more unstable because it made him widely disliked.

Sir John Egremont (born c1453; died c1505)
John Egremont was a member of the Percy family, being the son of Thomas Percy, first Baron Egremont (d. 1460). By the mid-1470s he was in the retinue of his kinsman, the earl of Northumberland, and served both Edward IV and Richard III, receiving rewards for good service. By 1486, however, he was in the service of Henry VII and may have hoped to have his father's barony restored by the new king. This did not happen, however, and may have been one of the reasons why he rebelled against the Tudor regime in 1489.

The Cornish rebellion of 1497: causes, events and impact

During the tensions surrounding James IV's support of Warbeck, and as Henry was preparing for war with Scotland, rebellion at home threatened the Tudor regime in the form of a revolt in Cornwall. This began in May 1497 and the key cause again appears to have been high taxation, this time to fund the military campaigns in Scotland that, for distant Cornwall, seemed rather irrelevant. The rebels marched to Somerset led by two obscure figures called Michael Joseph the Blacksmith and Thomas Flamank. On reaching Wells, however, they gained more illustrious support from Lord Audley, who became one of the leaders.

Lord Audley's reasons for disillusionment with Henry VII are unclear, but it seems that the gentry of Somerset were generally unimpressed by the Tudor regime as 24 other gentlemen from the area were also involved. It is possible Audley was still loyal to the Yorkists as his father had been a close friend of Edward IV, and his brother, John, was married to one of Edward's illegitimate daughters. This, however, seems to be a rather obscure motive, as King Edward was long dead by this stage. It is more likely that by promoting Warbeck's claim to be Edward IV's younger son, Richard of York, Audley wished to claim influence as he would have then been the new king's (alleged) brother-in-law.

Such a plan was extremely foolish and it is notable that the leaders of the Cornish revolt were unable to secure the support of Bristol for their cause in its early stages. Nonetheless, insurrection spread quickly through the South West, and the rebels seem to have called upon Warbeck to lead their revolt and marched on London. They travelled via Salisbury, Winchester, Farnham, and Guildford and did not meet with any significant opposition, although it seems that there was some fighting in Hampshire and Guildford. On 17 June, Henry fought the insurgents just before they reached the capital and defeated them at Blackheath, swiftly executing the ringleaders, including Audley, and then ordering careful investigations to discover, try and fine thousands of other lesser men who had taken part, a process that took a number of years and indicated Henry's determination to eradicate disloyalty. Even after the king's victory, however, Henry continued to be threatened from the South West as the rebels had called upon Warbeck to lead them. He sailed from Ireland and landed in Cornwall on 7 September, attacking Exeter with, according to contemporary claims, 8,000 troops. While ultimately Warbeck was unsuccessful, this posed a significant problem to the Tudor regime as, at around this time, James IV of Scotland was creating problems on the northern border, meaning Henry had conflict to deal with on two fronts. Royal troops defeated Warbeck and the rebels after two weeks, however, and Warbeck fled to sanctuary.

EXTEND YOUR KNOWLEDGE

The fate of Lord Audley and his family
Lord Audley's decision to lead the Cornish rebellion resulted in his execution and financial ruin for his family. He was captured at Blackheath by royal forces along with the other leaders and tried on 27 June. After being found guilty of treason, he was marched through the streets of London in a paper surcoat (a type of overgarment commonly worn in this period) which displayed his family coat of arms cut to shreds, symbolising the fall of his family as a result of his treachery. He was beheaded at Tower Hill. Henry seized his estates and his widow was taken into the care of her mother-in-law, apparently having a mental breakdown by 1515. His heir was allowed to regain his noble status in 1512, but the king charged so high a price for this restoration that the family remained crippled by debt and had to sell their lands in 1535. Lord Audley's story indicated the penalty of failed rebellion against the Tudor regime, and also demonstrates some of the more unattractive elements of Henry VII's financial policies.

SOURCE

6 From the entries for 1497 for the *Registrum Annalium Collegii Mertonensis* ('Annual register of the College of Merton'). Merton College is part of the University of Oxford.

Memorandum, in this year about the beginning of May, a great rising of the people occurred in the kingdom beginning in Cornwall where the ringleader was a [black]smith named Michael Joseph. A great multitude of people supported him, but there was none of noble blood except Lord Audley. Crossing the counties of Devon, Somerset, Wiltshire, Southampton, they came at length to Blackheath on 16th June, where they pitched their camp for the night. On the morrow, 17th June, Henry VII met them with a great multitude of nobles. He gained the victory without great slaughter on either side and the said captain and Lord Audley with others were captured and committed in chains to the Tower for their deeds. From there on the 27th of the month the said Michael and one Flammok, a lawyer, were drawn through the places of the city to Tyburn [a traditional site of punishment and execution] and there were hanged. Their bodies were taken down quartered, and by the king's orders were hanged in various cities and places in the kingdom. On the next day, the 28th, the said Lord Audley was drawn from Newgate through the places of the city to the place of punishment near the Tower, and there his head was struck off. His body was, by the king's grace, buried in the Preachers, but his head was fixed on London Bridge.

… Memorandum, in that year on 7th September, one Perkin, by nationality a Fleming, pretending that he was the second son of Edward IV, and calling himself Richard, duke of York, landed at the port of St Ives in Cornwall and proclaimed himself king of England. About 10,000 Cornishmen who hated Henry VII on account of their defeat at Blackheath on the previous 17th June, and who wished to avenge themselves on the king joined him, and they set out towards the east in battle array.

A Level Exam-Style Question Section A

Study Source 6 before you answer this question.

Assess the value of the source for determining the seriousness of the rebellions against Henry VII in 1497 and the reasons why the king was successful in subduing the insurrection.

Explain your answer, using the source, the information given about its origin and your own knowledge about the historical context. (20 marks)

Tip

Remember to not only focus on factors mentioned in the source, but also to discuss the passage's limitations using your own knowledge of Henry's reign and style of kingship.

Impact of the Cornish uprising

In the immediate aftermath of the rebellion, Henry secured his position by agreeing a truce with Scotland and quelling some of the cause of the Cornish unrest by cancelling the next round of parliamentary taxation. Warbeck left sanctuary on the condition that his life would be spared and he made full confession of his pretence and lack of a genuine claim to the throne. To emphasise his enemy's defeat and the illegitimacy of his claim, the king had Warbeck repeatedly paraded through the streets of London and also took him with him around the country, punishing Warbeck with the **stocks** when he tried to escape. In June 1498, he was condemned to spend the rest of his life in the Tower, in **shackles**. During his time in prison, he communicated with another inmate, Edward, earl of Warwick, who had been held in the Tower since childhood because he had a claim to the throne that would rival that of Henry VII. It is unclear exactly what plotting took place between the two men, but they seem to have aimed at escape and possibly wished to make an attempt on the throne with the help of a group of sympathetic Londoners. In the earl of Warwick's case especially, this may well have been an understandable and rather desperate bid for freedom. In November 1499, the two men were executed. It is suspected that Henry may have deliberately sought to entrap Warwick into treasonous discussion and plotting, in order to have an excuse for getting rid of his two rivals. Indeed, it is likely that the removal of alternative claimants to the throne – especially Warwick – was a pre-condition set by the Spanish monarchs before they would permit their daughter, Princess Katherine of Aragon, to marry the Tudor heir, Prince Arthur, in 1501 (see Source 7). In the longer term, therefore, the Cornish uprising had far-reaching consequences, including the death of two of Henry's key rivals and the securing of a crucial marriage alliance with Spain.

EXTEND YOUR KNOWLEDGE

Henry VII's choice of punishment for royal pretenders

In order to emphasise the falsity of the claims to be of royal birth, Henry VII was careful to ensure that both Lambert Simnel and Perkin Warbeck were treated in a way that emphasised their humble origins. This was done in part to humiliate those who had lent the pretenders their support.

In the case of Simnel, the boy was given a job in the royal kitchens and Henry was said to have remarked sarcastically upon the foolishness of the Irish, who would crown even a kitchen scullion.

In the case of Warbeck, he was punished in the stocks after one of his attempted escapes, a form of public humiliation that was usually only used for those of relatively humble birth, notably dishonest market traders. In 1499, after Warbeck's apparent conspiracy in the Tower with Edward of Warwick, it was notable that the earl was beheaded (which was considered to be a high-status form of execution, used only for nobles), while Warbeck was hanged, a method of execution traditionally used for lower-status criminals.

KEY TERMS

Stocks
A contraption designed to hold the ankles of a prisoner. They were situated in public places and were designed to allow the person being punished to be publicly humiliated. Crowds or passers-by could shame the prisoner further by shouting abuse, throwing refuse, etc. A similar device, which held the neck and wrists, was called the pillory and sometimes the words are used interchangeably. This type of punishment was normally used for relatively low-status prisoners.

Shackles
Iron chains placed around the ankles of prisoners who were deemed at risk of escape. Wearing shackles added significantly to the hardship of imprisonment.

SOURCE

7 From a letter from Rodrigo Gonzales de Puebla, the Spanish ambassador at the English court to Ferdinand and Isabella, the king and queen of Spain, dated 11 January 1500.

After kissing the royal feet and the hands of your Highnesses, I cause you to know that by the good fortune of your highnesses and of the lady princess of Wales [i.e. Katherine of Aragon, the Spanish princess, who was betrothed to the Tudor prince, Arthur], this kingdom is at present so situated as has not been seen for the last five hundred years till now, as those say who know best and as appears by the chronicles; because there were always brambles and thorns of such a kind that the English had occasion not to remain peacefully in obedience to their king, there being divers heirs of the kingdom and of such a quality that the matter could be disputed between the two sides. Now it has pleased God that all should be thoroughly and duly purged and cleansed, so that not a doubtful drop of royal blood remains in this kingdom except the true blood of the King and Queen and above all that of the lord Prince Arthur. And since of this fact and of the execution which was done on Perkin [Warbeck] and on [Edward, earl of Warwick] the son of the duke of Clarence I have written to your Highnesses by various ways, I do not wish to trouble you with lengthy writing.

A Level Exam-Style Question Section B

How significant were the challenges posed by Lambert Simnel and Perkin Warbeck to Henry VII in the late 15th century? (20 marks)

Tip

Remember to discuss the differences and similarities in both rebellions and to evaluate which imposter posed the more serious threat to the Tudor regime.

A Level Exam-Style Question Section B

'The rebellions of 1489 and 1497 clearly show that the primary threat to the stability of Henry VII's throne was his taxation policies.'

How far do you agree with this statement? (20 marks)

Tip

Remember to include information, not only about the two rebellions, but also Henry's other unpopular policies, such as his use of bonds, and other threats to his security that were not related to finance. You will also need to mention what the taxes were to be spent on – namely defence – and how threats from outside the kingdom were highly significant in this context.

Conclusion

The traditional image of Henry VII's reign, and one which Tudor propaganda was keen to emphasise, was that of a king who at long last had brought peace to a country previously divided by civil war. Certainly, the fact that Henry, with a rather dubious claim to the throne, managed not only to reign until his natural death but also to leave his throne to his unchallenged heir was a considerable achievement. Historians have long debated, however, how far this success was owing to Henry's skill as a politician or to his good fortune; few attribute it to Henry's personal likeability. His stringent financial policies, some of which amounted to extortion, gave him a reputation for avarice that was cemented shortly after his death when Henry VIII agreed to the execution of two of his father's most unpopular advisers on spurious charges. His regime twice experienced popular rebellions over taxation, but Henry also created resentment among the nobility by binding them to him through bonds that threatened financial ruin on any who disobeyed him. Some scholars have regarded these exactions, as well as Henry's complex spy network, as a sign that he ruled in a very different, and much less consensual, way than previous medieval kings. Others, meanwhile, have hastened to emphasise the continuity between the pre- and post-Bosworth periods. As ever, a middle ground between the two camps is probably the most accurate. Henry did rule differently from his immediate predecessors, Edward IV and Richard III, but this was probably less because he provided an intrinsically more 'modern' image of state than because, like all medieval kings, he stamped his own personality and experience on his reign. It is entirely unsurprising that a man in a weak position in terms of a legitimate claim, and who had spent most of his life away from the English court, should make alterations to political practice and endeavour to prevent opposition by all means available to him. That some of the methods he used were considered dangerously and unacceptably innovative, most notably his tax demands on the northern counties and his heavy use of bonds, indicates that the fundamental political fabric of the era remained wedded to custom and to the belief that, most of the time, a king should govern within the law. Nonetheless, Henry secured his realm by the eradication of many alternative claimants, rapid and harsh reprisals against members of the nobility who plotted rebellion and the careful use of a well-resourced intelligence network. While not all of these methods were innovative, the first Tudor king certainly made good use of them.

ACTIVITY
KNOWLEDGE CHECK

Henry VII's financial policies and his security on the throne

1 Consider the statement: 'Henry VII's financial policies undermined rather than strengthened his security'. Write a one-minute speech either agreeing or disagreeing with the statement, giving evidence to support your views. Then listen to a speech giving the alternative viewpoint from another member of your class and take notes.

2 Draw up a table comparing the significance of the Yorkshire rebellion of 1489 and the Cornish rebellion of 1497. Remember to focus on the importance of the events rather than just describing everything that happened. Once you have completed this, write a paragraph explaining which event was more significant in your view and why.

ACTIVITY
SUMMARY

1 Make notes about the advantages and disadvantages of each of the following features of Henry VII's reign. Example a) has been completed for you:

a) Careful use of spy network.

Advantages: Kept Henry secure on the throne and prevented plots from reaching completion in, for example, the 1490s.

Disadvantages: Demonstrated Henry's strong distrust of those around him and was liable to make people paranoid.

b) Henry VII married Elizabeth of York and had a number of children with her.

c) Arrested and executed those suspected of treason, even if their involvement was limited.

d) Made heavy use of bonds and recognisances in his dealings with the nobility.

e) Removed most alternative claimants to the throne via imprisonment and/or execution.

f) Charged heavy taxes that were in some cases levied contrary to established custom.

2 Create a timeline for the reign of Henry VII (1485–1509) and complete events of significance in these colours:

a) Red – events that seriously threatened the stability of his reign.

b) Orange – events that slightly threatened the stability of his reign.

c) Green – events that improved the stability of his throne.

Remember to include not only plots and rebellions, but also marriages, births and deaths, and diplomatic incidents.

WIDER READING

Arthurson, I. 'Espionage and Intelligence from the Wars of the Roses to the Reformation', *Nottingham Medieval Studies*, 35 (1991). Available online at www.deremilitari.org

Bennett, M. 'Simnel, Lambert (b.1476/7, d. after 1534)', *Oxford Dictionary of National Biography*, Oxford University Press (2004). Online edn www.oxforddnb.com/view/article/25569?docPos=1

Chrimes, S.B. *Henry VII*, Yale University Press (1999)

Goodman, A. *The New Monarchy: England, 1471–1534*, Basil Blackwell (1988)

Grant, A. *Henry VII*, Routledge (1985)

Gunn, S.J. 'Warbeck, Perkin [Pierrechon de Werbecque; *alias* Richard Plantagenet, duke of York] (c.1474–1499)', *Oxford Dictionary of National Biography*, Oxford University Press (2004). Online edn, Oct 2008 www.oxforddnb.com/view/article/28669

Lander, J.R. *The Wars of the Roses*, Sutton Publishing (2007)

Levine, M. *Tudor Dynastic Problems, 1460–1571*, Allen and Unwin (1973)

Pickering, A. *Lancastrians to Tudors: England, 1450–1509*, Cambridge University Press (2000)

Preparing for your A Level Paper 3 exam

Advance planning

Draw up a timetable for your revision and try to keep to it. Spend longer on topics that you have found difficult, and revise them several times. Aim to be confident about all aspects of your Paper 3 work, because this will ensure that you have a choice of questions in Sections B and C.

Paper 3 overview

Paper 3	Time: 2 hours 15 minutes	
Section A	Answer 1 compulsory question for the option studied, assessing source analysis and evaluation skills.	20 marks
Section B	Answer 1 question from a choice of 2 on an aspect in depth for the option studied.	20 marks
Section C	Answer 1 question from a choice of 2 on an aspect in breadth for the option studied.	20 marks
	Total marks =	60 marks

Section A questions

There is no choice of question in Section A. You will be referred to a source of about 350 words long, printed in a Sources Booklet. The source will be a primary source or one that is contemporary to the period you have studied, and will relate to one of the key topics in the Aspect of Depth. You will be expected to analyse and evaluate the source in its historical context. The question will ask you to assess the value of the source for revealing something specific about the period, and will expect you to explain your answer, using the source, the information given about its origin and your own knowledge about the historical context.

Section B questions

You will have a choice of one from two questions in Section B. They will aim to assess your understanding of one or more of the key topics in the Aspect of Depth you have studied. Questions may relate to a single, momentous year, but will normally cover longer periods. You will be required to write an essay evaluating an aspect of the period. You may be asked about change and continuity, similarity and difference, consequences, significance or causation, or you may be given a quotation and asked to explain how far you agree with it. All questions will require you to reach a substantiated judgement.

Section C questions

You will have a choice of one from two questions in Section C. Questions will relate to the themes of the Aspects of Breadth you have studied, and will aim to assess your understanding of change over time. They will cover a period of no less than 100 years and will relate either to the factors that brought about change, or the extent of change over the period, or patterns of change as demonstrated by turning points.

Use of time

1. Do not write solidly for 45 minutes on each question. For Section B and C answers, you should spend a few minutes working out what the question is asking you to do, and drawing up a plan of your answer. This is especially important for Section C answers, which cover an extended period of time.
2. For Section A, it is essential that you have a clear understanding of the content of the source and its historical context. Pay particular attention to the provenance: was the author in a position to know what he or she was writing about? Read it carefully and underline important points. You might decide to spend up to ten minutes reading the source and drawing up your plan, and 35 minutes writing your answer.

Preparing for your A Level exams

Paper 3: A Level sample answer with comments

These questions require you to analyse and evaluate source material with respect to its historical context.

For these questions remember to:

- look at the evidence given in the source and consider how the source could be used in differing ways to provide historical understanding
- use your knowledge of the historical context to discuss any limitations the source may have
- use your historical understanding to evaluate the source, considering how much weight you would give to its argument
- come to a judgement on the overall value of the source in respect to the question.

Study Source 7 in Chapter 4 (page 108).

Assess the value of Thomas Walsingham's description of the death of Henry V, analysing the character of Henry V and his political legacy.

Explain your answer, using the source, the information given about its origin and your own knowledge about the historical content.
(20 marks)

Average student answer

Henry V was famous for his military victories and was a very successful king, as Shakespeare demonstrated in his famous play. He won a lot of famous victories, such as the Battle of Agincourt when the English beat the French by using archers in a clever way. In this source, Thomas Walsingham explains that Henry was a really good king, who was justifiably admired.

> This gives some accurate background information and briefly summarises the source. To improve, it should make a more obvious link with the wording of the question, highlighting that the response will engage with both aspects of the enquiry.

The source is written by Thomas Walsingham, who was a monk based at St Albans' Abbey. It is quite reliable because he was writing at the time and was well informed about important political events, but maybe not so reliable because Henry V died in France and Walsingham was in England. He accurately shows that Henry died of dysentery, which is correct and this also makes the source seem more useful. Walsingham also discusses Henry's military victories when he says 'he had won victories in all his military engagements' which is true because he was a very successful warrior and won famous battles such as Agincourt and Harfleur. He also conquered most of France as Walsingham explains: 'All the French… had experienced the English king's just and prudent rule'.

Walsingham states that the French preferred Henry to their old king and this is a big testament to Henry because, if this is true, then he must have been a really able king. It might not be true, though, because Walsingham was English and so was probably quite biased. Also, Walsingham wasn't in France at the time. Henry was probably quite popular in Paris, though, because that is

> Here, too much material is copied from the information given on the exam paper, without much evaluation and the use of own knowledge. Instead, it would be better to write 'Walsingham clearly wrote this passage to praise Henry V. Most of his comments are fairly plausible – clearly, Henry was a strong warrior, for example, although arguably his victory at Agincourt was as much caused by luck as strong strategy.'

> Here, the candidate rightly highlights that the most unusual claim made by Walsingham is that the French preferred Henry to their own king and suggests that this might be inaccurate. To improve, the comments should be supported by reference to the problems Henry VI's minority council had controlling France after Henry V's death. The final sentence is the first direct link made with the second part of the question, so there should have been more emphasis on this point earlier in the essay.

where his young son was crowned a few years later, even though he was only nine months old when he came to the throne. This shows that Henry V left his son a strong political legacy.

Walsingham was a monk so probably would want to tell the truth because he was religious so the source is more accurate. This is supported by my own knowledge as I know that Henry was a good warrior and that he conquered most of France. The source also says Henry was very religious when Walsingham says that he was 'devoted to God', which would have been a good thing for a king at the time because in the medieval period they were very religious. It might be bad for a king to be religious though, because it would make him not want to fight.

Walsingham was very supportive of Henry V and said lots of positive things about him. This source is quite one-sided but it is true that he was a very successful king. This made things difficult for his son, Henry VI, because he was only a baby when Henry died and then he had a big reputation to live up to. When the king died in 1422, this meant a minority council had to take over to rule in place of Henry VI and this was a problem because they did not agree about how to run things in France especially. The baby's two uncles, John, duke of Bedford and Humphrey, duke of Gloucester, tried to run things and they did not get along so there was a lot of friction. There were particular problems because the French heir to the throne, the dauphin, did not accept that Henry VI should be king because he was English and a baby and so he stirred up trouble. There were a lot of military defeats under Henry VI and this was bad for his reputation because his father had been so successful. Everyone would have compared them and this wasn't really fair because Henry was so young and had a lot to live up to.

To conclude, this source is quite useful because it highlights lots of the things that Henry was good at and a lot of what it says about his character is true. It is quite biased, though, and this means that it is not entirely reliable. It doesn't say a lot about Henry VI's rule so it is not that useful for discussing Henry V's political legacy.

This paragraph is extremely weak and shows too much stereotyping and generalisation about religion in the medieval period; this is, however, a common error. For example, the fact that Walsingham was a monk does not necessarily mean he would tell the truth, but it does mean he was likely to emphasise Henry's piety and to praise the king's support for the Church as an institution. Also, during the medieval period, fighting wars and being a Christian were seen as entirely compatible by most people; indeed, it was widely believed that it was the Christian duty of a good king to protect his subjects.

The response is right to identify the one-sidedness of the source and to discuss Henry V's political legacy. The knowledge used here is generally accurate, although it could do with more detail, such as discussing the key treaties of Troyes (1420) and Tours (1444).

The conclusion focuses well on the question and the source. It is rather vague and naïve in its comments, however.

Verdict

This is an average answer because:

- the section on Henry V's political legacy is brief. It is important to ensure both aspects of the question are fully discussed
- the candidate's understanding of historical context is weak, a point that is especially evident in the discussion of medieval religion. The essay would benefit greatly from more discussion of the medieval concept of what made a good

monarch and the criteria contemporaries would have used to judge this
- there is some discussion of the strengths and weaknesses of the source's value as evidence, but this is not detailed enough and there needs to be more discussion of the source's limitations.

Use the feedback on this essay to rewrite it, making as many improvements as you can.

Paper 3: A Level sample answer with comments

Section A

These questions require you to analyse and evaluate source material with respect to its historical context.

For these questions remember to:

- look at the evidence given in the source and consider how the source could be used in differing ways to provide historical understanding
- use your knowledge of the historical context to discuss any limitations the source may have
- use your historical understanding to evaluate the source, considering how much weight you would give to its argument
- come to a judgement on the overall value of the source in respect to the question.

Study Source 7 in Chapter 4 (page 108).

Assess the value of Thomas Walsingham's description of the death of Henry V, analysing the character of Henry V and his political legacy.

Explain your answer, using the source, the information given about its origin and your own knowledge about the historical content. (20 marks)

Strong student answer

Walsingham was a famous late medieval chronicler and was noted for highly opinionated writing. This extract is no exception and an extremely positive view of Henry V is presented. The passage, written shortly after Henry's death in 1422, was designed to give an overview of the king's reign and provides insight into both the character of Henry and his political legacy.

According to Sir John Fortescue, it was the duty of a medieval monarch to 'maintain the peace, both inward and outward', in other words to defend the realm against external threats as well as to maintain law and order within his kingdom. It was also considered important that the king was seen to be religious. Henry V has often been regarded by both contemporaries and modern historians as the monarch who best conformed to this ideal. Walsingham's account of Henry's character expresses the view that he was a king who was exemplary in all three areas. There is clearly some truth in this – Henry was, above all, a highly successful warrior and his victories at Agincourt and Harfleur were legendary. Nonetheless, the fact that Walsingham's account of the king's character is so clearly based on the 'model king' stereotype is suspicious; it is likely that, to a certain extent, he was writing an account of stereotype rather than reality. This should be borne in mind when evaluating Walsingham's reliability as a source of factual information about Henry's character, but it does make the account very useful in assessing how the 15th-century hero-worship of Henry V made him a difficult act to follow for his much less-able son, Henry VI.

Although Henry V remains most famous for his military ability, it is significant that four paragraphs of this account focus mainly on his spiritual life. This partly reflects the author's own preoccupations; as a monk, Walsingham regarded the king's attitude towards the church as a factor of importance. The prioritisation of religious matters is a common factor in medieval sources, as the most literate group were the clergy so they have tended to author most of the contemporary sources. This can mislead historians into thinking that all other groups gave equal weight to religious matters. Nonetheless, there is other evidence which suggests that Henry V was considered by his contemporaries to be conventionally pious. It is likely, therefore, that information Walsingham gives about Henry paying his debts while on his deathbed, for example, were true as this was a common practice at the time as it was believed that those in debt could not move out of Purgatory in the afterlife.

The introduction demonstrates a clear engagement with both aspects of the question and gives a brief overview of the tone and purpose of the source. The opening line also demonstrates strong background knowledge.

Demonstrates detailed background knowledge of the historical context, allowing well-reasoned and sophisticated judgements about the usefulness of the source as a piece of evidence to be made. The discussion of the criteria by which a medieval king should be judged is excellent and firmly grounded in historical fact. It also clearly links to both aspects of the question.

The key themes are highlighted and the strengths and weaknesses of the author's interests are analysed. A strong

Another reason that Walsingham emphasises Henry's spirituality was to ensure his description of the king conformed to the traditional stereotype of a pious Christian ruler, who fought bravely against external enemies and was given victory over his opponents by God as a sign of divine approval. Clearly, criticism of a king whose son had just taken the throne in 1422 would be unwise. It must be noted, however, that many people at this time viewed Henry's military victories as a sign of God's approval and this was part of the reason why he faced no challenge to the throne after his famous battles despite the fact that he was part of a usurping dynasty, Henry IV having seized the throne forcibly from Richard II in 1399.

understanding of the context is shown, with a good grasp of the importance of medieval Christianity in the culture of the time, as well as the limitations of chronicles as a source type. Detailed own knowledge is used to support the judgements.

Henry's military successes were to prove a mixed blessing for his heir. On one hand, they ensured that the Lancastrian dynasty was secure on the throne by the end of his reign and there was considerable loyalty even to the infant king by the nobility in 1422. There were divisions in the royal council during Henry VI's minority government, notably between Gloucester and Bedford, and between Gloucester and Cardinal Beaufort, but given the length of the minority it is evident that all sides were unwilling to take the opportunity to overthrow Henry VI even though he was vulnerable. This basic loyalty to the crown continued until major English defeats in the Hundred Years War and Henry VI's total mental collapse in the 1450s, a point that has been particularly emphasised by historians such as John Watts and Christine Carpenter.

The precise political context of the date is evaluated here, with an explanation of how this impacts on the reliability of the evidence.

On the other hand, Henry V left an extremely difficult legacy for his son which anyone would have found very hard to cope with. The 1420 Treaty of Troyes made a baby king of both England and France by 1422, and in France there was plenty of opposition to English rule. This is ignored by Walsingham, who instead paints the implausible picture of the French lamenting Henry V's death. In reality, the dauphin was anxious to regain his lost kingdom and the English parliament became tired of providing money to establish law and order in France, instead arguing that the French should be taxed for this. This major financial difficulty is omitted in Walsingham's account, partly because Henry V was so popular parliament tended to do as he wished, but also because this author does not regard this matter of economic policy as so significant. In reality, however, the cost and complexity of continuing the Hundred Years War after 1422 was considerable and certainly beyond the feeble-minded Henry VI.

Demonstrates a strong understanding of the workings of Henry VI's minority government and the views of modern historians. Good grasp of the chronology of events and change over time is shown.

In conclusion, it is evident that Walsingham's account is useful in demonstrating a contemporary attitude towards Henry V's character, which was probably fairly typical at the time. Although the author was not present in France, he would have probably been reflecting popular feeling in England, at least among the educated classes. The value of the source is weakened, however, by the level to which it conforms to a stereotype of the 'ideal' king, reflecting the fact that Walsingham did not really have much 'insider' knowledge to share on this topic. Perhaps its greatest importance as a source is in revealing how difficult an act Henry V would be to follow for his son, as people were so impressed by military conquests in France. The fact that Walsingham does not mention the financial strain of the war with France reflects the fact that in 1422 this had not become a topic of serious popular concern, but it is clear to modern historians that the 1420 Troyes legacy was not sustainable.

The source's limitations are evaluated, using detailed knowledge to fill the gaps.

Judgements are made throughout this paragraph about the value of the source as evidence and the response prioritises which parts of the argument in the essay are the most significant in answering the question.

Verdict

This is a strong answer because:

- it focuses on the question throughout, answering both parts of the enquiry, and analyses the source thoroughly
- it uses the candidate's detailed and accurate own knowledge to ensure the source is evaluated and that judgements are reached about the strengths and weaknesses of the text

- it establishes valid criteria for judging medieval monarchs that are grounded in contemporary views and the historical context. It provides a sophisticated analysis of the source material, not simply reducing the analysis to describing a source as either 'biased' or 'not biased' but investigating degrees of accuracy and usefulness.

Paper 3: A Level sample answer with comments

Section B

These questions require you to show your understanding of a period in depth. They will ask you about a quite specific period of time and require you to make a substantiated judgement about a specific aspect you have studied.

For these questions remember to:

- organise your essay and communicate it in a manner that is clear and comprehensible
- use historical knowledge to analyse and evaluate the key aspect of the question
- make a balanced argument that weighs up differing opinions
- make a substantiated overall judgement on the question.

'The disappearance of the princes in 1483 was the result of Richard III's personal ambition.'

How far do you agree with this statement? Explain your answer. (20 marks)

Average student answer

Richard III is a king with a terrible reputation. After the sudden death of Edward IV in 1483, it was presumed that the throne would be inherited by his son, also called Edward. However, this didn't happen as Richard, duke of Gloucester interfered and delayed Edward V's coronation twice. Soon afterwards, Richard usurped his nephew and became king in June 1483. There was a serious backlash about this, with many people at the time claiming that he killed the two princes in the Tower to become king. This essay argues that the evidence is overwhelming that Richard killed his nephews.

There is a widely accepted view that Richard murdered the boys and this is influenced by Tudor propaganda in the 16th century. The main example of this is Shakespeare's play, 'Richard III' where Richard is shown to be an evil hunchback. Shakespeare was writing for Henry VII's granddaughter, Elizabeth I, so he would have had to make Richard look bad and Henry look good. Although Shakespeare's play is very exaggerated, when Richard's body was discovered by archaeologists the skeleton showed a curved spine, which shows Shakespeare knew some of the truth about Richard.

Shakespeare is also shown to be quite accurate because a lot of sources agree with his interpretation, including Dominic Mancini who is important because he is the only writer who was not writing with an agenda because he was a foreigner and so didn't need to be worried about not pleasing the king, Henry VII. He might not understand English well though so could be a bit biased, but he is not likely to be lying. He also got information from people like the doctor of the princes in the Tower, so he was quite well informed.

The introduction shows clear links with one aspect of the question, namely that Richard murdered his nephews, but does not engage with the idea that he did so because of personal ambition. It could be improved by writing: 'The motivations for Richard's actions have been debated by historians, with some arguing that the duke had reasonable concerns about the level of control the Woodville family would have over a child-king, but most emphasise the duke's overwhelming personal ambition as the cause for his crime.'

There are some good points here showing an understanding of the importance of Tudor propaganda. It would be greatly improved, however, by focusing on Tudor sources generally, including work by John Rous, Thomas More and Polydore Vergil, which provide more significant evidence as they were written closer to the time and were designed at least in part as historical accounts rather than fictional plays to entertain an audience.

Mancini is a very important source of evidence for this question and so the candidate is right to focus attention on him and to highlight why he is so significant. The use of the word 'bias' here is too basic; a person is not biased because they do not speak English, although they may be misinformed or inaccurate in some of their conclusions. To improve, the response should include more detail to support the view.

When considering a murder, it is important to consider motives. Richard had a lot to gain from killing the princes, because he could then become king once he had got rid of them. No one would have him as king if the boys were alive. It is proved that he didn't want Edward to be king because he delayed his coronation twice. He also had a family history of murder and probably helped to kill his brother George, duke of Clarence, in a vat of wine. Some people say he also killed his wife because she couldn't have children anymore and his son died, which wasn't a good thing at the time because having an heir was seen as important. Although this evidence is only circumstantial, it is very suspicious and shows that Richard had the personality to kill the princes.

Richard had a lot of opportunity to kill the princes because he was powerful and had access to the Tower. He also basically kidnapped the princes when they were travelling to London after Edward IV's death and put them in the Tower, showing evil intentions. He probably did this because he was greedy for power and didn't want the new king influenced by the Woodville family as he didn't like them. Although he personally seized the princes, he may not have been responsible for their murder himself as there is a vast amount of evidence supporting the notion that he hired someone else to do the job for him such as James Tyrell. Some writers at the time thought Tyrell killed the princes because Richard asked him to, but Richard is still responsible because if you hire someone to do the job you are to blame as well. Tyrell also confessed to murdering the boys, although he was tortured to say this so you can't rely on this too much.

To conclude, it is evident that Richard did kill his nephews because he was ambitious to be king. He had the evil personality to do so, plenty of motivation and almost everyone thought he had done it at the time. It is possible he got someone else to do the actual killing instead of doing it himself, but that's no excuse. He was also from a family who killed people who got in their way and he was ambitious to be king because that was how you were powerful at the time.

This paragraph is rather confused, as it starts by focusing on Richard's motivations, lists different murders he may have committed, and then reaches a judgement on his personality. It would be better to discuss these themes in separate paragraphs. There is also a lack of detailed knowledge here (for example: what was Richard's wife's name and why was he suspected of killing her? When did this happen and how well evidenced is this suspicion of murder?). The comment about George, duke of Clarence is very one-sided and does not show a full awareness of the facts; there is no clear evidence linking Richard to his brother's death, although he did not intervene at any point to stop it having been given substantial lands by Edward IV shortly beforehand. The theory that he was involved in the killing largely derives from Shakespeare's fictional account and it is also not definitely known that Clarence was drowned – this may well be a myth.

The question of opportunity and access is rightly highlighted here, but there is a lack of detailed evidence to support the key points. For example, why did Richard dislike the Woodvilles? It would also be worth pointing out that Tyrell was a loyal associate of Richard and that it was to discredit his former enemy that Henry VII was so keen to get Tyrell to confess to the murders, hence the use of torture. It is also important to avoid small factual inaccuracies; for example, Richard seized only Edward V on the journey from Ludlow to London, as his brother was elsewhere at time. Only later and after much persuasion did Elizabeth Woodville hand over the younger son.

The conclusion recounts the core arguments made and links with the question. To improve, the response should highlight which pieces of evidence are particularly compelling. The statement about Richard's family history is potentially relevant, but it is very generalised here. In essence, you cannot accuse someone of murder simply because their family was unpleasant; more evaluation than this is required.

Verdict

This is an average answer because:

- it is very one-sided. It is important that the argument is clear, but also that some consideration of alternative viewpoints/ evidence is shown
- it contains some slight factual inaccuracies, usually because the response is rather vague or makes generalisations. Instead, very precise, detailed knowledge should be used to support judgements

- it focuses mainly on one part of the question – the murder of the princes – and does not consider the question of Richard's personal ambition.

Use the feedback on this essay to rewrite it, making as many improvements as you can.

Paper 3: A Level sample answer with comments

Section B

These questions require you to show your understanding of a period in depth. They will ask you about a quite specific period of time and require you to make a substantiated judgement about a specific aspect you have studied.

For these questions remember to:

- organise your essay and communicate it in a manner that is clear and comprehensible
- use historical knowledge to analyse and evaluate the key aspect of the question
- make a balanced argument that weighs up differing opinions
- make a substantiated overall judgement on the question.

'The disappearance of the princes in 1483 was the result of Richard III's personal ambition.'

How far do you agree with this statement? Explain your answer. (20 marks)

Strong student answer

The accusation that Richard III was responsible for the deaths of the princes in the Tower because of his personal ambition is one that has blackened his reputation for centuries. Here it will be argued that while the evidence against him clearly has a number of flaws, the likelihood is that he was responsible for the murder of his nephews, although others may have carried out the actual deed. While there can be little doubt that a desire for power played its part, it is probably unfair to claim Richard was driven purely by ambition for the crown. In the hostile 15th-century political world, Richard would have justifiably regarded the Woodvilles as a very significant threat.

The most famous depiction of Richard III is by Shakespeare. This negative portrayal was so extreme and had such clear political motivations – he was writing, after all, for the granddaughter of Henry Tudor – that it created a backlash in the 20th century. The Richard III Society formed in the 1920s with the aim of rehabilitating this 'much maligned' king. While this provided a much-needed alternative to Tudor propaganda, the extremely positive assessments of Richard III that resulted were almost equally one-sided.

Instead, a more accurate image of Richard can be found through analysis of earlier sources. A key weakness in the case against Richard is that, with the exception of Dominic Mancini's account, all relevant chronicles were either written post-1485 or altered in Henry VII's reign to fit in with the new regime, such as the influential accounts by Thomas More and Polydore Vergil. This increases Mancini's importance; it is significant, therefore, that although he does not definitely accuse Richard, he makes it clear that Richard planned to usurp his nephews and was probably responsible for their deaths. Critics of Mancini have highlighted that he was an Italian visitor and so his weaker understanding of English may have reduced his understanding of the key events of 1483. In reality, however, these arguments are easily outweighed by the obvious advantages of the source, which was written by someone living in London at the time of the boys' disappearance, who was not writing with fear of displeasing a Tudor monarch and who had access to a number of sources of information including the account of the princes' doctor who visited them in the Tower regularly in 1483.

One important factor that most of the chronicle accounts highlight is the speed with which Richard seized Edward V and took control of him after the death of his father; indeed, the new king was removed from his Ludlow retinue while still travelling to London for his own

> A strong introduction that shows engagement with all aspects of the question. It also indicates the line of argument that will be taken, but demonstrates an awareness of a range of views on the issues.

> This demonstrates an awareness of the differing interpretations of Richard III and outlines the weaknesses in the arguments presented by recent scholars. It cross-references written and archaeological evidence and reaches a supported judgement.

> The significance and accuracy of different source material is compared and judgements are reached concerning the value of Mancini's account as evidence. An awareness of both sides of the argument is shown, yet the response convincingly argues the case using detailed knowledge.

> The response uses detailed knowledge to support the essay's

coronation. Such quick thinking on Richard's part indicates a strong determination to remove the child from the control of the Woodvilles. He later took care to remove the younger brother, Richard, from the dowager queen's supervision and to have him also placed in the Tower. In this matter, Richard may well have been acting rationally; the Woodvilles were a family who were widely regarded with hostility by the nobility owing to their influence with Edward IV, and their greed for money and advantageous marriages. They were also regarded as social upstarts, reflecting contemporary disapproval of Queen Elizabeth's relatively low social status when she married the king secretly. In allowing such a group to dominate a very young king, Richard would arguably have been acting unwisely not only from his personal perspective, but also in terms of the good of the country. There clearly was support within the royal council for Richard to become Protector of the Realm until the boy was of age, despite the Woodvilles' evident hostility to this.

> judgements. The argument is clear and shows a clear understanding of the historical context.

Richard's moves to remove power from the Woodville-dominated clique around the queen and to ensure the young princes were isolated was made evident in June when he undertook the callous destruction of Edward IV's most loyal supporters, notably William Lord Hastings and Anthony Woodville who were, among others, executed after dubious trials. At best, these actions show Richard would not broke any opposition in his role as Lord Protector, at worst they indicate that he had already decided upon usurpation of the throne. The latter alternative is more likely, as the killing of Hastings especially was highly controversial and probably only necessary if Richard intended to murder his nephews; Hastings, as Edward IV's closest friend and adviser, may well have supported Richard as Protector but not as a child-killer and usurper.

> The response shows strong knowledge of the chronology of the topic to develop the argument. Particularly significant events are highlighted and their importance clearly analysed.

Richard's desire to seize the throne probably had a range of motivations: it was, after all, the height of any medieval nobleman's ambition and the Wars of the Roses had shown Richard that force was often more important than legal rights in the politics of the period. He also may have convinced himself, with justification, that he was at risk of losing power, if not his own life, should he not swiftly deal with the Woodville threat; his own father, Richard of York, had served twice as Lord Protector under Henry VI and had ultimately been executed on the orders of an extremely power-hungry and vengeful queen – Margaret of Anjou. The parallels cannot have been lost on Gloucester, although there is no clear evidence of hostility between the two prior to 1483. Nonetheless, even by the bloody standards of the time, it is evident that Richard's killing of his nephews was considered immoral. Historians such as Horrox have highlighted that this stain on his character was to seriously undermine his position as king and helps to explain why he lost the throne by 1485 to Henry Tudor who, in reality, had a fairly weak claim to be king.

> Very strong contextual understanding shown here, demonstrating a thorough knowledge of the topic as a whole. The more complex aspect of the question – Richard's motivations – is discussed in depth and supported judgements are reached.

It seems probable that Richard was responsible for the deaths of the princes in the Tower, probably employing agents such as James Tyrell to carry out the actual deed. He was widely suspected of the crime at the time and no one else had as much to gain from the boys' deaths. His behaviour throughout indicated a desire to challenge other potential opponents early. He moved so swiftly to act after Edward IV's death in April that his actions indicate a level of premeditation, making the term 'murder' one that is justified here. Certainly, it suited Henry Tudor to emphasise Richard's wickedness and involvement in the crime, and he did everything in his power to blacken his enemy's reputation further, but he was simply building on what was widely believed when the boys disappeared.

> The conclusion reviews the argument and emphasises the most significant pieces of evidence. A clear overall judgement is reached.

Verdict

This is a strong answer because:

- it is structured and has a coherent argument, focusing on the question throughout
- it acknowledges alternative viewpoints but explains why they are less valid than the argument presented in the essay
- it makes frequent judgements that are supported by very detailed knowledge and shows a strong understanding of the historical context and significance of evidence in relation to the question.

Paper 3: A Level sample answer with comments

Section C

These questions require you to show your understanding of a subject over a considerable period of time. They will ask you to assess a long-term historical topic and its development over a period of at least 100 years, and they require you to make a substantiated judgement in relation to the question.

For these questions remember to:

- organise your essay and communicate it in a manner that is clear and comprehensible
- use historical knowledge to analyse and evaluate the key aspect of the question covering the entire period
- make a balanced argument that weighs up differing opinions
- make a substantiated overall judgement on the question.

'The key factor in maintaining a king's popularity and security on the throne in the years 1399–1509 was his military success.'

How far do you agree with this statement? (20 marks)

Average student answer

A good medieval king was expected to be a good warrior. This was considered very important and a sign of strength. Some kings were excellent fighters, like Henry V, but others were fairly useless on the battlefield, like Henry VI. In general, if you were a good warrior you tended to be popular, but sometimes this was not the case because a king like Richard III was meant to be good in battle even though he had a curved spine, but he still lost the throne.

Fighting was important for a king, as Fortescue pointed out when he said 'it is important to maintain the peace inward and outward'. An example of a king who did this was Henry V, who had victories at Agincourt and Harfleur because he was a very good warrior. His English forces were much smaller than French forces but he won because he made use of the longbow, which meant that archers caused confusion in the French lines. Henry was also an inspirational leader and the French panicked because they were running into mud. Henry was also ruthless about killing French prisoners to stop them helping their own side, which was effective but a lot of English soldiers weren't happy about killing the prisoners because they wanted to get money for them as a ransom.

Another king who was a good warrior was Edward IV, although he wasn't as sensational as Henry V. He won a lot of battles which helped him take the throne from Henry VI. Henry VI was a poor soldier which is further evidence that the statement in the question is right. Henry VI lost a lot of popularity because he lost Gascony in the Wars of the Roses which made people angry because the war had been very expensive. This meant that people would support Edward IV and so he won the throne from Henry VI who was also weak because he suffered from a mental breakdown which meant he couldn't make decisions.

Not all kings who were good warriors were popular, though, as evidenced by Henry IV who was good at fighting Owen Glendower in Wales but who was quite insecure and fought with his son Henry V a lot, which was quite unpopular because Henry V was very successful. Also,

> This provides some examples across the range of the time period and shows a fair understanding of the importance of a medieval king's military ability. To improve, it should make clear the difference between a king being popular and being secure – Henry VII, for example, was arguably unpopular but secure because of his use of spies and bonds.

> This paragraph opens with a quotation which is not quoted accurately and needs more explanation. Henry V is important, but the response has too much about Agincourt which is not relevant to the question. It is a common error for responses to side-track into describing battles in detail and not focus on the core arguments required.

> The structure of this paragraph is confusing as it begins with Edward IV but then focuses on Henry VI. Note the costly factual error when the candidate states that Henry VI lost Gascony as part of the Wars of the Roses – whereas the war with France was the Hundred Years War. There is a lack of detail; for example, instead of saying 'people' would support Edward IV, the response should name key noble supporters of the usurper.

Henry IV was ill for a long time so couldn't keep control easily and this made him unpopular. Similarly, Richard III was quite distrusted because he had scoliosis and so had a curved back. People at the time thought this meant he was evil because they were quite superstitious. Richard III was a brave warrior, though, but he lost to Henry Tudor at the Battle of Bosworth in 1485 so he wasn't perfect.

Fighting could make you more secure on the throne if you were a king, because if you weren't prepared to fight, then you could easily be overthrown and during the Wars of the Roses there was a lot of fighting so it was important to be strong in battle. During the reign of Henry VI, for example, there were loads of battles between the Yorkists and the Lancastrians and the king was useless at fighting so his queen had to organise things and this annoyed everyone because they didn't like it because she was a woman and they didn't agree with a woman running things. If you got a clear victory, that made it harder for people to rebel against you afterwards and, also, you had them in your power and sometimes in battles important people got killed on the other side so that got rid of threats from opponents which made the throne more secure.

Being a king was not just about fighting, but also you needed to be good at managing important people like noblemen and stopping fights between them. It was common at this time for noblemen to fight, such as the Percies and the Nevilles and, if a king did not stop these fights, then they could get out of hand. Henry VI wasn't good at dealing with situations like this and so this made him unpopular so they preferred someone like Edward IV who was stronger at fighting and could make people listen to him better. Also kings needed to be able to handle parliament and someone weak like Henry VI would just be pushed around by them.

If you were a successful warrior, then you had a lot of respect in medieval times and this would help you when you dealt with people and the king was supposed to be the head of the judicial system so people would be more likely to obey you if you were a strong fighter. Richard III was a good fighter but he was quite unfair in the way he killed some people like William Hastings and this was suspicious and also people thought Richard had killed the princes in the Tower so that made him unpopular. This shows that people didn't think a king should kill people unless there was a war.

In summary, medieval kings needed to be good at fighting because there was a lot of war and it was a violent time. People would take advantage of weakness in a king so there had to be respect for the monarch as a warrior. There were other important factors, such as managing finances to pay for war, but the main thing was that a king could win battles.

A good choice of examples from across the time period. During Henry IV's reign his son and heir should be referred to as the Prince of Wales; he only became Henry V when his father died. The comments about Richard III's deformity are not relevant and the claim that he was a brave warrior is accurate, but could do with supporting detail. The claims about the medieval period are too generalised; it is important not to talk about all people in the Middle Ages as if they held the same views, e.g. that they were all superstitious.

To improve, the response should include more precise detail and be written in a more formal, sophisticated manner. Sentences are often too long which makes the text hard to follow.

It is good that the response highlights other factors, not mentioned in the question, which would impact upon a king's popularity or security. Their treatment is very brief, however, and to improve, more detail should be used. Relations with parliament are important and are linked to taxation required for defence. More should be made of the fact that parliament had to grant taxes for war.

The link between gaining respect and a good military record is important. There were other methods of maintaining control, however, and Richard II and Henry VII are examples of leaders who tried these alternative ways, with varying success. The use of the execution of William Hastings as an example is good to show problems when kings abused the judicial system, but the material about Richard III is not clearly linked to the question.

The conclusion raises the important point about the need for funding for war, which had domestic political consequences. This is a very significant argument and should have been discussed in full earlier in the essay, not just mentioned in the final paragraph. Overall, the argument is clear but rather simplistic.

Verdict

This is an average answer because:

- it focuses mainly on the reigns of Henry V and VI. The reigns of Richard II and Henry VII are not mentioned and would provide useful examples
- the argument keeps emphasising the same points, rather than moving on to a different strand in the debate in each paragraph

- there is little analysis of the significance of key events or evaluation of which factors were more important in shaping a king's popularity/security.

Use the feedback on this essay to rewrite it, making as many improvements as you can.

Paper 3: A Level sample answer with comments

Section C

These questions require you to show your understanding of a subject over a considerable period of time. They will ask you to assess a long-term historical topic and its development over a period of at least 100 years, and they require you to make a substantiated judgement in relation to the question.

For these questions remember to:

- organise your essay and communicate it in a manner that is clear and comprehensible
- use historical knowledge to analyse and evaluate the key aspect of the question covering the entire period
- make a balanced argument that weighs up differing opinions
- make a substantiated overall judgement on the question.

'The key factor in maintaining a king's popularity and security on the throne in the years 1399–1509 was his military success.'
How far do you agree with this statement? (20 marks)

Strong student answer

For medieval kings, the ability to lead an army successfully was crucial to their security, as it enhanced their ability to maintain law and order. Military success also helped a monarch's relationship with parliament, as taxation was more likely to be easily granted after victories, as Henry V discovered after Agincourt, rather than to a leader who was seen to avoid battle, such as Richard II. Nonetheless, there were other factors which made a good king: respect for the Church, a suitable marriage, the ability to father sons, and the political strength to ensure the nobility especially did not quarrel too much among themselves. The military successes of a king were of paramount importance, but other qualities were also necessary.

A king who could fight successfully against an external threat was in a strong position. In 1399, Henry Bolingbroke was successful in usurping the throne from Richard II, a king whose reputation was weakened by his poor military leadership. Henry VI was another militarily incompetent king who was usurped. In both cases, the monarch's reluctance to lead men into battle made him look weak, encouraging others to aim for the crown. It is significant that Henry V suffered the Southampton Plot prior to his campaigns in France, but after his military success he was not challenged in this way again. As well as frightening other noblemen into submission, military victories against external threats also gave noblemen the opportunity to gain more wealth abroad, which was popular. Success also gained the king the support of the general public, reducing the risk of rebellion.

Henry V was unusual in the period, in that he was the only adult male to inherit the throne from his father. This made his position sufficiently strong that he could quickly subdue the Southampton rebellion and set sail to France. Other monarchs were in a weaker position because either they were a child, like Henry VI and Edward V, or they were usurpers. This meant that they could not swiftly gain prestige via speedy military victories. Most had to show their military abilities on the battlefields either against the Welsh and Scots, or during the Wars of the Roses. Henry IV earned respect for his ability to suppress the Glendower rebellion in Wales in the 1400s. This helps to explain why he was able to hold onto the throne despite being a usurper and developing a debilitating illness. Edward IV, however, was not in a position to engage in foreign war during the 1460s and this was a factor in him losing the throne in 1470.

One reason why military ability was important was because wars cost money and parliament would only grant taxation for defence (which included attacks on countries like France). Parliament was hostile to kings who did not lead campaigns themselves, notably Richard II who

Clearly focuses on the question and demonstrates a strong understanding of the historical context. It sets out the criteria by which a medieval king was judged and gives an indication of the line of argument the essay will take.

Strong knowledge of relevant key events is shown and different kings are compared to support the judgements made. The argument is logical and coherent. It makes links across the period and points out similarities and differences from different parts of the century.

Examples are used across the date range and an understanding is shown of which reigns are unusual and why. Links are made between different events. It is focused on the question, but makes different points from those highlighted in the first paragraph so the argument is developed.

showed considerable reluctance to fight, as evidenced by his refusal to move past Edinburgh during the 1385 campaign against Scotland. During Henry VI's reign, the defeats in France created a great deal of hostility towards the king as the amount of money given had been so large. Edward IV was also criticised during his second reign about the misuse of taxation granted to lead a campaign in France. Matters were made worse because the king pressured his subjects into granting large sums, via benevolences, and then did not fight but instead signed the 1475 Treaty of Picquigny. Edward's move, however, was an intelligent if unscrupulous one; from this treaty he gained a large pension from Louis XI, which meant he was no longer dependent on finance from the English parliament. This is an unusual example of a king finding financial support from elsewhere in order to help him make his throne secure.

Owing to the turmoil of the period, battles against alternative claimants to the throne, such as at Tewkesbury, Towton and Bosworth, were crucial to royal security. Surprisingly, the first usurper of the period, Bolingbroke, had to do little actual fighting to claim the crown, as Richard II was in Ireland with the bulk of his military support. In contrast, Tudor was obliged to fight hard to gain the crown from Richard III. This difference illustrates the importance contemporaries placed on a king being personally present to lead his men into battle. Unlike the king in 1399, in 1485 Richard III was vigorous in his defence of his title and even his enemies praised his bravery at Bosworth. Henry VII used his victory as a method of claiming that God favoured the Tudors, illustrating the propaganda importance of military success.

Another significant factor was a king's choice of bride. A king's wife rarely proved uniformly popular and some who intervened in politics, like Margaret of Anjou, were the subject of hostility. Her high level of political involvement earned her many enemies, but on the other hand she arguably was forced to take a higher-profile role than was usual because of her husband's incapacity. Certainly, she worked hard to secure the throne for Henry VI and his heir on a number of occasions and he may well have been deposed earlier without her. Another controversial marriage of the period was Edward IV's secret match with Elizabeth Woodville, which caused a great deal of international and domestic tension. This match arguably lost Edward the throne temporarily in 1470–71. It contrasted with Henry VII's marriage to Elizabeth of York, a match which could hardly have been more politically sensible, as it effectively ended the Wars of the Roses. Elizabeth of York also had the virtue of being fertile and the birth of an heir was crucial to the stability of any king on the throne. It is no coincidence that kings who were deposed were often childless, notably Richard II, Richard III and, in 1471, Henry VI.

It is fair to say that a king's military successes were the most important factor in ensuring his security on the throne. The 15th century was a time of considerable civil and foreign warfare, and so being able to fight well was essential to gaining the crown in the first place, and then holding onto it. The ability to put down internal rebellions was important, but, as Henry V's reign showed, success in battle abroad was the strongest method of ensuring loyalty and removing financial opposition from parliament. The need for taxes to fund war made it a topic of sensitivity if things went badly, as Richard II discovered in the 1380s and 1390s. Military ability, however, was not the only factor of importance. A careful use of espionage and bonds served Henry VII well in securing his throne, while a judicious choice of bride was also important. The presence of a male heir also made opposition less likely, although it did not entirely compensate for military incompetence, as Henry VI was to discover. In the final analysis, noblemen respected kings who could fight battles effectively, and losing the respect of the nobility was dangerous in an age where usurpation had become almost the norm.

The theme of financing wars is very important and the response argues the case clearly here. Relevant comparison is made between different kings and the significance of key events is highlighted. A high level of understanding of the context is shown, demonstrating a sophisticated evaluation of contemporary attitudes.

Examples from different reigns are used to highlight key points, focusing on the question. Excellent subject knowledge is used to support analytical judgements.

The argument is supported by detailed knowledge. The limitations of the statement in the question are explored and an analytical approach to historical information is maintained. The response has carefully selected information that is relevant to support the argument.

The conclusion provides a clear answer to the question and demonstrates understanding of the historical context. The full date range is discussed and there is analysis of the relationship between key factors in the period.

Verdict

This is a strong answer because:

- it analyses key themes of the period in relation to the question, and discusses both continuity and change over time

- detailed knowledge is used to support the argument. The argument is based on the criteria that contemporaries would have used to evaluate a monarch's success or failure.

Index

Acknowledgements

Acknowledgements

The authors and publisher would like to thank the following individuals and organisations for permission to reproduce photographs and text in this book.

Photographs

(Key: b–bottom; c–centre; l–left; r–right; t–top)

Alamy Images: National Geographic Image Collection 6, Ashley Cooper pics 24; **Bridgeman Art Library Ltd:** *Choosing the Red and White Roses in the Temple Garden*, 1910 (fresco), Payne, Henry A. (Harry) (1868–1940)/Houses of Parliament, Westminster, London, UK 9, Great Seal of Henry V (engraving), English School, (19th century)/Private Collection/© Look and Learn 11, 'Decrets de Gratien' (vellum), French School, (14th century)/Bibliotheque Municipale, Amiens, France 14, Royal 18 D. II, f.30v *Wheel of Fortune*, illustration from the 'Troy Book', c1455–62 (vellum), English School, (15th century)/British Library, London 37, The National Archives, London, England 48, Portrait of Richard II 'The Westminster Portrait', 1390s (oil on panel), English School, (14th century)/Westminster Abbey, London, UK 69, *Richard II Presented to the Virgin and Child by his Patron Saint John the Baptist and Saints Edward and Edmund*, c1395–99 (egg tempera on oak), Master of the Wilton Diptych, (fl.c1395–99)/National Gallery, London, UK 71, Seal of Owain, Prince of Wales (stone), French School, (15th century)/Centre Historique des Archives Nationales, Paris, France 81, Portrait of Henry V (1387–1422) (oil on panel) English School, (15th century)/National Portrait Gallery, London, UK 89, Ms 6 f.243 *Battle of Agincourt*, 1415, English with Flemish illuminations, from the 'St Alban's Chronicle' (vellum), English School, (15th century)/© Lambeth Palace Library, London, UK 93, Bridgeman/Nova 2644 fol.81r Domestic preparation, from 'Tacuinum Sanitatis' (vellum), Italian School, (14th century)/Osterreichische Nationalbibliothek, Vienna, Austria/Alinar 107, Add 42130 Margin illumination showing a wife beating her husband with a distaff, from the Luttrell Psalter, begun prior to 1340 for Sir Geoffrey Luttrell (vellum), English School, (14th century)/British Library, London, UK/© British Library Board. All Rights Reserved 114, *The Descendants of Countess Anne*, c1483 (pen & ink on paper), Dutch School, (15th century)/British Library, London, UK 134, *Richard III*, c1510-40 (oil on panel), English School, (16th century)/Society of Antiquaries of London, UK 146, *King Henry VII*, 1505 (oil on panel), Flemish School, (16th century)/National Portrait Gallery, London, UK/© Stefano Baldini 158, *Margaret of York* (1446–1503) Duchess of Burgundy, c1477 (oil on panel), Netherlandish School, (15th century)/Louvre, Paris, France 167; **The Trustees of The British Museum**. All rights reserved 21; **National Archives** 47; **TopFoto:** John Hedgecoe 84; **British Library Images Online:** Tetramorph, Matthew, in English, Wycliffite Bible, North Midlands, England, 1st quarter of 15th century 97, 121; **BARC, Archaeological Sciences, University of Bradford** 129; **National Galleries Scotland** 166.

Cover image: Mary Evans Picture Library: Interfoto/Friedrich

All other images © Pearson Education

Text

Quote p.10 from Kingship and Queenship in *Gothic: Art for England 1400–1547*, V&A Publications (Horrox, R. (Williamson, P. and Marks, R., eds) 2003) p.38, reproduced with permission; Extracts pp.26, 27 and 28 adapted from *The Paston Letters: A Selection in Modern Spelling,* Oxford University Press (Davis, N. (ed.) 1983) pp.148, 184, By permission of Oxford University Press; Quote p.27 from *Essential Histories: The Wars of the Roses: 1455–1485*, Osprey Publishing (Hicks, Michael 2003) p.66, © Osprey Publishing Ltd; Quote p.27 and Extract 2 p.32 from *Wars of the Roses,* Cambridge University Press (Carpenter, Christine 1997) pp.5, 184, Copyright © Cambridge University Press; Source 9 p.32 from The Council of the North, *History Today* (Cooper, S. 2015), www.historytoday.com/stephen-cooper/council-north#sthash.eRjm18eF.dpuf, reproduced with permission; Quote p.38 from *English Historical Documents,* vol. IV, Routledge (Myers, A.R. (ed.) 1995) p.267, reproduced by permission of Taylor & Francis Books UK; Extracts pp.15, 40 from *Transformation of England*, Routledge (Thomson, J.A.F. 1983) pp.265, 314, repr. 2014, reproduced by permission of Taylor & Francis Books UK; Extract p.41 from *King, Crown and Duchy,* Oxford University Press (Castor, Helen 2000) pp.309–10, By permission of Oxford University Press; Extract 3 p.51 from *The History of Parliament: British Political, Social and Local History* by Simon J. Payling, www.historyofparliamentonline.org/periods/medieval. We are grateful to the History of Parliament for permission to use this quotation; Extract 4 p.51 from The Place of Parliament in the King's Government in *The History of Parliament: The House of Commons, 1386–1421* (Roskell, J.S. (Roskell, J.S., Clark, L. and Rawcliffe, C., eds) 1993), Boydell & Brewer, www.historyofparliamentonline.org/volume/1386-1421/survey/ii-place-parliament-kings-government, reproduced with permission from The History of Parliament; Quote p.52 from Henry IV (1367–1413) in *Oxford Dictionary of National Biography*, Oxford University Press (Brown, A.L. (Matthew, H.C.G. and Harrison, Brian, eds) 2004), online edition (Goldman, Lawrence, ed. 2010), www.oxforddnb.com/view/article/12951, By permission of Oxford University Press; Extract p.59 from *The Wars of the Roses,* The History Press (Lander, J.R. 2009), reproduced with permission; Extracts pp.68, 70, Source 5 p.72, Extract 3 p.77, p.91, p.102, p.108, p.117, p.121, p.138, Quote p.139, p.140, p.142 from *Chronicles of the Wars of the Roses,* Weidenfeld & Nicolson, Phoebe Phillips Editions (Hallam, Elizabeth M., ed. 1988) pp.56–58, 72–76, 78, 89, 122–24, 119–26, 158–66, 194–96, 205, 273, 274, 279–82, 286 respectively, Dr Hallam, the Editor, grants permission in respect of those rights which she holds in the work; Extracts pp.75, 78 from *Richard II,* Yale University Press (Saul, N. 1999) pp.418, 419–20, Copyright © 1997 by Nigel Saul; Quotes pp.76, 77, Source 7 p.77 from Parliament Rolls of Medieval England, Henry IV, October 1399, Part I, www.sd-editions.com/AnaServer?PROME+0+start.anv+id=HENRYIV, reproduced with permission from Scholarly Digital Editions and PROME; Extract p.76 from *Lancaster and York: The Wars of the Roses*, Jonathan Cape (Weir, Alison 1996) p.37, reproduced by permission of The Random House Group Ltd.; Extract p.90 from *Agincourt: A New History*, The History Press (Curry, A. 2006) p.34, reproduced with permission; Extract p.95 from *Recueil des Chroniques et Anchiennes Istories de la Grant Bretaigne* (Jean de Wavrin (W. Hardy, ed.) 1891), reprinted in *Society at War: The Experience of England and France During the Hundred Years War*, Boydell Press (Allmand, C.T. ed., 1973) pp.107–08, reprinted by permission of Boydell & Brewer Ltd; Quote p.110 from *Nobility of Later Medieval England,* Clarendon Press (McFarlane, K.B. 1953) p.284, By permission of Oxford University Press; Extract p.112 from Beaufort, Edmund, First Duke of Somerset (c1406–1455) in *Oxford Dictionary of National Biography*, Oxford University Press (Richmond, Colin 2004), online edition, October 2008, www.oxforddnb.com/view/article/1855 [accessed 31 Oct 2015], By permission of Oxford University Press; Extract p.114 from *Politics*, Cambridge University Press (Everson, S., ed. 1996) pp.50–51, Copyright © Cambridge University Press; Extract p.122 from Proclamation of Grievances, 1450 in *Fordham Medieval Sourcebook*. Scanned and modernised from original by Prof. J.S. Arkenberg, Cal. State Fullerto (and further modernised by H. Carrel), http://legacy.fordham.edu/halsall/sbook.asp, reproduced with permission; Extract p.137 from Parliament Rolls of Medieval England, Appendix 1478, item 1, online (Given-Wilson, C. ed.), www.sd-editions.com/PROME/home.html, reproduced with permission from Scholarly Digital Editions and PROME; Extract 1 p.143 from *Richard III,* Yale University Press (Ross, C. 1999) pp.lvi-lvii, Copyright © C. Ross; Extract 2 p.143 from *Wars of the Roses*, Cambridge University Press (Carpenter, Christine 1999) pp.4–5, Copyright © Cambridge University Press; Extract 'Source 6' p.144 from *The Search for Richard III: The King's Grave*, John Murray (Langley, P. and Jones, M. 2013), Copyright © Michael Jones and Phillipa Langley reproduced with permission from John Murray Press, a division of Hodder & Stoughton Ltd. and The Viney Agency; Extract Source 8 p.145 from Thomas More's *History of King Richard III: A Reader's Edition*, pp.75–77 www.thomasmorestudies.org/docs/Richard.pdf, © Center for Thomas More Studies. The full text is available at www.thomasmorestudies.org/docs/Richard.pdf; Extract p.147 from *Richard III: From Contemporary Chronicles, Letters and Records, Print ISBN: 978-1781553138* Kindle Edition, Fonthill Media (Dockray, K. and Hammond, P. 2013), reproduced with permission; Extract p.148 from Parliament Rolls of Medieval England, Parliament 1484, Item 18 (22), online (Given-Wilson, C. ed.), www.sd-editions.com/PROME/home.html, reproduced with permission from Scholarly Digital Editions and PROME; Extract p.155 from Parliament Rolls of Medieval England, November 1485, Item 3, online (Given-Wilson, C. ed.), http://sd-editions.com/AnaServer?PROME+676437+text.anv+showall=1, reproduced with permission from Scholarly Digital Editions and PROME; Extracts pp.157, 165 from *Henry VII: The Importance of His Reign,* Routledge (Grant, A. 1985) pp.9, 10, 16, 7, Copyright © 1985 Routledge, reproduced by permission of Taylor & Francis Books UK; Source 3 p.159 from *Yorkists & Tudors, 1450–1603*, Blackwell (Newman, S. (ed.) 1989) p.10, republished with permission of John Wiley & Sons. Permission conveyed through Copyright Clearance Center, Inc.; Extract 2 p.159 from Espionage and Intelligence from the Wars of the Roses to the Reformation, *Nottingham Medieval Studies,* vol. 35 (Arthurson, I. 1991), reproduced online: http://deremilitari.org/articles/ reprinted by the kind permission of the Editorial Board; Quote p.160 from Henry VII (1457–1509) in *Oxford Dictionary of National Biography*, Oxford University Press (Gunn, S.J. 2004), online edition, January 2008 [accessed 31 October 2015] www.oxforddnb.com/view/article/12954?docPos=1, By permission of Oxford University Press; Extract p.161 from *Wars of the Roses,* Yale University Press (Hicks, M. 2012) pp.256–58, Copyright © 2010 Michael Hicks; Extract p.170 from *Lancastrians to Tudors,* Cambridge University Press (Pickering, A. 2000) pp.92–93, Copyright © Cambridge University Press.